LITERACY
IN THE
INTERMEDIATE GRADES

Best Practices for a Comprehensive Program

NANCY LEE CECIL

CALIFORNIA STATE UNIVERSITY, SACRAMENTO

JOAN P. GIPE

CALIFORNIA STATE UNIVERSITY, SACRAMENTO

Holcomb Hathaway, Publishers
Scottsdale, Arizona 85250

Library of Congress Cataloging-in-Publication Data

Cecil, Nancy Lee.
    Literacy in the intermediate grades : best practices for a comprehensive program / Nancy
Lee Cecil, Joan P. Gipe.
      p. cm.
    Includes bibliographical references (p.) and index.
    ISBN 1-890871-46-X
    1. Reading (Elementary)   2. Literacy.   I. Gipe, Joan P.   II. Title.

LB1573.C4334 2003
372.4—dc21

                                        2002191914

To my daughter, Chrissy—my most powerful literacy teacher —NC

To my fellow inhabitants of, and past and future visitors to, "The Treehouse" —JG

Holcomb Hathaway, Publishers, Inc.
6207 North Cattletrack Road
Scottsdale, Arizona 85250
(480) 991-7881
www.hh-pub.com

ISBN 1-890871-46-X

10 9 8 7 6 5 4 3 2 1

Printed in the United States of America.

CONTENTS

Brief Contents

Contents

4 VOCABULARY INSTRUCTION   93

5 READING COMPREHENSION   121

6 FOSTERING ORAL LANGUAGE IN THE CLASSROOM   159

9 DIFFERENTIATING INSTRUCTION FOR STUDENTS WITH SPECIAL NEEDS   271

10   FOSTERING LITERACY BEYOND THE CLASSROOM   299

11   CONNECTING PARENTS, TEACHERS, AND CHILDREN   325

12 LITERACY IN THE INTERMEDIATE GRADES   341

Orchestrating a Balanced and Comprehensive Program

Appendices

PREFACE
Preface

Intermediate-grade teachers in today's schools face many critical issues. Among the most pressing are the following: What strategies should teachers use to help *all* of their intermediate students make sense of printed text? How do teachers help *all* children become capable, fluent readers who choose to read—and read often—far beyond the classroom doors? What practices and instructional materials has research found to be the most effective? How can assessment inform instruction? In what ways do family and community influence children's success in reading? And how can state and district standards be used as a road map to guide effective instruction?

The need for answers to such questions resulted in the writing of *Literacy in the Intermediate Grades: Best Practices for a Comprehensive Program.* Clearly, the answers to these and similar questions profoundly affect what teachers do in the classroom. For example, if research findings, coupled with objective observations, identify certain strategies or materials as significantly more effective than others, teachers can make more intelligent decisions about day-to-day classroom activities. They are better able to distinguish potentially effective practices from professional folklore, yesterday's hit-or-miss traditions, and unexamined opinions about "what works," all of which are often little more than supposition.

Our challenge in writing *Literacy in the Intermediate Grades* was to show preservice and practicing teachers how to teach the language arts in a skillful yet motivational way; how to create a classroom climate where the joy of language, literacy, and learning thrives; and most important, how to inspire the heterogeneous garden of learners in today's intermediate classrooms to want to engage in literate behaviors, while believing they can.

Because of the extent of recent media coverage, it is probably clear to all that literacy instruction has been undergoing major changes and shifts in emphasis. Our research and recent experiences in schools have confirmed that the change is as profound as it is reported to be. As educators, we ask ourselves this question: Is this dramatic shift in practice a positive spiraling of knowledge or simply the educational pendulum swinging back yet again from opposite extremes, as many would have us believe?

If we behave as reflective professionals, then every time the model shifts, we learn much from where we have been. The most recent shift is a case in point. Many of the resultant instructional changes we see are causes for guarded optimism; in some classrooms, there is nothing short of a literacy Renaissance occurring. This positive turnabout has been spurred by a wealth of evidence from literacy and other educational researchers suggesting that a comprehensive and balanced, language-based, interactive program of direct instruction in the skills of literacy combined with an abundant exposure to quality children's literature create a program that has an extraordinary chance of developing learners who can read and write, and choose to do so. Instead of emphasizing bits and pieces of fragmented reading and writing skills, a comprehensive, balanced program focuses more on reading, writing, listening, speaking, viewing, visually representing, and thinking as interrelated communication processes—processes that are pivotal to all learning.

Readers of this book will be given strategies and procedures that suggest how to implement a balanced, comprehensive intermediate literacy program by integrating direct and indirect instruction in word study, vocabulary, comprehension strategies and speaking, listening, and writing skills within the context of rich and varied language arts experiences. *Literacy in the Intermediate Grades* addresses such issues as teaching to standards, differentiating instruction for readers of all levels, using assessment to inform instruction, working with English language learners and struggling readers, and connecting with parents.

The book presents many topics of particular interest to intermediate grade teachers including content area literacy, developing motivated, lifelong readers and writers, listening to learn, formal and informal speaking instruction, planning and implementing a differentiated lesson, and developing authentic learning experiences.

Countless programs, procedures, and strategies are available for literacy instruction in the intermediate grades today, and choosing among them can be challenging to the seasoned teacher and overwhelming to the beginning one. Therefore, we have selected prototypes that seem to represent the most effective practices according to current research and the reinforcing testimonies of a host of outstanding teachers who were observed and interviewed for the writing of this book.

Our goal is to offer a text that facilitates the development of reflective teachers who are empowered to think through the miasma of political debates that often focus solely on simplistic answers to the complicated task of teaching children to become literate. This text provides readers with the most consistent research of the last thirty years and translates it into practice. It presents evidenced-based perspectives in literacy education, describes a comprehensive range of instructional practices, and shows preservice and practicing teachers how to select practices that conform to the individual needs of their students. A caring teacher, armed with the knowledge of how to carry out the most effective practices in literacy, is what is most needed to develop eager and proficient young readers and writers.

SPECIAL FEATURES

Some of the special features of *Literacy for the Intermediate Grades* aid readers in understanding new concepts and vocabulary. Other features are designed to foster reflection and mastery of the material and to encourage readers to try out ideas in the classroom. The following features are particularly noteworthy:

- **In the Classroom.** Each chapter begins with a vignette in which readers observe an authentic classroom setting and see how a practicing teacher deals with the subject addressed in the chapter. These small glimpses of literacy instruction build vicarious background and trigger readers' prior knowledge about the chapter's topic. Throughout the chapter and in some of the activities we refer to the vignette, helping readers make the connection between new concepts and classroom instruction.

- **Activities.** More than 50 activities designed for use in intermediate classrooms are included in selected chapters. These specific, step-by-step procedures allow readers to put into practice in their field placement, practicum, or school the ideas and strategies they encounter in the chapter.

- **Questions for Journal Writing and Discussion.** Questions at the end of each chapter help readers reflect on and internalize key ideas. These questions are suitable for response in journal form or for stimulating lively discussion.

- **Suggestions for Projects and Field-Based Activities.** This special section makes the connection from research and theory to real classroom practice. At the end of each chapter, readers find several suggestions for surveying, interviewing, or observing local teachers to compare strategies presented in the chapter with actual practice. Other activities ask readers to try out a strategy or activity in the chapter with a small group of intermediate children.

- **Troubleshooting Sections.** Many chapters end with a brief section intended to help teachers consider alternative suggestions and activities appropriate for children for whom the literacy focus discussed in the chapter is a particular challenge. Ideas for corrective instruction are offered.

- **Chapter on Literacy and the Family.** Understanding the vast array of literacy practices in students' homes can lead to a partnership between home and school that will greatly enhance the literacy program at school. In exploring this connection, we look at the best ways to communicate with diverse families and foster their active involvement in helping their children become truly literate beings.

- **Chapter on "Orchestration."** In the final chapter of the book, we provide an intimate view of the urban classroom of an exemplary intermediate teacher who demonstrates many of the procedures, strategies, and ideals presented in the rest of the book. The reader receives a rare insider perspective on how a seasoned teacher makes decisions about classroom climate, materials, room arrangements, and how to maximize limited instructional time.

- **Glossary.** An extensive book-end glossary is included, allowing readers to review critical terms and concepts highlighted throughout the text.

- **Appendices.** Book appendices include reference for children's literature; current websites for literacy suitable for teachers, parents, or children; a variety of literacy checklists and assessment tools for classroom use; and a list of widely used commercial evaluation instruments.

- **Ancillaries.** A PowerPoint presentation and Instructor's Manual are available to adopters of this text. The Instructor's Manual provides several valuable tools for each chapter: a summary of key concepts, a list of key vocabulary, suggestions for in-class discussions and activities, and a range of assessment devices, including objective and subjective questions.

ACKNOWLEDGMENTS

We wish to extend our sincere thanks to the reviewers of the manuscript. Their comments were insightful and helpful, and the book is better as a result of their efforts. They include: Betty J. Conway, Baylor University; Angela M. Ferree, Western Illinois University; Leah Kinniburgh, Athens State University; Meryl K. Lazar, University of Pittsburgh; Pat Sharp, Baylor University; Carol Talbot, Marymount University; Sandra White, Mary Washington College; and Kathleen Shoop, University of Pittsburgh.

Special thanks to Colette Kelly and Gay Pauley of Holcomb Hathaway for their expertise, gentle pushing, and careful attention to detail. These two women are a delight to work with. Thanks, too, to Jennifer McQueary of Holcomb Hathaway for her work in constructing the PowerPoint presentation for this book.

Finally, hugs and high fives to our husbands, Gary and Charlie, who were ever patient and supportive as we took precious time away from family life to bring this book to fruition. Heartfelt thanks to you both.

CHAPTER 1

A Comprehensive Literacy Program for the Intermediate Grades

Focus Questions

- What is literacy?
- What are the major characteristics of the reading process?
- What are the major building blocks for development of literacy knowledge and enjoyment in the intermediate grades?
- How does a balanced and comprehensive literacy program for the intermediate grades differ from a more traditional one?

WHAT IS LITERACY?

Literacy is not something we do in school during English, reading, or language arts class. The term *literacy* has come to describe competence in a special field, such as computer literacy, and to include many types or multiple literacies, such as visual, media, cultural, emergent, family, and workplace, to name a few. While there can never be one definition of literacy that encompasses all that needs to be included in such a definition, the following description is useful to consider for this book. **Literacy** is a continuum of skills, including reading, writing, speaking, listening, viewing, visually representing, and critical thinking, applied in a social context to enable a person to function effectively in his or her group and community (Harris and Hodges, 1995).

LITERACY INSTRUCTION AND THE CONSTRUCTIVIST MODEL

The definition of literacy instruction to be used in the remainder of this book draws upon research on the nature of literacy and literacy learning best understood through the ideas of Vygotsky. This forerunner of current understandings of children and how they learn to read and write defined *instruction* as "helping the student to become interested and involved in a meaningful activity, then providing the student with the support needed to complete the activity successfully" (Vygotsky, 1978, p. 68).

At the heart of the **constructivist model of learning** is the belief that children must actively build their own understandings of all reading, writing, listening, and speaking activities. Vygotsky further asserted that all learning is basically a social and psychological process that takes place through interactions between children and others in their environment. Over time, children begin to internalize the skills and knowledge acquired through these social interactions.

Teachers whose teaching proceeds from a constructivist model generally include many discussions of literature, either in small, teacher-led groups, or in literature circles (see Chapter 5). While teachers generally help students to begin the group's meetings and may sometimes influence the course of the discussions, students are encouraged to share their own responses to

In the Classroom

Mr. Piper's fourth-grade class is learning about the desert. He uses a globe to show his students the many deserts that exist in diverse parts of the world. He then asks them to share what they already know about deserts. He writes their answers on the chalkboard under a column labeled "What We Know." Next, Mr. Piper asks them to think about anything they would like to know about the desert and desert life. Students respond enthusiastically and he writes their questions, such as "Does it ever get cold there?" and "Do they ever run out of water?" on the chalkboard under a column labeled "What We Want to Know."

Mr. Piper then invites the students to close their eyes as he takes them on a guided imagery of a trek across the arid desert of Israel's Negev region in the blazing noonday heat. They ride camels for several long, uncomfortable miles and finally stop to rest when the stubborn animals will go no farther. They encounter an angry scorpion behind a bush and, as the sun is at its brightest in the cloudless blue sky, they realize (oh no!) that their water canteens . . . are empty.

As they open their eyes, the teacher tells the students they will be reading a true story about a 10-year-old boy who gets lost in the harsh desert and must save himself from dehydration by drinking the juice of a giant cactus. He asks them to read silently, and to be thinking about what they would do in the same situation. After everyone has finished reading, a lively discussion ensues, inspired by Mr. Piper's provocative question, "What would you have done to survive if you had been lost in the desert?" Mr. Piper waits until all the students have had a chance to respond to this question in their journals, and then he calls on them, one at a time, until all who wish to respond have had a chance. All answers are validated and written on the chalkboard. Later, in writer's workshop, the students, divided into small groups, create their own desert survivor manuals using information gleaned from the Internet. Finally, the students revisited the chart on the chalkboard and share all that they have learned about desert life, while Mr. Piper records their responses under a column labeled, "What We Learned." Any answers not revealed in the reading of the passage lead to a discussion of where answers can be found and, ultimately, self-directed research using the Internet and media center resources.

the literature. Students often keep response journals in which they write their reactions to selections they have read. Finally, students may decide upon a multimedia project to share their reading with classmates, such as a PowerPoint presentation, a book poster, or a skit based on a scene from the story.

WHAT IS READING?

At first glance, it would hardly seem worth the trouble to answer the basic question, What is reading? because, in a sense, everybody knows perfectly well what it is: most people do it, in one form or another, every single day. But definitions underlie all intellectual endeavors. Definitions are assumptions that determine future educational activities. In other words, what teachers will do to teach reading will be determined, in large part, by what they believe reading is.

To define reading we must know exactly what is involved in this activity that sets it apart from other, similar activities. It is not enough, for example, to define reading as "a thought-getting process" because we can get thoughts just as easily from listening to a lecture or conversation, or from watching a film. There are, to put it another way, many similarities between reading a page of difficult text and hearing the same text read to us by another person. The problem of comprehension is paramount for both reader and listener.

No one would deny that a major purpose of reading is "to get information or enjoyment of some sort from the printed page." But since we get information in the same way from spoken language, this purpose does not define reading in a way that distinguishes it from engaging in conversation. As soon as we understand this point, the problem of definition begins to resolve itself. If we see that meaning resides in the relationship between the language and the receiver, we might then ask how writing (which we read) is related to language (which we hear).

If language, which is composed of sounds, carries the meanings, then what is writing? Writing is a device, or a code, for representing the sounds of a language in a visual form. The written words of a language are, in fact, just symbols of the spoken words, which are sounds.

So reading, then, becomes the process of turning these printed symbols back into sounds again. The moment we say this, however, some reasonable soul is bound to ask, anxiously, "But what about meaning? Can we propose to define reading as just deciphering the words without regard to the meaning?"

reading ●

The answer is yes, but only partly. **Reading** is, first of all, the mechanical skill of turning the printed symbols into the sounds of our language. Of course, the reason we turn the print into sound—in other words, the reason we *read*—is to get at the meaning. We decode the printed symbols to get what the author is attempting to *say* and then, more important, we make some meaning connection to the world as we know it (Pearson, 1993).

But there is even more to it than that. Reading entails both reconstructing an author's message and constructing one's own meaning using the print on the page as a stimulus. We can think of it as a transaction, or an exchange, among the reader, the text, and the purposes and context of the reading situation. A reader's reconstruction of the ideas and information intended by the author is somewhat like a listener's reconstruction of ideas from the combination of sounds the speaker makes. An artist creates a masterpiece that means one thing to him or her and a host of different things to different admirers of his or her piece. Likewise, the reader, like the listener, may create meanings that are different from those intended by the author. What readers understand from the reconstructed and constructed meanings depends on the readers' prior knowledge, prior experiences, and their maturity and proficiency in using language in differing social contexts.

CHARACTERISTICS OF THE READING PROCESS

A comprehensive approach to literacy instruction starts with the assumption that the purpose of reading is to create meaning from print. This meaning-making process contains four essential underlying characteristics. They are the assumptions that

- reading is a *holistic* process.
- reading is a *constructive* process.
- reading is a *strategic* process.
- reading is an *interactive* process.

Early readers focus a great amount of attention on acquiring fluency as they learn to decode print, whereas more proficient decoders in the intermediate grades have more energy with which to address more subtle facets of critical reading and responding. However, in either case, the reading process consists of similar fundamental properties whether the reader in question is an early reader who has just recently learned to "crack the code," or a child who is decoding fluently and is "reading to learn." If we explore these characteristics of the reading process, a better understanding of the complex nature of the activity emerges (Hyde and Bizar, 1989). The students in the opening classroom scenario were engaged in a literacy lesson that incorporated all these underlying characteristics.

Reading as a Holistic Process

The students in Mr. Piper's class were using reading as a *holistic* process: they put all their global decoding and comprehension skills together to think about the story. Observing such advanced readers as they read leads us to the realization that reading is not simply the sum total of the discrete skills that we have students practice in order to teach them how to read; rather, reading is a holistic process whereby the various subskills, such as decoding, finding the main idea, and using imagery, must be integrated to form a smooth, coherent whole (Baumann et al., 1998). The subskills, though crucial, must be applied to the act of reading by a competent reader who puts all the pieces together through constant practice. These subskills, and how they relate to each other, are outlined in Figure 1.1. As you can see from Figure 1.1, the subskills lead to recognizing and understanding words and ideas.

Reading as a Constructive Process

The students in Mr. Piper's class were seeing reading as a *constructive* process: they read to discover how the boy survived in the desert and compared it with what they might do under the same circumstances. As proficient readers engage in reading text while predicting what may happen next, meaning is constructed in their minds. (Rumelhart, 1977; Stanovich, 1980). That meaning lies not only on the page, but it is also negotiated with the imagination and experience of the reader. Readers need to use what is already in their minds and combine it with what they find on the printed page in order to construct a meaning based upon a kind of reconciliation of these two sets of input.

Reading as a Strategic Process

The students in Mr. Piper's class were using reading as a *strategic* process: they used mental imagery to "see" the desert in their mind's eye. Proficient readers use different strategies depending upon the purpose for reading and the difficulty and genre of the material. The purpose for reading may be to determine who stole the wallet, to appreciate the beauty of certain images, to memorize a poem, or to put together a model airplane. Having in mind the exact purpose for which they are reading helps students to utilize the appropriate strategies for the nature of the literacy task at hand.

Reading as an Interactive Process

Finally, the students in Mr. Piper's class used reading as an *interactive* process: they compared their own knowledge of the desert with the new information provided by the author. We have come to think of reading as a process in which the reader must actually interact, or negotiate meaning, with the author and text in order for true comprehension to occur (Buehl,

FIGURE 1.1   The reading subskills: An overview.

I. READINESS FACTORS

Concepts about print (orthographic knowledge)

Experiential background

Language development

Visual acuity and discrimination

Auditory acuity and discrimination

Phonemic awareness

II. RECOGNIZING AND UNDERSTANDING WORDS

Sight Words

Word Study Skills

Context clues

Phonic analysis (*single consonants, blends, vowels, digraphs, diphthongs, accents*)

Structural analysis (*root words, inflectional endings, compound words, contractions, prefixes, suffixes, syllables, morphemes*)

Vocabulary Development

Context clues

Multiple meanings

Synonyms and antonyms

Shades of meaning

Word origins (etymology)

Dictionary Skills

Locating words

Using pronunciation key

Finding appropriate definition

Oral Reading Skills

Phrasing and punctuation

Fluency (accuracy, rate, and expression)

Pronunciation and enunciation

Eye–voice span

III. RECOGNIZING AND UNDERSTANDING IDEAS

Comprehension Skills

Receptive (nonoral) reading

    Literal meanings (*details, main ideas, sequence, directions*)

    Implied meanings (*fact or fiction, characterization and setting, relationships, predicting outcomes, author's tone, mood and intent, comparisons and contrasts, conclusions and generalizations*)

Critical reading

    Fact or opinion

    Appraisal of author

    Biased statements

    Propaganda techniques

    Cause and effect

    Comparisons and contrasts

    Figures of speech

    Drawing conclusions

Creative reading

    Convergent (read to solve a problem)

    Divergent (go beyond author to new ideas)

Study Skills

Locating information

Selecting and evaluating sources

Organizing

Interpreting maps, graphs, etc.

Using SQ3R procedure

Rate of Comprehension Skills

Flexibility

Skimming

Silent reading habits

2001; Rosenblatt, 1983). What the reader brings to the text in terms of prior knowledge of content, writing style, and vocabulary determines how well he or she will be able to derive a rich meaning from the text. We have all had the experience of reading something about which we had little or no background knowledge, or **schema.** When this happens, we soon realize that although we may know many of the words, we cannot make sense of the material. We do not have the background we need to construct a rich meaning to take away from reading.

● schema

The Reciprocal Relation of Reading and Writing

Perhaps more than any other, an interactive model of reading and writing also helps us to understand exactly how reading and writing enjoy a highly reciprocal relationship. Both readers and writers are involved in similar, if not identical, thought processes during the synergistic acts of comprehending and composing (Squire, 1983). This phenomenon is not so surprising, however, since thought and language are virtually inseparable (Vygotsky, 1962, 1979).

Squire's model (1983) of how reading and writing are related is based on the notion that reading and writing place similar demands on one's thinking.

● Squire's model

These demands may best be illustrated by comparing the concerns of the reader and writer *during* the processes of comprehending and composing. For example, before reading a text, the reader prepares to comprehend by establishing a purpose for reading and recalling, or "activating," prior knowledge of the topic. Similarly, before writing text, the writer prepares to compose by establishing a purpose for writing and also activating all prior knowledge of the topic. Prereading and prewriting time are therefore critical to both the processes of reading and writing, because quality time spent during these initial stages prepares both readers and writers to construct meaning more effectively.

WHAT IS A BALANCED AND COMPREHENSIVE APPROACH TO LITERACY IN THE INTERMEDIATE GRADES?

In the past few years, teachers of young children have begun to reconcile their differences in terms of their perspectives on early literacy. Most teachers now agree that reading is a complex process incorporating the four characteristics (constructive, holistic, strategic, and interactive) evident in the opening scenario. Moreover, research has provided abundant support for the notion that a committed teacher who can integrate a program of explicit, systematic phonics instruction into a curriculum rich with quality literature, easily decodable text, and a variety of meaningful writing experiences will have the best chance of teaching children who will not only learn how to read, but do so willingly—far beyond the classroom door (Larsen-Blair and Williams, 1999; Stahl, 1992).

Most reading educators have long agreed that a certain amount of direct instruction in phonics is vital in learning how to decode automatically, but most have also maintained a belief that incorporating the basic elements of a holistic, meaning-based program with such instruction will have a more positive outcome on children's later attitudes toward reading as a chosen activity (Wink, 1996). To one degree or another, it seems, most competent teachers of early literacy in the new millennium are now trying to incorporate the best of both perspectives in a balanced and comprehensive approach to teaching literacy. They are seeing results, too, measured by rising test scores and their own observations, which have been brought about by infusing many meaning-based strategies with a structured, skills-based program, or by supplementing a holistic, literature-based program with a systematic phonics program (Cecil, 1999).

Now, however, attention has begun to focus not only on early reading instruction, with its major focus on teaching children *how to read,* but on another, equally important phase: when children have mastered the basic foundational skills of the reading act, they then need help learning *how to read to learn.* As children enter the intermediate grades, when most are armed with a compendium of automatic decoding skills, they require a program of literacy that is both balanced in instruction and comprehensive in breadth.

Balanced instruction means that, on a daily basis, students receive direct, explicit instruction in those literacy skills and strategies they have not yet mastered; such skills are taught to small groups of students who share a common need. These lessons are teacher-directed lessons and, though the teacher may use any of a number of resources, the main objective of the lesson is to teach that particular reading, writing, speaking, listening, viewing, or visually representing skill or strategy. The teaching is "explicit" in that the objective (the skill or strategy) is the teacher's focus.

In balanced instruction, however, indirect, implicit instruction is equally critical and leads to the joy of reading and writing. This instruction is student-directed and allows students, at other times of the day, to reinforce recently taught skills or strategies through much practice with teacher-chosen and self-selected literature via personal responses in oral, written, or visual form and group discussion. Such authentic literacy experiences certainly help to reinforce literacy skills and strategies, although indirectly, or in an embedded fashion. A balanced literacy program for the intermediate grades utilizes *both* approaches, at different times, in the instructional day.

As already stated, a literacy program for the intermediate grades must also be *comprehensive* in scope and include a number of critical components, with the ultimate goal of teaching students the skills to read and write and instilling in them the desire to do so because they have become pleasurable activities for them. It does not, however, concentrate on any of these components to the exclusion of the others (e.g., a fifth-grade teacher who lets students do independent reading, but teaches no reading strategies). To be truly comprehensive in scope, a comprehensive literacy program for the intermediate grades must include each of the following:

- quality literature with personal response and analysis
- ongoing assessment, using multiple measures
- instruction in word identification and vocabulary strategies, such as the morphology and etymology of words
- instruction in reading comprehension strategies
- fostering of independent reading
- development of oral and written language and visual learning

One basic difference between a balanced and comprehensive literacy program and a more traditional/skills-based view is the relative roles of the teacher and the students in such classrooms. In a balanced and comprehensive literacy program, the teacher's role is one of facilitator, offering students prompts and questions to focus their attention on strategies that will help them independently overcome challenges in present and future texts; in more traditional approaches, the teacher's role is directive, supplying short-term help by telling students exactly what to do as they need help. The aim of a balanced and comprehensive literacy program is to develop enthusiastic readers and writers who question, consider alternatives, and make informed choices as they seek meaning or to express meaning; the aim of the more traditional approach to literacy is often to draw students through a predetermined teaching sequence to ensure that all the basic skills of literacy are covered. Finally, a balanced, comprehensive literacy program is based on the understanding that it is the children themselves who are the readers and it is they who must bring meaning to and gain meaning from text as they read; in more traditional literacy programs the teacher more commonly adopts the role of interpreter, who makes the connections between the author and the readers and is responsible for checking that students have derived the correct meaning from text (Mooney, 1990) (see Figure 1.2).

A balanced and comprehensive literacy program in the intermediate grades also consists of five major affective and cognitive components. All of these components, offered separately, are crucial building blocks for literacy knowledge and enjoyment; when they come together as a whole entity, they are the essence of a strong literacy program for intermediate-grade youngsters. These five components are as follows:

- engagement

FIGURE 1.2 Comparison of two approaches to teaching reading/literacy.

BALANCED AND COMPREHENSIVE LITERACY PROGRAM	TRADITIONAL/SKILLS-BASED LITERACY PROGRAM
The teacher's role is to empower by providing instruction and questions that focus student's attention on:	The teacher's role is to supply short-term help by:

The teacher's role is to empower by providing instruction and questions that focus student's attention on:

- strategies that will help them to decode and understand text;
- becoming aware of textual cues that help students decode and comprehend.

Readers are taught directly how to overcome challenges in present and future text.

The goal of a balanced and comprehensive literacy program is to:

- create independent readers who question, consider alternatives, and make informed inferences as they search for meaning;
- entitle students to become independent problem solvers who can become long-term learners;
- show students how and why to choose and employ strategies to ensure that meaning is gained and maintained;
- use assessment to inform instruction.

A balanced and comprehensive literacy program is based upon the understanding that:

- students are the readers;
- students are the ones who must bring meaning to, and gain meaning from, the text they read.

The teacher is aware of the constant need for comprehension to be considered as the act of the reader engaging with, and responding to, the text during reading.

The teacher's role is to supply short-term help by:

- focusing student's attention on specific textual details;
- explaining the meaning of a word if they don't know it;
- explaining the meaning of text;

Readers become dependent upon the teacher to tell them exactly what to do in each reading situation.

The goal of a traditional, skills-based literacy program is to:

- lead students through a predetermined teaching sequence using a specific book to teach a particular skill;
- see that every student receives all the skills in a predetermined hierarchy, whether they are needed or not;
- frequently administer formalized assessment devices that provide information about progress in the specific program.

A traditional, skills-based literacy program is based upon the understanding that:

- connections between the reader and the author are depending upon the teacher as interpreter;
- the teacher is responsible for determining whether students understand.

The teacher oversees comprehension for students and alerts them to mismatches between the errors and the text, hoping the students will use this behavior in the future.

- a blend of transmission and transaction
- explanations and examples
- application and guided practice
- respect for each child's culture and background

Engagement

That a child must be engaged in the subject to learn most effectively is not a new concept, nor one espoused only by literacy experts. Many years ago Jerome Bruner expounded on the importance of getting the child interested and involved in learning (Bruner, 1966), and a plethora of motivational educational programs and learning theories have emanated from his early postulations. Educators are now convinced that when children are highly engaged in what they are doing and their experiences are meaningful and purposeful to them, learning is optimal (Guthrie and Wigfield, 1997).

Engagement with reading material, in fact, may be considered the key to learning in a balanced and comprehensive literacy program for the upper grades; however, it often seems apparent that as students go through school, their motivation for school—and reading—too often decreases. The less they like to do it, the less they will do of it, and a downward cycle is set in motion. Practice in literacy, as in anything else, results in greater proficiency. And, indeed, how much students read is, in fact, one of the best predictors of how well they read and write. Therefore, if we want all our students to read and write as well as they possibly can, we must find ways to combat the problem of decreasing motivation leading to the inevitability of aliteracy—a state of being able to read but choosing not to—especially as students move into the middle grades (Cunningham and Allington, 1999).

The answer to the question of engagement, however, lies not only in the method used, but in the effectiveness and enthusiasm of the teacher. **Engagement** involves a complex set of ongoing attitudes and activities that occur in the classroom environment. These attitudes and activities lead to the creation of a community of learners, including the teacher, who is excited about all aspects of the literacy process. Such a teacher is thoughtfully eclectic, modifying methods and programs to fit the needs of his or her learners. Teachers with the ability to engage learners do not rely on a single method or program for all children in their charge, because they know that good teaching requires "doing the right thing the right way and at the right time in response to problems posed by particular [students] on particular occasions" (Garrison, 1997, p. 132; Nelson-Levitt, 2000).

- engagement

The learning community conducive to engagement in the upper grades is an active, literate environment where reading, writing, speaking, listening, viewing, and visually representing are used as tools for almost all of the learning and problem-solving that occurs in the classroom. Although the teacher has thoughtfully created the literacy curriculum to reflect the needs of his or her learners and the dictates of the standards of the state in which they reside, there are also plenty of opportunities in such a program for students to choose their own reading materials and write connected text. In addition, students often collaborate as they work on reading and writing projects, and cooperative interactions among students are valued as critical to language learning and development, especially for English language learners (Slavin, 1989/1990).

Engagement also involves asking the kinds of questions that are provocative to students, or those that allow them to reflect on what they have read (Cecil, 1995). Such questions form the gateway to **grand conversations**. These kinds of open-ended questions and resultant discussions require students to come up with their own ideas about literature, as opposed to the more widespread "gentle inquisitions," which are mostly factually based questions used merely to determine whether students did, indeed, read the text and are able to recall verbatim the facts contained in it (Peterson and Eeds, 1990). To become proficient readers in the upper grades, students must be taught to actively solve problems with text; to respond to text critically and creatively in oral, visual, or written form; and to feel good about their ability to interact with the author's message (Tower, 2000). Such skills are acquired mainly through forming and responding to critical questions modeled by an effective teacher, or through "grand conversations" about text conducted by the teacher and, ideally, with their peers.

grand conversations ●

Transmission and Transaction: The Balance

At both primary and intermediate-grade levels, there must be a balance between the teacher directly imparting information through explicit instruction and systematic teaching—the **transmission model**—and a focus on negotiating with students about their individual thoughts and ideas about what they are reading and writing—the **transactional model** (Rosenblatt, 1978). A balanced and comprehensive approach to literacy in the upper grades uses both a transmission model and a transactional model at different times, for different purposes. These two models have similarities and differences in how they are used in the early grades. The latter approach is a more collaborative model that also integrates the four language modes of reading, writing, listening, and speaking and considers reading a transaction, or intellectual negotiation, between the reader and the author, where both parties bring their own experience to the text. In the transactional model, the teacher is not the only possessor of knowledge, but he or she takes on the role of facilitator in the literacy development process.

transmission model ●

transactional model ●

Using the transmission model in early literacy, the teacher assumes the responsibility of directly "transmitting" new information about letter sounds and symbols to students through explicit instruction and systematic teaching of the code that is the foundation of the English language. Other transmission responsibilities include rote instruction of **sight vocabulary,** or words immediately recognized, and the memorization of lists of **word families,** such as those words containing *oi:* voice, noise, moist, and so forth. By contrast, in the upper grades, when most decoding of new words has become automatic, the teacher must then show students how to gain information from text by explicit, systematic teaching of such comprehension strategies as summarizing, generalizing, using the context, making predictions, and visualizing (see Chapter 5). Additionally, the teacher must directly teach advanced decoding and morphological skills, such as the meaning and derivation of word parts, that can help students figure out the meanings of unknown words (see Chapters 3 and 4).

● sight vocabulary
● word families

In a balanced and comprehensive approach to literacy in the primary grades, the process of transaction, or learning to negotiate meaning with the author of the text, begins in early literacy instruction even before children themselves are able to read. As they are sharing reading with a teacher, individual predictions and opinions are solicited, and children learn to bring their own set of experiences to all language-related situations. In the upper grades, these negotiations are continued, but refined, as children collaborate with the teacher and each other not only to think about the meaning of the text as the author intended it but also to consider how it appears to them, with all the personal experiences and background information that they now are able to bring to it.

Explanations and Examples

In a balanced and comprehensive literacy program in the intermediate grades, students need to be explicitly taught how proficient readers construct text in order to comprehend written material. Explicit teaching still occurs at this level and involves making clear to learners what the particular skill is that they are learning, how they can best learn it, when and under what conditions to utilize the skill, and how they will know when they have been successful at employing it. They must be shown how effective comprehension strategies work, and then they must be given examples of how each strategy can help them as they read to make meaning from the written page. As basic a truth as this may appear to be, such explicit teaching has not always occurred in U.S. schools. Too often in classrooms, many students have been left alone to figure out how to go about understanding text and exactly what they have to do to become successful readers and writers (Hancock, 1999).

Delores Durkin, in a landmark study of comprehension instruction in American schools, found that little, if any, explanation of how to use comprehension strategies was offered in elementary schools; instead, much time was devoted to assessing how well students comprehended, using reams of basal workbook pages to do so (Durkin, 1990). In other words, students seem to have been expected to "intuit" comprehension strategies without anyone ever having taught them, directly, how to employ them! The results of this study caused a flurry of reform, dedicated to directly teaching comprehension strategies to students, in a systematic, step-by-step fashion.

Lectures, definitions, general descriptions, and overviews rarely give students the complete raw material they need to construct meaning. Students need both **deduction**—going from the general to the particular, through explanation—and **induction**—going from the particular to the general, with the help of examples (Hyde and Bizar, 1989). Both explanations and examples are useful and necessary in a balanced and comprehensive literacy program to foster construction of text, and most teachers are now aware of the need to teach strategies directly to students. However, there is usually tremendous pressure on teachers to hurry through certain packaged literacy programs, perhaps causing teachers to provide to students minimal explanations of how, when, and under what conditions to use comprehension strategies and to offer few, if any, examples of what the strategies look like in actual practice. This time crunch is a significant hindrance to teaching students to construct text in a thoughtful way. Creating examples that will have meaning for students takes more time and effort than merely memorizing linear explanations of strategies. If a teacher does not take the time, students often lose a true grasp of the concepts behind the strategy. Additionally, students have fewer opportunities to think about and internalize such strategies.

Several examples of how comprehension strategies are used can be offered most effectively through teacher **modeling,** or scaffolding, as most human behaviors are acquired in this way (Bandura, 1986; Vygotsky, 1978) (see Chapter 5). Modeling, or showing children exactly how to perform a specific reading behavior, can be done at various times within a balanced and comprehensive literacy program for the upper grades. First, implicit—or indirect—modeling can occur many times during the day as students are engaged in reading and writing activities and the teacher takes the opportunity to share pertinent information. Second, modeling can occur during **writer's workshop,** as the teacher directly demonstrates the various steps needed to publish a piece of written work. Third, using the vehicle of the **guided reading procedure,** the teacher has the opportunity to introduce literature, think aloud through a compendium of decoding and comprehension strategies, and demonstrate his or her own response to the text. Finally, **minilessons,** developed on the basis of the individual needs of students, are ideal opportunities for the teacher to model the exact literacy strategies that are needed for the literacy context (Cooper, 2000).

deduction

induction

modeling

writer's workshop

guided reading procedure

minilessons

Application, Guided Practice, and Personal Response

A review of the important research on successful literacy programs in the last few years offers teachers surprisingly consistent findings about what factors are critical in setting the stage for a successful balanced and comprehensive literacy program that enables students to construct meaning. Fielding and Pearson (1994), synthesizing the findings of research on reading comprehension, offer three critical findings to teachers. This important summary of research makes the following suggestions:

1. Teachers must provide a large block of time for application of newly acquired literacy skills. The amount of time devoted to actual reading and writing practice, according to Fielding and Pearson (1994), should be greater than the sum total of all specific skill instruction. In other words, after a skill or comprehension strategy has been introduced, there should be ample time immediately after these sessions for students to internalize their new understandings; the students should be actively adding them to their burgeoning literacy understandings through extensive teacher-guided practice. To ensure that such practice actually translates into enhanced comprehension, however, students should sometimes be given some choices about what they read. Additionally, the material used should be appropriate in difficulty, that is, not so difficult as to be frustrating, yet not so easy that nothing challenging is encountered.

2. Teachers must provide opportunities for students to practice literacy skills in a social setting. The absolutely quiet, teacher-directed classrooms, proudly heralded in some traditional schools, should be a thing of the past, according to these researchers—at least for certain times in the school day. Students, especially English language learners, learn best when they are able to talk about what they are reading and writing. Besides enhancing their learning by adding sensory input and vocabulary development afforded by oral discussion, reading, when it becomes a social activity, is more enjoyable for most students. Therefore, in a balanced and comprehensive literacy program for the upper grades, a continuum of literacy instructional configurations should be offered in most classrooms. While **shared reading** and guided reading, where the teacher is prominent and working with small groups, are ideal formats for direct transmission of skills, other more collaborative approaches, such as **dyad reading** or simple **partner reading, literature response groups,** and **interest groups** should also be instituted (see Chapter 5 for discussion of these concepts).

- shared reading
- dyad reading
- partner reading
- literature response groups
- interest groups

3. Teachers must ensure that students are given myriad opportunities to respond personally to text. To act on this suggestion, teachers must ensure that they do not limit themselves to only factual-type questions that require only a monosyllabic answer, but allow time for the type of critical and creative questions for which there is no one "correct" answer, and for which every student has an opportunity to voice an opinion emanating from his or her own life (e.g., "What would *you* have done if the boy treated you that way?"). It is also helpful for teachers to sometimes pose provocative questions about text for which they themselves do not have an answer, not seeking a response they have in mind, or one provided by the basal teacher's manual. Moreover, in a truly balanced and comprehensive program for the intermediate grades, adequate time should be set aside for sharing journal reactions to literature, or original writing, in small groups, where the climate is risk free and conducive to personal conversations about text.

Students in a balanced and comprehensive literacy program can also use modern technology to share their responses about books they are reading using electronic dialogues. Using a computer, students can write their thoughts and feelings about books and e-mail them to students reading the same material in other classrooms, older students in the same school, or even preservice education students at a university. The "computer pal," if chosen wisely, can encourage students to elaborate on their entries, make personal connections with text, and reflect more deeply on their reading (Moore, 1991).

Respect for Each Child's Culture and Background

Finally, perhaps the most pressing issue in a balanced and comprehensive approach to literacy in the intermediate grades is for each teacher to possess a deep sensitivity and appreciation for children of all diverse backgrounds. Diversity must never be merely tolerated, but actively celebrated by the teacher as well as the students. We simply cannot hope to be successful with all learners in today's heterogeneous classrooms without first understanding each child's reasons for becoming literate. Without that knowledge, we may fail in our attempts to fully engage the child as an equal partner in his or her own pursuit of knowledge. As teachers, we must somehow lead children to fall in love with books and, as Lucy Calkins (1994, p. 111) suggests, we must get them to "write from the heart about their own unique experiences with the world." Then they will be able to see the purpose of concomitant skill instruction and, consequently, become actual co-conspirators in the quest for literacy.

Instruction in literacy for students in the upper elementary grades, in order to be successful, must take into account each child's culture and understand each child's particular way of learning. All human beings learn according to their existing understandings and cultural backgrounds in socially constructed settings, particularly through conversations with family and loved ones. Therefore, any instructional plans in literacy must be developed with great care, using observation, home visits, formal and informal assessment, along with all other available background information about each child's language, culture, values, knowledge, and interests.

SUMMARY

The past decade has seen a major emphasis on creating a balanced and comprehensive literacy program designed to teach young children how to read. Now, the focus is also on older children, most of whom have mastered the early skills necessary for automatic decoding and are now ready to turn their attention to reading to learn. For either developmental level, the fundamental characteristics of the process are basically the same. Reading is a holistic process, not just a sum of all its parts. It is a constructive process whereby the reader predicts the meaning. Additionally, reading is a strategic process, in which the reader must choose which strategies in his or her repertoire are appropriate to the task. Reading is also an interactive process, with the reader and the author negotiating the joint meaning of the text.

A balanced and comprehensive approach parts company from a more traditional approach to literacy mainly in its view of who holds responsibility for meaning-making from text. In a balanced and comprehensive approach, the teacher accepts the role of facilitator—prompting, advising, questioning, and providing direct instruction on instructional strategies, yet allowing the student the freedom to interpret text according to his or her own background of experiences.

A balanced and comprehensive approach to literacy in the upper elementary grades differs from a similar approach used for early readers in that the focus is now less on decoding and more on making sense of the world through print. While many of the underlying beliefs remain the same, the focus shifts slightly in subtle ways. While there must continue to be a transmission of strategies—in this case more related to comprehension than decoding—there must also be an emphasis on transaction, or a personal meaning-making with text. In addition, engagement is crucial in the upper grades to ensure that children, now able to read, do so willingly as a chosen recreational activity. Clear explanations and examples are critical in the upper grades to make sure children know exactly how to apply the comprehension strategies that proficient readers use. Abundant guided practice and opportunities to apply the skills that have been taught will help to solidify understandings and increase confidence as well as enjoyment. Whole texts and authentic literature, both fiction and nonfiction, can be utilized for these purposes. Finally, a clear respect and appreciation for the culture and background of each learner will enable the teacher to understand what each child needs to become a literate individual.

In the following chapters we explore the specific components needed in a balanced and comprehensive literacy program for the upper grades that will help to develop readers and writers who have the tools to read, write, and incorporate technology—and joyfully do so—to explore their worlds.

Questions

1. Reflect upon your own experience with reading and writing in the intermediate grades. Do you believe you received a balanced and comprehensive or a more traditional model of instruction? Give examples. In retrospect, can you think of any measures your teachers might have employed to make your literacy instruction more meaningful?

2. Think about your own definition of what it means to be a literate person. How do you think your definition will influence how you teach reading, writing, listening, speaking, viewing, and visually representing?

3. Discuss with a classmate what you consider to be the three most striking differences between literacy instruction today and literacy instruction in the recent past. What do you think caused these changes?

Suggestions

1. Make notes while observing a literacy lesson in an intermediate classroom. Analyze the lesson in terms of the components of a balanced and comprehensive literacy program proposed in this chapter.

2. Ask a group of intermediate-age children to discuss the characteristics they feel a good teacher of literacy should possess. Then ask them how they feel when they are allowed to select their own books or topics to read, write, discuss, or analyze. Do they seem to find it easier or more difficult to create without first being given an idea and/or a direction?

3. Try to recall the most significant literacy development activity you experienced in the intermediate grades. With your instructor or a classmate, discuss how a similar experience could be designed into a lesson for you to teach to a small group of intermediate students.

References

Bandura, A. (1986). *Psychological modeling: Conflicting theories.* Chicago: Aldine-Atherton.

Baumann, J. F., Hoffman, J. V., Moon, J., & Duffy-Hester, A. M. (1998). Where are the teachers' voices in the phonics/whole language debate? Results from a survey of U. S. elementary teachers. *The Reading Teacher, 51,* 636–650.

Berliner, D., & Biddle, B. (1996). *The manufactured crisis.* White Plains, NY: Longman.

Bruner, J. (1966). *Toward a theory of instruction.* Cambridge, MA: Harvard University Press.

Buehl, D. (2001). *Literacy-building strategies for content teachers.* Newark, DE: International Reading Association.

Calkins, L. M. (1994). *The art of teaching writing.* Portsmouth, NH: Heinemann.

Cecil, N. L. (1995). *The art of inquiry: Questioning strategies for k–6 classrooms.* Winnipeg, Manitoba: Peguis.

Cecil, N. L. (1999). *Striking a balance: Positive practices for early literacy.* Scottsdale, AZ: Holcomb Hathaway.

Cooper, J. D. (2000). *Literacy: Helping children construct meaning.* Boston: Houghton Mifflin.

Cunningham, P. M., & Allington, R. L. (1999). *Classrooms that work: They can all read and write* (2nd ed.). New York: Longman.

Darling-Hammond, L. (1997). *Doing what matters most: Investing in quality teaching.* New York: National Commission on Teaching and America's Future.

Durkin, D. (1990). Delores Durkin speaks on instruction. *The Reading Teacher, 43,* 472–476.

Fielding, L. G., & Pearson, P. D. (1994). Reading comprehension: What works. *Educational Leadership, 2,* 62–68.

Garrison, J. (1997). *Dewey and Eros: Wisdom and desire in the art of teaching.* New York: Teachers College Press.

Guthrie, J. T., & Wigfield, A. (Eds.). (1997). *Reading engagement: Motivating readers through integrated instruction.* Newark, DE: International Reading Association.

Hancock, J. (Ed.). (1999). *The explicit teaching of reading.* Newark, DE: International Reading Association.

Harris, T. L., & Hodges, R. E. (Eds.). (1995). *The literacy dictionary: The vocabulary of reading and writing.* Newark, DE: International Reading Association.

Hyde, A. A., & Bizar, M. (1989). *Thinking in context: Teaching cognitive processes across the elementary curriculum.* White Plains, NY: Longman.

Larsen-Blair, S. M., & Williams, K. A. (1999). *The balanced reading program: Helping all students achieve success.* Newark, DE: International Reading Association.

Mooney, M. E. (1990). *Reading to, with, and by children.* Katonah, NY: Richard C. Owens.

Moore, M. A. (1991). Electronic dialoguing: An avenue to literacy. *The Reading Teacher, 45,* 280–286.

Nelson-Levitt, J. (2000). *Why Jeannie can't teach: Reflections of a first-grade mentor teacher.* Unpublished master's thesis, California State University, Sacramento.

Pearson, P. D. (1993). Teaching and learning reading: A research perspective. *Language Arts, 70,* 502–511.

Peterson, R., & Eeds, M. (1990). *Grand conversations: Literature groups in action.* New York: Scholastic.

Rosenblatt, L. (1978). *The reader, the text, the poem: The transactional theory of the literary work.* Carbondale: Southern Illinois University Press.

Rosenblatt, L. (1983). *Literature as exploration* (4th ed.). New York: Modern Language Association.

Rumelhart, D. E. (1977). Toward an interactive model of reading. In S. Dornic (Ed.), *Attention and performance* (vol. 6). Hillsdale, NJ: Erlbaum.

Slavin, R. E. (December 1989/January 1990). Research on cooperative learning: Consensus and controversy. *Educational Leadership, 47*(4), 52–55.

Squire, J. R. (1983). Composing and comprehending: Two sides of the same basic process. *Language Arts, 60*(5), 581–589.

Stahl, S. A. (1992). Saying the "P" word: Nine guidelines for exemplary phonics instruction. *The Reading Teacher, 15,* 33–50.

Stanovich, K. (1980). Toward an interactive-compensatory model of individual differences in the development of reading fluency. *Reading Research Quarterly, 16,* 22–71.

Tower, C. (2000). Questions that matter: Preparing elementary students for the inquiry process. *The Reading Teacher, 53*(7), 550–557.

Vygotsky, L. S. (1962, 1979). *Thought and language.* Cambridge, MA: MIT Press.

Vygotsky, L. S. (1978). Mind in society. In M. Cole, V. John-Steiner, S. Scribner, & E. Souberman (Eds.), pp. 128–173. Cambridge, MA: Harvard University Press.

Wink, J. (1996). Jonathan: Linking critical pedagogy and literacy. *Clip: A Journal of the California Literacy Project, 2*(4), 27–30.

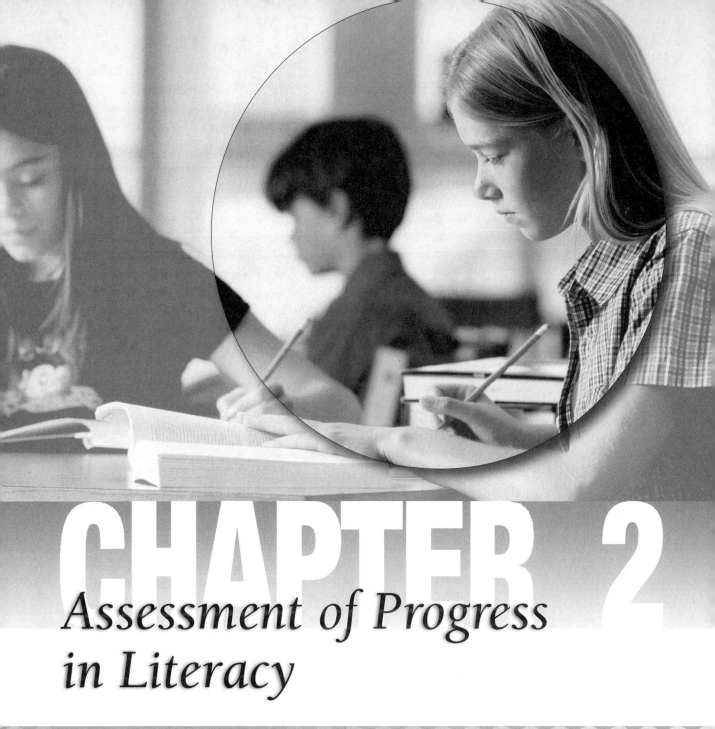

CHAPTER 2

Assessment of Progress in Literacy

Focus Questions

- How is assessment different from evaluation?
- What are the types of assessment possible for intermediate-grade literacy?
- In what ways can literacy assessment inform instruction?

CURRENT VIEWS OF ASSESSMENT

Many in the field of education today believe that "our nation is test crazy" (Glazer, 1998, p. 1) and participating in a testing frenzy (O'Sullivan and Jiang, 2002). Each day it seems that more and more testing is being required of students at all levels. Achievement test scores for area schools are published in the local newspaper and used by realtors to market homes. The commonsense thinking is that if we want our students to perform better we need to test them more. Everyone wants students to perform at their best, but is testing the way to achieve this? According to Daniels and Bizar (1998), "since most standardized test scores correlate highly with socioeconomic status, any new round of testing will usually reconfirm the unworthiness of the underclasses and comfort the privileged" (p. 205). Testing is about **evaluation,** or placing a value on a performance. Evaluation is not, however, synonymous with assessment.

Defining Assessment

Assessment is the process of gathering information (data) about students' abilities that will help teachers, parents, and other caregivers know more about a learner's strengths and weaknesses so that they may provide appropriate instruction or assistance for the learner. As such, assessment certainly can include tests since they provide one piece of data, but assessment is about more than just testing. It is about looking at instruction in terms of how it impacts student learning. It is about self-evaluation much like what Artis did in preparing his portfolio. It is about performing to a set of identified criteria. Thus, assessment is a much broader and richer concept than testing. But, as Neill (2000) states, "Assessment is at a crisis point: the old model is incapable of meeting real needs, and a new approach is not yet clear. . . . Whatever forms of exams are eventually used, they cannot provide much help for teachers in learning to integrate assessment with instruction in a continuous flow—and that is the heart of assessment in the service of learning" (p. 145).

Ongoing assessment of literacy development refers to the use of multiple instruments, daily observation, and many work samples to measure progress. It also refers to the ongoing analysis of the data from these

In the Classroom

Small groups of about four to five students arrange their desks in circles around Ms. West's fourth-grade classroom. Within each group one student will present his or her language arts portfolio to the others. Ms. West scheduled this sharing of portfolios as a kind of dress rehearsal in preparation for student-led conferences with parents later in the week. Let's eavesdrop on one student, Artis, and listen to his portfolio introduction.

My name is Artis. I hope I will be going to the fifth grade next year. I created this language arts portfolio during fourth grade. My teacher's name is Ms. West.

I began working on things and saving things for my portfolio on September 15 and put my portfolio together on May 20. I began deciding what to include in my portfolio in April and May.

I picked items that were important to me to include in this portfolio. I wanted to show what I had learned and I put all of my favorite projects in the portfolio. I also wanted to show that I am a hard worker.

The way I decided which things would go first in my portfolio was easy—I picked my favorite thing first. I had a list of everything I wanted in my portfolio and I just put it in order starting with my favorite item.

This portfolio shows that I kept a book list for my readings. It also shows that I have a prediction log that I use when I am reading stories. My portfolio

shows what I learned through reading. I learned about hurricanes and sand dollars. It also shows that there are some things about my reading that I still have to work on.

My portfolio shows the different types of writing I can do. I included a book that I wrote and illustrated. I also included some comic strips that I wrote the story for as well as a story that uses new vocabulary.

I think that my best items are the comic strips, my hurricane book, and my movie review. These activities were all fun and I learned a lot from completing each of these.

My portfolio shows the improvements I have made this year. It shows what I can do. I can write a book if I use my imagination! It shows I can improve with practice and it shows that I am a hard worker.

Artis proceeds to share individual items from his portfolio with his group members. He tells why each item is special to him and what he has learned from that item. Later, he will also be asked to share with his parents those areas for which he feels he needs to learn more. By the end of this day, all Ms. West's students will have an idea of what their classmates have accomplished and will see each one at his or her best. The students are proud of their efforts and it is truly a literacy celebration. Following the sharing, students are invited to have pizza and cold drinks in the cafeteria, compliments of Ms. West.

instruments and observations concerning individuals, small groups, and the entire class so that the teacher can customize instruction and, when necessary, plan appropriate interventions. This type of ongoing assessment is also referred to as *formative assessment;* it helps us know how we are progressing. **Summative assessment** is a compilation of formative assessment data, or summary data provided at program endings, units of study, or other intervals (e.g., midterm, final, every eight weeks) to report progress (e.g., report cards).

The assessment in Ms. West's classroom is ongoing and dynamic; it is the basis on which she makes all of her instructional decisions. In an effective intermediate classroom, instruction is based on information acquired through valid assessment procedures. Moreover, students in the class are also involved in their own assessment and, like Artis, are able to recognize their own strengths and limitations and are encouraged to use strategies designed to increase their literacy competence. Finally, in a classroom like Ms. West's, the teacher is able to use and interpret the results from a variety of curriculum-based and standardized assessment tools and effectively communicate those results to students, their parents or caretakers, and relevant school personnel. Artis knows how well he is doing, and so does everyone who cares about his learning process.

Standards and Assessment

Teachers today are being held accountable for meeting a wide array of standards. These standards are of two basic types: **professional teaching standards** (i.e., related to how well the teacher performs), and *curriculum* or *content standards* (i.e., related to what the teacher must teach). In addition to national standards for both teachers and content (see the National Board for Professional Teaching Standards at www.nbpts.org/ and the NCTE/IRA English Language Arts Content Standards at www.ncte.org/standards/), individual states have developed their own sets of standards. In California the standards for teachers are referred to as the California Standards for the Teaching Profession (www.ctc.ca.gov/), and in Louisiana they are called the Louisiana Components of Effective Teaching (www.doe.state.la.us/DOE/asps/home.asp). Content standards for any state can be found online at that state's

Department of Education web page. Individual school districts usually adopt the state content standards or include a few additional standards. When standards are referred to in this chapter, it is content standards that are the focus.

The assessment tools discussed in this chapter can coordinate easily with state-mandated content standards. English language arts standards need not be viewed as something above and apart from the practices of actual classroom teachers. Rather, well-designed standards represent what "teachers and the many others involved in English language arts education agree is the best and most productive current thinking about teaching and learning" (Smith, 1996, p. v). Hill et al. (1998) provide an appropriate analogy: "Classroom based assessments provide sign posts to document growth. The [standards] provide the roadmap to show where we are going" (p. 175).

PRINCIPLES OF ASSESSMENT

As a result of reflective practice, lesson observations, checklists, and other measures, teachers perform assessments, and in turn these assessments inform teachers as to what needs to be taught, or retaught. The following five principles of assessment reveal this reciprocal, synergistic relationship between assessment and teaching. Careful study of these assessment principles can help teachers determine whether their assessment plan will be complementary to instruction (adapted from Cooper, 1997).

The Core of Assessment Should Be Daily Observation

Teachers, who frequently observe and take notes on each aspect of literacy development, know much more about the status of their students than can be obtained from any standardized testing, no matter how reliable the testing is purported to be. It is imperative that assessment be a daily event, occurring as the student reads and writes. Through observing patterns of growth over time, the teacher is in the ideal position to get a clear picture of how students are progressing.

Assessment Should Take Many Different Forms

Different types of assessment tools should be used for different purposes to ensure that the most accurate measure of each learner's literacy progress is obtained. For example, writing samples, checklists about summaries of text, and anecdotal notes give insights that are not scientific but based solely upon the teacher's judgment. Although these data are critical to effective planning and decision making, the teacher also needs standardized test results that have accepted statistical *reliability* (i.e., dependability and consistency) and *validity* (i.e., soundness); in other words, the tests consistently measure what they claim to be measuring. To get a truly multidimensional overview of a student's performance in any dimension of literacy, teachers need to took at the data from all available sources.

Assessment Must Avoid Cultural Bias

Learners from different cultures, linguistic groups, and backgrounds may have different language issues as well as varied experiences and styles of learning. When planning assessment procedures, and particularly when interpreting and reporting them to others, these factors should be judiciously considered.

The importance of considering cultural bias can be illustrated by a situation encountered by a teacher who had a student in her class from the Virgin Islands. It had been determined that the student had a severe reading disability. However, upon examining the test items and the test results, the teacher realized that the student was certainly not reading disabled: she had scored poorly because she had not known many vocabulary words, such as *chimney* and *caboose*—words that have little meaning for residents of a tiny tropical island!

Students Themselves Should Be Actively Engaged in the Assessment Process

Although students cannot be involved in every aspect of literacy assessment, sometimes asking for input when evaluating their work can be a key factor in encouraging students to take charge of their own learning, and it invites ownership of their successes. Since teaching and learning are ideally collaborative processes, we do not want students to view assessment as an uncomfortable practice that the teacher "does" to them. Therefore, by allowing students and teachers to work and think together, assessment becomes a shared responsibility, with learners participating enthusiastically as team players in their own learning.

Assessment Should Focus on Students' Abilities

Assessment should focus on determining what learners *can* do, not what they *cannot* do. When teachers really understand the reading and writing abilities of their students, it becomes much easier to decide which new literacy experiences should be offered to help them develop further. Not only is this a more constructive way of looking at learning, but students benefit in other crucial ways. They are able to progress more readily when the atmosphere is one where mistakes are viewed as building blocks rather than failures that must be avoided (Cousin et al., 1993).

TYPES OF ASSESSMENT

Teachers have at their disposal an almost overwhelming array of instruments to use as part of the assessment process. Many of these instruments blend naturally into instruction; others provide a separate means to assess literacy progress, in either more or less direct ways as related to actual classroom instruction. Think of assessment as a continuum—with teacher

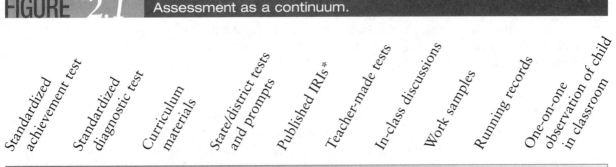

FIGURE 2.1 Assessment as a continuum.

Standardized achievement test · Standardized diagnostic test · Curriculum materials · State/district tests and prompts · Published IRIs* · Teacher-made tests · In-class discussions · Work samples · Running records · One-on-one observation of child in classroom

LEAST DIRECT   MOST DIRECT

(Formal)   (Informal)

* IRIs = informal reading inventories.

observation being most direct and standardized tests being least direct (Johnston, 1992) (see Figure 2.1). Traditionally, these distinctions in assessment have been referred to as informal and formal, respectively.

Because so many assessment tools are available, it is impossible to discuss each one in this chapter. Therefore, we explore a sampling of some of the most pervasive assessment devices that are compatible with a balanced and comprehensive literacy program. An example of a balanced and comprehensive framework for guiding the assessment process is presented in Figure 2.2. Here, the assessment process is guided by two questions: What kind of information do I need? and How am I going to gather this information? For each area of literacy, decisions must be made about the best ways to obtain the desired information. The options presented are (1) *direct,* which refers to teacher-developed or one-on-one observations of what the student can do; (2) *ongoing,* which refers to a set of direct data collected over time; and (3) *indirect,* which refers to data that come from standardized instruments or instruments devised by someone outside the classroom setting. Once the teacher has determined the area for which he or she needs information, the framework provides several alternatives for obtaining that assessment data.

Most of the techniques discussed in the remainder of this chapter can be used easily on the basis of the information given; others require reviewing an examiner's handbook. Appropriate references are given for those that require more detailed study, and samples of others are presented in Appendix D.

Four categories of assessment are used in intermediate-grade classrooms: standardized testing, curriculum-based assessment, standards-based performance assessment, and process-oriented assessment. While each category offers a unique perspective for a balanced and comprehensive literacy program, the assessment tools presented in this chapter may accommodate more than one category. For example, checklists could be utilized across all four categories.

| A framework for guiding the literacy assessment process.* | | | FIGURE 2.2 |

What kind of information do I need?	How am I going to gather this information?		
	DIRECT	**ONGOING**	**INDIRECT**
Structural analysis/ word analysis	One-on-one observation Word games	Anecdotal notes Running records	Stanford Diagnostic Subtest Published word lists
Vocabulary	Observation Pretest Free writing Class presentations	Daily discussions Anecdotal notes Weekly tests Writing samples	Stanford Achievement Test Carver Vocabulary Test
Fluency	One-on-one observation Paired reading	Anecdotal notes Running records Tape recordings IRI/miscue analysis	State/district developed instruments
Spelling	Free writing Pretests Dictations	Writing samples Journals Weekly tests	Standardized test
Reading comprehension	Retellings QARs Discussions Cloze tests	Paraphrases Summaries Class contributions Sketchings	Standardized tests (Stanford Achievement, Metropolitan Achievement)
Writing	Free writing Journals Quickwrites Editing checklist	Writing samples Daily work	Rubrics that accompany curriculum materials (scaled scores)
Reading/writing attitudes	Reading logs Number of books read/written Teacher interviews	Conferences Reading response journals	Questionnaires Attitude surveys Interest inventory (all published)
Student views of own literacy	Books chosen Self-evaluations Response journals Teacher interviews	Portfolio choices Dialogue journals Reflection log	Attitude survey Reading survey Questionnaires (all published)

* IRI = informal reading inventory; QARs = question–answer relationships.

Standardized Testing

standardized testing ●

Standardized testing focuses on the use of norm-referenced tests to measure reading and writing skills as well as the subskills of these areas. (See "Standardized, or Indirect, Assessment Procedures" later in this chapter for specific, technical information about tests that fall under this category.) These tests are administered by the teacher or reading specialist and usually provide numerical scores that represent a student's rank compared to the performance of other learners at the same age or grade. The data obtained from these tests can be, but are not always, related to the content of instruction.

norm-referenced tests ●

Because they are **norm-referenced tests**—that is, administered to a large group of students to establish the reference scores to which subsequent scores are compared (refer to Figure 2.3)—they have not been developed to assess a specific curriculum. Therefore, some items may address material a teacher has taught, but there might also be items about topics not taught. Or, the test might measure the content of the curriculum, but in ways different from the instructional format used by the teacher. For instance, synonyms might be taught by the teacher within the context of sentences, whereas the standardized test might assess knowledge of synonyms through word matching.

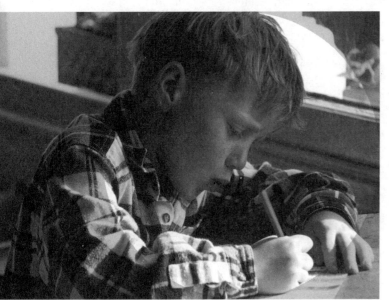

Examples include tests such as the Stanford Achievement Test (The Psychological Corporation) and the Stanford Diagnostic Reading Test (SDRT) (Karlsen and Gardner, 1995). The forms of these instruments appropriate for the intermediate grades offer subtests that provide a systematic appraisal of a student's ability to recognize meaningful word parts (roots, affixes, and compounds), to determine main ideas and supporting details, to correct sentences that are poorly written, as well as an accounting of vocabulary words the student knows compared with age-matched peers. The Green (grades 3.5–4.5), Purple (grades 4.5–6.5), and Brown (grades 6.5–8.9) Levels of the SDRT cover the range of intermediate grades.

The results of standardized tests are most appropriately used to get an overall sense of how well a group (school, class) is performing, and what general academic areas might need more focus in the classroom. These indirect assessments are often viewed by teachers before they have had an opportunity to get to know their students' strengths and needs better. As a result, they are used to make initial placements in instructional groups *until more direct information can be obtained with the actual materials the students will be using in the classroom*. It would be unfortunate if these initial placements were left unexamined once the teacher learns more about his or her particular students!

| Comparison of norm- and criterion-referenced assessments. | FIGURE 2.3 |

NORM-REFERENCED ASSESSMENTS ...	CRITERION-REFERENCED ASSESSMENTS ...
1. Assess students' knowledge of particular subject matter.	1. Assess student ability to perform a specific task.
2. Compare performance with that of a **norm group** (large number of students representative of the students for whom the test was designed in order to establish scoring values for the test).	2. Determine whether the student has the skill needed to progress to the next level of learning.
3. Are used annually as pretests/posttests to determine student gain and compare gains with those of the norm group.	3. Are used as often as needed to determine skills to be taught and skills that have been mastered.
4. Contain items considered to be precise, valid, and reliable for the purpose of selecting and sorting low-achieving and high-achieving students.	4. Contain items that determine whether the student is able to use a learned skill in a variety of situations.
5. Have high **construct validity** (items assess the skills, knowledge, and understandings that most experts agree comprise the area being tested).	5. Have high **content validity** (items assess the ability needed to perform the behaviors expected in the course, or in the curriculum).
6. Have high **reliability** (consistently measure the same behavior with each administration of the test).	6. Are not concerned with reliability; students are not expected to show the *same* behavior, but *improved* behavior.
7. Are interpreted by comparing students' scores with those obtained by the norm group.	7. Are interpreted by noting whether the student is able to perform a specific task, and to what degree.
8. Yield global measurements of general abilities.	8. Yield analytical data regarding specific objectives.
9. Provide scores that are statistically compared with those of a norm group (e.g., percentiles).	9. Provide a score that is considered acceptable by the teacher (e.g., 80% accuracy); incorrect items can be further examined.
10. Are written to create variability among individual scores in a group for the purpose of sorting students.	10. Are designed to assess ability to perform a specific task as stated by a specific objective or curriculum content standard.

Source: Adapted from Eddie Kennedy, *Classroom Approaches to Remedial Reading,* 1977. Itaska, FL: F.E. Peacock Publishers.

Curriculum-Based Assessment

Curriculum-based assessment uses school district–adopted curriculum materials to provide information about students' abilities. This category of assessment relates directly to the teacher's literacy curriculum to identify instructional needs and to determine what is required for learners to "master" a concept. Such assessment also may include **criterion-referenced tests**—tests that compare a student's performance to standards (the criteria) deemed appropriate for mastery in a particular area. Scores from such tools

● curriculum-based assessment

● criterion-referenced tests

typically offer a number, or percentage, for the amount of material each student has mastered. These scores are then compared with the criterion score required; usually 80 percent accuracy determines "mastery." See Figure 2.3 for a comparison of norm-referenced and criterion-referenced assessments.

Curriculum-based assessments are usually administered in the classroom using items and materials derived from the curriculum. Examples of curriculum-based assessments include asking a student to read a passage aloud from a text and counting the number of words read correctly per minute, or culminating a thematic unit on exploration by asking students to quickly write down as many words related to the study of exploration as they can. The first example represents a criterion-referenced test in that students are expected to be able to read a certain number of words correctly per minute at particular grade levels (refer to Figure 3.8). The teacher is evaluating whether this criterion has been met. The second example is more direct in that the results will inform the teacher how effectively the thematic unit increased students' vocabulary for a particular area of instruction. The teacher might have certain expectations for a minimum number of words that should be listed by each student, but these expectations can also vary according to the student. A second language learner might be expected to list at least 5 words, whereas a native English learner might be expected to list 10.

Standards-Based Performance Assessment

standards-based
performance
assessment ●

Relatively new to classrooms, **standards-based performance assessment,** a type of criterion-referenced assessment, describes assessment that views standards as the criteria on which performance is evaluated. These standards are most often devised by state curriculum committees, and several states have addressed the national standards for the English Language Arts (NCTE/IRA, 1996) within their own sets of standards. Standards can be met in a variety of ways, or performances (e.g., essays, exhibitions, performance by a group, short story writing), and students can reflect on their progress toward achieving the standards (Wilhelm, 1996). In other words, *using standards-based performance assessment does not dictate the type of tools that might be used for assessment.* Any of the tools found in Figure 2.2 could be used; each standard provides only the criterion for the assessment. Rather than ask what students know and can do in relation to other students (norm-referenced), standards-based performance assessment asks what students know and can do in relation to a set of standards (see Figure 2.4).

Beverly Falk (2000) provides a clear statement of the purposes and benefits of standards-based performance assessments:

> Standards-based performance assessments support teaching by providing teachers with a guide for their teaching and with information about *what* students can do as well as *how* they do it. They support student learning by offering students opportunities to demonstrate their understandings in a variety of ways and, because of their open and clear expectations, by giving students a fair shot at demonstrating what they know. At the same time,

standards-based performance assessments are useful accountability measures because they allow the public to see student and school progress in relation to valued goals. (p. 83)

Teachers using standards-based performance assessment are continually thinking of how they can organize a set of experiences that will help their students meet the standards. They try to use what they know about their students' interests, abilities, and competencies. The term *authentic assessment* has some relevance here. **Authentic assessment** is often understood to mean assessment that represents literacy behavior found in the community and in the workplace. Instruction focuses on learning that has direct application in the real world. For example, students concerned about the environment may engage in service-learning projects centered around recycling. (See Chapter 10 for more about service learning.) In this example, authentic assessment would focus on how successful their projects were in the eyes of the community. Teachers involved in such projects, just as those using standards-based performance assessment, often rely on anecdotal records, checklists, and scoring rubrics to help them determine how well their students have met the standards. The checklist in Figure 2.4 is one way a teacher can record evidence that his or her students are working toward each of the standards.

- authentic assessment

Process-Oriented Assessment

Process-oriented assessment refers to a teacher's direct observations of students' actual reading and writing abilities for the purpose of noting which specific behaviors or strategies students use. In process-oriented assessment, the literacy behavior being examined is documented in the learning context in which it normally occurs. For example, a process-oriented assessment could consist of anecdotal notes or a checklist designed by the teacher that asks such questions as, "Is the learner able to separate affixes from root words to assist decoding?" or "Is the learner able to use word parts to determine word meaning?" The assessment then might take place when the student reads one-on-one with the teacher from a content area text, such as a social studies text. The use of *running records* or an *informal reading inventory* (IRI) (both discussed later in this chapter) with follow-up miscue analyses also falls under this category. Such assessments are quite compatible with standards-based performance assessment.

- process-oriented assessment

STANDARDIZED, OR INDIRECT, ASSESSMENT PROCEDURES

There are advantages and disadvantages to using standardized assessment devices in the classroom. Although standardized group tests can be used, in a very broad way, to compare student performance with that of a cross-section of students in other areas of the country, such tests provide little or no usable information about the specific needs of individual students in a par-

FIGURE 2.4 Checklist for observations of progress toward standards.*

NAME: Luke   **GRADE:** 6

STANDARDS	CONTEXT	DATE OBSERVED	CONTEXT	DATE OBSERVED	CONTEXT	DATE OBSERVED
1. Reads a wide range of print and nonprint texts	Reading book of poetry before writing own poem	9/5	Internet material	10/4		
2. Reads a wide range of literature (many time periods, many genres)	Read Whitman's "Song of Myself"	9/5	Read daily newspaper	9/7		
3. Applies a wide range of strategies to comprehend, interpret, evaluate, and appreciate texts	Reading journal	9/12	Peer conferences	9/23		
4. Adjusts use of spoken, written, and visual language to communicate effectively	Presented culture report using photos and drama	10/4	Listens to radio shows—said "I want to get ideas for my readers theatre. Other people will be listening and I want to get it right."	10/20	Readers theatre	11/6
5. Employs a wide range of strategies for writing and different writing process elements to communicate effectively	Used galley sheet to formulate a creative story	9/15	Using word processing and desktop publishing and time lines	10/21		
6. Applies knowledge of language structure, conventions, media techniques, figurative language, and genre to create, critique, and discuss print/ nonprint texts	Used punctuation in effective ways— added to the punctuation chart in the writing area	9/28	Engaged in PQP† with a partner	10/12		

STANDARDS	CONTEXT	DATE OBSERVED	CONTEXT	DATE OBSERVED	CONTEXT	DATE OBSERVED
7. Conducts research by generating ideas and questions, and by posing problems	Began research KWH† chart about whales	10/3	Wrote a business letter to request more information on whales	10/10		
8. Uses a variety of technological and informational resources to gather/synthesize information and create/commu-nicate knowledge	Visited WWW museum sites	10/4	Worked on hypermedia stack	10/22		
9. Understands and respects diversity in language use, dialects, cultures	Contributed a question related to family life in culture study	9/3	Helped team collect artifacts (maps, clothing) related to culture study	9/4		
10. If ELL, makes use of native language to develop English competency			.			
11. Participates in a variety of literacy communities	Small group & whole class	9/13	Book Club	10/3	Pen pal	10/24
12. Uses spoken, written, and visual language to accomplish own purposes	Requested information from Kay	10/6	Shared informa-tion with Kay that helped her answer one of her research questions	10/7	Used free time to read article about Keiko the whale	10/15

*The standards used in this checklist are the NCTE/IRA Standards for the English Language Arts. Any state standards could be used and the checklist can be made grade-level specific as well.

† PQP = Praise, Question, Polish; KWH = Know, Want to know, How to find out.

An Assessment Program

Ms. West, the teacher we met at the beginning of this chapter, has created an assessment program that incorporates data from a wide variety of assessment tools to evaluate the literacy growth of Artis and the other students in her class. The tools listed here are discussed elsewhere in this chapter.

- Once a year, usually during spring, the students take a norm-referenced achievement test called The Stanford Achievement Test (The Psychological Corporation). Reviewing these results at the beginning of the school year allows Ms. West to obtain general literacy information about her new class and an indication of how well the students in her school are doing in comparison with other students of the same age and grade across the nation (standardized testing).

- At the beginning of the year Ms. West first gives students a *group cloze* test developed from the material they will be expected to read to evaluate their ability to handle the content area texts (curriculum-based).

- For students who score below 30 percent accuracy on the group cloze test, Ms. West administers an *informal reading inventory* to more carefully evaluate their reading strategies, determine their reading levels, and identify specific strengths and needs in comprehension and word analysis. Eventually, Ms. West will administer an informal reading inventory to all her students (process-oriented).

- Twice a month Ms. West listens to each student alternately read from either narrative or expository material and takes *running records* to check their comparative reading fluency (curriculum-based, standards-based).

- Every day Ms. West observes her students and takes *anecdotal notes* monitoring anything she considers significant in their struggles, their successes, and their attitudes; she sometimes uses checklists to make these observations more structured when determining their knowledge of multisyllabic words, ability to answer a range of comprehension questions, or progress toward state standards (process-oriented, standards-based).

- At the end of each content area unit, Ms. West gives students an oral or a written *cloze test* to determine their comprehension and their understanding of grammatical structures and content vocabulary (curriculum-based, standards-based).

- Once a week Ms. West listens as students *summarize* and *paraphrase* both narrative and expository material to evaluate their English language fluency, knowledge of story structure and organizational patterns, and comprehension skills (process-oriented, standards-based).

- Once or twice a week Ms. West and her students examine and briefly discuss the work in their *writing portfolios* (process-oriented, standards-based).

- Every six to eight weeks Ms. West administers a *structural analysis word list test* to those students who need it to measure growth in structural elements; she also gives a quick survey of *specialized vocabulary words* to determine which words students still need to master (standards-based, curriculum-based).

ticular classroom context. As with any assessment device, teachers must first determine what information they are seeking and then decide whether the standardized instrument is appropriate to those goals. As Cunningham and Allington (1999) so wisely remind us, "Tests that do not help us teach better are generally a waste of time and resources" (p. 263).

Achievement Tests and Their Application by Teachers

In most schools, reading achievement is evaluated by a standardized, or norm-referenced, test. These tests have been administered to a large group of students, representative of those for whom the test is intended, in order to establish the norm, or reference, group. This, then, is the group with which the scores of other students taking the test are compared. Standardized tests also have a standardized set of directions that must be followed for valid comparisons to be made.

Achievement tests are generally administered in a group and offer the teacher a "ballpark" estimate of their students' reading performance. The results are more helpful for comparing groups than for making judgments about how to meet the specific needs of individual students. As mentioned earlier, teachers often use the results of these tests to help with *initial* placement of students into instructional groups. Scores can be charted and decisions for planning general areas for instructional focus can be made (see Figure 2.5). A diagnostic test, however, such as the SDRT, would need to be administered in order to obtain more specific information from a standardized test. Teachers also use standardized test scores as confirmation of the results from their own direct assessments. Nevertheless, standardized tests present the teacher with a variety of types of scores that must be interpreted cautiously.

Interpretation of Standardized Test Scores

The most commonly reported score from a standardized test is the percentile score. **Percentile scores** range from 1 to 99, with an average score of 50, but they do *not* represent the percentage of items answered correctly on the test. They are scores that have been converted from the raw scores to allow comparisons among students of the same age or grade in the norm group, or in the same classroom or school. Each test's technical manual explains the manner in which this conversion was done. For example, students receiving a percentile score of 76 did not answer 76 percent of the items correctly. This score means that these students have done as well as or better than 76 percent of students in the norm group and in their own classroom on this test. An individual's subtest scores can be compared, but not averaged. In other words, a comprehension subtest score of 65 and a vocabulary subtest score of 43 means the student performed better in comprehension than in vocabulary and may benefit from enhanced instruction in vocabulary, which, in turn, might help both scores. However, we *cannot* say the student's average reading score is the 54th percentile (the average of 65 and 43).

● percentile scores

FIGURE 2.5 Graphic profile for examining class standardized test scores.*

TEACHER: Ms. G   GRADE LEVEL: 4   DATE: September

NAME OF TEST: CAT/6   DATE TEST ADMINISTERED: April

PUPIL'S NAME	WORD ANALYSIS		VOCABULARY		COMPREHENSION		COMMENTS
Carolyn B.	39	4	37	4	35	4	steady progress
Artis C.	34	4	53	5	36	4	good progress
Mary D.	49	5	23	③	23	③	vocabulary & comprehension
Isaac D.	63	6	83	8	74	7	could peer tutor?
Doug F.	18	②	29	③	18	②	use vocab. to build skills
Raul H.	38	4	38	4	6	①	focus on comprehension
Brandon L.	53	5	18	②	40	4	verify vocabulary
Cory M.	56	5	39	4	9	①	twins—but very different
Kerri M.	29	③	56	5	54	5	could Cory lean too much on Kerri?
Kalisha P.	36	4	26	③	3	①	focus on comprehension
Darlene P.	30	4	24	③	27	③	some comp. & vocab. work
Marcus R.	10	②	57	5	58	5	verify word analysis skills
Brenda R.	99	9	98	9	85	8	could peer tutor?
Sara R.	6	①	8	①	5	①	ELL
Carmen T.	12	②	14	②	11	②	ELL
Luis T.	37	4	31	4	14	②	comprehension strategies
Patricia W.	8	①	34	4	25	③	verify with an IRI
Mark W.	38	4	26	③	21	③	some comp. & vocab. help
Greg W.	57	5	38	4	37	4	good, steady progress
Linda Y.	36	4	35	4	16	②	comprehension strategies
	% ile	stanine	% ile	stanine	% ile	stanine	

*Below average stanine scores are circled. Twelve of twenty students, more than half, are below average in comprehension. The instructional focus needs to be on comprehension.

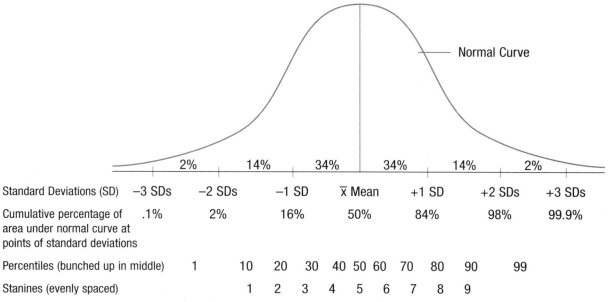

Scoring distributions for the normal curve. FIGURE 2.6

	−3 SDs	−2 SDs	−1 SD	x̄ Mean	+1 SD	+2 SDs	+3 SDs
Standard Deviations (SD)							
Cumulative percentage of area under normal curve at points of standard deviations	.1%	2%	16%	50%	84%	98%	99.9%

Percentiles (bunched up in middle) 1   10   20   30   40 50 60   70   80   90   99

Stanines (evenly spaced)   1   2   3   4   5   6   7   8   9

Another type of reported standardized test score are **stanine scores.** These are scores that have been converted into nine equally spaced units, with 1 being the lowest and 9 the highest. A stanine of 5 is considered average, so stanines 1, 2, or 3 represent below average performance; 4, 5, or 6 represent average performance; and 7, 8, or 9 represent above average performance (see Figure 2.6).

- stanine scores

When interpreting test scores it is important to know the reported standard deviation (SD) for the test. The **standard deviation** is the number (usually (±1, 2, or 3) used to refer to the variability in the scores as indicated by their distance from the mean, or average. The higher the SD, the more variability in the scores. The importance of the SD becomes clearer when comparing different types of scores (see Figure 2.6).

- standard deviation

If we consider percentile scores and the SD markings in Figure 2.6, 1 SD above the mean (50 + SD of 30) gives a score of 80 and 1 SD below the mean (50 – SD of 30) gives a score of 20. This large SD indicates much variability in percentile scores. This may be why percentile scores are often reported simply as a percentage of students scoring above the mean of 50. There is so much variability in percentile scores that to say the 80th percentile is much better than the 70th percentile or even the 60th is not really true. It is not until students score beyond the 90th or below the 10th percentile that they are beyond or below 1 SD from the average.

Another example involving SDs that might be more familiar relates to scores on intelligence tests. The Wechsler has a mean of 100 and a SD of 15, so an IQ score of 100 is average, 115 is 1 SD above average (or +1 SD), 130 is 2

SDs above average, and 145 is 3 SDs above average (which is a criterion for joining Mensa), while 85 is 1 SD below average, 70 is 2 SDs below average, and 55 is 3 SDs below average. Similarly, the Stanford-Binet intelligence test has a mean of 100 and a SD of 16 (116 = 1 SD, 132 = 2 SDs, 148 = 3 SDs, etc.).

It is important for interpreting test results to know not only what the mean and SD are, but also to know how much error is associated with the test. All tests have some error, and that error is represented by a number known as the **standard error of measurement** (SEM). Using this number provides a range of scores that a student's "true" score will likely fall within. For example, let's say the standardized test score for a student is the 77th percentile, but the SEM for this test is 12. This means that the student's "true" score falls somewhere between the 65th (77 − 12) and the 89th (77 + 12) percentile. This is quite a range. With so much room for error, we might wonder why so much emphasis is placed on standardized test scores. Of course, the SEM may be lower than the one in this example, but it is important for those reporting test results to also report this information to aid in interpretation. Information about the mean, SD, and SEM is available in the test's technical manual.

standard error
of measurement ●

DIRECT ASSESSMENT PROCEDURES

Literacy assessment devices that provide a teacher with information *directly* applicable to instructional planning are numerous and include IRIs; running records; interest and attitude surveys; interviews; teacher-made activities such as cloze tests; curriculum material placement tests; retelling tasks; word list and spelling tests; and written teacher observation procedures such as checklists, anecdotal notes, and scoring rubrics. Instructional lessons themselves are inextricably intertwined with direct assessment, as teaching and assessing continually inform one another. A discussion of all the assessment devices available is beyond the scope of this chapter and it is not necessary or possible for a teacher to use every device contained in this chapter. Because a teacher has limited instructional time, choosing which tools to use should be based on the specific literacy needs of his or her class, and the type of information the assessment tool provides. For example, teachers who wish to use interest groups when studying particular content area units would administer an interest inventory developed to help identify potential groupings (see Appendix D). The descriptions that follow should help teachers decide what tools would be best to use for their particular purposes.

Informal Reading Inventory

informal reading
inventory ●

An **informal reading inventory,** or IRI, is one of the most valuable diagnostic tools for assessing the reading progress of each student in the class as well as diagnosing specific reading strengths and needs. These inventories are referred to as "informal" because they are not norm-referenced. The IRI is an individual diagnostic reading test composed of lists of leveled sight words or sentences and a set of graded reading passages (both narrative and expository) from preprimer through grade 8 or even grade 12, with accompanying comprehension questions for each passage. Most basal reader series include their own IRI (sometimes called a *student placement test*) as part of their evaluation program, but devices such as the *Analytical Reading Inventory* (Merrill/Prentice Hall), the *Basic Reading Inventory, Preprimer–12* (Kendall/Hunt), the *Flynt–Cooter Reading Inventory for the Classroom* (Merrill/Prentice Hall), and the *Qualitative Reading Inventory* (HarperCollins) are also available (see Appendix C for a list of these and other assessment tools). Teachers can also design their own IRI by compiling a series of graded passages from their own curriculum materials by using readability formulas and taxonomies (tools that provide a classification of types of knowledge, such as Bloom's Taxonomy) for developing appropriate questions. Because they actually listen to the student reading aloud, observant teachers are offered a kind of "window into the learner's brain" to see what strategies for word analysis and construction of meaning are used. The IRI is an invaluable tool because it enables the teacher to:

- identify a student's independent, instructional, frustration, and listening comprehension levels;
- determine strengths and needs in word analysis and comprehension abilities;
- understand how a student is using syntactic (structure), graphophonic (visual–sound), and semantic (meaning) cues to make sense of reading;
- compare how a student decodes words in isolation with how that student decodes words in the context of meaningful sentences.

The IRI takes about 20 to 30 minutes to administer and is often taped; the student reads aloud while the teacher records the reader's **miscues**— deviations from the actual text—by using a kind of shorthand. After the oral reading, the teacher asks for a retelling followed by a series of comprehension questions. The **retelling,** which asks the reader to describe what he or she just read, gives insight into the reader's general ability to recall, interpret, and draw conclusions from the text. The follow-up comprehension questions assess specific aspects of the reader's understanding of the material read. Because comprehension of text is a critical issue in the intermediate grades, it is also helpful for teachers to ask for retellings and follow-up questions after students have read passages silently. These results can then be compared with results following an oral reading. Additionally, since most reading in the intermediate grades and beyond is done silently, the results are important data for the classroom teacher. In addition to providing both narrative and expository passages, published IRIs provide several forms, so it is an easy task to use one form for oral reading and another for silent reading. The following questions, modified as appropriate, can be asked to elicit a thorough retelling for both narrative (stories) and expository (informational) material.

- What can you tell me about (topic of passage or story)?

● miscues

● retelling

- What else was this passage/story about besides (the topic student mentioned already)?
- What happened after (event mentioned in retelling)?
- What do you think the author(s) is (are) trying to tell us (in the part mentioned in retelling)?
- How was (event or fact mentioned in retelling) important to this passage/story?
- How do you think you might use this information?
- How is this reading like anything you have read about before?

Retellings should be done prior to asking the comprehension questions provided in a published inventory. If a retelling is complete enough, very few comprehension questions may need to be asked because they would essentially have been answered already. If this is not the case, then the comprehension questions should be asked directly. In reviewing published IRIs it is important to look for 8–10 questions per passage and a balance of the following question types:

- *Literal*—The student recalls or recognizes information directly stated in the text.
- *Inferential*—The student recognizes or discovers relationships in the text that are not directly stated.
- *Critical/evaluative*—The student uses original and logical thought and previous knowledge or experiences to solve a problem or make a value judgment.

Analysis of results can indicate strengths in literal comprehension, but weaknesses in inferential or critical/evaluative thinking. Such information certainly helps a teacher plan appropriate instruction.

After beginning the IRI with an easy passage, the student continues to read progressively more difficult passages. When the student falls below about 90 percent in word recognition accuracy for oral reading, or achieves less than 60 percent accuracy in comprehension, or appears frustrated, the test is terminated; the passage level at which this occurs is called the **frustration level.** After the student reaches the frustration level, the teacher reads aloud passages at successively higher grade levels until the student is unable to correctly answer at least 75 percent of the comprehension questions (this percentage may vary depending on the IRI being used). The purpose of this last step is to determine the learner's reading capacity level, also called *listening comprehension level.* A **reading capacity level** is the highest level of material a student can understand when the passage is read to him or her.

Material is at the student's **independent level,** appropriate for recreational reading, when that student can read the passage without stress and correctly pronounce 97 percent, or most of the words, and correctly answer at least 90 percent of the comprehension questions. The passage at which the student can correctly pronounce between 91 and 96 percent of the

frustration level ●

reading capacity
level ●
independent level ●

Summary of informal reading inventory percentages.* FIGURE 2.7

	WORD RECOGNITION	COMPREHENSION
Independent level	97% or above	90% or above
Instructional level	91–96%	60% or above
Frustration level	90% or below	Below 60%
Listening comprehension level		75% or above

*Percentages may vary among inventories and for grade levels. These percentages of accuracy are suggested for intermediate grades (Cooper, 1952; Gipe, 2002).

words and correctly answer at least 60 percent of the comprehension questions is the student's **instructional level,** the appropriate level of difficulty for classroom instruction in reading (see Figure 2.7).

● instructional level

After analyzing decoding and comprehension errors to establish what instruction is needed in these skill areas, the teacher conducts a *miscue analysis* to determine how the learner is using language clues (i.e., syntactic, semantic, graphophonic) to think about reading. The teacher looks for patterns of miscues, such as those that retain the meaning (e.g., *Dad* for *father*), those that retain the syntactic pattern (e.g., *being* for *begging*), or those that simply retain the visual/sound similarities (e.g., *father* for *feather*). Miscues such as repetitions of words or phrases usually do not signify errors but indicate that the student may be rereading to try to rework a word or passage that did not seem to make sense.

Teachers should choose a commercial IRI that corresponds as closely as possible to the instructional materials used in the classroom and should agree with what the inventory considers a text deviation (e.g., a *repetition* is usually considered a positive second search for meaning). Additionally, by noting the types of comprehension questions, the number asked, and how scoring is handled, teachers can examine how the inventory evaluates comprehension. Teachers should also look at the clarity of instructions for administration, scoring, and interpretation and select one with which they feel most comfortable. See Figure 2.8 for an example of a completed IRI protocol (Woods & Moe, 1999) demonstrating coding, scoring, retelling, comprehension, and miscue analysis for one student.

Running Records

Another method for analyzing a reader's miscues are **running records** (Clay, 1985, 2000). Running record assessments use a system of checks and other marking conventions to represent what a reader says and does while reading

● running records

FIGURE 2.8 Example of a completed IRI protocol.

FORM C, LEVEL 4	READER'S PASSAGES PAGE 31

Prior Knowledge/Prediction

☐ Read the title and predict what the story is about. A sick pony.

    Q: What do you know about a sick pony?

    SR: I don't know. I've never been on a pony.

☐ Read the first two sentences and add more to your prediction.

    A boy is really worried about his pony. The pony's sick.

Prior Knowledge

☐ a lot

☐ some

☑ none

A Sick Pony*	O	I	S	A	Rp	Rv
1 Jody was so/worried that he didn't even want to eat. He had stayed						
2 in the barn all day/to take care of his sick pony, ~~Gabilan~~. The pony's/condition [Gab / Gabil] [cold]			/	/	/	
3 was growing worse as/his/breathing grew louder and harder. [breath]			/		/	
4 At nightfall, Jody/brought a blanket from the house so he could sleep/ [night] [horse SC]			/		/	
5 near/Gabilan. In the middle of the night/the wind whipped around the barn [wind SC]					/	
6 and blew the door open.						
7 At dawn Jody awakened to the banging of the barn door. Gabilan						
8 was gone! In/(alarm) he ran from the barn following the pony's tracks. [follow]	/		/			
9 Looking upward he saw buzzards, the birds of/death, flying overhead. [up] [buzz SC]			/			
10 Jody stood still, then ran to the top of a small hill. In a clearing below, he [clear]			/			
11 saw something that filled his heart with anger and hate. A/buzzard/was [anjer]			/		/	
12 perched on his (dying) pony's head. [pointed]	/		/			
TOTALS Number of miscues ___16___ Number of self-corrections ___3___						

O = omission   S = substitution   Rp = repetition

I = insertion   A = aided by teacher   Rv = reversal

*This passage is a retelling from the novel, *Tuned Out,* by Maia Wojciechowska.

Continued.

FIGURE 2.8

FLUENCY: Does the reader . . .

- ☐ read smoothly?   ☑ word-by-word?   ☐ read words in meaningful phrases?
- ☐ use pitch, stress, and intonation to convey the meaning of a text?
- ☑ repeat words and phrases because he or she is monitoring the meaning (self-correcting)?   *some*
- ☑ repeat words and phrases because he or she is just trying to sound out the words?
- ☑ use punctuation to divide the text into units of meaning?   *Some WR difficulties are beginning to interfere.*
- ☐ ignore the punctuation?

RATING SCALE

1 = clearly labored, disfluent reading, very slow pace   →   3 = poor phrasing/intonation/reasonable pace

2 = slow and choppy reading/slow pace   ←   *2.5*   4 = fairly fluent reading/good pace

Cueing Systems				
LINE #	Miscue	Graphophonically Similar Initial Medial Final (word level)	Syntactically Acceptable Unacceptable (sentence level)	Semantic Change in Meaning (CM) No Change in Meaning (NCM) (sentence level)
2	cold	I	A	CM
3	breath*	IM	A	*slight* CM
4	night*	IM	A	*slight* CM
8	follow*	IM	A	*slight* CM
9	up*	I	A	NCM
10	clear*	IM	U	CM
11	anjer	IF	U	CM
12	pointed	IF	A	CM
	* Note the omissions of word endings.			

SUMMARY

- ☑ Most, ☐ few, ☐ no   miscues were graphophonically similar to the
  some   word in the passage.
- ☐ Most, ☐ few, ☐ no   miscues were syntactically matched.
- ☐ Most, ☑ few, ☐ no   miscues maintained the author's meaning.
- ☑ The self-corrections demonstrate that the reader monitors the meaning.   *(continued)*

FIGURE 2.8 Continued.

RETELLING

It's about a pony. Jody is really worried about the pony. It's sick. And the barn door started banging.

Q: Can you tell any more?

SR: That night Jody stayed with the horse. He saw something buzz around. The pony was gone.

Q: Can you tell more?

SR: No

RETELLING SUMMARY: ☐ many details, logical order
☐ some details, some order ☑ few details, disorder

Note: Indicate any probing with a "P"

Story Elements	All	Some	None
Main Character(s)	✓		
Time and Place		✓	
Problem		✓	
Plot Details in Sequence			✓
Turning Point			✓
Resolution			✓
Reader's Thumbnail Summary:	A pony is sick.		

COMPREHENSION QUESTIONS AND POSSIBLE ANSWERS

(RIF = Retells in fact; PIT = Puts information together; CAR = Combines author and reader; EAS = Evaluates and substantiates)

+ (RIF) 1. Who are the two main characters in this story? (Jody and his sick pony, Gabilan)

+ (RIF) 2. Where does this story take place? (<u>in a barn</u>, in the country)

1/2 (PIT) 3. What is the problem in this story? (<u>the pony is sick</u> and getting worse)

− (CAR) 4. What do you know about the phrase the **pony's condition**? (state of health, Gabilan is sick, his health was poor) He has a cold.
What does the phrase **pony's condition** have to do with this story? (the pony's condition was growing worse as his breathing grew louder and harder) He's sick.

+ (RIF) 5. Why did Jody take a blanket from the house? (<u>so he could sleep</u> near Gabilan) with his pony

− (CAR) 6. What do you know about the word **dawn**? (sunrise, the start of the day) I don't know.
What does the word **dawn** have to do with this story? (Jody woke up at dawn)

− (PIT) 7. Why was the barn door banging? (in the middle of the night a wind whipped around the barn and blew the door open; at dawn some wind was still blowing) It's loose.

− (EAS) 8. Do you think Jody's pony was dying? You think this because . . . (yes, he was really sick; it didn't say that the veterinarian had been to treat the pony; his breathing was loud; when Jody found Gabilan he saw buzzards perched on his head) No. It ran out of the barn.

READER TEXT RELATIONSHIP (RTR)   From the Text   ☐ adequate ☑ not adequate
From Head to Text ☐ adequate ☑ not adequate

Scoring Guide Summary			
Word Recognition		**Comprehension**		**Emotional Status:**
Independent	2	Independent	0–1	Uncertain, signs of stress
Instructional	7 −16	Instructional	2 −4½	and tension
Frustration	14+	Frustration	4+	

text aloud. Analysis of running records reveals whether the reader uses the language cue systems (V = visual, or graphophonic; S = syntactic; M = meaning, or semantic) and engages in self-correction of errors. Running records may appear easier to administer than IRIs and more expedient because no special materials are needed other than paper and pencil. The IRI, however, is a more thorough assessment, because it generally requires the student to read more than one passage and allows for comparisons of the student's oral reading with the silent reading of both narrative and expository material. It is important to keep in mind that multiple samples will always offer a clearer picture of any student's "true" reading ability, but at times the expediency of the running record makes it more appealing, especially as a means of tracking reading fluency, or measuring reading rate if the reading of the passage is timed.

With the running record, students orally read text passages ranging from easy to difficult. Although comprehension is not assessed with comprehension questions, teachers often ask readers to do a retelling after the passage is read to check for understanding. Teachers are able to examine students' strengths and limitations in the use of various decoding strategies by making a check mark on a piece of paper as the student reads each word correctly, and by writing the word diacritically to denote substitutions, repetitions, mispronunciations, or unknown words. Refer to Figure 2.9 for an illustrative example. *R* indicates repetition. The arrow shows what was repeated. Words in the original text are written below the horizontal lines and what the reader said is written above the lines. *SC* means self-correct, and these miscues are analyzed under a separate column because they give us important information, but they will not count as words read incorrectly for scoring purposes; *E* means errors. Alternatively, teachers can duplicate a copy of the pages the student will read and record errors next to or on top of the text copy.

After identifying the words that the student read incorrectly, the teacher calculates the percentage of words read correctly. For the example in Figure 2.9, this would be 92/96, or 96 percent accuracy. Teachers use the percentage of words read correctly to determine whether or not the material is too easy, too difficult, or at the appropriate instructional level for the student at that time using the same percentages discussed for the IRI determination of reading levels.

As with the IRI, the teacher can then do a miscue analysis, categorizing the student's miscues according to the graphophonic, semantic, and syntactic cueing systems, in order to examine what word identification strategies are being used. The letters *V* (for visual cues), *M* (for meaning cues), and *S* (for syntactic cues) are used, respectively. Errors can then be classified and charted and instructional decisions made accordingly.

Anecdotal Notes

Many teachers incorrectly assume that their own observations about a student's literacy status are not as important as the results of standardized tests.

FIGURE 2.9   Example of a coded and analyzed running record.

CLAIRE'S READING

Claire made a number of errors on this text but she often self-corrected without any assistance. (Only a portion of the record is shown.)

Analysis of errors and self-corrections
Information used

CLAIRE'S RECORD

Page of Text	Running Record	E M S V	SC M S V
"Because I'm years older," Hannah smirked.	✓ ✓ ✓ ✓ R ✓ ✓.		
He gave up arguing and stomped off towards his	✓ ✓ ✓ ✓ ✓ ✓ ✓ ✓		
room. "See you in the morning," he said to	bedroom. She | SC ✓ ✓ ✓ ✓ ✓ ✓ room. See	Ⓜ Ⓢ Ⓥ Ⓜ Ⓢ Ⓥ	M S Ⓥ
his mother to emphasize that he was ignoring	✓ ✓ and | SC emphases ✓ R ✓ ✓ ✓ to emphasize	Ⓜ Ⓢ V M S Ⓥ	M S Ⓥ
Hannah.	Anna | SC Hannah |	Ⓜ Ⓢ Ⓥ	M S Ⓥ
He posed in front of his bedroom mirror. If	✓ possed ✓ ✓ ✓ ✓ ✓. ✓ posed	M S Ⓥ	
Hannah was a damsel in distress, she couldn't	✓ ✓ ✓ ✓ ✓ district | SC ✓ ✓ distress |	M S Ⓥ	Ⓜ Ⓢ Ⓥ
expect him to come galloping to her rescue.	✓ ✓ ✓ ✓ ✓ ✓ ✓.		
She could stay tied to the stake. He would	✓ ✓ ✓ died | SC ✓ ✓ ✓. ✓ ✓ tied |	M S Ⓥ	Ⓜ Ⓢ Ⓥ
charge in cutting this way and that with his	✓ ✓ ✓ the ✓ ✓ ✓ ✓ ✓ this	M Ⓢ Ⓥ	
fearsome sword. All would fall before him and	✓ sWord | SC ✓ ✓ ✓ ✓ ✓ ✓ sword. |	M S Ⓥ	Ⓜ Ⓢ V
he would fight his way to where she was tied	✓ ✓ ✓ ✓ ✓ ✓ ✓ ✓ ✓		
and then . . .	✓ ✓ . . .		

Her teacher summarized the analysis of the reading like this:

Claire uses meaning, structure, and visual information, repeats word occasionally, self-corrects most of her errors, picking up more visual information, and attempts all words.

Claire needs to take more responsibility for making all the information match. She needs to be encouraged to recognize when meaning is lost, and self-correct.

Researchers strongly dispute this belief (Cambourne and Turbill, 1990). One of the most powerful and reliable parts of any teacher's assessment and evaluation process, researchers claim, is teachers' daily, systematic observation of their students, using either a clipboard or a tape recorder. Ideally, some observation time should be scheduled every day to focus on particular students and take brief logs, or **anecdotal notes,** about these students' involvement in literacy events (Rhodes and Nathenson-Mejia, 1992). Teachers should observe students in every possible language context: one-on-one interactions, small group discussions, and large class settings. The focus should always be on what learners *do* as they read and write. The most useful notes

● anecdotal notes

- describe specific events.
- report rather than evaluate.
- relate the events to other information about the student.

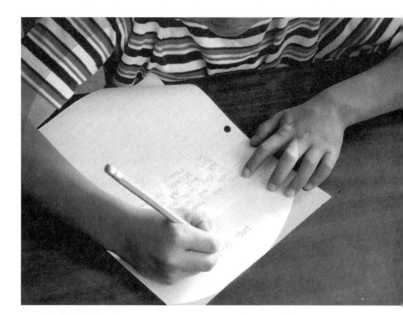

Teachers can make observations about learners' attempts to use word parts, their success with daily reading and writing activities, the questions they ask, the books they are reading, what they seem to like and dislike in reading, and whether they use strategies and skills fluently or indicate some level of confusion.

These anecdotal records provide truly dynamic documentation of students' growth over time while also directing the teacher's attention to problem areas needing direct instruction for individuals, and possible minilesson topics for small groups. Based on the anecdotal notes provided in Figure 2.10, Luke's teacher concluded that he

- is learning to use his prior knowledge and the context of the passage to determine new words' meanings.
- is developing positive reading habits.
- still needs to expand his vocabulary but is developing more confidence in using background knowledge, context, and word parts.
- has an interest in the topic of planets.
- has a well-developed spatial intelligence.

This information helps Luke's teacher provide appropriate instruction for him that might include the use of literature circles, which allow students to choose the books they wish to read and discuss with their peers (see Chapter 5), and to provide opportunities to create artistic responses to what he has read.

FIGURE **2.10** Example of anecdotal notes for Luke.

DATE	NOTES
12/4/02	During independent reading, Luke attempted a guess at a new word's meaning, <u>spectacles</u>. He said he remembered his brother talking about his glasses as his "specs."
1/6/03	Luke asked to return to the library to find a different book after starting one that he said was not interesting.
1/14/03	During guided reading, Luke came across the word <u>tireless</u>. He immediately recognized the <u>-less</u> ending and said "without tire." After a brief time, he said, "Oh, they wanted to make enough money to get a gift for their mother and they were working as if they were not tired."
1/25/03	Luke assembled a set of nonfiction literature and located several websites on the topic of planets. He has chosen drawings, charts, and diagrams as the activities he will use to show what he has learned.
2/16/03	Luke created an attractive and accurate mobile of the sun and the planets to share with the class as a visual for his oral report.

Checklists

Often teachers use checklists as a starting point for documenting their observations. These checklists can be teacher developed, or located in other professional references. A checklist is especially helpful in providing guidance to novices for what to observe. Checklists should also provide for multiple observations and use in a variety of contexts so that conclusions are more accurate. They can be used quite effectively to gather large amounts of data that are easily compiled and reviewed. For example, the teacher can use school district content standards to develop a checklist of strategies that students are being taught. The checklist includes columns for marks (e.g., checks, plus signs, minus signs) and space for comments. Checklists can be used while observing individuals or groups, with dates or students' names inserted as column headings. Such checklists can be used periodically to monitor students' progress. Figure 2.11 is an example of a checklist for observing intermediate-grade literacy behaviors for either individuals over time or for groups of students.

Checklists can also be constructed for students to use for self-assessment. Such checklists help students recognize the specific elements of performance that are expected of them. They also provide a kind of "road map" for completing their work. Figure 2.12 is an example of a checklist used with intermediate-grade students for effective writing.

Intermediate-grade literacy observation checklist.   FIGURE 2.

GRADE LEVEL: 4   TEACHER: Mrs. B

CONTENT STANDARDS	Brad	Sasha	Jen	Mark	Raul	Jack	COMMENTS
Reads narrative text with fluency		9/8	9/8	9/11	9/11		partner Jack & Raul
Reads expository text with fluency			9/20		9/20		
Identifies main events of the plot		9/8	9/8	9/11	9/11	9/11	
Makes inferences using text		9/8		9/11			
Makes inferences using illustrations			9/8			9/11	work with Brad 1-on-1
Identifies structural patterns in expository text:							Do more in next grading period
—compare and contrast							
—cause and effect							
—order (enumeration or sequential)			10/4	10/4			
Asks questions				9/16			
Makes predictions	9/16	9/16	9/16	9/16	9/16	9/16	
Monitors own understanding			9/20				
Applies appropriate fix-up strategies			9/20				
Creates mental images while reading							
Retells to include salient points		10/12	10/12	10/12	10/12		focus more on this
Makes text-to-self connections	10/4						
Uses clues to determine word meanings:							
—word clues							work on affixes
—sentence or paragraph clues			9/16	9/16			
—background knowledge				9/16			

FIGURE 2.12 | Student self-assessment checklist for effective writing.

Name: _Mark_

Title(s) of Work Assessed: _The Solar System_

Did I . . . ?

☑ have a plan before I started writing?

☑ write complete sentences that are not run-on sentences?

☑ write some compound sentences that are connected with *and, or, but?*

☑ write a good topic sentence for each paragraph?

☑ write supporting sentences that help support the topic sentence in each paragraph?

☑ write accurate nonfiction that is also interesting?

☑ provide good transitions between paragraphs?

N/A write a story that has a beginning, a middle, and an end?

N/A write a story with a problem and a solution?

N/A describe the main character well?

N/A include dialogue in my story?

N/A use correct punctuation in any dialogue?

☑ use interesting and vivid words?

☑ confer with others to revise?

☑ edit my drafts?

Scoring Rubrics

scoring rubric ●
performance ●
descriptors ●

A **scoring rubric** describes the levels of performance that a student must demonstrate related to a particular achievement goal, whether it be written or oral. These criteria, or **performance descriptors,** help communicate to both teachers and students the standards that will be used to evaluate students' work. Scoring rubrics help provide for consistency in evaluating students' written work and oral performances (see Figures 2.13 and 2.14, respectively). Scoring rubrics represent a more analytical assessment of student work in that specific areas of strength and weakness can be readily identified.

CRITERIA	NEEDS WORK (1)	MAKING PROGRESS (2)	DOING GREAT (3)	ABOVE AND BEYOND (4)	SCORE
Understanding of Material	Apparent misunderstanding of material.	Limited understanding of material displayed by vague, unclear language.	Developing understanding of material.	Clear understanding of material displayed by clear, concrete language and complex ideas.	1 2 3 4
Structural Organization	Essay lacks logical progression of ideas.	Essay includes brief skeleton (introduction, body, conclusion) but lacks transitions.	Essay includes logical progression of ideas aided by clear transitions.	Essay is powerfully organized and fully developed.	1 2 3 4
Sentence Fluency (Flow)	Repetitive sentence patterns. There are no connecting words between sentences. Many sentences run into each other.	Sentence patterns are generally repetitive, with occasional variance. There are usually connecting words between sentences, where appropriate. Some sentences should be merged; others should be made into two or more sentences.	Sentence patterns are generally varied, but sometimes variations seem forced and inappropriate. There are connecting words between sentences, where appropriate. Each sentence contains a complete thought; there are no run-on sentences.	Varied and interesting sentence patterns. There are connecting words between sentences, where appropriate. Sentences are complete thoughts, with no run-ons.	1 2 3 4
Support	Few to no solid supporting ideas or evidence for the essay content.	Some supporting ideas and/or evidence for the essay content.	Support lacks specificity and is loosely developed.	Specific, developed details and superior support and evidence in the essay content.	1 2 3 4
Mechanics	Frequent errors in spelling, grammar, and punctuation.	Errors in grammar and punctuation, but spelling has been proofread.	Occasional grammatical errors. Spelling has been proofread.	Nearly error free. Reflects thorough proofreading for grammar and spelling.	1 2 3 4

FIGURE 2.14　Scoring rubric for oral presentation.

CRITERIA	NEEDS WORK (1)	MAKING PROGRESS (2)	DOING GREAT (3)	ABOVE AND BEYOND (4)	SCORE
Speaking	Monotone; speaker seemed uninterested in material.	Little eye contact; fast speaking rate, little expression, mumbling.	Clear articulation of ideas, but apparently lacks confidence with material.	Exceptional confidence with material displayed through poise, clear articulation, eye contact, and enthusiasm.	1 2 3 4
Creativity	Delivery is repetitive with little or no variety in presentation techniques; lacks visuals.	Material presented with little interpretation or originality; visual aid fails to grab attention and/or fails to communicate information.	Some apparent originality displayed through use of original interpretation of presented materials visually and/or orally.	Exceptional originality of presented material and interpretation both visually and orally.	1 2 3 4
Content	Results are unclear and information appears randomly chosen.	Results are clear, but supporting information is not available.	Results are very clear; many relevant points, but they are unaddressed.	Exceptional use of material that clearly relates to a focused thesis; abundance of varied supportive materials.	1 2 3 4
Clarity	No apparent logical order of presentation; unclear focus.	Content is loosely connected; transitions lack clarity.	Sequence of information is well organized for the most part, but more clarity with transitions is needed.	Development of thesis is clear through use of specific and appropriate examples; transitions are clear and create a succinct and even flow.	1 2 3 4
Presentation Length	Greatly exceeding or falling short of allotted time.	Exceeding or falling short of allotted time.	Remained close to the allotted time.	Presented within the allotted time.	1 2 3 4

Cloze Tests

A **cloze test** is an easy-to-use assessment device that consists of a representative 250–300 word passage from any relevant reading material, making it a useful tool across the curriculum, as the example in Figure 2.15 illustrates. To construct a cloze passage, the first sentence is left intact, followed by an every *n*th word (*n* = 5, 7, or 10) deletion pattern to achieve 25–50 blanks to be filled in. Cloze tests are used to determine a student's ability to comprehend the ideas in the sentences as well as in the entire passage (Taylor, 1953). Students must read the passage and supply the missing words. Besides establishing whether or not the text is at the appropriate instructional level (or *suitability*) for a student, this procedure may be used to assess the student's ability to use context clues in reading (see Chapter 4). By examining each incorrect response made by the student, the teacher can determine whether the response makes sense syntactically or semantically. Often, a response may be both semantically and syntactically correct without being the exact keyed response (e.g., for "The boy *stroked* the dog" the reader substitutes "The boy *petted* the dog"), which would be considered acceptable as evidence of using these two cueing systems. However, for determining appropriateness of the material in terms of reading level, only the exact keyed response can be accepted as correct. A score of 30 to 50 percent accuracy is considered instructional level, quite a lenient score as a result of only accepting exact keyed responses. A score above 50 percent is considered independent level, and a score below 30 percent is considered frustration level. The cloze can be designed in written form or orally, on tape, for struggling readers. A variation on cloze, called maze, provides three word choices for deleted words instead of a blank. Students must choose the best word that fits the passage. The same deletion patterns that are used with cloze can be used with maze, but word choices are very specific (the correct word, a word of the same part of speech, a word of a different part of speech), and the scoring changes to 85 percent for independent level, 60 to 75 percent for instructional level, and below 50 percent for frustration level (Guthrie et al., 1974).

● cloze test

Writing Folders

The **writing folder** is a folder where students keep all their rough drafts in various stages of the writing process and other daily compositions or reports, topics for future pieces they might like to write, and notes from minilessons. Students also include their own assessments and reflections about any piece they have completed. Pieces can be assessed using an analytic approach (see Scoring Rubrics section) or a holistic approach. A **holistic approach** to writing assessment judges the whole piece rather than just its individual parts. Important characteristics of good writing are considered, such as the impact of the piece (does the paper engage the reader in a clear, imaginative, convincing way?), its inventiveness (does it surprise or is it clever?), and its individuality (does it have a voice?) (Kirby et al., 1988). Material from writing folders is the basis for teacher–student conferences on

● writing folder

● holistic approach

FIGURE 2.15

Example of group cloze test for social studies material about Joseph Cinque.*

Directions: On the line in front of each line of text, write one word that you think best fits the blank. Read through the entire selection before you begin. This will give you clues for filling in the missing words.

MISSING WORDS	TEXT
	Human bondage has always been part of civilization.
1. _____	The ancient Egyptians enslaved the people _____
2. _____	conquered. So did the ancient Romans _____ Greeks.
3. _____	Moslem traders of the eleventh _____ exported
4. _____	their North African captives to _____ Moslem
5. _____	countries. Long before Europeans came _____ the
6. _____	scene, a small percentage of _____ Africans
7. _____	enslaved fellow black Africans. But _____
8. _____	was a difference between ancient and _____
9. _____	slavery. In ancient times, slavery was _____
10. _____	about race. Most victims were convicted _____
11. _____	or captives in wars and religious _____. They
12. _____	usually remained in the same _____ area or at
13. _____	least on the _____ continent.
14. _____	The global economy did not _____ the
15. _____	African slave trade until Spain _____ Portugal
16. _____	discovered the New World. Even _____, the
17. _____	Spanish first tried to enslave _____. They failed
18. _____	because Indians were nomadic _____, not laborers or
19. _____	farmers, and fiercely _____. As forced laborers, they
20. _____	tended to _____ and die. In fact, so many
21. _____	_____ that in 1517 a missionary named

*To be used to determine the suitability of the text for the students. *Source:* Adapted from K. Abdul-Jabbar and A. Steinberg, "Resistance," in *Black Profiles in Courage,* pp. 40–45. Copyright © 1996 by William Morrow & Co.

Continued.   FIGURE 2.15

22. _____   _____ Bartolome de las Casas suggested substituting
23. _____   _____ blacks instead. And that's what happened.
24. _____   _____ blacks were better suited. Most lived
25. _____   _____ settled villages, towns, and cities. They
26. _____   _____ expert farmers who grew permanent crops,
27. _____   _____ the men were used to laboring
28. _____   _____ the fields. Also, Africans understood that
29. _____   _____ could become a slave at any
30. _____   _____ . And once enslaved, especially in a
31. _____   _____ culture, they knew they could not
32. _____   _____ and hide in the crowd. In
33. _____   _____ Caucasian society, where could a black
34. _____   _____ hide? . . . So African blacks quickly became the
slaves of choice. (A minimum of 25 blanks are scored.)

ANSWER KEY:

1. they	13. same	25. in
2. and	14. impact	26. were
3. century	15. and	27. and
4. other	16. then	28. in
5. on	17. Indians	29. anyone
6. black	18. hunters	30. time
7. there	19. independent	31. different
8. modern	20. sicken	32. escape
9. not	21. died	33. a
10. criminals	22. Bishop	34. person
11. feuds	23. African	
12. geographic	24. African	

individual instructional needs, and minilesson topics are chosen from observations during these sessions.

For special displays, publications, or parent–teacher meetings, the teacher often meets with each student to make collaborative decisions on what piece(s) should be selected to put in a special "showcase portfolio" (see Using Portfolios for Managing Assessment Data later in this chapter) that will be shown to parents. Writing folders are often proudly decorated and personalized by students and kept in a special place in the classroom where they are easily accessible. Anecdotal notes, checklists, or scoring rubrics regarding the contents of these folders provide important assessment data on students' writing progress.

Word Lists

Teachers in the intermediate grades may wish to periodically and informally assess their students' recognition of particular words and especially their use of structural elements often found in multisyllabic words. To keep an account of known structural elements for each student, 3 × 5 index cards can be numbered and arranged in the same order as the words on a list of polysyllabic words such as *The Nifty-Thrifty-Fifty* (Cunningham and Hall, 1998). While holding the cards for a student to respond to, the teacher uses an accompanying checklist to note which words the student recognizes and reads successfully. (Figure 2.16 lists the Nifty-Thrifty-Fifty; Figure 2.17 shows a partial checklist; Appendix D includes the full checklist.) The student must say the entire word

FIGURE 2.16 Nifty-Thrifty-Fifty words.

1. antifreeze	14. employee	27. invasion	40. semifinal
2. beautiful	15. encouragement	28. irresponsible	41. signature
3. classify	16. expensive	29. midnight	42. submarine
4. communities	17. forecast	30. misunderstand	43. supermarkets
5. community	18. forgotten	31. musician	44. swimming
6. composer	19. governor	32. nonliving	45. transportation
7. continuous	20. happiness	33. overpower	46. underweight
8. conversation	21. hopeless	34. performance	47. unfinished
9. deodorize	22. illegal	35. prehistoric	48. unfriendly
10. different	23. impossible	36. prettier	49. unpleasant
11. discovery	24. impression	37. rearrange	50. valuable
12. dishonest	25. independence	38. replacement	
13. electricity	26. international	39. richest	

Cards and partial checklist for assessing the Nifty-Thrifty-Fifty. **FIGURE 2.17**

NIFTY-THRIFTY-FIFTY*	TRANSFERABLE	CHUNKS
1. ✔ antifreeze	1. ✔ anti	
beauty-ful 2. ___ beautiful		2. ✔ ful (y - i)
class - class - classy 3. ___ classify		3. ___ ify
com - tees 4. ___ communities	4. ✔ com	4. ✔ es (y - i)
com - ty 5. ___ community	5. ✔ com	5. ✔ y
composition 6. ___ composer	6. ✔ com	6. ___ er
continent 7. ___ continuous	7. ✔ con	7. ___ ous (drop e)
8. ✔ conversation	8. ✔ con	8. ✔ tion
deodorant 9. ___ deodorize	9. ✔ de	9. ___ ize
10. ✔ different		10. ✔ ent
11. ✔ discovery	11. ✔ dis	11. ✔ y
12. ✔ dishonest	12. ✔ dis	
13. ✔ electricity	13. ✔ e	13. ✔ ity
14. ✔ employee	14. ✔ em	14. ✔ ee
encourage 15. ___ encouragement	15. ✔ en	15. ___ ment
expense 16. ___ expensive	16. ✔ ex	16. ___ ive
17. ✔ forecast	17. ✔ fore	
18. ✔		. ✔ en (double t)
19. ___		. ___ or
20. ✔		. ✔ ness (y - i)

1. antifreeze

2. beautiful

3. classify

4. communities

quickly, with no hesitation or sounding out in order to receive a check for knowing that particular word. For each correct response, the teacher makes a check next to the corresponding word. If the student cannot say the entire word correctly, but does say any of the transferable chunks, these recognized parts should be checked, but the word will not be considered correct in the final scoring. The teacher can also write above the word any attempts, parts recognized, mispronunciations, or substitutions for later analysis. The student's score is the total number of words, not chunks, checked. This raw score can then be converted easily to a percentage since there are 50 words in the list.

Interest and Attitude Inventories

interest and
attitude inventory ●

The interests and attitudes of students about reading, writing, and school in general have been found to be highly correlated with success in literacy. **Interest and attitude inventories** provide information about these factors and should therefore be included in any comprehensive assessment program. Given the importance of these factors, they should be monitored incidentally, using anecdotal notes, and deliberately through an interview or questionnaire, administered orally or in writing, to the whole class or to individuals. A sample reading interest inventory and an attitude survey are found in Appendix D. Teachers can design their own inventories appropriate to the age and developmental level of their learners, but the questions should be designed to solicit at least the following critical information:

- the subject areas that are motivating to the student
- the student's favorite book
- what the student does in his or her spare time
- what sports or hobbies the student enjoys
- the student's favorite television program
- the student's preferred instructional arrangements; for example, teacher directed, or working alone, with a small group, or with one other student
- the student's attitudes toward reading and writing
- what reading materials and experiences the student has been exposed to

Teachers then use these data to form interest groups or establish "partners" for reading, or to provide appropriate selections for students to choose books for participation in book clubs (see Chapter 5).

USING PORTFOLIOS FOR MANAGING ASSESSMENT DATA

Teachers and students work together toward literacy development, so they each have responsibilities for managing assessment data that document that development. As in Ms. West's classroom, portfolios offer a management system for classroom work. They provide a way for students to take on some responsibility for organizing and self-evaluating their work.

Portfolios are defined here as a collection of selected products accompanied by evidence of self-evaluation; that is, each artifact, or selected product, within the portfolio is explained by a caption. The caption provides a brief description of the artifact and why it has been included. This latter part of the caption is referred to as a *reflective statement* because it requires the portfolio-maker to reflect on why the artifact is important to include, and to self-evaluate his or her growth in the area represented by the artifact. Use of checklists, such as that seen in Figure 2.12, will help students prepare their reflective statements. The process of constructing a portfolio helps students understand what they know and what they still need to learn. With defined categories, a portfolio keeps products systematically sorted and can guide the daily work schedule.

● portfolios

For example, one portfolio system could define categories that match the curriculum framework or state standards. Thus, an upper-grades portfolio might use comprehension, composition, vocabulary and word study, and independence as its defined categories (Glazer, 1998). This kind of system enables both the teacher and the students to maintain an organized daily schedule, and it provides a point of entry for regular student–teacher conferencing. Selected artifacts are generally a combination of items the teacher designates for the portfolio (e.g., an attitude survey administered at the beginning of a school year to be compared with end-of-school-year attitudes), and those the student self-selects for particular reasons that are explained by the student. An example of one fifth grade student's table of contents is provided in Figure 2.18.

Usually, students develop and maintain two types of portfolios: working and showcase. The **working portfolio** contains completed work samples or works in progress. It is the holding place for artifacts that may eventually be selected for placement in a showcase portfolio. The **showcase portfolio** is a collection of artifacts chosen to demonstrate excellence in achievement. Selected from the working portfolio, these artifacts are few but represent a student's best efforts and are accompanied by a reflective statement that explains the importance or value of the artifact to the portfolio owner.

● working portfolio

● showcase portfolio

The portfolios Ms. West's students were sharing at the beginning of this chapter are examples of showcase portfolios. These portfolios were being prepared and finalized for presentation to parents and guardians as a way of demonstrating to significant people the student's achievements for the school year.

Many excellent resources provide information on how to start portfolios, what they might include, how they can be organized, and student examples. Some of these are as follows:

Clemmons, J., Laase, L., Cooper, D., Areglado, N., & Dill, M. (1993). *Portfolios in the classroom: A teacher's sourcebook.* New York: Scholastic Professional Books.

FIGURE 2.18 Table of contents for a fifth-grade student's portfolio.

TABLE OF CONTENTS

INTRODUCTION TO THE PORTFOLIO

Comprehension

- Written retelling for *The Music Teacher from the Black Lagoon*
- Science project drawing of the Planet Mobile and summary report
- Tape recording of Book Club discussion

Composition

- Original story: "How the Red Cabbage Became Red"
- Persuasive letter to school principal for change in recess time
- Research report
- PowerPoint presentation

Vocabulary and Word Study

- Word sort sheets for contractions, prefixes, and suffixes
- Idiomatic expressions and what they really mean
- Roots and branches (Greek and Latin roots)
- New terms for math
- New terms for social studies
- New terms for science

Independence

- Self-assessment of writing checklist
- List of books read and time sheet initialed by parent

Danielson, C., & Abrutyn, L. (1997). *An introduction to using portfolios in the classroom.* Alexandria, VA: Association for Supervision and Curriculum Development.

DeFina, A. A. (1992). *Portfolio assessment: Getting started.* New York: Scholastic Professional Books.

Fiderer, A. (1995). *Practical assessments for literature-based reading classrooms.* New York: Scholastic Professional Books.

Jenkins, C. B. (1996). *Inside the writing portfolio: What we need to know to assess children's writing.* Portsmouth, NH: Heinemann.

Myers, M., & Spalding, E. (Eds.). (1997). *Exemplar series grades 6–8.* Urbana, IL: National Council of Teachers of English.

Myers, M., & Spalding, E. (Eds.). (1997). *Standards exemplar series: Assessing student performance grades K–5*. Urbana, IL: National Council of Teachers of English.

Sunstein, B. S., & Lovell, J. H. (2000). *The portfolio standard: How students can show us what they know and are able to do*. Portsmouth, NH: Heinemann.

SUMMARY

The major goal of literacy assessment is to determine how each student is progressing in particular areas at a given time and to make instructional adjustments that are focused on students' needs. The best way to achieve this assessment goal is to use a variety of direct and indirect assessment tools; that is, to take a multidimensional approach for examining students' strengths and needs.

The use of indirect measures, or standardized instruments, provides important comparative data that have been proven to be valid and reliable but that do not always provide accurate and specific information for individual students. Data from such measures should, therefore, be interpreted cautiously, especially when the test-takers are culturally or linguistically diverse learners.

Direct assessments such as observations, anecdotal notes, and checklist data can support or refute standardized test data. Data compiled frequently and interpreted carefully by means of direct assessments are excellent for continually informing instruction.

The value of the assessment tools presented in this chapter depends largely on reflective analysis and how the devices are used for communicating literacy progress and resultant instructional plans with the students and their caregivers. By recognizing the strengths and limitations of different types of assessment tools, teachers can maximize their value within a balanced and comprehensive literacy program.

Questions
FOR JOURNAL WRITING AND DISCUSSION

1. Interview a local intermediate-grade teacher to determine what assessment strategies he or she uses. What components of literacy does the teacher assess? How are these areas assessed? Does the teacher rely more on direct or indirect assessment, or is there a balance? Discuss your findings with your classmates to compare your findings to theirs.

2. Daniels and Bizar (1998, pp. 207–209) offer 12 ideas to keep in mind for making sure our assessment methods enact the ideals of best practice. Using the content of this chapter, and other readings or information you have, consider these ideas. In your journal, choose two or three of

the 12 statements and indicate whether you agree with the statement, and why or why not. Then, in class with a partner or small group, discuss the statements you chose.

a. Assessment should reflect, encourage, and become an integral part of good instruction.

b. Powerful evaluation efforts focus on the major, whole outcomes valued in the curriculum (real things such as writing, researching, reading, experimenting, problem solving, creating, speaking).

c. Most school assessment activities should be formative (to ensure students learn better and teachers teach more effectively).

d. Traditional norm-referenced, competitive measures that rank students against each other provide little helpful formative assessment and tend to undermine progressive instruction (constructive programs rely more on self-referenced growth measures).

e. A key trait of effective thinkers, writers, problem solvers, readers, researchers, and other learners is that they continually self-monitor and self-evaluate (self-assessment).

f. Skillful and experienced evaluators take a developmental perspective (stages).

g. Teachers need a rich repertoire of assessment techniques.

h. It is never enough to look at learning events from only one angle; rather, we now use multiple measures, examining students' growth from several different perspectives (for a "thick" picture of students' learning).

i. Teachers need to reallocate the considerable time that they already spend on assessment, evaluation, record keeping, testing, and grading activities (less time scoring, more time saving and documenting—new assessment procedures do not require any more time, nor any less).

j. Sound evaluation programs provide, where necessary, a database for deriving legitimate, defensible student grades (however, norm-referenced grading should be deemphasized).

k. It takes many different people working cooperatively to effectively evaluate student growth and learning (external test-makers, teachers, students, parents or guardians, school support personnel).

l. The currently available state and national standardized tests yield an exceedingly narrow and unreliable picture of student achievement, are poor indicators of school performance, and encourage archaic instructional practices (professional teachers avoid teaching to standardized tests).

3. It is no longer enough to provide students with opportunities to learn and develop their literacy skills; schools must now provide proof in the form of standardized test scores that learning has actually taken place. Discuss this pervasive approach to measuring learning. What implications does it have for other forms of literacy assessment?

Suggestions
FOR PROJECTS AND FIELD ACTIVITIES

1. Arrange to meet with a teacher and examine the report for one student's achievement test results. Analyze the report with the teacher as if you were trying to use the data for planning instruction. What additional information do you feel might be helpful?

2. Administer a reading or writing attitude survey to an intermediate-grade student. Tabulate and analyze the responses. The following questions are provided to help you analyze the information. What are the implications for instruction?

   a. What are the student's perceptions about reading/writing?

   b. What does the student feel are important characteristics of good reading/writing?

   c. How insightful is this student in terms of how he or she perceives reading/writing?

   d. What other relevant information did you discover about the student?

   e. Do your data indicate that the student has a healthy attitude toward reading/writing?

3. Observe a classroom teacher as he or she administers a specific literacy assessment tool (e.g., running records, cloze test, word lists, spelling test, district writing prompts). Discuss the interpretation of the results with the teacher. Why was the assessment given? What was learned? How will the teacher adapt instruction as a result of the information gained?

References

Cambourne, B., & Turbill, J. (1990). Assessment in whole language classrooms: Theory into practice. *Elementary School Journal, 90,* 337–349.

Clay, M. (1985). *The early detection of reading difficulties* (3rd ed.). Auckland, New Zealand: Heinemann.

Clay, M. (2000). *Running records for classroom teachers.* Portsmouth, NH: Heinemann.

Cooper, J. D. (1997). *Literacy: Helping children construct meaning.* Boston: Houghton Mifflin.

Cooper, L. J. (1952). *The effect of adjustment of basal reading materials on achievement.* Unpublished doctoral dissertation, Boston University.

Cousin, P. T., Weekly, T., & Gerard, J. (1993). The functional uses of language and literacy by students with severe language and learning problems. *Language Arts, 70,* 548–556.

Cunningham, P. M., & Allington, R. L. (1999). *Classrooms that work: They can all read and write* (2nd ed.). New York: Longman.

Cunningham, P. M., & Hall, D. P. (1998). *Month-by-month phonics for upper grades: A second chance for struggling readers and students learning English.* Greensboro, NC: Carson-DeLosa.

Daniels, H., & Bizar, M. (1998). *Methods that matter: Six structures for best practice classrooms.* York, ME: Stenhouse.

Falk, B. (2000). *The heart of the matter: Using standards and assessment to learn.* Portsmouth, NH: Heinemann.

Gipe, J. P. (2002). *Multiple paths to literacy: Classroom techniques for struggling readers* (5th ed.). Upper Saddle River, NJ: Merrill/Prentice Hall.

Glazer, S. M. (1998). *Assessment IS instruction: Reading, writing, spelling, and phonics for ALL learners.* Norwood, MA: Christopher Gordon.

Guthrie, J. T., Siefert, M., Burnham, N. A., & Caplan, R. I. (1974). The maze technique to assess, monitor reading comprehension. *The Reading Teacher, 28,* 161–168.

Hill, B. C., Ruptic, C., & Norwick, L. (1998). *Classroom based assessment.* Norwood, MA: Christopher-Gordon.

Johnston, P. (1992). Nontechnical assessment. *The Reading Teacher, 46,* 60–62.

Karlsen, B., & Gardner, E. F. (1995). *Stanford diagnostic reading tests* (4th ed.). San Antonio, TX: Harcourt. (Also available online at: www.hemweb.com/trophy/readtest/sdrt4.htm)

Kirby, D., Liner, T., & Vinz, R. (1988). *Inside out: Developmental strategies for teaching writing.* Portsmouth, NH: Boynton/Cook.

National Council of Teachers of English. (1996). *Standards in practice* (series of 4 books: K–2, 3–5, 6–8, 9–12). Urbana, IL: National Council of Teachers of English.

Neill, D. M. (2000). Transforming student assessment. In R. D. Robinson, M. C. McKenna, and J. M. Wedman (Eds.). *Issues and trends in literacy education* (2nd ed., pp. 136–148). Boston: Allyn & Bacon.

O'Sullivan, S., & Jiang, Y. H. (2002, Summer). Determining the efficacy of the California reading instruction competence assessment (RICA). *Teacher Education Quarterly, 29*(3), 61–72.

Rhodes, L. K., & Nathenson-Mejia, S. (1992). Anecdotal records: A powerful tool for ongoing literacy assessment. *The Reading Teacher, 45,* 502–511.

Smith, K. (1996). Foreword. In M. Sierra-Perry (Ed.), *NCTE standards in practice: Grades 3–5* (p. v). Urbana, IL: National Council of Teachers of English.

Taylor, W. L. (1953). Cloze procedure: A new tool for measuring readability. *Journalism Quarterly, 30,* 415–433.

Wilhelm, J. D. (1996). *Standards in practice: Grades 6–8.* Urbana, IL: National Council of Teachers of English.

Woods, M. L. & Moe, A. J. (1999). *Analytical Reading Inventory* (6th ed.). Upper Saddle River, NJ: Merrill/Prentice hall.

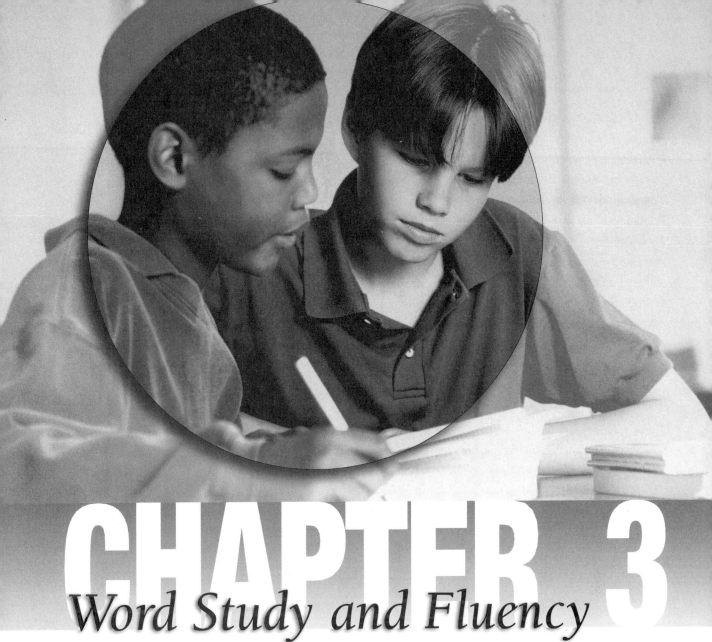

CHAPTER 3
Word Study and Fluency

Focus Questions

- What are the key components of word study at the primary and at the intermediate grade levels?

- In what ways do elements of word study for intermediate grades differ from the elements of primary grade word study?

- How is word study related to fluency?

In the Classroom

Mrs. Diaz's sixth-grade students come to school on Monday morning talking about seeing the movie *Jurassic Park III* over the weekend. The classroom reading center includes several magazines with articles about dinosaurs and the making of the Jurassic Park movies, as well as several copies of the book *Jurassic Park* (Crichton, 1990). The students are very interested in exotic animals and places. Knowing her students as well as she does, Mrs. Diaz recognizes an opportunity to teach her students about more advanced word parts, and something about the morphology, or internal structure, of words through the use of their interest in exotic animals. She has prepared an activity called "Create an Exotic Animal" that involves students putting meaningful parts of words together to form a new, exotic animal (Johnson and Pearson, 1984). By the time each student has created a new animal, and shared his or her animal with classmates, most of the students will know what the word parts mean and can apply this new skill to unknown words they may meet in other texts. Mrs. Diaz's activity, with example animals, follows.

CREATE AN EXOTIC ANIMAL

Directions: You are a scientist in charge of creating exotic animals for a Jurassic-type adventure park. You must create names for your animals that are understood by scientists and people around the world. This means you must use the prefixes, suffixes, and roots that come from ancient Latin and Greek. For example, a unicorn is an animal that has one horn (uni = one + cornis = horn). Use the following chart of prefixes, suffixes, and roots to help you name your animal. You also need to draw the animal so we will know what it looks like.

Scientist's Vocabulary Chart

mono = one	macro = large, long	melano = black	uni = one	poly = many
leuco = white	bi = two	micro = small, short	erythro = red	tri = three
lineatus = lined	bruno = brown	quadro = four	punctata = dotted	ocu = eye
pento = five	pedi, pod = foot	dent, dont = tooth	dec = ten	cephalus = head
corp = body	-let = small	cornis = horn	cord, cardi = heart	-kin = small
-ling = small	-trix = female			

Once students finish sharing their exotic animals, Mrs. Diaz discusses other more commonly used words found in their readings that derive from the roots and affixes in the chart (e.g., gosling, ocular, microcosm, dentist). In this way students can see how they might use structural analysis (identification of meaningful word parts such as roots, affixes, and compounds) to figure out unknown words. Some of the students' creations were a *punctata tricephalopentopod*, a *polymicroocutrix*, and a *bruno macrocorpmicroped,* seen here.

punctata
tricephalopentopod →

bruno macrocorpmicroped

polymicroocutrix

DEFINING WORD STUDY

Word study is a systematic, conceptual learner-centered approach to instruction in spelling, word analysis (to include phonics), and vocabulary (Bear et al., 2000). Instruction of approximately 10 to 15 minutes daily links directly to the texts and other materials being used in the classroom and provides many opportunities for students to manipulate word parts. Word study teaches students how to look at words and should be approached developmentally. At the primary-grade level, word study is mainly about

● word study

1. developing an understanding of the **alphabetic principle** (knowing that each speech sound has a distinctive graphic representation).

● alphabetic principle

2. helping students learn about and use phonics to decode words unknown in print.

At the intermediate-grade level, word study is primarily about

1. developing spelling at the **syllables and affixes stage** and the **derivational relations stage** (stages of spelling development characterized by polysyllabic words that often contain **affixes** [prefixes and suffixes], and derive from Greek or Latin roots, respectively).

● syllables and affixes stage
● derivational relations stage
● affixes

2. helping students determine word meanings using the meaningful parts of words (Henderson, 1990; Kemper and Brody, 2001).

Thus, word study is developmental. While we would hope that all intermediate-grade students would be ready to study words at the syllables and affixes stage, this will not be the case. It is advisable for a teacher to directly assess his or her students using a spelling inventory (see Appendix D) to look at the way each student spells words. By analyzing what the learner does when he or she spells, the teacher can determine that learner's conceptual understandings of our English word system and the level at which he or she is able to study words.

Following is a brief review of reading and spelling stages. This information is provided to help teachers determine a student's readiness for intermediate-grade-level word study based on his or her spelling/reading stage.

A REVIEW OF READING AND SPELLING STAGES

Briefly, emergent readers demonstrate a lack of understanding of the alphabetic principle, and they do not have a concept of letter–sound correspondences. Their "spelling" consists of scribbles, random marks, drawings, or mock letters (see Figure 3.1). As learners develop an understanding of the alphabetic principle and become beginning readers, they demonstrate the **letter name/alphabetic stage.** They spell by using letters they hear in words, usually consonants, even if it might be only one letter per word. Further development produces the **transitional reader,** who understands there are letter pattern units, or word families, or frequently occurring **rimes** (vowel[s] with any following consonants in a single syllable) such as

● letter name/ alphabetic stage
● transitional reader

● rimes

FIGURE 3.1   Stages of reading/spelling development.

READING/SPELLING STAGE	AGES	GRADES	CHARACTERISTICS
Emergent	1–7	pre–K to mid-1	scribbles, random marks, drawings, mock letter
Beginning/Letter Name	4–9	K to early 3	M or MN for man; L or LD or LED for land; B or BP or BOP or BUP or BOMP for bump
Transitional	6–12	1 to mid-4	MEET or METE for meat; NALE for nail; SOKE for soak; SMOAK for smoke; FOWT for fought; FODE for food; CAFE for cough; CLOKE for clock
Intermediate/Syllables and Affixes	8–18	3 to 8	GRIPING for gripping; MIDLE for middle; CONFUSSHUN for confusion; PLESURE for pleasure; RUPSHUR for rupture; MONKY for monkey; BARBAR for barber; DISPOSUL for disposal
Advanced/Derivational Relations	10+	5 to 12	SOLEM for solemn; ANAMAL for animal; OPISITION for opposition; CRITASIZE for criticize; BENAFIT for benefit; TELEGRAM for telegram; APPEARENCE for appearance; AMMUSEMENT for amusement

-at, -in, -ot, -and and spells words using these patterns, although not always correctly. For example, the letter name speller might spell boat as BOT, but the transitional speller will try to use a long *o* pattern and might produce BOTE, BOWT, BOOT, or BOAT. At the intermediate and advanced stages of reading development, students recognize single syllable patterns automatically and have already been reading and writing polysyllabic words, so they begin to apply this knowledge for spelling words containing syllables and affixes and word derivations—thus, the respective spelling stages.

In addition to this review of reading/spelling stages, a brief overview of primary-grade-level word study elements is in order because not all intermediate grade students will have reached an advanced word study stage.

EARLY WORD STUDY INSTRUCTION

phonemic awareness ●

Instruction in word study begins in the primary grades with activities that develop **phonemic awareness,** that is, the ability to attend to sounds in the context of the spoken word independent of the visual representation or meaning of the word. These activities usually focus on rhyming, blending, segmenting, and manipulating sounds in spoken language. From there students learn to recognize the relationships between the 44 sounds in the English language and the 26 graphic symbols (the letters of the alphabet) used to represent those sounds. This focus on learning letter–sound correspondences is called **phonics.**

● phonics

Because there is not a one-to-one match between the sounds and letters in English orthography, some letters will represent more than one sound, or combine with other letters to form a sound. For example, the letter *m* (as is true for most of the 21 consonant letters) has only one sound; however, the letters we call vowels (*a, e, i, o, u*) typically represent at least two sounds, referred to as long and short. The two letters *w* and *y* do double duty by sometimes acting as consonants (i.e., in the initial position in words such as *yes, you, yellow*), and sometimes acting as vowels (e.g., *day, buy, cow, sew, try*). The letter *c* does not have its own sound but represents the sound of either *s* or *k*. Certain letter combinations represent additional sounds such as *ch, sh, th, wh, au, oi, oo, ou* or contain silent letters as in words such as *know, lamb,* and *fight.* What adds to the confusion that some learners experience is that there are sounds that can be represented by more than one letter or letter combination. Take the long sound of /a/. It can be represented by *a, ai, a_e, ay, eigh, ey.* There are many other examples like these, and young readers must begin to recognize these letter–sound patterns that make up the content of phonics.

Word study instruction, then, in the primary grades, focuses on helping students learn phonics and apply it most often to single syllables or to one-syllable, decodable words. For example, students are directed to remove the beginning consonant(s) (the **onset**) from the rest of a one-syllable word (e.g., h—at). They then say the sounds indicated by the rime, or /at/. They are directed to say, and finally add, the sound for the beginning consonant(s) to the rime (/h/ + /at/ = hat). At this point, they have pronounced the word and must cross-check it within the context of what they are reading to be sure it makes sense: He wore a hat on his head.

● onset

ADVANCED WORD STUDY INSTRUCTION

Students in the intermediate grades must continue to learn to recognize increasingly complex words quickly and accurately. While some students still need instruction with phonics, or decoding (see "Troubleshooting"), a major focus of word study instruction in the intermediate grades is having students

1. learn to syllabicate multisyllable words.
2. study the internal structure of words that includes (a) affixes and **roots** (**base words**) and the forms of various parts of speech (morphology; also structural analysis), and (b) the origins and derivations of words (**etymology**).

● roots
● base words

● etymology

The focus on the internal structure of words will also enhance spelling development because these word parts will be learned and spelled as whole units. Additionally, much of this work will be helpful for learning new word meanings, so it can also be intertwined with instruction for **vocabulary** development (see Chapter 4).

● vocabulary

Syllabication

The process of analyzing a polysyllabic word is the same as that for one-syllable words, except the process is applied more than once. Multiple applications are based on the total number of syllables in the word; that is, the process will be applied twice for a two-syllable word, three times for a three-syllable word, and so forth (Gipe, 2002). Basically, the learner must first divide the unknown word into individual syllables, then pronounce each syllable, and finally put the syllables back together. The steps are as follows:

1. To begin to locate syllables in a polysyllabic word, locate the vowels.
2. Try to make syllables by using the consonants just before and after the vowels.
3. Attempt to pronounce these trial syllables.
4. Try to blend the trial syllables together.
5. Cross-check the pronounced word within the context of what is being read to see whether it makes sense. If the resulting pronounced word does not seem right, try segmenting the syllables in another way (see Figure 3.2).

listening vocabulary ●

This strategy is not always precise, but if the word is part of the student's **listening vocabulary** (words understood in speech, but not recognized in print), it may provide a close enough approximation that the context will help identify the word. In the case of a totally new word, students will need to be told what the word is and that word can become part of a personal dictionary for further vocabulary study and assistance with spelling if the word is later needed for writing purposes.

FIGURE 3.2 Analyzing a multisyllabic word.

STEP	WORD: HOSPITAL
1. Find the vowel(s).	o i a
2. Make syllables with the consonants just before and after the vowels.	"hos" "pit" "tal"
3. Try to say these syllables.	"hos" "pit" "tall"
4. Blend the syllables together.	"hospit" "tall" . . . "hospital"
5. Cross-check with the context.	"Oh yes, it makes sense. His father was sick so he went to the hospital."

Morphology

In addition to syllabication, students need instruction on morphology to help them recognize words. **Morphology** refers to the internal structure and forms of words. The structural features of words that need to be taught are *roots* (base words), *prefixes* (affix that precedes root), *suffixes* (affix that follows root), **inflections** (plurals, past tense endings, possessive form), and **compound words** (two base words together, e.g., sidewalk). Roots, prefixes, and compound words are most directly tied to meaning so they provide the most helpful information related to vocabulary. Suffixes and inflections also carry meaning, but it is more general in nature (Ruddell, 1993). Consider the differences by examining the word *dentist*. If the reader recognizes the "ist" suffix and knows "ist" means "one who" but does not know that the meaning of the root "dent" is "tooth," then recognizing "ist" is not much help other than to know the word is a noun.

- morphology
- inflections
- compound words

Intermediate grade students should be shown how to figure out the meaning of unknown multisyllabic words by recognizing the many meaning-bearing affixes that are added to the base, or root, of other words. Figure 3.3 presents some common meaning-bearing prefixes, roots, and suffixes that, if memorized, will go a long way toward helping students discover the meaning of hundreds of words. Activities that require students to use these word parts, such as naming the exotic animals found at the beginning of this chapter and the class dictionary activity presented next, will assist in their memorization.

Meaning-bearing affixes and roots.* FIGURE 3.3

auto (self)
anti (against; opposite)
tele (far)
bi (two; twice)
dia (through)
con (together)
trans (across)
re (back; again)
in, im, in (not; within)
pre (before)
circum (around)
graph (writing)
phon (sound)
hydr (water)
therm (heat)
meter (measure)

dic (say)
post (carry)
vit, viv (life)
vert (turn)
sol (sun)
mania (fondness for)
phobia (fear of)
ist (one who)
ic (pertaining to)
ism (condition of)
able, ible (able to)
ment (state of)
er (one who)
tion, ion (act of)
less (opposite of)

* A more detailed list of such word parts can be found in *The Reading Teacher's Book of Lists,* 4th ed. (Fry et al., 2000).

ACTIVITY *The Class Dictionary*

For this activity, students are involved in a science unit on ecology. They are engaged in service-learning projects (see Chapter 10) related to the environment and cleaning up their surrounding community. Throughout the unit students keep a record of the words they are learning and that they need to use when speaking and writing about ecology issues, as well as creating words that have potential meaning to gain practice using the word parts. Here are guidelines for creating a class dictionary on this or any topic.

1. Over several weeks, introduce each of the chosen word parts with example words for each. Extend this list as desired using additional meaning-bearing word parts; for example, ology: ecology; ment: environment; aero: aerate; aqua: aquifer; cosm: cosmos; bio: biosphere; ics: politics; ish: flourish; off: offshore; bene: beneficial; re: recycle.

2. Conduct a word hunt for words containing each part as they are introduced.

3. Put students in groups of three and ask them to create three original words by combining a prefix, a root, and a suffix from the list.

4. Instruct each group to creatively define their new words by considering the meaning of each of the parts. Explain that the definitions can be serious or humorous.

5. Have a spokesperson for each group share each of their new words with the rest of the class, encouraging the other class members to hypothesize what the meanings of the words might be based on their knowledge of the meaning of the individual components.

6. Invite each group to create an illustration to accompany each of their new words. For example, see the classroom scenario at the beginning of this chapter.

7. As a whole class, help students to alphabetize all the groups' words, decide on the part of speech for each entry, and enter them into an illustrated class dictionary.

structural analysis ●   A direct approach for teaching **structural analysis** (identification of meaningful word parts) is to identify a structural element found in a critical word from students' reading assignments. For example, in a social studies unit dealing with forms of government, the element "cracy" in the words aristocracy and autocracy might be chosen. Instruction proceeds by examining the more familiar word *democracy*. The important element "cracy" should be highlighted and students invited to provide a meaning for that part based on their understanding of the word *democracy*. Most students can define a democracy as majority rules, or a government of the people, by the people, and for the people; in short, rule by the people. Then students are told that "cracy" comes from the Greek *"kratia"* and means strength or power; in other words, who rules. Whatever is attached to "cracy" tells who does the ruling. The form of government, democracy, contains the roots "demo" and "cracy," so students can deduce that "demo" means people, and, in fact, "demo" is from the Greek, *"demos,"* meaning people.

Other forms of government can now be examined in the same way (e.g., aristocracy, autocracy, theocracy, bureaucracy). Additionally, it would be useful for this example to introduce and discuss the membership structure for each of these forms of government, that is, aristocrat, autocrat, theocrat, and bureaucrat, respectively.

Related words should be introduced and discussed at this time. These might be posted on a word wall, or become part of a word study notebook that students maintain. Both of these methods will assist with spelling development because the words are written and a visual representation is also readily available. Some examples are demography, demagogy, epidemic, aristocratic, autobiography, autonomy, automatic, bureau, bureaucratic, theology, theocentric, and atheism.

Learning the words on a word list such as the Nifty-Thrifty-Fifty (Cunningham and Hall, 1998, discussed in Chapter 2 and Appendix D) will provide students with morphological patterns for figuring out many other words. These 50 words include common affixes (see Figure 3.3 for others) as well as reveal common spelling changes that occur when suffixes are added to root words. These words can be introduced in groups of five each week using daily activities as follows. The words chosen should also be used within their authentic contexts so students will not only be able to recognize the words, but also know how they are used.

A Typical Week's Word Study Plan

Monday. Display the five new words on a word wall large enough to be seen by students from their seats. **Word walls** are charts or bulletin boards on which important vocabulary words are placed, usually alphabetically, to be referred to during word study activities (see below). Use thick, bold permanent markers for printing the words. Model the decoding of these five words.

● word walls

Write a sentence using a new word on the board:

If your pet licks the <u>antifreeze</u> off the garage floor, it could become very sick, and even die.

Teacher: The underlined word contains a word you might already know and a prefix. A prefix is a word part that is added to the beginning of a word. Can anyone tell me the word without the prefix? (If not, draw a circle around freeze and ask again.)

Then discuss the meaning of the word, and other words that begin with "anti." Continue this process for the other four words of the day.

Tuesday. Come back to the five words introduced on Monday. Practice the five new words by saying the letters and syllables in these words as a rhythmic chant, almost like a song, or a cheer that a cheerleader might lead at a football game. For example, antifreeze might develop into

a - n - t - i anti
a - n - t - i anti
a - n - t - i anti
anti antifreeze

Again, the meanings of the affixes and the whole word should be discussed.

Wednesday. Return to the five words introduced on Monday. Examine the composition of each of the five new words. Focus on how the spelling of the root words may change when an affix is added. Have each student create a written chart such as the following:

WORD	PARTS	SPELLING CHANGES
antifreeze	= anti + freeze	no changes
beautiful	= beauty + ful	y changes to i
classify	= class + ify	no changes
communities	= com + unity + es	m doubles, y changes to i
community	= com + unity or com + unit + y	m doubles

Then ask questions about these words to focus on their meanings, or other special characteristics:

1. Which word is the opposite of ugly?
2. Which word means the opposite of freezing?
3. Which two words have unity as their root?
4. How do you write the plural of community?
5. Which word tells what you do when you group things that are similar?

Students should check the spellings of the words they wrote using the word wall.

Thursday. Chant again (see Tuesday) the five new words introduced on Monday. Now help students see how knowing these words can help them recognize and spell other words they may not yet know. Using related forms of the words taught (Cunningham and Allington, 1999) (see Figure 3.4), ask students to decode, spell, and discuss meanings for these words. For example, have students pronounce *declassify*, note its spelling (add "de" to "classify"), and talk about its meaning as undoing what had been done, or classified. Other words to use could be *classification, freezer, subfreezing, beautifully, powerful, hopeful, communication, mystify,* and *certify.*

Friday. Cover up the word wall. Administer a spelling test on the five new words, or include these in a weekly spelling test. The format might proceed as follows: Say the word, use the word in a sentence, and repeat the word. Then go on to the next word. Students can correct their own papers by writing the correct spelling from the word wall next to any misspelled words.

After 10 weeks all of the words will have been learned. Because these 50 words contain morphological patterns for so many other words, they should be overlearned. The various elements will then be recognized and recalled automatically when needed during reading and writing. The transfer words in Figure 3.4 contain parts of the Nifty-Thrifty-Fifty words. Many other words can also be used as transfer words. Intermediate-grade students and teachers alike will find www.sentex.net/~mmcadams/spelling.html to be a useful website for word study.

There is a general pattern that teachers can use when teaching the morphology and etymology (see below) of words:

1. Begin with the known and move to the unknown.
2. Provide a means for making the transfer. Talk through the process. With practice and repetition, the process becomes internalized.
3. Discuss related words so that knowledge increases in an exponential way as opposed to just one word being studied at a time.
4. Value the content of particular disciplines by using the critical language in that discipline as a means of teaching a functional skill—word analysis.

Etymology

Exploring the histories or derivations of words (etymology) with students not only helps them with spelling (e.g., knowing that *ballet* and *buffet* are both French words helps them to understand the "et" making a long /a/ sound), but also provides interesting multicultural word walls and lessons as well. Many dictionaries, such as *The New Webster's Dictionary,* offer

FIGURE 3.4   Transfer words for the Nifty-Fifty-Thrifty.

NIFTY-FIFTY-THRIFTY TRANSFER WORDS

Here are just some of the words students should be able to decode, spell, and discuss meanings for by using parts of all fifty words:

conform	relive	declassify	powerlessly
conformity	repose	decompose	powerlessness
inform	reclassify	deform	superpower
informer	revalue	deformity	finalize
informant	recover	prearrange	finalizing
information	rediscover	resign	finalization
misinform	electrical	resignation	weighty
uninformed	displease	designation	weightier
formation	discontinue	significant	weightiest
formal	disposal	significance	weightless
transform	musical	freezer	undervalue
transformation	continual	freezing	friendlier
performer	employer	freezable	friendliest
responsibility	employment	subfreezing	friendliness
responsive	unemployment	underclass	unfriendliness
responsiveness	unemployed	overexpose	unpleasantness
honesty	employable	underexpose	historical
dishonesty	unemployable	superimpose	historically
honestly	difference	undercover	expressive
legally	consignment	forecaster	impressive
illegally	nationality	forecasting	repressive
responsibly	nationalities	forecastable	invasive
irresponsibly	internationalize	miscast	noninvasive
arranging	interdependence	antidepressant	invasiveness
rearranging	depress	overture	hopefully
placing	depression	empower	hopelessly
replacing	depressive	empowerment	predispose
misplacing	deport	powerful	predisposition
report	deportation	powerfully	deodorant
reporter	deportee	powerfulness	beautician
refinish	devalue	powerless	electrician

Source: From Cunningham, P. M. & R. L. Allington. *Classrooms That Work: They Can All Read and Write,* 3/e. Published by Allyn & Bacon, Boston, MA. Copyright © 2002 by Pearson Education. Adapted by permission of the publisher.

information as to the language from which each word derives. Additionally, books on the history of words found in any school library can provide entertaining stories of words' origins. For example, the word *tank,* which is defined as a heavily armored vehicle, was originally used as a secret code word to keep the Axis powers from knowing about its existence during World War I. The sharing of such information adds a spark to the study of history, and it can also help students to remember the concept and meaning of the word (Rasinski and Padak, 2000). Many prefixes and suffixes in the English language are also derived from other languages, and understanding these word parts will often give students an idea as to their meaning.

Greek and Latin are common ancient languages from which many of the words in our language derive; however, they are not the only languages of word origin. Students will be interested in studying the etymology of our words. One example is *lagoon,* which derives from the French (*"lagun"*) and Italian (*"laguna"*) languages and means a shallow lake or pond. Another, from one of the author's past experiences living in New Orleans, is the word *lagniappe,* whose origins are in the Creole French (*"la"*) and Spanish (*"napa"*) languages, and the combination results in a word meaning a small present given to a customer with a purchase, or, as the store owners would say, "a little something extra." English language learners especially would be interested in identifying words originating from their native language.

ADDITIONAL INSTRUCTIONAL PRACTICES FOR ADVANCED WORD STUDY

The following practices were chosen because they are especially geared toward intermediate-grade students.

Word Walls

One way to emphasize new, essential, or troublesome words is to post them on word walls, as described earlier, so students will have ready access to these words. It is especially helpful in the intermediate grades for word walls to focus on particular syllabic elements. Word walls can be organized into the prefixes, suffixes, and roots most appropriate for a particular topic of study, by meaning, or as identified by grade-level curriculum groups. Another way to present word walls is to introduce a word part that has a large family of words associated with it and encourage students to add words to this group as they find them in their reading. They can place the word on a word card, share it with the class along with its meaning and where they found the word, and then place it on the word wall. These word groupings can also become the spelling words to be studied. For instance, "ology" is a good example of one such family. Many subjects will contain words that have "ology" in them. Science is the most obvious perhaps (e.g., biology, dermatology, ecology, entomology, hydrology), but there are other subjects as well (e.g., sociology, theology, morphology, anthropology). Students can be told that the suffix "ology" means "the study of" or "the science of" whatever it is preceded by (e.g., geo = earth + ology = the study of) (see Figure 3.5).

FIGURE 3.5   Example word wall.

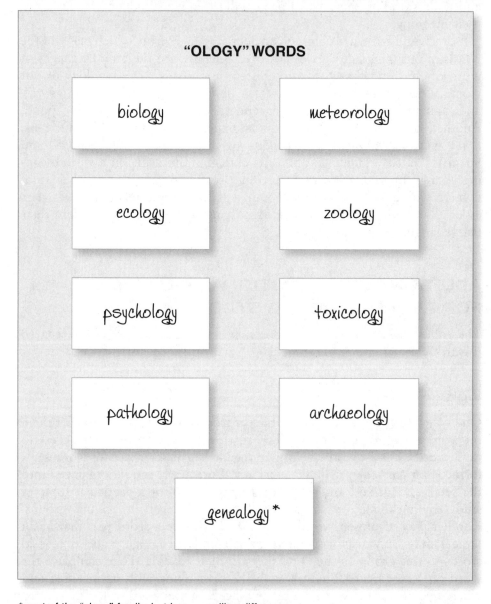

* part of the "ology" family, but has a spelling difference

Roots and Branches   (Bloodgood et al., 2001)   ACTIVITY

This word study technique focuses on Greek and Latin roots, from which a preponderance of our words derive, to discover within-word patterns that will help with word recognition, meaning, as well as spelling.

1. Present a root written within a circle on a large piece of poster paper without revealing its meaning (e.g., graph).

2. Ask students to provide words they already know that contain that word part. Write these on the poster paper as branches off the central root (see Figure 3.6).

3. As students discuss these words they can infer the meaning of the root (e.g., "graph means to write"); write that meaning within the circle.

Additional words can be added to the posters as they appear in material read over the course of time. Several of these "Roots and Branches" posters can be prepared and hung around the classroom for students to add to as they finish other assignments. As posters are added, the meaning of the root written within the circle is discussed, and as new words are added to these posters, the new words are discussed as to their relationship to the central root.

FIGURE 3.6   Roots and branches.

ACTIVITY *The Word Family Tree* (Buehl, 2001)

An excellent strategy for etymological exploration, the word family tree involves students connecting word origins, key terms from a unit of study, common roots, and other current meanings of the word. Using the analogy of a family tree, the teacher introduces the concept of the word family as listing the individual word's "ancestors," or origins, direct descendants, and related words, or "relatives," that contain the root. Words that have similar meaning that are already known words can also be introduced.

1. Begin with a word that is found in students' text material; for instance, from a social studies selection the word *segregation* could be selected.

2. Give students the original word forms: the Latin "se" (apart) + "greg" (herd), the Latin "com" or "con" (with), and the Latin "ag" (the "ad" becomes "ag" when followed by the letter *g*, and means *to*). Students will notice root forms and may be able to give related words (e.g., congregate and segregate).

3. Ask students to speculate about the word's connection to other words. A "What's the Word Connection?" activity establishes how the word's origin can help determine its current meaning:

   What's the word connection . . .

   . . . between a flock of sheep and a group of outcasts?

   . . . between a crowd and a loner?

   . . . between concrete and a group of people who attend the same church?

4. Introduce the word family tree (see Figure 3.7). Explain how the word is linked to a meaningful root to help students speculate about the kinds of contexts in which this word or its relatives will likely appear. It might help to think about who would use these words and what they might say (see "Who would use this word, or a relative of it?" in Figure 3.7).

5. Provide other target words that students can investigate (e.g., *concert, genetics, sonar, treaty*). Students can work with a partner, or in small groups, to complete word family trees for these words to share with the entire class.

FIGURE 3.7   A word family tree for the word *segregation.*

Who would use this word, or a relative of it?

Judge: <u>Segregation</u> is against the law.

Minister: I am happy to see all of my <u>congregation</u> at church.

Sentence: Expecting Rosa Parks to sit at the back of the bus was a form of <u>segregation</u>.

Definition: noun. The isolation of a race, class, or ethnic group by forced or voluntary residence in a restricted area, by barriers, or by separate educational facilities or other discriminatory means.

Segregation
(Direct Descendant)

<u>Pronunciation Key</u>
seg-ri-gā-shen

<u>Ancestor (Root Word[s])</u>
"greg" means gather
"se" means apart

<u>Relatives</u>
congregation
aggregate
gregarious

<u>Memory Clue</u>
- 4 syllables with accent on third syllable
- isolation by discrimination

Word Play/Word Formation

Students need to realize that the English language is a living, growing language. New words are continually added to our language. There are words in our dictionaries today that were not there a few short years ago. And the word parts students are learning in the intermediate grades are generally how new words come into existence. Prefixes and suffixes are added to existing root words to form new words (e.g., *preview, Americanism*). Sometimes two words are combined to create a new word. These are called **portmanteau words,** or words that are blended together (e.g., *motel* from *motor* + *hotel,* or *smog* from *smoke* + *fog*). Intermediate-grade students get excited about creating potential new words and they enjoy sharing them and their definitions with classmates.

portmanteau words ●

The following examples of "created" words were found, unclaimed, on the Internet (modified from Johnson, 2001, p. 162). They could be used as examples for challenging students to create their own words:

> **Aquadextrous** (ak wa DEKS trus) adj. Having the ability to turn the bathtub faucet on and off with your toes. Susan was able to relax in her reclined position as she used her *aquadextrous* ability to warm up her cooling bathtub water.
>
> **Elevacelleration** (el a VA cel er AY schun) n. The mistaken idea that the more you press the elevator button the faster it will arrive. The businessman tapped his foot impatiently as he demonstrated *elevacelleration.*
>
> **Elboatics** (el bo AT iks) n. The physical maneuvering two people engage in for trying to use the one armrest between them at the movie theater. Because they were engaged in *elboatics,* the couple missed an important part of the movie.

Students can work in teams or alone to create the new words. Each new word should be presented like a dictionary entry with the pronunciation key, part of speech, a definition, and a sample sentence, as seen in the examples. If an illustration is appropriate, this can also be provided.

INCREASING FLUENCY

As students advance through the grades, the texts they are expected to read contain increasingly complex linguistic and syntactical features. A reader who up to now has been able to read with **fluency**—that is, speed, accuracy, and prosody (or appropriate pacing, intonation, expression)—may suddenly begin to read more slowly, or less accurately, and with less confidence. In fact, reading rate charts do show a drop-off at grade four, when reading requires more emphasis on expository text (see Figure 3.8).

fluency ●

The structure of the texts that students now encounter is often different from that of earlier text. Students need to learn new functions for some words. They need to learn what is preferred and what is to be avoided in inflection and syntax. The use of more varied punctuation will likely reduce fluency until those new patterns can be practiced. Teachers in the interme-

Reading rate ranges for instructional-level reading.   FIGURE 3.8

Reading rate is measured in words read correctly per minute. This rate is used to evaluate automaticity of word recognition. Words per minute (WPM) is determined by multiplying the number of words in the passage by 60 and then dividing by the number of seconds taken to read the passage. This measure can be used with both oral and silent reading; use of a stopwatch is recommended. For silent reading, direct the student to indicate when he or she is starting to read, and to look up when he or she has finished the selection.

INSTRUCTIONAL LEVELS	ORAL RATE RANGE	SILENT RATE RANGE
Preprimer	13–35 WPM	NA*
Primer	28–68 WPM	NA
First	31–87 WPM	NA
Second	52–102 WPM	58–122 WPM
Third	85–139 WPM	96–168 WPM
Fourth, Fifth	78–124 WPM	107–175 WPM
Fifth, Sixth	113–165 WPM	135–241 WPM

*NA = not available.

diate grades would do well to read aloud to students to model these new patterns (Richardson, 2000).

Students also need time reading so they can gain experience and practice with the more complex forms of written language. A minimum of 20 minutes per day of silent reading, more if possible, will go a long way toward providing the necessary practice for increasing fluency. In schools that have higher achievement levels, students spend more than 75 percent of the time scheduled for reading instruction actually reading. Thus, if instruction were scheduled for 100 minutes, then 75 minutes of that time students would actually be reading, not working with a group or with the teacher on skill lessons (Allington and Cunningham, 2002, p. 134).

One effective strategy for improving fluency and oral reading that many students also find motivating is readers theatre. Sloyer (1982) defines **readers theatre** as "an interpretative reading activity for all the children in the classroom. Readers bring characters to life through their voices and gestures. . . . Readers Theatre becomes an integrated language event centering upon oral interpretation of literature" (p. 3). As such, readers practice oral reading and address all the areas of fluency (speed, accuracy, prosody)

● readers theatre

through "rehearsals" of the material to be read before an audience. To provide an appealing performance, the reader must not only comprehend the material and read it accurately, but dramatize his or her interpretation through appropriate intonation and expression.

ACTIVITY *Readers Theatre*

In this type of group-reading activity, a narrator speaks directly to the audience, establishing the basic premise of the story and linking the various segments. The narration text is created with the help of the other students. The narrator also simplifies the language and abstract concepts. The other actors read the dialogue of the characters, and each actor may take the part of more than one character. The success of the readers theatre production depends on the oral aspects of the presentation rather than on acting skills or props. The actors will read their parts fluently. The actors use facial expressions and tone of voice to convey the emotions and moods of the characters. Action is merely suggested; the audience must visualize the activity in their mind's eye. Readers theatre usually omits stage properties, lights, and costumes, so that nothing distracts the audience's attention from the characterization.

The story chosen should require a minimum of rewriting, or a prepared readers theatre script could be used (see www.aaronshep.com/rt/). The kind of story best adapted for readers theatre contains characters who have multidimensional features and unique personalities. The language of such a story should be thought provoking, colorful, and rhythmic. The plot should have an element of conflict and/or suspense. The completed script may be made into a laminated booklet and placed in a learning center for children to enjoy as a free-time oral reading activity.

The development of a script requires two distinct steps: (1) selecting material with strong dramatic appeal, and (2) adapting the selection to bring about a positive audience response. Almost any piece of literature containing lots of dialogue will do, but folktales are especially well suited to the vehicle.

An adaptation of readers theatre is books on tape, which are recorded literature selections for an unseen audience. Using this method, small groups of students select a piece of quality literature and practice reading it until it has become fluent and expressive, adding sound effects and including various voices for different characters. One teacher in Sowams School in Barrington, Rhode Island, asked businesses to contribute the literature as well as the blank tapes. The tapes, with the books and biographies of the different readers, were then sent to children's hospitals in the surrounding area as a class service-learning project.

Stories can also be adapted into more traditional plays portraying the physical actions of the characters for classes seeking more formal productions. The following seven steps briefly outline a more spontaneous process for creating an adaptation of readers theatre that allows students' own words to "bring literature to life":

1. After setting a purpose for listening, read the story aloud for comprehension. Then have students reread the story aloud with all the dramatic intensity they can muster.

2. Have several students relate the story in sequence from memory with the aid of a story grammar or story frame.

3. Select a scribe to write down the story, section by section, in the students' own words. Distribute copies of this new version to each student, thus providing each with a "script." (In a traditional play, this script is memorized; in readers theatre, it is simply read.)

4. Have small groups of students act out, or "block," each section of the play as another student reads it.

5. As a group, discuss how different characters might talk, walk, look, and behave. The roles of all characters should be considered in this discussion—from narrator to those involved in crowd scenes.

6. While the play is in the rehearsal stage, tell the music teacher the theme of the upcoming performance and ask him or her to select several songs that might enhance the script. Also ask the teacher if he or she would be willing to set aside some class time to help students create scenery to enhance the setting.

7. Encourage students to design invitations that include the theme of the performance and allow them to distribute the invitations to those who will be in the audience (e.g., parents, classmates, other classes within the school).

TROUBLESHOOTING

It would be wonderful if we could assume that all students in the intermediate grades possessed the decoding ability needed to focus on comprehension strategies. Unfortunately, we cannot make this assumption. For students still having difficulty decoding, it is imperative that they continue to receive instruction that will enhance their decoding ability so they can increase their sight vocabulary, in turn permitting rapid access to word and text meaning. Generally, older students still having trouble with decoding will

- not pronounce the word at all.
- pronounce the word like some other word they know.
- pronounce the word differently each time they encounter it.

They are demonstrating that they do not have a decoding strategy or that they are not focusing on and/or recognizing the letters and letter clusters within the word. Techniques for intermediate-grade students that directly address these decoding difficulties follow.

No Decoding Strategy

Students who demonstrate no use of a decoding strategy in the intermediate grades often benefit from using a structured approach for figuring out an unknown word in print. DISSECT is a decoding strategy that offers students step-by-step alternatives for learning unfamiliar words (Bryant et al., 1999; Lenz et al., 1984; Sadler, 2001). There are seven steps to the strategy, and after the teacher has modeled the steps, they can be printed on index cards, laminated, and used as bookmarks for a ready reference during reading. Of course, if a word is identified without using all seven steps, it is not necessary to continue with the remaining steps. The seven steps are as follows:

D   Discover the word's context by using the clues in the text around the word.

I   Isolate the prefix if there is one and think of its meaning.

S   Separate the suffix if there is one.

S   Say what is left. This is the root, or stem.

E   Examine the stem by separating letters to make decoding easier. Try to look for a part you can say.

C   Check with someone if necessary.

T   Try the dictionary pronunciation key.

Assume that the word causing difficulty is *unsaturated*. The student is reading a section of a health or science text that deals with good eating habits. This word is being used to describe a type of fat. The student recognizes, or is told to remove, the prefix *un*. The teacher might ask, "What does the prefix *un* do to the word it is attached to?" The student may respond with "It means *not* or it changes the word to its opposite, like unfinished means *not* finished, or the opposite of finished is *not* finished." Next, the student separates the suffix. In this word the suffix is identified as *ed*. It might help the student to actually write down what is left after removing the prefix and the suffix. The word would now look like *saturat*. But it may need to be pointed out that sometimes when *ed* is added to a word, the original word already had an *e* (relate to a known word like fade/faded). In this case, when *ed* is added, the last *e* in the word is dropped, so it needs to be replaced when the *ed* is removed. Hence, the stem, or root, is actually written *saturate*. The teacher has now provided a mini spelling lesson as well as a decoding strategy. However, the word cannot yet be pronounced by the student, so further examination is needed. The student recognizes the syllables "sat" and "ate." The teacher might point out that what is left is "ur," and say that syllable. Now the student can put the three syllables together: "sat"—"ur"—"ate." If this word is unknown in terms of listening or meaning vocabulary, then this process will not trigger an "aha." The dictionary will be needed to check both pronunciation and meaning. It would be useful for the teacher to also relate the word to the context in which it has occurred: if *saturate* means capable of absorbing, then *unsaturated* means *not* capable of absorbing. The meaning of the new word will be reviewed as a final step. The student can then list other words already known, or found during reading, that have some of these same syllables, such as *Saturday, satisfied, Saturn, create, mediate,* or *delegate*.

Mispronounces Words

Direct instruction in decoding the most consistent aspects of our written language, such as syllables, and then blending these syllables to form whole words and using these words in context should be provided for older students who consistently mispronounce words. The following activity, called Sylla-Search, is adapted from a phonics exercise used by classroom teacher Barbara Panza with second and third graders.

Sylla-Search   ACTIVITY

This activity uses multisyllabic words and focuses the learner on the syllables that are pronounced most consistently either in isolation or within other words.

1. Write the multisyllabic word *attendance* on the board. Then ask the following series of questions about the syllables in this word:

       What two letters make the /at/ sound?   A-T

       What three letters make the /ten/ sound?   T-E-N

       What five letters make the /dance/ sound?   D-A-N-C-E

       How would you say the syllable T-E-N?   /ten/

       How would you say the syllable A-T?   /at/

       How would you say the syllable D-A-N-C-E?   /dans/

   Is there another word you can think of that contains the syllable A-T or /at/? The syllable T-E-N or /ten/? (write these words on the board for students to see):

   cat bat mat sat fat . . . tend tens tense

How about words with more than one syllable? (write these words on the board for students to see):

attack   matter   attend   tension

2. Ask students to look through some of their books for other words that contain these syllables.
3. Ask students to write these words in their personal dictionaries with a definition or sentence that will help them remember the word.

Another approach involves the use of creative thinking-reading activities (CT-RAs). CT-RAs are brief, small-group activities designed to generate many solutions to a problem, and then to combine possible solutions into one "best" solution to be shared with the whole group (Ruddell, 1993). Standard starters such as "Think of all the ways . . ." or "What would happen if . . ." are used. Only about 10 to 15 minutes at the beginning or end of a class are needed to complete these activities. To focus on decoding, starters might include "Think of all the ways you can figure out an unknown word," "What would happen if the prefix *un* was added to this list of words?" "Think of as many words as you can that start with the syllable 'con'," or "Think of all the words you can find in the word *assignment.*"

ACTIVITY *CT-RA*

A modification of the classroom scenario activity that begins this chapter could serve as a CT-RA (Tierney, 1985).

1. Using copies of the pictures of the animals created by the students in the In the Classroom vignette, have students cut them out, cut off the head, and pass the head to the student sitting next to them.
2. Ask students to tape the new head onto the animal they are holding.
3. Using the scientist's vocabulary chart, ask each student to rename the animal they have now created.
4. Move the students into small groups and have them develop habitats and behaviors for their animals, finally sharing this information with the entire class.

This activity can help students with decoding and spelling difficulties to gain practice with useful and consistent Greek and Latin roots as well as demonstrate to them how manipulating word parts leads to the creation and pronunciation of other words.

SUMMARY

Word study is presented as a continuum of development in spelling, word analysis, and vocabulary abilities. The focus in the intermediate grades changes from attention to mapping sounds onto letters to recognizing units that make up whole words. Of most importance are units that hold meaning such as prefixes, suffixes, roots, and endings. These units are also very consistent in their pronunciation and meaning, thus aiding both decoding and spelling. Because the nature of word study at the intermediate-grade levels involves word parts that hold meaning, instruction is also closely tied to meaning vocabulary. It would be extremely difficult to avoid talking about the meanings of words when providing instruction in roots, prefixes, suffixes, compound words, and derivational words. While students in the primary grades learn to decode words that are for the most part in their speaking and listening vocabularies, students in the intermediate grades are learning to decode many words for which they have no conceptual knowledge. Instruction in word recognition, then, must also be closely related to instruction in meaning vocabulary to be most effective and efficient. As intermediate-grade students encounter text with structures different from the more familiar narrative structures of primary-grade materials, their fluency levels drop off. Teacher modeling of fluent reading for more complex materials is helpful, as is providing time for students to practice reading these more complex materials.

Questions
FOR JOURNAL WRITING AND DISCUSSION

1. Describe in your own words the stages of reading/spelling development. What characteristics might a student demonstrate in each of the stages? Explain how being aware of these stages might help a teacher plan appropriate spelling instruction for each learner.
2. Discuss how word study may be of particular value to English language learners.
3. What is the value in teaching morphology to students? Use examples to support your response.

Suggestions
FOR PROJECTS AND FIELD ACTIVITIES

1. Administer a spelling inventory (see Appendix D) to three intermediate-grade students. Analyze their responses as to what reading/spelling stage is represented most often in their spelling. What are some instructional activities that would benefit these students?

2. Develop a list of 15 words based on similar or related roots, affixes, or derivations. Invite a small group of intermediate-grade students to sort the words as they think they should be sorted. Then have these students make statements about their findings. Present your list and your findings to your classmates. What were the students able to learn from the sorting activity?

3. Observe a word study lesson taught to intermediate-grade students. Through discussion with the teacher and your direct observation, answer the following questions:

   a. What strategies are students being taught about how to spell new words?

   b. How are students being taught about syllables, affixes, and derivations?

   c. How is word study applied in reading and writing situations in the classroom?

References

Allington, R. L., & Cunningham, P. M. (2002). *Schools that work: Where all children read and write* (2nd ed.). Boston: Allyn & Bacon.

Bear, D. R., Invernizzi, M., Templeton, S., & Johnston, F. (2000). *Words their way: Word study for phonics, vocabulary, and spelling instruction* (2nd ed.). Upper Saddle River, NJ: Merrill.

Bloodgood, J. W., Pacifici, L. C., & Rullman, A. (2001, December). *Bringing word study to upper elementary and preservice teacher classrooms.* Alternative Session presented at the annual meeting of the National Reading Conference, San Antonio, TX.

Bryant, D. P., Ugel, N., Thompson, S., & Hamff, A. (1999). Instructional strategies for content-area reading instruction. *Intervention in School and Clinic, 34*(5), 293–302.

Buehl, D. (2001). *Classroom strategies for interactive learning* (2nd ed.). Newark, DE: International Reading Association.

Crichton, M. (1990). *Jurassic Park*. New York: Knopf.

Cunningham, P. M., & Allington, R. L. (1999). *Classrooms that work: They can all read and write* (2nd ed.). New York: Longman.

Cunningham, P. M., & Hall, D. P. (1998). *Month-by-month phonics for upper grades: A second chance for struggling readers and students learning English.* Greensboro, NC: Carson-DeLosa.

Fry, E. B., Kress, J. E., & Fountoukidis, D. L. (2000). *The reading teacher's book of lists* (4th ed.). Paramus, NJ: Prentice Hall.

Gipe, J. P. (2002). *Multiple paths to literacy: Classroom techniques for struggling readers* (5th ed.). Upper Saddle River, NJ: Merrill-Prentice Hall.

Henderson, E. (1990). *Teaching spelling* (2nd ed.). Boston: Houghton Mifflin.

Johnson, D. D. (2001). *Vocabulary in the elementary and middle school.* Boston: Allyn & Bacon.

Johnson, D. D., & Pearson, P. D. (1984). *Teaching reading vocabulary* (2nd ed.). New York: Holt, Rinehart and Winston.

Kemper, L. W., & Brody, F. (2001). Advanced decoding and fluency. In F. Brody (Ed.), *Teaching reading: Language, letters and thought* (2nd ed., pp. 144–167). Milford, NH: LARC.

Lenz, B. K., Schumaker, J. G., Deshler, D. D., & Beals, V. L. (1984). *The word identification strategy.* Lawrence, KS: University of Kansas.

Rasinski, T., & Padak, N. (2000). *Effective reading strategies: Teaching children who find reading difficult* (2nd ed.). Upper Saddle River, NJ: Merrill-Prentice Hall.

Richardson, J. S. (2000). *Read it aloud!* Newark, DE: International Reading Association.

Ruddell, M. R. (1993). *Teaching content reading and writing.* Boston: Allyn & Bacon.

Sadler, C. R. (2001). *Comprehension strategies for middle grade learners: A handbook for content area teachers.* Newark, DE: International Reading Association.

Sloyer, S. (1982). *Readers theatre: Story dramatization in the classroom.* Urbana, IL: National Council of Teachers of English.

Tierney, B. (1985). In the fifth grade, they all raise their hands. *Learning, 85,* 34.

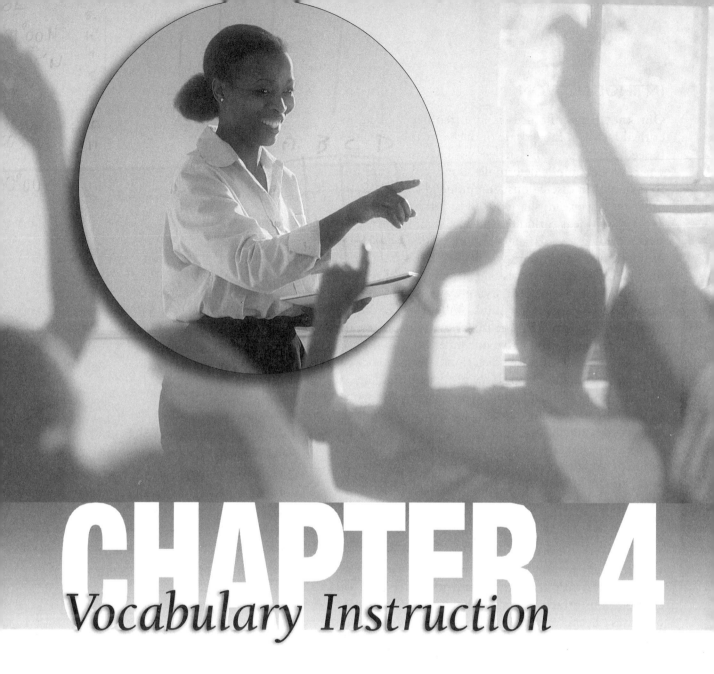

CHAPTER 4
Vocabulary Instruction

Focus Questions

- What are important factors to keep in mind when teaching vocabulary?
- What are some research-based instructional strategies to teach vocabulary directly to children?
- How can teachers assist students in learning how to figure out the meanings of new words on their own?

INTRODUCTION

Our knowledge of words is an often overlooked, yet critical factor in the mosaic of our entire personalities. Indeed, the word knowledge we have stored somewhere in our minds determines how well we are able to take part in discussions; comprehend the books and other texts we read; share our most intimate thoughts; explain our ideas for others; and, in sum, form a cohesive worldview. A larger vocabulary does not mean only that we know more words but, more important, that we are able to express our thoughts and feelings in a more complex and satisfying way. We may use our storehouse of words to think and even to dream; therefore, it follows that the richer our vocabulary, the more potentially productive our inner life can be.

In a more specifically educational setting, vocabulary is absolutely integral to proficient reading. If children do not understand the meaning of the words in text, the process of reading is reduced to meaningless word calling, or "barking at print." No child should ever have to struggle along producing only a series of verbal nonsense. As teachers, we want children to understand a wide range of words. A fundamental part of critical thinking necessary for adequate reading comprehension is rapid access to the necessary word meanings (Anderson and Freebody, 1981; Graves, 1986).

Proficient readers are able to connect new words with other words they know and to understand the connotations attached to them by virtue of their various uses. Because each proficient reader's particular background varies, for every passage a social history and context is created that continually attaches personal meaning to it. Encountering words over and over again, both through text and in conversation, builds a fabric of understandings that clarifies the meanings of familiar words and then makes it even easier to solve the meaning of new words, creating a snowballing spiral of vocabulary acquisition. Indeed, Nagy and Anderson (1984) estimated that by fifth grade, average readers read 10 times more than poor readers, and that voracious readers read up to 50 times as many words! As a result, by merely encountering more words, good readers learn much more about language.

In the Classroom

Mrs. Chase briefly explains the term *eternal life* to her students and gives them a few seconds to imagine what it would be like to live forever. She then leads a lively discussion about what the students believe are the possible advantages and disadvantages of living forever, writing all their comments on the chalkboard. Jennifer believes that living forever would be a wonderful thing because "you wouldn't have to die and make people sad"; Ethan counters that all his friends would be gone and he might become "lonely and bored."

Following the discussion, Mrs. Chase's sixth-graders begin reading Natalie Babbitt's *Tuck Everlasting* (1975) in heterogeneous literature groups. During this time, Mrs. Chase uses a clarifying table to anchor the meaning of the term *eternity* within the context of the book. She writes the word *eternity* under the heading "Core Idea" and writes below it that this term means "an endless period of time." She then asks if someone can give an example of what eternity means from his or her own life experience. "When you're waiting for the mail to arrive because you are expecting a special birthday present from your aunt. It seems like an eternity! But it's not, really," exclaims Raul. Next, Mrs. Chase asks the students to offer examples of another word with which the term might be easily confused. Rachel suggests, "Anything that has a life span that you can predict would not be a good example of eternity. Recess lasts for about 15 minutes, a fixed amount of time—not an eternity." After this, the teacher asks for "clarifiers," or phrases that will help the students to think more clearly about what the term does and does not mean. After the students brainstorm in small groups, the teacher writes down their responses:

"You don't know the beginning and you don't know the end."

"Some religions believe that we live on for an eternity after we die."

"Always and forever."

"Events that go on longer than you want them to seem to take an eternity, but that's an exaggeration."

At this point, Mrs. Chase asks the students to think about how the term *eternity* was used in the book. They offer that the Tuck family had drunk from a spring that gave them everlasting life; in this case they never grew older and would exist for "all the time that will ever exist in the world." Finally, the teacher asks the students to create a sentence using the term *eternity*. Now all the students are able to quickly complete this task, offering sentences that reflect their own lives or the book they have just read. Andy's contribution is typical:

"An eternity is an amount of time that has no end, or just feels like it will never end."

Mrs. Chase's use of the *clarifying table* has solidified the students' understanding of the most critical concept in the book. (See pp. 102–104 for a discussion of clarifying tables.)

TYPES OF VOCABULARY

Two major types of vocabulary are relevant in the upper-grades classroom: meaning vocabulary and reading vocabulary. **Meaning vocabulary,** as the name implies, is the sum total of a child's understanding of the meaning of words. Meaning vocabulary is extremely important, because readers need to draw from this store as they emerge into reading to learn. Meaning vocabulary can therefore be likened to a vast reservoir from which readers draw known meanings and use these to figure out new meanings as they read. **Reading vocabulary,** on the other hand, is gained when children learn to decode words whose meaning they already know, in other words, the words are already in their meaning vocabulary.

Vocabulary can be further broken down into three subcategories, or tiers, that have major implications as to how the various words encountered could most effectively be introduced to children in the intermediate grades. These three subcategories are

- basic words
- general-utility words
- low-utility words

The exact words that we decide to teach students directly is influenced by the occurrence of those words. How frequently the words will be seen in text and therefore afford opportunities for practice by students should be in direct proportion to the time we spend introducing the words (Beck et al., 1987). Once we are aware of which words are the most instructionally significant, then we can consider a variety of methods for teaching those words, either directly or by assisting students in using strategies that aid in new vocabulary acquisition.

Basic words are the building blocks of everyday language. They are so commonplace and are used so often that their meanings do not require specific instruction except in the case of second language learners, who usually will have the concept but will require a new English label for the word. Examples of such words are *am, boy, said,* and *from.*

General-utility words are more complex terms that proficient readers and speakers use often in speech, but these words tend not to be specific to any one subject area. Instruction in common root words, prefixes, and suffixes can often help students to discover the meaning of words in this category; the majority of vocabulary study during a reading lesson would be directed at this tier of words. Words such as *create, combine, examine,* and *transfer* are examples of this tier of vocabulary.

low-utility words ●

Low-utility words, the third tier of vocabulary, are the words that are encountered less frequently, and they are usually found in particular content areas. Such words should be introduced before students engage in their content area texts and tasks and grouped according to the particular concept with which they are identified. Examples of such words include *tropism, solar, biped,* and *crater.*

LEVELS OF WORD KNOWLEDGE

Knowing a word is *not* an all or nothing proposition. Researchers (Dale, 1965; Beck et al., 1987) have created a continuum of word understanding ranging from being completely unfamiliar with a word to having a rich network of meaning attached to it. Words often have both a denotation and a connotation and can also evoke a constellation of meanings and ideas to different people depending on their own experiences and cultural settings. Moreover, knowing a word in context is different from knowing a word in isolation, and being able to use a word in daily conversation is different from merely being able to understand the word in written format (see Figure 4.1).

Knowledge of a word, then, can be best viewed in terms of the extent or degree of understanding that a person has about it. By pointing out to children the continuum of ways it is possible to be familiar with a word, they

FIGURE 4.1 Four stages of word knowledge.

1. I never heard/saw the word before.
   (I have never before seen nor heard the word *torii.*)

2. I have heard/seen the word, but I don't know what it means.
   (I have seen the word *torque* in a body shop.)

3. I recognize the word in context, or . . . it has something to do with . . .
   (An "ovipositor" has something to do with a sea animal laying eggs.)

4. I know the word.
   (A "kinkajou" is a yellowish-brown mammal of Central and South America.)

1	2	3	4

COMPLETELY UNFAMILIAR · RICH NETWORK OF MEANING

Source: Adapted from Stahl, 1999.

can begin to experience both how working with words and reading widely support growth in meaning vocabulary. For example, a child comes across an unfamiliar word (*extinction*) but can associate it with something with which she is familiar (preservation of animals). This partial recognition, supported by context, may let her continue to read without interrupting the "flow" of her understanding of the passage. In fact, encountering a partially known word in context and relating it to the meaning of a whole text is the kind of literacy event that will gradually enhance her knowledge of that word and help her to move it along the continuum toward a richly known word. As the child encounters the word again and again, recognition of the word's meaning will grow at a relatively constant rate, depending upon the helpfulness of the context (Schwanenflugel et al., 1997). Finally, Beck et al. (1987) have suggested that when readers reach the stage where they feel they truly "know" a word, they are even able to provide an original sentence containing the word, or a restatement of the definition in their own words.

PRINCIPLES OF VOCABULARY INSTRUCTION

A major task in vocabulary instruction should be to choose words for students that include known words as well as unfamiliar words so that personal connections can be made. Such a task is not accomplished through traditional vocabulary acquisition methods of having students copy the words, look them up in the dictionary, memorize definitions, and then use the words in contrived sentences. Rather, some guiding principles for effective vocabulary instruction are the following (Fountas and Pinnell, 1996):

New words should be integrated with familiar words and concepts. There are a wide variety of ways that students can create knowledge connections between new words and their own background knowledge. For example, teachers can help them to identify how the new words are related to previous subject matter they have learned (e.g., "a novel is like a long story"), to identify something from their personal life experiences that reminds them of a particular word (e.g., "filibuster reminds me of my talkative Uncle Buster"), to create metaphors or similes for a term (e.g., "a chrysanthemum is like a yellow mum"), or to lead a discussion about how some of the words might relate to solving some real-life problem they have had (e.g., "because I always procrastinated about feeding my hamster, I taped a sign on his cage to help me remember").

Students should experience words in repeated, meaningful encounters. New words should be taught in the context of a meaningful subject matter lesson and discussions with students should then center around the use of the new words. For example. the word *phototropism* could best be taught after an experiment in which plants are observed growing toward the sun. At some point, students should be encouraged to use the new terms themselves in multiple contexts—through reading, writing, listening, and

Teacher behaviors that enhance vocabulary learning

LINK	Relate students' past experiences with present ones.
ELABORATE	Add more information about familiar content, or suggest a rewording of the content.
INPUT	Introduce new vocabulary and reinforce through constant use.
CONNECT	Tie new words to the activity or the activity to the new words.
CLARIFY	Add examples, illustrations, or descriptions.
QUESTION	Stimulate thinking about terms through questioning.
RELATE	Show how new words compare with those students know.
CATEGORIZE	Group new words, ideas, and concepts.
LABEL	Provide names for concepts, ideas, and objects.

speaking. In short, they should frequently use the words in sentences within the context of discussing broader issues that are meaningful to them.

Students should immediately apply the words they learn in other contexts and associate them with other knowledge. Comprehension is greatly enhanced when students can quickly identify examples of the words or ways the new words can be appropriately applied in the context of a discussion of an already familiar concept. For example, the teacher could relate the word *propaganda* to a sales pitch with which students are familiar, such as a car salesperson's spiel, and then lead a discussion of other high-pressure, and often misleading, advertisements they have seen on television, with the students taking notes on some of the most offensive ones they have seen. The teacher could then end the discussion with an informal survey about which propaganda techniques the students like the least and why.

Vocabulary instruction should engage students in active processing of word meanings. Whereas some students can acquire new vocabulary through listening and discussion, many others need more active engagement in order to process the new words. Using the new terms in essays or creative writing affords students an even greater opportunity for reflection and thinking about how the words are used. Other forms of active engagement include acting out the words, creating mnemonic devices, or drawing pictures that capture the essence of the word's meaning.

Ellis and Farmer (2000) offer suggestions for selecting vocabulary to teach:

1. *Teach words that are essential to the unit or theme of study.* Instead of teaching all words that appear in a list at the end of a text chapter, teach the ones that are so critical that it would be impossible to understand the chapter without knowing them.

2. *Go for depth and connections.* Don't try to teach a large quantity of words that children will probably not encounter again; instead, teach a few words in a manner that results in deep understandings by connecting to concepts with which children are already familiar.

3. *Teach only key concepts.* Although a chapter of study may contain 15 or more highlighted vocabulary terms, there may be only 4 or 5 that address crucial concepts in the chapter.

4. *Reinforce words that will be used often during the school year.* General-utility words that will be revisited often provide a foundation upon which much information will be built over time.

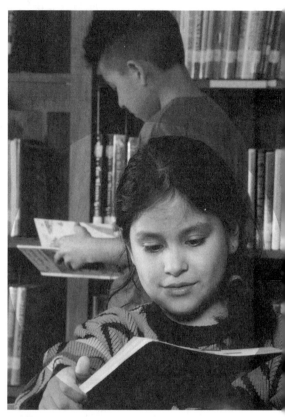

TEACHING WORD MEANINGS

Teachers always seem to be looking for better ways to increase their students' vocabularies because they are aware that the old ways, for the most part, did not result in long-term retention of new words. Traditionally, students copied a list of words from the chalkboard, looked up their meaning in the dictionary, memorized a definition (usually a simple synonym), and then wrote sentences that were supposed to demonstrate an understanding of the word's essence. Here is an example of a product from such a method: "I was exhausted." This method of memorizing isolated vocabulary one word at a time is not only ineffective, as the example suggests, but it is also impractical. While students may remember approximately 200 words a year through this rote method, Anderson and Nagy (1992) advise that students must acquire more than 3,000 words a year to keep up with the demands of content area material! Clearly, teachers must offer a variety of approaches to vocabulary instruction to assist students in their substantial vocabulary needs.

Although there are many approaches to teaching students the meaning of a word, the approach a teacher should take depends on three discrete factors (Stahl, 1999):

- the nature of the word—concrete or abstract?
- the possibility for grouping the word with others
- the possibility for graphically illustrating the word

Nature of the word. First, the word itself should be considered. If the word is one requiring little explanation (e.g., *mountainside*) or one that can be easily shown to students (e.g., *rutabaga*), then little extended elaboration is required. However, if the word is more abstract and difficult, such as *propaganda*, a lengthier explanation would be more appropriate.

Additionally, an instructional strategy designed to help students to focus on what the word is as well as what it is not, in relationship to words they already know, is often illuminating.

Grouping the word with others. Second, since teaching words as single units is decidedly inefficient, teachers should look for ways to link words and ideas together so that students encounter a group of similar, or related, words at one time. For example, if students are studying the newspaper, it would make sense to introduce all the parts of the paper—obituaries, headlines, editorial, classified advertisements, and so forth—because all these elements are related to the same concept, or belong to the same "semantic field." Similarly, as mentioned in the previous chapter, it may be possible to introduce students to many medical words that share the same suffix when introducing the word *cardiologist,* so that they are encountering—and mentally filing— the words *ophthalmologist, psychologist,* and *optometrist* at the same time.

Graphically illustrating the word. Finally, a word should be acted out or in some other way made graphic to students when the word in question lends itself to such treatment. Such words as *meandered* or *exhausted* can be immediately made clear through pantomime; likewise, the word *chrysanthemum* is instantly accessible through a photo or through examining the live flower. Moreover, such multisensory approaches to vocabulary development, with their deemphasis on oral language, help encourage English language learners to be active participants in the learning and comprehension process.

VOCABULARY INSTRUCTION: EFFECTIVE STRATEGIES

Through effective, formal vocabulary instruction, children will acquire new words to their meaning vocabulary; in addition, the stress of an overwhelming number of new words and concepts encountered in instructional reading material will be reduced. The end result is that by reducing the number of unfamiliar words with which the children must struggle, the teacher increases the chances of creating a positive literacy experience. In this section, we explore five different ways in which teachers can provide effective instruction in vocabulary.

To ensure the maximum acquisition of new words throughout the school years, we must provide instruction that helps students

- relate new words to what they already know.
- figure out partially known words by using the context.
- decide when they need to consult a resource (e.g., a dictionary).
- infuse the words they read into writing and speaking.
- commit to learning new words.

In the remainder of this chapter, we explore these issues by addressing the assumptions about vocabulary knowledge that underlie practice. We then examine the most effective methods of teaching word meanings according to current research. Through an understanding of the issues involved in teaching vocabulary, preservice and practicing teachers will be able to make informed instructional choices in this critical area.

Using Tools to Relate New Words to Known Words

Incidental learning opportunities in the classroom are clearly not sufficient to teach students the number of words necessary for them to learn when that load appears to be roughly 3,000 words per year, or approximately 8 words per day (Baumann and Kame'enui, 1991; Beck and McKeown, 1991; Graves, 1986). Baumann and Kame'enui report that studies employing direct definition or synonym instruction conclude that the number of words learned in even this way is greater than the number acquired through incidental teaching. Therefore, recent studies have explored the benefits of using alternative vocabulary-learning techniques, such as semantic maps and graphic organizers, to directly teach the meaning of important words.

Two major methods for clarifying and enriching the meanings of known words are (1) graphic organizers, such as semantic maps; and (2) semantic feature analysis.

Graphic Organizers

Graphic organizers, also referred to as graphic representations and structural overviews, work well for meaning-related concepts. A graphic organizer visually represents a body of knowledge that includes the critical concepts, ideas, events, generalizations, and/or facts pertaining to the word, using a diagram, cluster, or other type of visual display. Examples of graphic organizers are semantic maps and clarifying tables.

● graphic organizers

Semantic maps (Johnson and Pearson, 1986) help children visualize related information and develop new words for the same concept (see the following activity and Figure 4.2). Semantic mapping can also be used as a valuable prewriting strategy. The steps outlined in the activity can be adapted for individual purposes.

● semantic maps

Semantic Map

ACTIVITY

Using the following instructions, help students create a semantic map.

1. Choose a key word or concept from a book, story, or passage students will be reading soon.

2. Write the core idea on the center of a large sheet of chart paper, on an overhead transparency, or on the board.

3. Ask students to think of as many words as they can that are related to the word. As you list them, place them in broad categories (see Figure 4.2). You may wish to add related categories that have been overlooked.

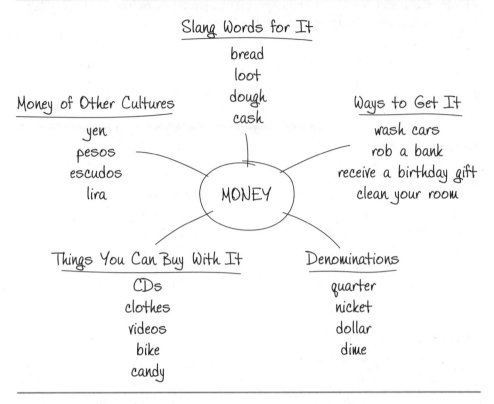

FIGURE *4.2* A semantic map for "money."

4. Lead students in a discussion of the broad categories and invite them to help you label these. Some words may fit into more than one category.

5. When the map is completed, discuss the categories and focus attention on those that will be highlighted in the passage to be read (e.g., students will be reading material about minting currency after completing the semantic map in Figure 4.2).

6. After reading the passage, revisit the map and augment it with new categories and words that were not mentioned in the original map-creating discussion.

clarifying table ● A **clarifying table** is a graphic-organizing strategy teachers may use to preteach, or "clarify," vocabulary terms—usually low-utility words—students will encounter in an upcoming lesson, or to anchor the meanings of terms that have already been explored through content area lessons. As a rule, clarifying tables work best when the meanings of the new words are introduced at the beginning of the lesson, are explored more thoroughly during the content area lesson, and then the terms that are most critical to the lesson are solidified using the clarifying table (see Figure 4.3). The following activity illustrates how to construct a clarifying table and the steps used to employ it.

A clarifying table.	FIGURE 4.3

TERM:	Propaganda
CORE IDEA:	"A plan to spread opinions or beliefs"
CLARIFIERS:	It's used by people who want you to think the way they do for some reason.
EXAMPLES:	Political candidates give lots of facts and figures of why you should vote for them. Advertisements tell you why you should buy their product.
CONFUSED WITH:	An opinion. Jennifer believes cats make better pets than dogs. However, she is not trying to make others believe this.
KNOWLEDGE CONNECTIONS:	Door-to-door salespeople offer propaganda. Salespeople on the telephone. Activists. Lobbyists.
EXAMPLE SENTENCE:	The senator used lots of propaganda—like telling us he had reduced crime in the state by 18%—to convince us we should reelect him.

Source: Adapted from Ellis and Farmer, 2000.

Constructing and Using a Clarifying Table

ACTIVITY

(Ellis and Farmer, 2000)

1. From the content area selection, identify several low-utility words that are particularly critical to the understanding of the selection.
2. Write one of those words on chart paper with its core idea, or simple definition. For example, *propaganda*'s core idea would be "a plan to spread opinions or beliefs."
3. Under the core idea, label a column "Clarifiers." With students, brainstorm some descriptions of propaganda, such as "it's used by people who want you to think the way they do for some reason."
4. After discussing the word with students, brainstorm some examples of propaganda and write down one or more that epitomizes the essence of the concept most clearly. Example: "Political candidates give lots of facts and figures of why you should vote for them." List these under the heading "Examples."
5. With students, brainstorm some instances that might easily be confused with the term, but are substantively different. Discuss how the

instances differ. Example: "Jennifer believes cats make better pets than dogs. However, she is not trying to make others believe this." Use the heading "Confused with:" for these entries.

6. Brainstorm some everyday examples of how propaganda is used and list these under the heading "Knowledge Connections." Examples from a child's background might be a door-to-door salesperson, or members of an activist group.

7. Place students in small groups and have them create a sentence for the term *propaganda*, illustrating that they understand its meaning. With group consensus, select a sentence that captures the sense of the word to write on the chart and complete the clarifying table. Example: "The senator used lots of propaganda—like telling us he had reduced crime in the state by 18 percent—to convince us we should reelect him."

Semantic Feature Analysis

semantic feature analysis ●

Semantic feature analysis can be used when the concepts fall into one category (e.g., kinds of trees, breeds of dogs, past presidents). The procedure can also be used to compare two versions of the same story, or to compare a video to the source novel (Pittelman et al., 1991). Semantic feature analysis works best for words that form a group that are similar in meaning. The following activity outlines steps for creating a semantic feature analysis (Nagy, 1988).

ACTIVITY *Creating a Semantic Feature Analysis*

1. Select words that form a semantically close group (e.g., words that represent precipitation: rain, snow, sleet, hail, slush, fog). At least some of the distinctions in meaning should be immediately understandable to students.

2. On the board or overhead, use the selected words as column heads in a two-dimensional matrix (see Figure 4.4).

3. For the horizontal rows, decide on a number of words or phrases describing components of meaning shared by some of the words, or phrases that distinguish some words from others, such as round, solid, liquid, cold, frozen, and white.

4. One square will represent the intersection of a given word and a semantic feature. One by one, ask students if the feature is shared by the given word. Discuss why or why not.

5. Record in the square whether or not, or to what extent, the feature applies to each word.

FIGURE 4.4 Semantic feature analysis.

	rain	sleet	hail	fog	snow	slush	mist
solid	no	yes	yes	no	yes	sort of	no
liquid	yes	no	no	no	no	sort of	sort of
cold	sometimes	yes	sometimes	no	yes	yes	no
frozen	no	yes	yes	no	yes	yes	no
white	no	yes	sort of	sort of	yes	yes	sort of
clear	yes	no	yes	no	no	no	yes

Using the Context

Proficient readers use many strategies to identify and pronounce words that might be unfamiliar to them in print. Often, such words are in a reader's speaking or listening vocabularies but it may be the first time they have been encountered in written material. Readers often use context clues to identify and pronounce these words. The syntactic (grammar) and semantic (meaning) information provided in the words, phrases, sentences, and paragraphs in a text are called **context clues.** Context clues include the use of surrounding information to help identify a word. They are very important to word analysis and, ultimately, comprehension. But context clues do not always offer enough information in a sentence to help children actually learn the meaning of an unknown word. The clues may be obvious to someone who already knows the meaning of a word, but context clues often provide only limited information, which can be misleading, or no help at all. For example, consider the following two sentences: "Dyan looked over the members of her team. Each looked more hapless than the next." No real clue as to the meaning of the word *hapless* can be gleaned from the context of the sentences. However, researchers still recommend that children be taught how to use context clues because certain context clues can be helpful; moreover, context clues can be tools to help children develop word-learning strategies that they can use independently (Nagy, 1988).

● context clues

In a related study, Gipe (1980) asked children to read new words in meaningful contexts and had them apply these words to their own experiences. She then compared this method with three other methods for teaching children to use the context: having children pair an unknown word with a synonym, having children categorize words, and having them look up the words in the dictionary. She found that having children apply the new words to their own experiences in a written response after deriving the meaning of the word from context was most effective.

To summarize what we know about using the context, there are four key points to keep in mind when teaching students to use this important skill:

1. Acknowledge that context may not always be enough.
2. Only select examples of text that allow students to discover the word.
3. Model for students a strategy for thinking through how to get the meaning from context, using a "Think Aloud."
4. Encourage students to immediately apply the new word to their own experience in written form (e.g., have them write about a time they felt "rejected").

Context clues can sometimes help students find the meaning of an unfamiliar word in the following ways:

- by directly defining the word
- by providing an appositive or comparison of the word
- by contrasting the word with a known word

Readers are also using context clues when they:

- think logically through the rest of the sentence
- consider examples provided in the sentence

Sentences with one or more of these features should be used to directly show students how word meaning can be gleaned through context. Examples of each of these context clues are as follows:

A <u>gendarme</u> is a police officer in France and several other European countries who has had military training. (definition)

She was <u>exhausted,</u> or extremely tired, after being up half the night. (appositive)

Rather than being famous in his homeland for defeating the enemy in the war, the man found he was <u>notorious.</u> (contrast)

Sandra said <u>morosely,</u> "This town will be the death of us." (logic)

Cats, dogs, and hamsters are all examples of <u>domestic</u> animals. (illustration)

Context clues can be found in sentences other than the one in which the new word appears, so students should be encouraged to read surrounding sentences for clues to meaning. Sometimes an entire paragraph embodies the explanation of a word, as in the following example:

"The climb took far longer than Sara and Michelle had thought. But when they arrived at the top, they were greeted by the most spectacular sight they had ever imagined. Their whole five-mile hike had been worth it. They were <u>exhilarated</u>!"

Finally, the following instructional activity, C(2)QU (which stands for context and two questions) can help teachers show students how to work through the use of context clues to discover the meaning of an unfamiliar word.

C(2)QU   (Blachowicz, 1993)   **ACTIVITY**

1. Provide a broad, meaningful context for an unfamiliar word using one of the five context types: definition, appositive, contrast, logic, illustration. Example: "When it was time to help clean up the house, the little girl vanished." Invite students to offer suggestions about the meaning of the word through the hints provided by the way it is used in the sentence(s).

2. Provide one or two sentences that offer more explicit contextual information for the word. Example: "Ramon watched as the horse grew smaller and smaller and finally vanished from sight. Now it was really gone." Now ask students to reconsider their original hypotheses about the word.

3. Ask students direct questions that involve the meaning of the word. Example: "When something vanishes, do you expect to see it again? What kinds of things might vanish?"

4. Invite students to use the word appropriately in oral or written form. Example: "The puppy was so hungry that the food we put out for her vanished in an instant."

Consulting Resources to Discover the Meanings of Words

Proficient readers use various strategies to discover the meanings of unknown words. For example, they might ask someone, read around the word, use the context, or look up the word in the dictionary. Although the latter option is the one that directly leads to autonomy in acquiring vocabulary, if we ask children to look up every unknown word, they may lose the continuity of what they are reading and, eventually, lose interest in reading. Allen (1999) offers 12 options children can consider as resources to figure out the meaning of unfamiliar words:

1. See how the word fits into the sentence.
2. Use the dictionary to find the meaning of the word.
3. Say the word out loud to see if it can be recognized.
4. Read the sentence again to see if it becomes clearer.
5. Look at the beginning of the sentence again.

6. Think about what other word would make sense in the sentence.

7. Look for other words in the sentence that give clues.

8. Ask someone else to read the sentence out loud.

9. Look at the picture, if there is one.

10. Read around the word and then go back to it.

11. Skip the word if it isn't needed.

12. Ask the teacher, another adult, or a classmate.

polysemantic ●

Many words in the English language are **polysemantic;** that is, they have multiple meanings. If we include shades of meanings or related meanings as multiple meanings, then nearly every word in the English language in some way has more than one meaning associated with it. It is often perplexing for children to find a word they thought they knew used in a context that is unfamiliar to them.

The dictionary, while an excellent source for discovering the meanings of unknown words, can be confusing when children are attempting to determine the appropriate meanings of words that have multiple meanings, or specific, technical definitions. In some cases, children may be familiar with several common meanings of a word, but not with the specialized meaning found in content area subjects, such as science, social studies, and mathematics. For example, a child may understand the word *change* and be able to use it appropriately when discussing replacing school clothes with play clothes after school, but be unaware that the word can also be used to discuss a process of metamorphosis in science, a financial transaction system in mathematics (making change), and a transition to a different political system in social studies (Burns et al. 1999).

Because polysemantic words can have different meanings depending on the context in which they are used, such words can be extremely confusing to children, especially those for whom English is a second language. The following two activities can help show children how to select the appropriate dictionary definition for a polysemantic word.

ACTIVITY *How Is It Used?*

1. Write the following sentences on the board:

   The man had to pay room and board at the country inn.

   She was on the Board of Education in her city.

   The board was made of the finest redwood.

   We got on board just as the train was departing.

   The board member offered advice on the proposed idea.

2. Distribute student dictionaries to pairs of students.

3. Ask each pair of students to look up the word *board* in the dictionary and find the specific definition to fit each sentence.

4. With the whole class, discuss each meaning as it is located.

5. Have students create new sentences of their own that fit each definition.

6. Invite pairs of students to read other dictionary definitions for the word *board* and compose sentences for these meanings as well.

7. Use the same procedure for other multiple-meaning words as they are encountered.

If a new meaning for a word does not represent a difficult concept, it can be taught simply by discussing with children their current understanding of the word's meaning, presenting the word's new meaning, and then noting the similarities and differences when the word is used in the variant way. However, if the new meaning is more complex, then the method outlined in the following activity, ideal for expository text, may be more helpful.

Possible Sentences (Stahl and Kapinus, 1991) ACTIVITY

1. From an upcoming reading assignment, choose several key terms that might be difficult because they are being used in a way that is unfamiliar to students. For example:

   base, run, board

2. Provide short explanations for the words as they will be used in the upcoming assignment. For example:

   A character in literature can have *base,* or evil, motives for doing seemingly good deeds.

   A person decides to *run* for, or pursue, a political position, such as *mayor.*

   A *board* of directors is a group of people who get together to oversee a project.

3. Have the students form small groups and ask them to create *possible sentences,* using the words as they believe they might be used in the passage they are about to read.

4. Write the suggested sentences on the board. Read and discuss them together.

5. After reading the assignment, revisit the *possible sentences* and discuss whether the sentences reflect the appropriate meaning of the specified word, based on the new information from the passage.

6. If students decide any of the sentences do not reflect the appropriate meaning of the word, help students revise them to make the meanings match. For example:

The men will <u>run</u> for their life when they are chased by the lion. (would not be a meaning match)

The woman was the first female to <u>run</u> for governor of Kentucky. (revised)

Although we have come a long way since the days when we simply asked students to copy definitions of words or look up every unknown word, we still need to teach students the value of using the dictionary to learn about the meanings of words and thesauri to teach them how to locate synonyms and antonyms. Teachers can provide structured opportunities for students to use these important tools during minilessons and other word study activities. Additionally, students can be encouraged to use the dictionary through the use of the ongoing activity that follows.

ACTIVITY   *VIT Word Book*

1. Give each student a special notebook or bind several sheets of paper together with a cover. Have students decorate the cover and label it "Very Important Term (VIT) Word Book."

2. During free reading time, encourage students to write in their books terms for which they cannot get the meaning through context, rereading, or other avenues. Also have them record the sentence in which the word occurred.

3. Once a week, provide a time when students can use the dictionary to look up all the terms they have accumulated in their notebooks over the week. You may wish to offer assistance, or specific minilessons in dictionary usage prior to these sessions.

4. In small share groups, have students share one or two of the new words they have "discovered" in these dictionary usage sessions.

Infusing New Vocabulary into Writing and Speaking

Teachers can encourage students to expand their speaking vocabularies, or the words they use in oral language, by actively recognizing and praising appropriate word usage in the classroom, as well as by allowing ample time for spontaneous word play, in which students experiment with words that they discover and choose to share. Children often have words in their reading and listening vocabularies that they have never used in speaking or writing. Through specific word games such as Camouflage, they can be urged to stretch their speaking vocabularies by telling stories, deliberately selecting words for which they are just beginning to grasp the meaning. Semantic gradients, used with a dictionary or thesaurus, can help older students think about and discuss relationships among similar and different words (synonyms and antonyms) as well as discern slight shades of meanings between words.

The following activities will help expedite this process of moving words into children's speaking vocabularies.

Camouflage   (Cecil, 1994)   ACTIVITY

1. Pass out to each student a 3 × 5 card with a word written on it that may be in the student's reading and listening vocabularies but that has not yet entered the student's speaking vocabulary.

2. Tell students they may look at their own card, but not at each other's. Also instruct them that they may use a dictionary or a thesaurus if they want to get a clearer understanding of the word and clues about its usage.

3. Have students take turns creating a story or personal anecdote that "hides" their word in it. For example (fifth-grader hiding the word *pallid*):

   My sister and I went into a haunted house last weekend. I was so apprehensive I could barely converse, and my sister's face was pallid when she heard eerie sounds coming from the upstairs. Eventually we spotted a diminutive feline and realized that that must have been what we heard!

4. When a student has finished telling his or her story, encourage the other students to try to guess the word the student has "camouflaged." If the number of incorrect guesses is greater than the number of correct guesses, the storyteller wins. (Hint: Advise students that the best strategy is to use the most sophisticated words they can think of to throw off the other students. Encourage them to use the dictionary or thesaurus.)

Semantic Gradient   ACTIVITY

1. Have students form small groups and encourage them to choose two known words with opposite meanings, such as race/crawl, gigantic/minuscule, and frigid/torrid.

2. Have students write one of the words toward the top of a sheet of paper and the opposite word toward the bottom. The space in the middle will be used for placement of other words according to how closely they fit meaning wise.

3. With the help of a dictionary and/or thesaurus, invite students to discuss the meanings of the two words and then list other words in the continuum according to how closely they match the meaning of the first two words. Explain that each word on their paper must be the same part of speech as the original two words. Also stress that there are no right or wrong answers but that they should be able to defend their placement of words. For example (for fifth-graders):

fly	walk
race	stroll
skedaddle	saunter
run	meander
jog	shuffle
power walk	crawl
strut	stand still

4. Invite students to share their lists and explain why they placed the words where they did by giving examples of how such words could be used in sentences.

5. Place the lists on charts around the classroom so that they can be added to as children encounter other words that are related to the original two words. Optional: Have students act out words.

Committing to Learning New Words

Because of the sheer number of words that children must acquire every year, as noted earlier in this chapter, perhaps the most proactive instructional approach teachers can take with vocabulary is to encourage children to individually commit themselves to building their word knowledge. Having such a personal commitment is, of course, especially critical for children who face the extraordinary task of learning English as a second language.

One way teachers can get students to make such a commitment is to discuss with the whole class a variety of ways that they can learn new words. During this discussion, teachers should not only offer their own ideas but also incorporate those that the students suggest. Some ideas to consider are the following:

- Have students make a commitment to learn one new word a day, from any source.

- Have students make a commitment to look up in the dictionary one word a day that has been heard in conversation or on the news.

- Have students "adopt" a certain prefix or suffix, or Greek or Latin root, and learn and use words containing these elements over a few weeks' duration.

- Have students agree to acquire at least two or three new words each week from their context, and record both the words and the context from which they were derived.

- Have students make a list of "tired" words, or words that are used too often in one's own writing and speaking. Look these up in a thesaurus and commit to using newly discovered synonyms for these words, one a week.

- Each day, have a different student find one word that he or she believes will "stump the teacher." Allow the student to write this word on the board for you to try to define. Keep a running list of the new words found—and your success at defining them.

Finally, we believe it is the teacher's own fascination with words—their history, sound, origin, and so forth—that can make all the difference in children's curiosity about and interest in acquiring them. Ultimately, a love for our language is "caught" rather than "taught." Consequently, a teacher who frequently stops reading a passage to dramatically repeat a phrase filled with imagery, or one who often shares favorite words, puns, riddles, and other word play with students, will help to create learners who notice words and remember them. Word play can be done incidentally during any literacy activity, or it can consist of structured word games, such as crossword puzzles, Scrabble, or Password. The following activities are prototypical of the kind that help instill a love of language in children. (See also Chapter 3.)

Hinky Pinkies   ACTIVITY

Hinky Pinkies is a word play activity that fosters appreciation of rhyme, requires students to use the dictionary or thesaurus to look up unknown words, and motivates them to add the new words to their speaking vocabularies. Additionally, the game provides important practice in determining what is and is not an appropriate synonym. The activity proceeds as follows:

1. Explain to students that Hinky Pinkies are rhyming definitions for terms with either one syllable (hink pinks), two syllables (hinky pinkies), or three syllables (hinkety pinketies).

2. Have students form pairs and pass out a dictionary and a thesaurus to each pair.

3. Show the following example to students:

a thicker arachnid

4. Explain to students that in order to find the answer, they must find a synonym for both the word *thicker* and the word *arachnid*. Advise them that they may use the dictionary or thesaurus if they do not know the meaning of a word and also to help them with appropriate synonyms. Further, explain that the synonyms for the original words must rhyme and be the same number of syllables. In this example, each word will be two syllables, a hinky pinky.

5. Ask students to look up the word *arachnid* in the dictionary or thesaurus. Write the words they discover on the board (the most prominent definition will be *spider*).

6. Ask students to think of a two-syllable word that rhymes with spider and means the same thing, or is a synonym for, the word *thicker*. Write the answer on the board:

   a thicker arachnid = a wider spider

7. Do this exercise for several other examples, making sure to use one word that is unfamiliar to students in each definition:

   an evil pastor (sinister minister)

   an ebony slit (black crack)

   a mean gem (cruel jewel)

8. Create 20 of these word plays for students to do in pairs. Then ask each pair of students to create their own hink pinks, hinky pinkies, or hinkety pinketies with the help of the dictionary or thesaurus.

9. Have each pair of students read their examples to the class so that the other students can guess the answers. Make a class book of their contributions.

ACTIVITY *Paraphrastics*

Children are intrigued by adages in which synonyms have replaced the original words and phrases, although the original meaning has been kept intact. Additionally, the need for a dictionary and a thesaurus makes it an excellent activity to increase vocabulary and awareness of appropriate synonyms.

1. Place students into small groups and give each group a dictionary and a thesaurus.

2. Using the board or overhead projector, show students several adages that they are most likely to be familiar with, but that have been modified by different words and phrases so that the adage sounds entirely different. For example:

Members of an avian species of identical plumage congregate. (Birds of a feather flock together.)

All articles that coruscate with resplendence are not necessarily auriferous. (All that glitters is not gold.)

The stylus is more potent than the claymore. (The pen is mightier than the sword.)

Male cadavers are incapable of yielding any falsehoods. (Dead men tell no lies.)

3. Ask students to try to figure out the original adage by looking up unfamiliar words in the dictionary. After they have come up with the solution, write the original adage under the paraphrased one.

4. Brainstorm some other adages that they have heard. Invite students, in their small groups, to paraphrase these adages using the thesaurus for synonyms.

5. When all groups have finished this exercise, have them read their revised adages to the rest of the class so that the other students can try to guess the original adage. Create a class book with the paraphrased adages. Encourage students to try to stump their parents and other family members with the paraphrased adages.

6. For an added challenge, encourage students to take the original adages and design new phrases that mean just the opposite of the originals. For example, "All that glitters is not gold" would become "None that tarnishes is silver."

TROUBLESHOOTING

Inadequate vocabulary is often the result of a limited background of experiences and intellectual stimulation, as well as a lack of reading habit. Lack of oral stimulation, limited experiences with print, few books in the home for recreational reading, or no desire to read can all contribute to a vocabulary deficit. Speech defects or hearing difficulties may also be factors in slow or weak language development (Crawley and King, 2000). Fortunately, the following three suggestions will not only be helpful for those children with inadequate vocabularies but will enrich the vocabularies and intellectual lives of all students in a class, and will be especially valuable for English language learners.

Limited Interest/Experience in Independent Reading

The importance of wide reading for its impact on vocabulary development cannot be overemphasized. Just reading a few minutes each day will make staggering differences in the number of words children encounter in the course of a school year (see Figure 4.5).

FIGURE 4.5

Effect of time spent reading independently on number of words encountered.

Reading Minutes Percentile	Independent Reading	
	Minutes Per Day	Words Read Per Year
98th	65.0	4,358,000
90th	21.1	1,823,000
80th	14.2	1,146,000
70th	9.6	622,000
60th	6.5	432,000
50th	4.6	282,000
40th	3.2	200,000
30th	1.3	106,000
20th	0.7	21,000
10th	0.1	8,000
2nd	0.0	0

The graph in Figure 4.5 indicates that the average child who is at the 90th percentile of minutes spent reading recreationally reads almost 2 million words outside of school—or more than 200 times more words than the child at the 10th percentile, who reads merely 8,000 words per year on his or her own. Although all words encountered are not necessarily "learned," it has been suggested that children acquire approximately 1 in 10 new words from reading (Cunningham and Stanovich, 1998).

Therefore, children who read widely will come across a plethora of new words and, with every subsequent encounter with each word, begin to move the words through the four levels of word knowledge (refer back to Figure 4.1), from never having heard it before to knowing it well. Teachers can encourage students to read widely by continuing throughout the upper grades to read aloud to them, from books selected from a variety of different genres and representing diverse ethnic groups. Providing a good selection of literature in the classroom and allowing ample time during the school day for students to read self-selected material helps to foster an interest in reading. Finally, students tend to encourage each other to read when time is set aside for them to share and respond to what they are reading in meaningful ways.

Limited Schema for Remembering New Vocabulary

Schema is a child's organized knowledge of the world. This knowledge provides the basis for understanding and remembering new vocabulary words. If the child already has some relevant background and/or word knowledge about the topic being introduced, new vocabulary can be enhanced by activating, or bringing to the surface, the child's existing schema. The more actual, concrete experiences teachers provide for their students, especially those for whom English is a second language, the more teachers will be adding to this schema upon which students can attach new words and concepts. Words seldom exist in a vacuum, and offering such experiences tends to allow children to greatly expand their knowledge of the words associated with the topic under consideration in a relatively short amount of time. Book talks, art in all its forms, cooking, experiments, and objects associated with reading and discussion are forms of realia that engage children in questioning, discussing, and thinking about new words and incorporating them into their meaning vocabularies.

Sometimes a child has no knowledge of or background about a certain subject being introduced. In that case, the teacher must actually construct a schema for that child. Since it is not always possible to offer the child "virtual reality," or an opportunity to experience an event directly, sometimes vicarious, or "simulated," experiences provide another way to show a context for new vocabulary. For example, a chapter on the Amazon would clearly be best enhanced by a field trip there to actually show students the rain forest, the canopy, and the different flora and fauna; however, because such a journey is not always feasible, a video clip, television excerpt, or pictures from books and magazines are usually more practical activities and, with appropriate explanation and description from the teacher, can result in almost as much new vocabulary acquisition.

SUMMARY

Acquiring the meaning of many new words may not be all there is to reading, but because words can be considered the "building blocks" that comprise all written and spoken text, their importance in a balanced and comprehensive literacy program must not be underestimated. Students need to learn the meanings of approximately 3,000 new words a year—and more if those students are learning English as a second language—so teachers need to do more than simply have them memorize a list of vocabulary words and their meanings. They must also provide effective meaning vocabulary development strategies such as helping students to appreciate words and their origins and to make a personal commitment to find out about them. Furthermore, teachers must encourage wide reading and provide strategies for independently figuring out the meaning of unknown words. Above all, teachers themselves must share their fascination with and curiosity about words. Ultimately, the goal of all vocabulary instruction should be to inspire children to become independent word collectors who actively enjoy learning new words. Such learners become the students who comprehend best, and thus, read the most, entering into a self-perpetuating cycle of success.

Actively learning the meanings of many new words, through a wide variety of means, is unquestionably an integral part of a balanced and comprehensive literacy program for the intermediate grades. The more numerous the reading, writing, listening, and speaking experiences children of this age are offered, the more they will come into contact with intriguing new words. And it is through just such experiences that children's stores of vocabulary steadily grows, just as it is through the excitement of abundant reading and writing that they become proficient readers and writers.

Questions
FOR JOURNAL WRITING AND DISCUSSION

1. From a page in this chapter, create three columns of words: the first one entitled "Basic Words," the second, "General-Utility Words," and the third, "Low-Utility Words." With a partner from the class, arrange the words from this page in the three different categories. Defend your choices in a discussion with other classmates. Why do you think it is important to classify the words you would teach to children in this manner?

2. Review the graph of the relationship between the time spent on recreational reading and the number of words encountered in a year in Figure 4.5. Based on this evidence, how important would you consider efforts to motivate children to read for their own enjoyment? How would you make sure this occurs in your intermediate classroom?

3. As you are reading for work or pleasure, make note of several words that are unfamiliar to you. What strategies would you use to determine the meaning of these new words? Are the strategies you would use always the same? What factors determine when you would resort to looking up the words in the dictionary? How are your own habits relevant to your future classroom teaching?

Suggestions

FOR PROJECTS AND FIELD ACTIVITIES

1. With the other members of your class, list 10 words from a newspaper. From this chapter, consider the different instructional strategies you might use to teach these words to children. In an intermediate classroom, use one of the strategies to teach the selected words to a small group of students. How successful were you? Compare your experience with that of other classmates who chose to use a different instructional strategy.

2. Spend a day discovering the interesting words that intermediate-grade students are naturally curious about. Can you categorize these words? How would you incorporate these concepts into the daily curriculum to encourage curiosity about words?

3. Prior to reading a short story to a group of intermediate-age children, ask them to guess the meaning of three or four words that you deem to be especially difficult. During the reading, ask them to determine the meaning of each word after it occurs in the story. Are the responses enhanced with the additional contextual information? What does this experience teach you about the value of discussing words as they occur when reading aloud?

References

Allen, J. (1999). *Words, words, words*. Portsmouth, NH: Heinemann.

Anderson, R. C., & Freebody, P. (1981). Vocabulary knowledge. In J. T. Guthrie (Ed.), *Comprehension and teaching: Research reviews*. Newark, DE: International Reading Association.

Anderson, R. C., & Nagy, W. E. (1992). The vocabulary conundrum. *American Educator, 16*(4), 14–18, 44–47.

Baumann, J. F., & Kame'enui, E. J. (1991). Research on vocabulary instruction: Ode to Voltaire. In J. Flood, J. J. D. Lapp, & J. R. Squire (Eds.), *Handbook of research on teaching the English language arts*. New York: MacMillan.

Beck, I., & McKeown, M. (1991). Conditions of vocabulary acquisition. In R. Barr, M. Kamil, P. Mosenthal, & P. D. Pearson (Eds.), *Handbook of reading research* (vol. 2, 789–8l4). New York: Longman.

Beck, I. L., McKeown, M. G., & Omanson, R. C. (1987). The effects and uses of diverse vocabulary instructional techniques. In M. G. McKeown & M. E. Curtis (Eds.), *The nature of vocabulary acquisition*. Hillsdale, NJ: Erlbaum.

Blachowicz, C. L. Z. (1993). C(2)QU: Modeling context use in the classroom. *The Reading Teacher, 47*, 268–269.

Burns, P. C., Roe, B. D., & Ross, E. P. (1999). *Word recognition and meaning vocabulary: A literacy skills primer*. Boston: Houghton Mifflin.

Cecil, N. L. (1994). *Freedom fighters: Affective teaching of the language arts*. Salem, WI: Sheffield.

Crawley, S. J., & King, M. (2000). *Remediating reading difficulties* (3rd ed.). Boston: McGraw-Hill.

Cunningham, A. E., & Stanovich, K. E. (1998, Spring/Summer). What reading does for the mind. *American Federation of Teachers.*

Dale, E. (1965). Vocabulary measurement: Techniques and major findings. *Elementary English, 42*(8), 895–901.

Ellis, E., & Farmer, T. (2000). *The clarifying routine: Elaborating vocabulary instruction.* Kansas City, MO: Edge Enterprises.

Fountas, I. C., & Pinnell, G. S. (1996). *Guided reading: Good first teaching for all children.* Portsmouth, NH: Heinemann.

Fry, E. B., Fountkidis, D. L., & Polk, J. K. (1985). *The new reading teacher's book of lists.* Upper Saddle River, NJ: Prentice Hall.

Gipe, J. P. (1980). Use of a relevant context helps kids learn new word meanings. *The Reading Teacher, 33,* 398–402.

Graves, M. F. (1986). Vocabulary learning and instruction. In E. Z. Rothkopf (Ed.), *Review of research in education* (vol. 13). Washington, DC: American Educational Research · Association.

Graves, M. F., Watts, S., & Graves, B. (1994). *Essentials of classroom teaching: Elementary reading.* Boston: Allyn & Bacon.

Johnson, D. D., & Pearson, P. D. (1986). *Teaching reading vocabulary* (3rd ed.). New York: Holt, Rinehart and Winston.

Nagy, W. E. (1988). *Teaching vocabulary to improve reading comprehension.* Newark, DE: International Reading Association.

Nagy, W. E., & Anderson, R. C. (1984). How many words are there in printed school English? *Reading Research Quarterly, 19,* 233–253.

Pittelman, S. D., Heimlich, J. E., Berglund, R. L., & French, M. P. (1991). *Semantic feature analysis: Classroom applications.* Newark, DE: International Reading Association.

Rasinski, T., & Padak, N. (2000). *Effective reading strategies: Teaching children who find reading difficult* (2nd ed.). Upper Saddle River, NJ: Merrill.

Schwanenflugel, P. J., Stahl, S. A., & McFalls, E. I. (1997). *Partial word knowledge and vocabulary growth during reading comprehension* (Research Report No. 76). Athens, GA: University of Georgia, National Reading Research Center.

Stahl, S. A. (1999). Vocabulary development. *Reading research to practice: A series for teachers.* Cambridge, MA: Brookline.

Stahl, S. A., & Kapinus, B. (1991). Possible sentences: Predicting word meanings to teach content area vocabulary. *The Reading Teacher, 45,* 36–43.

CHAPTER 5
Reading Comprehension

Focus Questions

- What are the key factors that affect reading comprehension?
- What are the five most effective reading comprehension strategies?
- How can teachers use guided reading to help students learn comprehension strategies?

121

DEFINING COMPREHENSION

You might want to first think about what the term *comprehension* means to you. Is it the ability to recall text? Is it knowing the answers to questions asked about the text? Does it mean the ability to critique what has been read, or to summarize it, or to cull a theme or characters' motives? Certainly comprehension includes all of these abilities. **Comprehension** is currently thought of as the construction of meaning, and it is the ultimate goal of exemplary reading instruction.

The theoretical framework for reading comprehension instruction that we support in this chapter views comprehension instruction as an active process; that is, it encourages students

- to relate text to their own prior experiences, or make predictions about what might happen.
- to construct mental images during their reading.
- to question themselves about text ideas while they read.
- to summarize the big ideas in what they read. (Pressley, 2002)

Our framework also recognizes that meaning is socially constructed; in other words, students need to engage in conversations about what they read to help clarify and broaden their understandings of the text. We support a *strategic reader model* for comprehension instruction that implies teachers will demonstrate for their students strategies that help them to actively process text (e.g., relate to prior experiences, question, form images, predict, clarify, summarize, make inferences). A combination of direct explanation and teacher modeling, or "thinking out loud," can work well as a form of explicit teaching for comprehension strategies (Duffy, 2002). In addition, reading comprehension strategies need to be modeled and practiced, one strategy at a time, using a variety of text in order to teach and practice the strategy at a deep level, with the teacher gradually allowing the student to take over use of the strategy (Pearson and Gallagher, 1983).

In the Classroom

Mr. Perez is preparing for Monday's science lesson and wants to use the technique of *questioning the author* (Beck et al., 1997) to better engage his fifth-grade students in their expository reading *while* they read material from a new unit on mammals. He reads the following paragraph from his science materials:

What are mammals?

The name "mammal" refers to the female's mammary glands, which provide milk for her young. This characteristic sets off mammals among the warm-blooded, back-boned animals. Mammals are hairy; young are born alive. Most have varied teeth, for cutting, tearing, or grinding. The mammal's skull is unique; the brain is more complex than in other animals.

Mr. Perez realizes that this paragraph contains the major characteristics of mammals. He decides he will first direct his students' attention to the essential characteristic of the mammary glands. Following this he will focus their attention on the other features found in mammals.

Mr. Perez then plans a set of queries. To begin discussion, Mr. Perez decides to ask at the end of the first paragraph, "What has the author told us about mammals?" If students do not mention the main characteristic, his follow-up query will be, "What does the author mean by saying that the word *mammal* refers to the female's mammary glands, and that this characteristic *sets off* mammals?" Next, Mr. Perez will use the query "What else does the author tell us about mammals?" to begin a discussion that compares mammals with other warm-blooded, back-boned animals, and with other animals in general. He will use a visual, probably a T-chart (see Figure 5.9 later in this chapter), to keep track of students' ideas for later use.

As Mr. Perez proceeds through his science material, he anticipates where he will need to assist his students in constructing their understanding of this material. He is aware that he may need to interpret what his students try to say (revoice), model how to arrive at meaning, or provide additional information not available in the text (annotate). He may also need to draw attention to particular students' ideas (marking), or turn students back to the text for further thinking or clarifying. Once students indicate they have understood the essential meaning and are ready to move on, Mr. Perez will recap, or summarize, the major ideas, or he may ask another student to recap. With this lesson plan in mind, Mr. Perez now feels ready to begin the new science unit about mammals.

FACTORS AFFECTING READING COMPREHENSION

Fortunately, there has been quite a bit of research on reading comprehension. This research has found that there are a number of factors that affect comprehension, including factors external to the reader and characteristics within the reader.

Factors External to Readers

Reader-friendliness of text. It seems logical to expect that text clearly written with a minimum level of abstractness would be easier to comprehend. In fact, research studies do support this notion. For example, a study by Jorm (1977) demonstrated that texts using high-frequency words and high-imagery words are easier for all students to comprehend. Englert and Thomas (1987) found that texts organized sequentially are easiest to comprehend, followed by those that are enumerated, descriptive, and comparative/contrasting, in that order (see Chapter 8 for descriptions of these text structures). We refer to text that is easy to comprehend as user- or reader-friendly.

Context. The context, or environment, in which reading takes place can also affect comprehension. Consider how your own reading differs when you read within a classroom setting compared with when you read at home, or in a library. The classroom environment itself can affect comprehension (Gipe, 2002). Opportunities for reading practice, access to appropriate materials, availability of modeling and direct instruction, and a risk-free atmosphere are all factors that teachers can influence in a positive way.

Characteristics Within Readers

Ability to construct a mental representation. It has become more and more apparent that the reader's ability to construct a mental representation, or picture, of the information read and its interpretation is a major aspect of comprehension. The research on mental representations of text indicates that such representations resemble a network of nodes (the individual text elements) and connections (the meaningful relations between the elements) (van den Broek, 1990; van den Broek et al., 1996). The two most important types of connections for establishing coherence and enhancing the construction of meaning are referential (e.g., pronouns) and causal/logical relations (e.g., if . . . then; this . . . because) (Britton and Graesser, 1996). That is, when events or statements have more clear connections to other events or statements in the text, generally in the form of pronouns, direct references, or as cause/effect relationships, they are more easily recalled. Readers proceed through text attempting to make sense of it by connecting explicitly stated information to two main sources of information: related concepts in their background knowledge (or *schema*), and a subset of concepts from the preceding text. As noted in the section "Factors External to Readers" above, a coherent, well-written text is reader-friendly and easy to comprehend. A coherent, well-written text also helps the reader make the necessary referential and causal/logical connections and facilitates a clear mental representation of the text. But, even with reader-friendly text, the reader still needs to develop the ability to actually make the connections.

Ability to make connections. A reader who can make meaningful connections between the text information and related background knowledge will better comprehend the text. Readers need to be able to relate what they read to their own lives (text-to-self connections), and make connections between the text they are reading and other similar texts (text-to-text connections), or to events or concerns that occur in the world at large (text-to-world connections) (Moravcsik and Kintsch, 1993; Harvey and Goudvis, 2000).

Ability to attend to information in the text. The general ability to attend to the information in the text is influenced by short-term memory, concentration, and motivation. In addition, the approach to the comprehension process will vary depending on how the reader interprets the level of attention necessary when reading for pleasure or for some educational, or informational, purpose. The reader might decide that the book he or she has chosen to read for pleasure does not need a high level of attention in order to understand it, especially when the reader is already very familiar with the author's writing style. On the other hand, the reader may decide that upon opening his or her statistics textbook the night before a test, a high level of attention is needed.

Amount of background knowledge. A reader that has the background knowledge relevant to the text being read has a head start on comprehending the text. Such background knowledge may include, but is not limited to, knowledge of the text structure the author has used, familiarity with the literary genre, recognition of the vocabulary, and possession of information about the topic. This prior knowledge constitutes a schema for the topic. Try reading a topic about which you know very little (quantum physics?) and see how much you comprehend!

Engagement with the text. It is quite likely that the major issue in comprehension for students in the intermediate grades is engagement with the text (Wilhelm, 1997). To construct meaning, the learner needs to be purposefully and actively involved with the text. Activating relevant background knowledge, making connections to their own lives, collaborating with other students, and realizing when comprehension has occurred or has broken down are all important aspects of being involved with the text.

Knowledge of basic skills. Well-developed basic skills such as letter/sound recognition, word decoding, and knowledge of grammar will increase the amount of cognitive energy available for constructing coherent mental representations of the text. In general, for the intermediate-age group, word-decoding abilities are sufficient (see Chapter 3 for advanced word analysis skills). Ongoing vocabulary instruction (see Chapter 4) will enhance comprehension, especially in content areas where there is so much specialized vocabulary.

Knowledge of reading strategies and metacognition (or metacomprehension). Knowledge of reading comprehension strategies is a crucial factor (see next section), but one that also requires **metacognition** (understanding how one knows, or thinking about thinking) and **meta-comprehension** (realizing when one has or has not understood) abilities to ensure that readers will recognize when and under what conditions a comprehension strategy needs to be used. Students who demonstrate good metacomprehension, or comprehension-monitoring ability, know when they do and do not understand what they have read. They use fix-up strategies to resolve their comprehension difficulties. They can identify where their difficulty lies—"I don't understand the last section on page 45"—and what the difficulty is—"I am confused by the phrase *cornhusk mattresses*. What kind of mattress is this?" They may try to use their own words to restate a difficult sentence or passage: "So the author meant the quiet forest became noisy with the sounds of crickets and a howling wolf when he said the stillness of the forest was broken." Students who use fix-up strategies do not hesitate to look back through the text for clues that might help them understand: "I think I remember something about how old Abe Lincoln was when he went to school, but by the time he was 16 he only had one year of school? I need to look back to see how old he was when he first went to school." And they also look ahead in the text for information that might help them: "This sentence says Abe Lincoln's first home was a one-room log cabin and that he was born in Kentucky. I thought he lived in Illinois? He must have moved. . . . Oh, I see the next section is

● metacognition
● metacomprehension

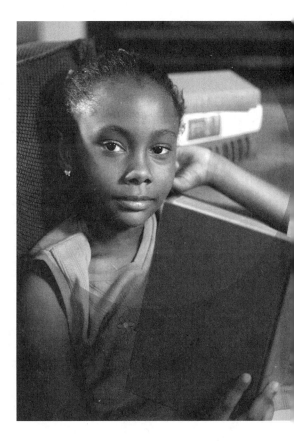

called 'The Lincolns Move to Indiana.' That will tell me more about his later life and where else Lincoln may have lived."

COMPREHENSION STRATEGIES FOR READERS TO USE

As stated in the previous section, readers at the intermediate-grade level need to know and be able to independently use reading comprehension strategies. A relatively small, but powerful, set of strategies is recommended (Pressley, 2000):

- Predicting
- Generating questions
- Checking back
- Imagery/visualizing
- Summarizing

These five strategies should be taught directly through considerable teacher explanation and modeling of their use (see the Think Aloud procedures described in the next major section). Then, extensive, long-term student practice within a print-rich context, across content areas, and with a variety of text types must be provided (see Appendix A for children's literature resources).

Predicting

Proficient readers make mental predictions, or calculated hunches, about what might happen next in the text they are reading. Their hunches are based on what they already know about the topic, what they know about the literary structure the author is using (e.g., narrative, expository, fairy tale, historical fiction, or autobiographical), and what they have learned thus far in the text. As skilled readers continue to read, they tend to confirm or deny their previous hunches, according to new understandings that occur. With expository text, they often preview the text to get an overview of what information will be covered and look through the text to see if it matches their expectations. Skilled readers also ask themselves questions for which they hope to find answers as they read, thus setting their own purposes for reading the text. (See the DRTA and Jigsaw: Read a Book in an Hour activities for example lessons that encourage students to use predicting.)

Generating Questions

One of the most valuable ways proficient readers construct text meanings is by asking and answering important questions about text as they read. They are aware of the difference between "thinking-type" questions and "locating information–type" questions, and they are able to reflect later on the caliber of the questions they have asked themselves. (See the Reciprocal Reading, Dyad Reading, QAR, and Jigsaw: Read a Book in an Hour activities for example lessons that require students to recognize question types and generate questions.)

Checking Back

Proficient readers are continually checking their own understanding as they read, making sure what they are confronting conforms to what they already know as well as ensuring that they have not missed something. It is, therefore, quite normal for skilled readers to make frequent regressions, or to go back and reread a sentence or passage, to check that they initially "got it right." Such monitoring of understanding can best be described as the encounter that takes place when a skilled reader is reading an unstimulating text late at night and suddenly realizes that not a word has been understood—a phenomenon to which most readers can relate! (See the GIST and DRTA activities for examples that encourage the use of checking back.)

Imagery/Visualizing

Proficient readers tend to create pictures in their mind's eye as they read text, especially text containing elaborate descriptions or well-developed story characters. Placing themselves in the story's setting or time period, and/or imagining themselves as the main character, facing the same trials and tribulations, helps them appreciate, remember, and internalize the story that is unfolding before them. The experience of mental vision is so personal and intense that readers skilled in this strategy are often disappointed when they see the film version of a story they have read, because it frequently pales in comparison to what occurs in their rich imaginations. (See the Sketch to Stretch and Going Beyond Visualizing activities for example lessons that utilize imagery.)

Summarizing

Proficient readers tend to remember important ideas and information they discover throughout a text and formulate them into a "big picture" of the reading material. Such a strategy is the basis on which skilled readers are able to summarize what they have read, or to articulate the main idea in expository text and separate it from the supporting details. Summarizing also includes the ability to identify particular underlying themes in literature. In addition, summarizing can reveal personal opinions about the text. Proficient readers internalize the meanings certain works have held for them, review ideas frequently, and evaluate what they have read compared with other texts and what they had hoped to gain from the text. Summarizing text can thus be influenced by these previously internalized views. (See the GIST, Reciprocal Teaching, and Dyad Reading activities for example lessons that use summarizing.)

EFFECTIVE DIRECT INSTRUCTIONAL PRACTICES

The activities and instructional frameworks offered in this section incorporate and support the five comprehension strategies just discussed. Where appropriate, specific aspects of an activity have been designated as prereading, during reading, or postreading. The activities can be used with students of all abilities with some appropriate modifications. For instance, if written responses are called for, they can be included as soon as students have the required writing proficiency; in the meantime, oral responses are an acceptable option. Encourage oral discussions during the activities, accompanied by pictures, objects, or other visuals, for the added benefit of allowing English language learners to listen to the way others are thinking and participate as they feel comfortable.

Think Aloud

think aloud ●   **Think aloud**—the oral verbalizing of one's thinking—is one of the most effective ways a teacher can model the comprehension strategies a reader uses to gain meaning from the printed page (Davey, 1983). The teacher may utilize this strategy with the following activity.

ACTIVITY *Think Aloud*

1. Ahead of time, make copies of the text passage that will be demonstrated or prepare it for an overhead projector.

Prereading

2. After looking at the title on the cover and any illustrations in the passage, ruminate aloud as to what the passage might be about. (Figure 5.1 represents an example of a teacher using think aloud to model the strategy of visualizing.)

During Reading

3. Read the passage aloud as the students track. Continually organize images by explaining the passage after every sentence or paragraph.

4. Answer aloud such questions as:

   "What am I reminded of here that I already know?" (tapping prior knowledge)

   "What are some ways I can get help in understanding unfamiliar words and/or ideas?" (monitoring understanding)

   "What does this remind me of in my own life?" (making connections)

5. After modeling the reading of several paragraphs in this fashion, invite students to add their own problem-solving tactics and personal impressions by reading succeeding passages in pairs.

FIGURE 5.1 — Teacher modeling of the think aloud procedure for the strategy of visualizing.

Note: text material is in bold; teacher think aloud comments are in italics.

The title of the story is "The Desert Man". . . . I have a pretty good picture in my mind of what the desert looks like. Miles and miles of sand, blazing hot, very little vegetation.

The old man was hot and tired. His long white robe billowed in the dry desert wind.

My picture in my head is of a very old man. . . . He is dressed in a long white robe, and the material must be light enough to be blown by the wind. I can see his robe blowing in the wind.

He wiped his brow as he started to trudge up yet another of the endless dunes of the desert. He saw only a sea of sand surrounding him.

I can see in my own mind what the old man sees . . . hills and hills of hot sand . . . he is wiping his forehead and is bent over because he is so tired and weary.

The sun beat down on him mercilessly. He would not give up. He knew the camp was near.

The look on the old man's face is very clear to me now. He has a look of determination. He is very determined to make it to the camp. . . .

The pictures I made in my head about this passage helped me understand the story, and they will help me remember what I have read. This is a comprehension strategy that good readers use to help them learn and remember. It is a strategy that you can use to improve your comprehension.

Source: Gambrell, L. B., & Bales, R. J. (1987). Visual imagery: A strategy for enhancing listening, reading and writing. *Australian Journal of Reading, 10*(3), 147–153.

Guided Reading

Students need to be directly shown how to process text so that they can become independent readers. **Guided reading** is an instructional framework that provides direct teacher support for developing effective strategies for comprehending text independently at increasingly difficult levels. The teacher generally works with a small group of students who are reading at a similar level of difficulty. A guided reading lesson involves three stages: prereading, during reading, and postreading. Prereading deals with building schema for the reading selection. During reading is the core of the lesson in

● guided reading

which important strategies are modeled and practiced. Students are encouraged to read silently during this stage and request help as needed. Postreading is a time to check for understanding, invite personal response, check the accuracy of predictions, and generally interpret and clarify what was read.

As a type of guided reading (teacher-led, small-group reading instruction that focuses on questioning and predicting to aid comprehension), the **directed reading thinking activity (DRTA)** is one of the most commonly used approaches for enhancing comprehension with both narrative and expository materials, and especially with literature-based instruction. The objective of the DRTA, developed by Stauffer (1975), is to improve comprehension by having students focus on a particular passage and to make predictions about it based on its textual features.

directed reading thinking activity ●

ACTIVITY *DRTA*

Although a DRTA lesson can be conducted in various ways, the steps include the following:

Prereading

1. Direct students' attention to the title of the selection and ask them to predict its content. After students have volunteered their predictions and the reasons for their responses, ask a preselected group whether they agree or disagree and why.

During Reading

2. Read to, or have students read silently, several sentences, and then ask students what they think the text is about based on this new information.

3. Direct the students' attention to particular vocabulary or phrases that are prominent to the meaning of the text. Ask them to use these words to hypothesize what the text will be about.

4. Ask students to look at pictures, graphs, and figures and make more predictions based on this new information.

Postreading

5. Ask students to reread or review the text to confirm or negate their predictions and hypotheses. Discuss their findings. See Figure 5.2 for an example of a teacher–student discourse that occurred during a DRTA conducted with social studies material.

Example discourse from a DRTA lesson for social studies.   FIGURE 5.2

Prereading:

Ms. Clark: Based on the title of this chapter section, "Abe Lincoln Grows Up with America," what do you predict that you might learn in this section and why?

Brian: I predict this section will tell me where Abe Lincoln grew up because it says "grows up" in the title.

Jennifer: I think it will tell me where he was born and where he lived because in the picture it shows him sitting inside a house.

Ms. Clark (to other students): Do you agree with these predictions? Why or why not?

Students: Yes, agree. The title talks about growing up, so this section will talk about Abraham Lincoln when he was a young boy.

During Reading:

Ms. Clark: After reading the first page in this section (four paragraphs), do you want to change any of your predictions, or make any new ones?

Brian: Well, we now know where Abe Lincoln was born—Kentucky.

Timothy: And he lived in a one-room log cabin, so we know that is where he is sitting in the picture. Inside the log cabin.

Jennifer: And we found out he was born on February 12, 1809.

Ms. Clark: So it sounds like we need to make some new predictions.

Brian: The book talks about his mother and father and uses the word *children*, so I think Abe Lincoln had a brother or sister. I think we will find that out in the next part.

Ms. Clark: Timothy told us Abe Lincoln lived in a one-room log cabin. Look at that sentence in your text. It says, "His first home was a one-room log cabin." Does that tell you anything or make you think of another prediction?

Brian: It makes me think he moved into a another home sometime. This was just his first home.

Jennifer: I think Abe Lincoln moves to Washington, D.C., and then he became president since Kentucky was where his first home was.

Ms. Clark: Look at that picture again. Where is Abe sitting, and why is he sitting there?

Brian: He is sitting by the fireplace. He might be cold. It might be winter.

Timothy: But he has a book in this hand. He looks like he is trying to use the glow of the fireplace to see the book.

Jennifer: Maybe the electricity went out!

(continued)

FIGURE 5.2 Continued.

Ms. Clark: Do you think there was electricity in Abe's first house?

Brian: No, because the book says the house had deerskin windows, a door with leather hinges, and the floor was hard-packed earth. I think Abe Lincoln's family was too poor to have electricity.

Ms. Clark: What do you think we will learn on the next page?

Brian: If Abe Lincoln has a brother or sister.

Timothy: Where the family moved to.

Jennifer: How Abe Lincoln became president.

Ms. Clark: Let's read the next page.

Postreading:

Ms. Clark: Now that you have finished this section, were your predictions supported? What did you find out?

Brian: We learned more about Lincoln's family. His father's name was Thomas Lincoln, and his mother's name was Nancy Hanks Lincoln. His father was a farmer and they had a cow.

Timothy: Abe Lincoln went to school when he was seven.

Jennifer: The family was very poor.

Brian: It just kept saying "children." I still don't know if Abe Lincoln had a brother or sister!

Timothy: But it did tell us that the family moved to Indiana when Abe was still seven. And two years after they moved his mother died. So he was nine when his mother died.

Jennifer: His father married a woman who had three children, so we know Abe had either brothers or sisters, or both, but not what they were. His stepmother's name was Sarah Johnston Lincoln.

Brian: Abe Lincoln only had about one year of school! But the book said that many people never went to school at all! Wow!

Timothy: Abe grew up tall in Indiana. He was six feet, four inches by the time he was 16.

Ms. Clark: You learned quite a bit about the young Abe Lincoln. How do you think his early life may have helped him to become president of the United States?

Brian: Since he was poor, he would know what poor people need.

Jennifer: He had to work real hard when he was young, so he knew how to work hard to become a president.

Timothy: He read books and wrote things, so he was smart enough to be president.

GIST

The GIST procedure (generating interactions between schemata and text) is intended to improve students' comprehension and provide a tool for guiding student summary writing (Cunningham, 1982). **GIST** is a teacher-directed, small-group strategy that takes students from writing a summary of no more than 15 words for paragraphs to a written summary of 20 or fewer words for short passages. Beginning with the paragraph version, students are asked to compose a summary sentence of no more than 15 words following the reading of each sentence in the paragraph. That is, after reading the first sentence they summarize what is said. Then, as each new sentence is read, students incorporate the additional information into a new summary statement of no more than 15 words. Paragraphs should have from three to five sentences.

● GIST

GIST   ACTIVITY

Using a paragraph from the chapter section read for the DRTA lesson in Figure 5.2, GIST might proceed as follows:

1. Choose an appropriate paragraph. For example,

   Abe's father, Thomas Lincoln, worked hard to raise crops in the stony soil of his little farm. His mother, Nancy Hanks Lincoln, was a good housekeeper. When hunting was good, Thomas Lincoln could shoot deer, bear, rabbits, and turkeys in the woods. The family also had corn bread, greens from the garden, and potatoes.

2. Present only the first sentence to the students. The sentence should have 15 blanks underneath.

   Abe's father, Thomas Lincoln, worked hard to raise crops in the stony soil of his little farm.

   _____ _____ _____ _____ _____

   _____ _____ _____ _____ _____

   _____ _____ _____ _____ _____

3. Cover or remove the displayed sentence and have students, as a group, generate a summary from memory. After the summary statement has been created, reveal and reread the sentence. Students can decide at that time to revise their statement. Do not evaluate the statement or interfere with the group decision. Once the students are satisfied with their statement, go on to step 4. One summary statement for the first sentence might appear as

Abe's	hard-working	father	raised	crops
on	his	farm.		

4. Ask students to read the first two sentences and retell them using the same 15-word limit as they had for just the first sentence.

5. Have students create a summary statement for sentences one and two that is no longer than 15 words. Again have students revise until they are satisfied from memory of the text. Then allow them to look at the text before proceeding to the next step. The new summary statement might look like this:

Abe's	hard-working	father	raised	crops
on	his	farm	and	his
mother	kept	house.		

6. Continue in the same manner for the rest of the paragraph. Students will soon realize that they are using up their allotted 15 words too quickly and will need to think of new ways to combine information, as well as to decide what information is most important to keep. The summary statement for the next two sentences might become

Abe's	hard-working	parents	provided	a
well-kept	house	and	food	from
crops	raised	or	from	hunting.

7. Now that students are becoming adept at sentence-by-sentence summarizing, have them write paragraph summaries using short passages. Explain to students that the procedures are the same, except the number of words they can use is now 20.

This technique can be motivating for students if not overly used. Pretending to write telegraph messages is another way to create summary statements. When each word used costs money, it becomes more critical to focus on and choose only the most important ideas for a summary. (Also see "Writing in the Content Areas" in Chapter 8 for more information on writing summaries.)

Reciprocal Teaching

reciprocal teaching ●   **Reciprocal teaching** is an interactive procedure that fosters comprehension by helping students actively monitor their thinking (Rosenshine et al., 1996). Students are taught to summarize text, anticipate questions, clarify unclear text, and make predictions about upcoming text. During reciprocal teaching, the teacher demonstrates how to monitor reading comprehension, how to observe the thinking process while reading, and how to determine when reading is successful and when it is not (Palincsar, 1987). The teacher then asks the students to attempt the same activities on their own, offering them feedback on their performance. Teacher involvement remains high until students can summarize and ask main idea questions on their own.

Reciprocal Teaching   ACTIVITY

This activity requires extensive modeling and guidance from the teacher and is initially conducted as follows:

During Reading

1. Read a paragraph from a passage of text, usually expository, aloud. (*Note:* As students learn these procedures, they will work in small groups, with each student taking on the teacher role for each new paragraph; thus the term *reciprocal.* At that point, reading will be done silently, or with partners in the case of struggling readers.)

Postreading

2. Model how the paragraph might be summarized. Focus on the main ideas in the paragraph, include the topic sentence, and point out that a summary should be no more than one-third of the original paragraph.

3. Ask the group an important question about the paragraph, one that focuses on the key issue. Solicit other questions from the group.

4. Think aloud about any unclear concepts or new vocabulary. Attempt to determine meanings from context. Also think about the need for clarifying information that might help students to understand the paragraph more completely. (*Note:* This step is not always necessary for well-written paragraphs that are appropriate for the reader's skill level.) Solicit other ideas about what information might be needed.

5. Predict aloud what might be expected to be in the next paragraph or in the remainder of the passage. Explain the reason for this prediction. Solicit other predictions from the group.

6. Proceed to the next paragraph. According to Palincsar and Brown (1984, 1986), these modeling sessions should last about 30 minutes.

Dyad Reading

Dyad reading is a form of paired oral reading (also called "buddy reading," "partner reading," or "say something") that has the added dimension of reinforcing the important comprehension strategies of summarizing and questioning (Cecil, 1995).

● dyad reading

ACTIVITY *Dyad Reading*

This activity consists of the following format:

1. Select two students to demonstrate the activity. Have one read a sentence or a paragraph aloud.

2. As that student reads, have the other student listen carefully and then summarize (orally or in writing) what was in the sentence or paragraph. For variation, the second student may simply draw what was read and then describe the picture.

Postreading

3. Have the reader ask the listener critical comprehension questions.

4. Encourage the students to discuss the answers and, where there is disagreement, have them refer to the text selection to support their answers.

5. Have the students change roles with succeeding material.

Question–Answer Relationships

question–answer relationships ●

Question–answer relationships, or QARs (Raphael, 1982), help students enhance their comprehension by learning to answer a range of questions and understand each question's relationship to the text, the author, and to themselves. With this strategy, students ask themselves, "Where would I find an answer to this question in the text?" and use the following hierarchy of questions and answers to help them decide.

Literal question (type 1). The answer is "right there." This tells the student that the answer to the question is easy to find in the text. In fact, the exact words in the question are contained within the text.

Inferential question (type 2). The answer can be found if you "think and search" or "put it together." This tells the student that the answer is in the text, but two ideas will have to be brought together; that is, the words used in the question may be a bit different from the words used in the text, so the answer will be slightly harder to find.

Critical question (type 3). The answer is in the mind of "the author and you." The answer is not directly stated in the text, but if students bring their own ideas to the text and combine them with the opinion the author seems to hold, they will be able to answer the question.

Creative question (type 4). The answer has to be determined "on your own." The student will not find a direct answer to the question in the text. There is no right or wrong answer to the question; it must emanate from the student's imagination or from information he or she already has about the topic.

QAR

Following is an outline of how students can be guided to incorporate the use of these questions to boost their own comprehension:

Prereading

1. Give students four passages with questions for which the question types have already been determined. (Figure 5.3 shows a sample passage and questions.)

FIGURE 5.3 QAR sample passage and question types.

An introductory QAR lesson must first define all the question types. Using the familiar nursery rhyme *Jack and Jill,* examine the following questions to note the characteristics of each type.

Jack and Jill went up the hill
to fetch a pail of water.
Jack fell down and broke his crown
and Jill came tumbling after.

1. Where did Jack and Jill go?
   Response: Up the hill to get some water
   QAR: Right there

2. Did Jill get the pail of water?
   Response: No, she fell down the hill too.
   QAR: Putting it together (or think and search)

3. What could have caused Jack's crown to break in his fall down the hill?
   Response: I bet the pail full of water hit him in the head.
   QAR: Author and me

   Or

   What happened to Jill?
   Response: She fell down the hill after Jack did and hurt herself too because when she fell, she rolled right into Jack.
   QAR: Author and me

4. Do you think Jack and Jill ever got the pail of water they went up the hill to get?
   Response: I think they got the water but it all spilled out when they fell down the hill. Then they were too badly hurt to go back up to get more water.
   QAR: On my own

2. Using the first passage, model how the answers to each question might be found in the text by identifying the appropriate QAR.

During Reading

3. Read the second passage aloud to students. Ask the questions aloud and have volunteers explain which kind of question is being asked and how they would find the answer in the text.

During/Postreading

4. Divide the class into small cooperative groups. Ask them to read the third passage and answer the questions identifying the appropriate QARs.

5. Have students follow the same procedure individually, while going around the classroom offering assistance as needed.

IMPLICIT INSTRUCTION

In addition to direct instruction in comprehension strategies, students learn to comprehend through more implicit types of instruction. Implicit instruction includes independent reading and activities that are often called *reader response activities* (Beach, 1993). There is much overlap between independent reading and reader response activities, as you'll see later in the section on literature circles and book clubs.

Independent Reading

It is theorized that students need to be given time to read if we expect them to be able to practice using comprehension strategies, to include those that have been taught directly, and also simply to enjoy reading. Independent reading is a central factor to developing lifelong enjoyment of reading. According to the landmark study *Becoming a Nation of Readers* (Anderson et al., 1985), "Children should spend more time in independent reading. Independent reading, whether in school or out of school, is associated with gains in reading achievement. By the time they are in third or fourth grade, children should read independently a minimum of two hours per week. Children's reading should include classic and modern works of fiction and nonfiction" (p. 119).

Book Contracts

book contract ●

Teachers who are held more accountable for how their students spend their independent reading time as well as encourage reader response may wish to consider the concept of a book contract. A **book contract** is a packet of required and alternative activities, such as journal writing; cross-curricular activities that involve art, science, math, and/or social studies projects; and author research; from which a student will choose in order to fulfill a contract with the teacher (see the Extension Activities later in Figure 5.5). The student may be expected to complete 6 of 8 activities, but the student will choose the 6 he or she wishes to complete. The required activities usually consist of a chart for documenting the pages read each day, a page for maintaining new vocabulary, and any other documentation that a teacher may be responsible for collecting. The packet may include a cover page made from a photocopy of the book's cover for the student to personalize (N. L. Cecil, personal communication, July 26, 2002). Book contracts can be helpful to the teacher in individualizing instruction because there can be several different book contracts at several different readability levels functioning at the same time.

Literature Circles and Book Clubs

Daniels (2002) defines **literature circles** as "small, peer-led discussion groups whose members have chosen to read the same story, poem, article, or book. While reading each group-assigned portion, members make notes to help them contribute to the upcoming discussion, and everyone comes to the group with ideas to share" (p. 2). **Book clubs** are student-led groups who read literary selections, write reactions and questions in a reading log, and engage in both small-group and whole-class discussions (McMahon and Raphael, 1997).

● literature circles

● book clubs

Though literature circles and book clubs are not exactly the same thing, they are more alike than different. They both recognize the social nature of learning and the transactional nature of the reading process. Their success depends on students being given a choice of material to read and discuss with peers. In this way, the text read is reentered and explored by a group of readers for a more thorough and complete understanding. The discussion group negotiates the meaning of the text, combines and connects ideas, and constructs meaning that one person reading alone might not ever achieve.

Literature circles and book clubs usually involve a written component—individual readers maintain written logs that document special passages or issues, or they place stick-on notes with brief comments on particular pages that will be shared with group members. Readers also document interpretations of their reading with sketches, illustrations, and diagrams. Often teachers will initiate literature circles by using role sheets as a "getting started" tool for helping students understand how to participate in peer-led discussion groups (see Figure 5.4). There are four components to the book club program: daily reading in a book of one's choice, daily writing in a journal or log related to the reading, student-led discussion groups, and community share—the whole class component. This last component provides the opportunity for teachers to be able to model for, or explicitly teach, their students how to lead and maintain good group discussions as well as ideas for what to write in a journal (Raphael, 2000).

FIGURE 5.4 Role descriptions for readers to use with their book club reading.

DISCUSSION LEADER

Develop a set of questions that you will ask your group members to discuss the material you read for today. Think about what your own feelings are or areas that confused or concerned you. Ask questions about what was read, or try some general questions such as, How did you feel about what you read? Did it remind you of anything? Were you surprised by anything? What do you think were the most important ideas?

VOCABULARY MASTER

Choose about three or four words from the reading that you find especially important, interesting, unusual, confusing, or totally new. Try to learn as much as you can about these words. Learn what they mean, and then help your group members learn these words also.

ARTIST

Draw a picture, sketch, diagram, or cartoon that is related to what you read. The drawing should be a representation of what the text was about. Show the drawing to your group members without telling them what it means to you. After they each have had a chance to say what they think it means, tell them what you intended.

CONNECTOR

Make connections between what you read and your life experiences. You might make a connection to something you experienced as a student, or to something that has happened in the community, in another place or time, or to other people. You could also make a connection to something else that you have read. Sharing these connections with your group members may help to trigger other connections that they can share.

SUMMARIZER

In a one- or two-minute statement, summarize what today's reading was about. Focus only on the main points and give the essence of the reading assignment. You might wish to list the main points if there are several.

LITERARY LUMINARY

Locate one or two special sections of today's reading. There might be a part of the reading that is especially interesting, funny, sad, confusing, controversial, thought-provoking, or important. Decide which parts are worth rereading or revisiting. Then think about how to share them again with your group members. You might wish to read them aloud, or have group members reread them silently and follow up with a discussion.

Source: Adapted from Daniels, 2002.

Literature Circles/Book Clubs

ACTIVITY

Literature circles and book clubs are powerful activities for intermediate-grade readers because these "students find that peers provide important support for their comprehension and interpretation of text, and that the literate activities . . . help develop their ownership over literacy" (Raphael, 2000, p. 85). Steps for implementing literature circles and book clubs follow:

Prereading

1. Provide students with a selection of books from which they can choose to read and discuss with classmates (see Appendix A). Titles can be presented in the form of a **book talk** (reading aloud a brief selection and/or sharing positive impressions from a book to arouse interest in reading the book). Students can freely choose a book, but sometimes a student will have to make a second choice if no one else chooses the same book. The optimum discussion group should have four or five members to ensure "a variety of perspectives on the text, a range of responses that enlivens discussion" (Daniels, 2002, p. 19).

   ● book talk

2. Have students choose their books and meet with others reading the same book to determine how much they will read for their first discussion meeting. Meetings are regularly scheduled, daily or weekly, and should allow at least 30 to 45 minutes for group discussion for intermediate-grade students.

During Reading

3. Have students read the agreed-upon pages of the text. For the written preparation, have students record their comments about the text, listing important page numbers, drawing pictures, noting difficult words or passages, making connections to their own lives, and developing questions to ask their group members. The nature of these comments is an individual one; however, they should help prepare the student for the upcoming group discussion.

Postreading

4. Have groups meet to discuss their reading. Students generally take turns leading the discussion, but all students must be involved. At the end of the discussion, have students decide on the amount of reading for the next discussion period. At this point, how well the groups are functioning and whether each member is participating fully should be apparent. The student-led discussions can indicate areas that need to be addressed during community share (book club), or whole-class sharing.

5. Have the whole class meet to listen to what the other groups have been discussing. This also provides an opportunity for explicit instruction or scaffolding on the part of the teacher.

6. If desired, ask students to complete self-assessments at the end of each discussion, or at the end of a complete book, to evaluate their own goals, roles, and performance as a group member.

ACTIVITY *Jigsaw: Read a Book in an Hour*

Teachers in the intermediate grades find it especially difficult to provide the depth of coverage necessary to achieve thorough understanding for the breadth of content knowledge expected. One approach that takes full advantage of collaborative working groups for the purpose of learning new material is jigsawing (Aronson and Patnoe, 1997). A specific jigsaw activity called Read a Book in an Hour (Cecil, 1990; Childrey, 1980) allows students to share responsibility for reading specific material. The material is divided into small portions and assigned to members of the class to read. Later, class members share the information to achieve the whole of the material. In other words, an individual student, or partnership, takes the responsibility of reading and learning a small amount of material well enough to summarize it for others, and as this information is shared, all members of the class learn the required material.

Prereading

1. Identify a topic of study and its components. Then develop a sign-up list that identifies enough "portions" for all members of a class to be involved.

2. Have students sign up for, or assign them, one portion of the topic/material.

During Reading

3. Allow students ample time to read the material.

4. Students are responsible for understanding the material for which they are accountable. Instruct them to identify and learn new vocabulary and concepts. Ask them to formulate ideas for how to present this information to classmates.

Postreading

5. Have "expert" groups (those who have read the same material) come together and prepare for their "teaching" of the new material. This

might involve preparing visuals as well as an oral presentation. Conferencing with the teacher is acceptable.

6. Have students present their material and answer questions.

While jigsawing is typically used with expository material, the modification, Read a Book in an Hour, can be used with narrative material for the express purpose of engaging students with a literary piece that they might not otherwise read on their own. Often students in upper grades are required to read particular works of literature as part of state content standards. Many students do not have either the confidence in themselves or the motivation to complete these required texts. Using this strategy, which adapts the jigsaw concept, enables these students to participate more fully in reading these texts. The anticipated benefit of this experience is that students will get a sense of the entire piece and thus have the schema necessary to read the book on their own, confident that they will be successful. And, much like book talk activities, by using high-quality literature, this technique will increase students' interest and desire to read the entire book on their own. A sample Read a Book in an Hour lesson with suggestions for integrating other areas of the curriculum is presented in Figure 5.5.

Reader Response Activities

Support for reader response activities as part of a comprehensive program for comprehension instruction is based on the work of Vygotsky (1978, 1986) and Rosenblatt (1978, 1983, 1994). Vygotsky's work views comprehension as socially constructed through negotiation among text, readers, teachers, and other members of the classroom community; Rosenblatt's work views comprehension as the result of the interaction, or transaction, between the reader and the text. The instructional frameworks and strategies that follow support the development of comprehension through independent reading.

Students can respond to what they read in an infinite number of ways. Many teachers and students are already familiar with written forms of responding such as journals, paraphrases, and summaries. Students also write letters to authors, or to a character in a story that they have read. Some students write as if they were the character in the story. Personal essays, poems, scripts for a readers theatre, and short stories are additional forms of written response. There are spoken forms of response as well. In addition to readers theatre, students might be asked to teach the text, or discuss in small groups, retell the text, or role play. Engaging in panel discussions or in a student–teacher conference are also spoken ways of responding to text. Finally, there are visual ways to respond that involve artistic endeavor and the use of graphic organizers.

Book: *The Summer of the Swans,* by Betsy Byars. Grade Level: 6th

Goals: To help students learn how to summarize and how to develop one key question from a passage; to encourage students to read *The Summer of the Swans* in its entirety on their own.

Content Standard(s): Reading-Language Arts Content Standard 2.4: Clarifying an understanding of texts by creating outlines, logical notes, summaries, or reports; and Standard 3.2: Analyzing the effect of the qualities of the character on the plot and the resolution of the conflict.

FACTORS TO BE CONSIDERED:

1. Motivation for the lesson cannot give away the story line.
2. Students should be grouped according to their reading abilities.
3. The number of chapters and the number of students should be compatible.
4. Books should have dramatic intensity and be of high literary quality; those that are very predictable are not good choices.

OTHER STORIES BY BETSY BYARS:

The Eighteenth Emergency and *Pinballs*

OTHER STORIES ABOUT DISABILITIES:

Take Wing, by Jean Little; and *A Racecourse for Andy,* by Patricia Wrightson

ANTICIPATORY SET/MOTIVATION:

Relate feelings of awkwardness, loneliness, or simply being different. "Is everyone the same? Is it wrong to be different? Are people always happy? Have you ever felt you weren't good enough? Or simply that you just can't fit in? I'd like to introduce you to a girl named Sara and let's see what problems she encounters and how she attacks and solves her problems."

THE PROCESS:

1. Pair students and assign chapters/sections.
2. Tell students that partners may move to another location while doing their paired reading but must return to their seats when the reading is completed.
3. Remind the class of the rules for partner reading, which include shoulder-to-shoulder reading and a *12-inch voice* (voice cannot be heard beyond 12 inches from mouth) maximum.
4. Read the first chapter to the entire group to establish setting.

SUMMARIZING:

5. Review the meaning of *to summarize*. Summaries should be no more than 2 minutes long.
6. Summarize the chapter and ask a prediction question for the upcoming section. Students are now ready to do their paired reading and prepare their

summaries and a prediction question from their assigned section. *Note:* The prediction question is posed to the following group during the sharing phase.

THE PROCESS CONTINUES:

7. Once students have read their sections and prepared their summary and prediction question, allow the process to continue. This should take about 15 to 20 minutes depending on the reading abilities and the length of the chapters assigned.

8. Repeat the prediction question to the first group. The first group then addresses the question and answers, if possible, and summarizes their reading. (These summaries may be written down and read, read from a prepared outline, or merely recited from memory, depending on the grade level.) This group then asks their prediction question to the following pair.

9. Allow the process to continue until the last group has participated.

10. For the last chapter, either read it aloud or assign it to the students to read.

COMPREHENSION CHECK:

- Literal
  1. What made Charlie leave his home in the middle of the night?
  2. Why did Sara dislike Joe Melby?
  3. What did Charlie lose while he was lost?
  4. Why was Aunt Willie nervous when Frank came to pick up Sara's sister, Wanda?

- Inferential
  1. Is Sara happy at the end of the story? Why do you think so?
  2. Why did Sara decide to accept Joe Melby's invitation to Benny Hoffman's party?
  3. Why do you think Sara knew that Charlie had gone out in the night to see the swans and that he had taken the one he had into the forest?

- Critical
  1. What does it mean to care more about someone else than you care about yourself?
  2. Often characteristics are revealed about a person when he or she reacts to a situation. When Gretchen called Charlie a "retard," Sara squirted water on her. When Sara believed Joe had stolen Charlie's watch, she became angry at Joe and would not believe him when he denied being the thief. What do these incidents tell you about Sara?
  3. On page 140, Betsy Byars writes that Sara "suddenly saw life as a series of huge, uneven steps." What do you think the author meant by this?
  4. Could Charlie really relate to the swans? Why or why not?

(continued)

FIGURE 5.5 Continued.

- Creative
    1. Charlie found the place where the swans were to be beautiful and serene. Create and describe a place that you think would be like this, a place where you might go at a time like this.
    2. Create a character who is in a situation that makes him or her feel awkward or out of place. Describe the situation and help the character cope with his or her feelings.
    3. Describe Aunt Willie's next ride on a motor scooter. Will she ever ride solo?
    4. What happened to Sara at the party? Did she enjoy herself?

ENRICHMENT ACTIVITIES:

1. Reread the entire novel on your own.
2. Keep a diary for Sara during the summer that Charlie is lost. Write entries for her dated at the beginning of the summer, during Charlie's absence, and at the end of the summer. Show her cares and concerns. Does she mature?

EXTENSION ACTIVITIES TO CHOOSE FROM FOR BOOK CONTRACT:

- Art
    1. Using poster paints, mix the paints to create puce (brownish-purple) and then paint a picture using this new color.
    2. Create a mobile of scenes from *Summer of the Swans* (swans, lakes, puce tennis shoes, watch, Sara, Charlie, etc.)
- Science
    3. Prepare a research report on birds and swans.
    4. It became very cold the night Charlie was lost. Conduct a study of weather and why temperature drops at night. Record at least six daytime and six nighttime outdoor temperatures for a week, but try to use the same times of day.
- Math
    5. Graph the outdoor temperatures from their science work in choice #4.
    6. Solve math problems finding kilometers walked by Sara, Joe, and Charlie. (The problems use decimals and the directions north, south, east, and west.)
- Social Studies
    7. Author Betsy Byars used West Virginia for the location of her story. Conduct a study of the geography of West Virginia. Decide where in the state the story took place, and write a paper supporting this answer.
    8. Conduct research on disabilities. Then choose one and write a paper on that one disability.

Sketch to Stretch

In Sketch to Stretch (Harste et al., 1988), students create a simple line drawing that depicts their interpretation of the material read. This sketch is then shared with a small group of peers who give their interpretations of each other's sketches. The guidelines are as follows:

1. Place students in groups of four or five. Ask them to think about the selection and draw a sketch of what the selection meant to them or what understanding they took from the selection.

2. When sketches are complete, have students in the group share their sketches with the other group members.

3. Have the group members give their interpretations of the sketch before the artist tells his or hers. What is important about this activity is that it allows readers that struggle with verbally oriented procedures the opportunity to demonstrate understanding and alternative interpretations. Examples are presented in Figure 5.6.

Example sketches for Sketch to Stretch. FIGURE 5.6

Sketch for <u>Fox Song</u>

Sketch for <u>The Bracelet</u>

ACTIVITY   *Going Beyond Visualizing*

This activity encourages the reader to use all the senses to comprehend and respond to text, not just visualizing. The reader is directed to create mental images that involve all of the senses when he or she reads. Using the sentence starters I see . . . , I hear . . . , I feel . . . , I smell . . . , and I taste . . . , students are asked to write, tell, or draw what they saw, heard, felt, smelled, and tasted as they were reading.

The sentences one fifth-grade student generated after reading a *National Geographic* article about sea turtles follows. The result is almost poetic:

I see turtles trying to get to the water. Thousands.

I hear the sound of thumping against their flippers.

I can feel all of the sand kicking into my eyes.

Some turtles died so I can smell the rot.

I can taste other turtles' backs. I can taste sand flinging into my open mouth.

(Harvey and Goudvis, 2000, p. 104)

Graphic Organizers

Graphic organizers, defined in Chapter 4 as visual ways of representing a body of knowledge, can also be used to help students focus their thoughts for responding to text. In general, they help students:

- categorize words, ideas, and characters.
- organize a sequence of events.
- compare what they read to something else.
- identify important elements in a text.
- examine the organizational pattern of the information or story read.

Graphic organizers can use only drawings or pictures, only written words, or some combination of both. Examples of a target organizer, so called because of its shape, and a conversational roundtable (Burke, 2000) are presented in Figure 5.7. Here, these graphic organizers compare two versions of the same story and demonstrate story features, respectively, in writing. Drawings could be used instead of words. Generally speaking, organizers are flexible enough to be used for a variety of purposes. For example, the target organizer could also be used for vocabulary development by placing a word such as *independence* in the center of the target, and writing other words in the next level that represent varying aspects of this concept. In the outermost circle, synonyms, antonyms, definitions, explanations, or instances of use could be written. Likewise, the conversational roundtable could be used to explore essential and nonessential characteristics, with examples and nonexamples for the concept located in the center circle. Additional examples of graphic organizers can be found in Chapters 4 and 8.

Graphic organizers: target organizer and conversational roundtable. FIGURE 5.7

Target Organizer

Conversational Roundtable

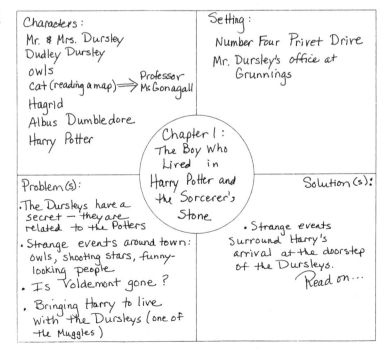

Characters:
Mr. & Mrs. Dursley
Dudley Dursley
owls
Cat (reading a map) ⟶ Professor McGonagall
Hagrid
Albus Dumbledore
Harry Potter

Setting:
Number Four Privet Drive
Mr. Dursley's office at Grunnings

Chapter 1: The Boy Who Lived in Harry Potter and the Sorcerer's Stone

Problem(s):
• The Dursleys have a secret — they are related to the Potters
• Strange events around town: owls, shooting stars, funny-looking people
• Is Voldemont gone?
• Bringing Harry to live with the Dursleys (one of the Muggles)

Solution(s):
• Strange events surround Harry's arrival at the doorstep of the Dursleys.
Read on...

Target Organizer content (Cinderella inner circle and Yeh-Shen outer circle):

Inner circle (Cinderella):
1. Beautiful Cinderella lived with her stepmother and two stepsisters
2. Only friend was her fairy godmother
3. Not allowed to go to king's ball
4. Fairy godmother, "Be home before Midnight."
5. A hit of the ball, running at midnight and lost a glass slipper.
6. Prince found slipper, then found Cinderella. They lived happily ever after.

Outer circle (Yeh-Shen):
1. Beautiful Yeh-Shen lived with her stepmother and one stepsister
2. Friend was a beautiful golden fish with golden eyes and magic bones
3. Not allowed to go to Festival celebration.
4. Magic fish bones, "Do not lose the golden shoes."
5. Avoiding stepmother and stepsister ran at the Festival and lost a golden shoe.
6. Golden shoe found and sold to the King. King sought owner, found Yeh-Shen, and they got married.

TROUBLESHOOTING

Students of all ages can have difficulty with comprehension for a variety of reasons. Comprehension will obviously be difficult if the reader cannot quickly and automatically pronounce many of the words that he or she is trying to read. In addition, the reader needs some prior knowledge of the topic being read to be able to adequately comprehend the material. Assuming the reader has access to material at an appropriate level of difficulty, he or she needs to be able to relate, or make connections, to the text for it to be meaningful. This is why prereading strategies are so important—to activate, build or enhance background knowledge prior to beginning a lesson. Readers who have difficulty with comprehension often are not making meaningful connections to the text. The following recommendations are for those students who have a difficult time making connections to the text.

Difficulty Making Connections During Prereading

anticipation guides ●

Students need to begin thinking about connections to the text even before they start to read. Used before reading, **anticipation guides** consist of a set of three to five statements that serve two basic purposes: (1) to activate the student's background knowledge for the topic by asking the student to either agree or disagree with the statement and be prepared to explain their position, and (2) to provide guidance for the upcoming reading. Anticipation guides are also intended to arouse curiosity about the topic by presenting statements that are potentially controversial or challenging. Students become motivated to read the material to prove their choice, or to resolve conceptual conflicts or lack of understanding. The anticipation guide can thus serve as a postreading activity as well, to revisit the statements and allow for changes in viewpoints.

The teacher prepares an anticipation guide by

- reading the text to identify the major concepts students should learn.
- considering students' current knowledge about these concepts.
- creating statements that students have sufficient knowledge to understand what they say, but not enough to conceptually understand the statements, or the rationale behind them.
- listing the statements in a particular order; one that follows the order presented in the text is usual, but not mandatory.

Once completed, the anticipation guide can be presented as an individual handout accompanied by a visual using an overhead transparency or multimedia. The teacher should read aloud the directions and the statements for the students. Students should respond individually to each statement by agreeing or disagreeing, and explaining why. In order to do this, students must make connections to their own background knowledge related to the topic they are about to read. A group discussion follows with the teacher first tallying the responses for agreement and disagreement with each statement. Discussion should include at least one explanation for each point of view. Following this discussion, the material is read, keeping the anticipation guide in mind. After the reading, the students may return to the guide and respond once more. This time they will have the actual text to use to support or refute points expressed in the earlier discussion (Duffelmeyer, 1994; Readence et al., 1998). Figure 5.8 shows an anticipation guide for a book entitled *Outside and Inside You* (Markle, 1991), which is used with struggling readers to help them learn more about their bodies.

Difficulty Making Connections During Reading

Comprehension improves when students actively seek to connect the content of what they read with what they already have experienced or have learned (Brown, 2002). The strategy called "It reminds me of . . ." (Richards and Gipe, 1992) encourages students to verbally make connections between what they read and their background knowledge *while they are reading*. To be able to state what the passage "reminds me of . . ." a connection has to be made between the material and the student's own background knowledge.

The teacher models this strategy by reading a portion of a text selection, stopping, and saying aloud, "It reminds me of . . .". Modeling works best if realistic fiction, a memoir, or a version of a familiar tale is used because these will be more likely to provide situations that readers can recall or relate to in their own lives. For example, the story *Fox Song* (Bruchac, 1993) tells of a young girl who is experiencing the recent death of her beloved grandmother. As the girl walks around her community, she is constantly reminded of the things she did with her grandmother, and what she learned from her. After reading an early section of how sad the girl feels when she is told of her grandmother's death, the teacher might say, "It reminds me of the time when I heard my mother on the phone with my grandmother. She had just learned

FIGURE 5.8

Anticipation guide for use with *Outside and Inside You.*

Directions: Below are some statements about parts of your body. Read each statement carefully and write Agree or Disagree on the line before each statement. Be prepared to explain why you agree or disagree with the statement.

_____ 1. If you scrub too hard, you might wash your skin away.

_____ 2. Muscles are more important than bones.

_____ 3. You don't really see with your eyes, but with your brain.

_____ 4. It would be best if you just drank liquids to nourish your body.

that my grandfather, her father, had died. This sad, empty feeling just came over me." Then students are given the opportunity to respond to the same passage. The teacher might also use just the cover of a children's book and ruminate about what it reminds her of as a way of modifying this activity for use during prereading. After a few examples, students will soon be able to identify parts in other content with which they connect.

Difficulty Making Connections After Reading

The possibilities for making connections following the reading are many. The simplest connections are most likely to be to our own experiences. These text-to-self connections come more naturally and are similar to the "it reminds me of . . ." during reading connections. But we also can make connections to other things we have read, or to events that happen in the world. Some common types of text-to-text connections, from easiest to more difficult, include

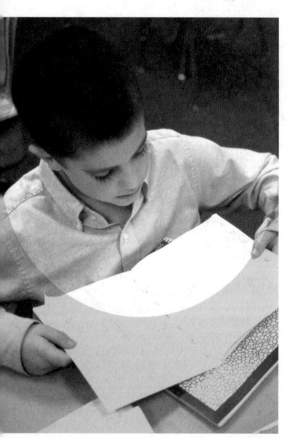

- comparing characters, their personalities, and actions.
- comparing story events and plot lines.
- comparing lessons, themes, or messages in stories.
- finding common themes, writing style, or perspectives in the work of a single author.
- comparing the treatment of common themes by different authors.
- comparing different versions of familiar stories. (Harvey and Goudvis, 2000, p. 73)

Teachers can model text-to-text connections by choosing to share books that have similar themes, or that are actually versions of the same story. It is best to model with the easier material first. For example, the teacher might read the more familiar *Little Red Riding Hood* and then share *Lon Po Po*, a Chinese version of the same story (Young, 1989). These books would not be too difficult for struggling intermediate-grade students to grasp the connections. A T-chart can be used to list the connections, with the teacher beginning the list and students contributing to it (see Figure 5.9).

As students become comfortable making text-to-self and text-to-text connections, they may naturally begin to make connections to more global issues, or they can be encouraged to make these text-to-world connections through modeling. Additionally, as Harvey and Goudvis (2000) point out, "Encouraging students to make text-to-world connections supports our efforts to teach students about social studies and science concepts and topics" (p. 75). They share an example of a fourth/fifth-grade teacher who introduced *The Lotus Seed* (Garland, 1997) to his students. This book

	FIGURE 5.9
T-chart listing text-to-text connections for *Little Red Riding Hood* and *Lon Po Po*.	

LITTLE RED RIDING HOOD	LON PO PO
One child.	Three children.
Child goes to see grandmother.	Mother goes to see grandmother.
Mother gives directions.	Children figure out what to do.
Wolf is clever and outsmarts grandmother and Little Red Riding Hood.	Wolf is not smart and is killed by the clever children.
Huntsman is the hero.	Children are the hero.
Food is bread, wine, and sweet butter.	Food is gingko nuts.
People are eaten.	No one is eaten.
Wolf dies.	Wolf dies.

relates the story of a Vietnamese family fleeing their home for the United States during the Vietnam War. Most of the students had little knowledge about, or direct experience with, the content of this book, but there was one particular text-to-self connection that enabled the teacher to illustrate a text-to-world connection. As the class discussed the book, one student shared, "My uncle fought in Vietnam and he told me all about it." In response to this statement another student looked rather confused and then looked back to a picture in the book that showed bombs falling on a rice paddy. She exclaimed, "You mean *we* were the ones dropping the bombs on Vietnam?" At this point the teacher interjected with a text-to-world connection and some information about the war: "The rice paddy is probably in North Vietnam and U.S. planes may have been doing the bombing. The North Vietnamese were fighting for communism and the South Vietnamese were fighting for freedom."

It is important to note that these connections can often overlap. It is not that crucial for students to accurately distinguish among what is a text-to-self, text-to-text, or text-to-world connection, or to come up with a long list of these connections. In the process of contemplating and making some connections, students begin to monitor their understanding, think about what they are reading, and thus enhance their comprehension. That is the purpose.

SUMMARY

Comprehension is the reason we read. But comprehension cannot occur without the simultaneous use of all the language cue systems (semantic, syntactic, graphophonemic). That is, the reader has to simultaneously construct meaning from the words that have been decoded while connecting what is read to prior knowledge as well as connecting new information to previously known information. It is a complex and arduous process best consummated through a program that offers guidance in specific comprehension strategies and many opportunities to apply them with quality literature as well as expository text. For a literacy program to be balanced and comprehensive, it must not only enable learners to decode text, but also to offer them guidance in strategic reading and provide ample opportunities for independent reading using techniques such as those presented in this chapter.

Questions
FOR JOURNAL WRITING AND DISCUSSION

1. Think about what you do when you read. What comprehension strategies did you use while reading this chapter? Make a list of the strategies that you can identify. Then spend a few minutes reading a novel or other narrative material. Make a second list of the strategies you used with the narrative text. Compare the two lists. Are there major differences? Discuss the lists with your classmates.

2. Prepare an argument for why you allow students in your classroom the time to read self-selected material and then to discuss it in small groups. How would you change this argument for your administrator and for a parent?

3. How does your definition of reading impact the importance of comprehension instruction to your total reading program?

Suggestions
FOR PROJECTS AND FIELD ACTIVITIES

1. Select one of the comprehension strategies from this chapter. Locate a selection from an intermediate-grade classroom that would be appropriate material for teaching this strategy. Teach the strategy to a small group of classmates. Discuss their reactions. How would you modify your teaching for intermediate-grade students? What feedback helped you the most?

2. Teach a comprehension strategy to a small group of intermediate-grade students, or to an individual student. What problems did they have with the lesson? What problems did you have with the lesson? What did they like and dislike about the strategy? Discuss the results with your class.

3. Observe an intermediate-grade classroom teacher during reading lessons for at least five days (try to observe a full week, or different days). Make a list of all the activities the teacher and students engage in during this time. Keep track of how much time is spent on each activity. How much time was spent on direct teaching of comprehension strategies? How much time was spent on the application of these strategies? How much time was spent on actual reading by the students?

References

Anderson, R., Hiebert, E., Scott, J., & Wilkerson, I. (1985). *Becoming a nation of readers.* Washington, DC: National Institute of Education.

Aronson, E., & Patnoe, S. (1997). *The jigsaw classroom: Building cooperation in the classroom* (2nd ed.). New York: Longman.

Beach, R. (1993). *A teacher's introduction to reader-response theories.* Urbana, IL: National Council of Teachers of English.

Beck, I. L., McKeown, M. G., Hamilton, R. L., & Kucan, L. (1997). *Questioning the author: An approach for enhancing student engagement with text.* Newark, DE: International Reading Association.

Block, C. C., & Pressley, M. (Eds.). (2002). *Comprehension instruction: Research-based best practices.* New York: Guilford.

Britton, B. K., & Graesser, A. C. (Eds.). (1996). *Models of understanding text.* Mahwah, NJ: Erlbaum.

Brown, R. (2002). Straddling two worlds: Self-directed comprehension instruction for middle schoolers. In C. C. Block and M. Pressley (Eds.), *Comprehension instruction: Research-based best practices* (pp. 337–350). New York: Guilford.

Bruchac, J. (1993). *Fox song.* (P. Morin, Illus.). New York: Putnam.

Burke, J. (2000). *Reading reminders: Tools, tips, and techniques.* Portsmouth, NH: Boynton/Cook.

Cecil, N. L. (1990). Read a book in an hour: A smooth transition to multi-chaptered texts. *Reading Improvement, 27*(3), 188–191.

Cecil, N. L. (1995). *The art of inquiry: Questioning strategies for K–6 classrooms.* Winnipeg, Manitoba: Penguis.

Childrey, J. (1980). Read a book in an hour. *Reading Horizons, 20,* 174–176.

Cunningham, J. W. (1982). Generating interactions between schemata and text. In J. A. Niles & L. A. Harris (Eds.), *New inquiries in reading research and instruction* (pp. 42–47). Thirty-first Yearbook of the National Reading Conference. Washington, DC: National Reading Conference.

Daniels, H. (2002). *Literature circles: Voice and choice in Book Clubs and reading groups* (2nd ed.). York, ME: Stenhouse.

Davey, B. (1983). Think aloud—Modeling the cognitive processes of reading comprehension. *The Reading Teacher, 27,* 44–47.

Duffelmeyer, F. A. (1994). Effective anticipation guide statements for learning from expository prose. *Journal of Reading, 37,* 452–457.

Duffy, G. G. (2002). The case for direct explanation of strategies. In C. C. Block & M. Pressley (Eds.), *Comprehension instruction: Research-based best practices* (pp. 28–41). New York: Guilford.

Englert, C. S., & Thomas, C. C. (1987). Sensitivity to text structure in reading and writing: A comparison between learning disabled and non-learning disabled students. *Learning Disabilities Quarterly, 10,* 93–105.

Gambrell, L. B., & Bales, R. J. (1987). Visual imagery: a strategy for enhancing listening, reading and writing. *Australian Journal of Reading, 10*(3), 147–153.

Garland, S. (1997). *The lotus seed* (T. Kiuchi, Illus.). New York: Harcourt.

Gipe, J. P. (2002). *Multiple paths to literacy: Classroom techniques for struggling readers* (5th ed.). Upper Saddle River, NJ: Merrill/Prentice Hall.

Harste, J., Short, C., & Burke, C. (1988). *Creating classrooms for authors*. Portsmouth, NH: Heinemann.

Harvey, S., & Goudvis, A. (2000). *Strategies that work: Teaching comprehension to enhance understanding*. York, ME: Stenhouse.

Hyman, T. S. (1986). *Little red riding hood*. New York: Holiday House.

Jorm, A. (1977). Effect of word imagery on reading performance as a function of reader ability. *Journal of Educational Psychology, 69*, 46–54.

Markle, S. (1991). *Outside and inside you*. New York: Scholastic.

McMahon, S. I., & Raphael, T. E. (1997). The book club program: Theoretical and research foundations. In S. I. McMahon & T. E. Raphael (Eds.), *The book club connection: Literacy learning and classroom talk* (pp. 3–25). New York: Teachers College Press.

Moravcsik, J. E., & Kintsch, W. (1993). Writing quality, reading skills, and domain knowledge as factors in text comprehension. *Canadian Journal of Experimental Psychology, 47*, 360–374.

Palincsar, A. (1987, January). Reciprocal teaching: Can student discussions boost comprehension? *Instructor*, 56–60.

Palincsar, A. S., & Brown, A. L. (1984). Reciprocal teaching of comprehension-fostering and comprehension-monitoring activities. *Cognition and Instruction, 1*(2), 117–175.

Palincsar, A. S., & Brown, A. L. (1986). Interactive teaching to promote independent learning from text. *The Reading Teacher, 39*, 771–777.

Pearson, P. D., & Gallagher, M. (1983). The instruction of reading comprehension. *Contemporary Educational Psychology, 8*, 317–344.

Pressley, M. (2000). Comprehension instruction in elementary school: A quarter-century of research progress. In B. Taylor, M. Graves, & P. van den Broek (Eds.), *Reading for meaning: Fostering comprehension in the middle grades* (pp. 32–51). New York: Teachers College Press.

Pressley, M. (2002). Comprehension strategies instruction: A turn-of-the-century status report. In C. C. Block & M. Pressley (Eds.), *Comprehension instruction: Research-based best practices* (pp. 11–27). New York: Guilford.

Raphael, T. E. (1982). Question-answering strategies for children. *The Reading Teacher, 36*, 186–190.

Raphael, T. E. (2000). Balancing literature and instruction: Lessons from the Book Club Project. In B. Taylor, M. Graves, & P. van den Broek (Eds.), *Reading for meaning: Fostering comprehension in the middle grades* (pp. 70–94). New York: Teachers College Press.

Readence, J. E., Bean, T. W., & Baldwin, R. S. (1998). *Content area reading: An integrated approach* (6th ed.). Dubuque, IA: Kendall/Hunt.

Richards, J. C., & Gipe, J. P. (1992). Activating background knowledge: Strategies for beginning and poor readers. *The Reading Teacher, 45*, 474–476.

Rosenblatt, L. M. (1978). *The reader, the text, the poem*. Carbondale: Southern Illinois University Press.

Rosenblatt, L. M. (1983). *Literature as exploration*. New York: The Modern Languages Association of America.

Rosenblatt, L. M. (1994). The transactional theory of reading and writing. In R. B. Ruddell, M. R. Ruddell, & H. Singer (Eds.), *Theoretical models and processes of reading* (4th ed., pp. 1057–1092). Newark, DE: International Reading Association.

Rosenshine, B., Meister, C., & Chapman, S. (1996). Reciprocal teaching: A review of the research. *Review of Educational Research, 64*, 479–530.

Stauffer, R. G. (1975). *Directing the reading-thinking process*. New York: Harper & Row.

van den Broek, P. W. (1990). The causal inference maker: Towards a process model of inference generation in text comprehension. In D. A. Balota, G. B. Flores d'Arcais, & K. Rayner (Eds.), *Comprehension processes in reading* (pp. 423–445). Hillsdale, NJ: Erlbaum.

van den Broek, P. W., Risden, K., Fletcher, C. R., & Thurlow, R. (1996). A "landscape" view of reading: Fluctuating patterns of activation and the construction of a stable memory representation. In B. K. Britton & A. C. Graesser (Eds.), *Models of understanding text* (pp. 165–187). Mahwah, NJ: Erlbaum.

Vygotsky, L. S. (1978). *Mind in society*. Cambridge, MA: MIT Press.

Vygotsky, L. S. (1986). *Thought and language* (A. Kozulin, Trans.). Cambridge, MA: MIT Press.

Wilhelm, J. D. (1997). *"You gotta BE the book": Teaching engaged and reflective reading with adolescents*. New York: Teachers College Press.

Young, E. (1989). *Lon Po Po: A Red Riding Hood story from China*. Daly City, CA: Philomel.

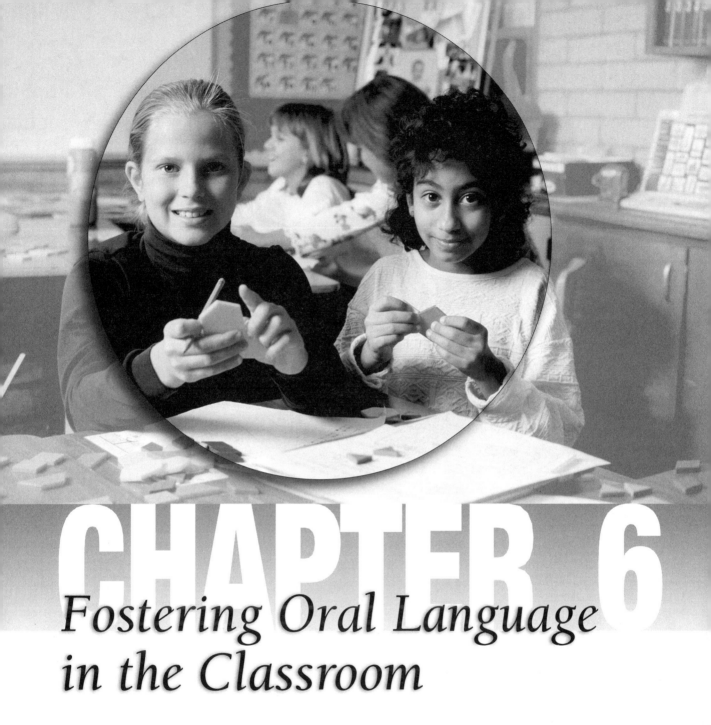

CHAPTER 6

Fostering Oral Language in the Classroom

Focus Questions

- What should be the major objectives of an oral language program in the intermediate grades?
- What are some evidence-based strategies to foster the development of both informal and formal oral language?
- How can drama be used to make language accessible for second language learners?

159

In the Classroom

Mr. Pollard is preparing for a guided reading selection about tornadoes with his fourth-grade class. The school in which Mr. Pollard teaches is on the coast of North Carolina and, although most of the students have had firsthand experience with a hurricane, he wonders how much they know about tornadoes, another severe, but similar natural disaster. To prepare the students for the selection, Mr. Pollard leads a discussion:

Mr. Pollard: We were all affected by hurricane Floyd last summer, but how many of you have ever known anyone who was in a tornado? (Several students raise their hands.) So what do you know about tornadoes, Josh?

Joshua: We lived in Kansas when I was a baby. My mother told me there was a special kind of cellar you go into when a tornado is supposed to come. A tornado can pick a house right up in the air—or even a car—but a cellar is level, so you're safe there.

Mr. Pollard: Yes, tornadoes are very strong and can do a great deal of damage.

Patricia: Did you guys see the film *Twister*? A huge tornado threw a cow way up in the air and even a semi! Do you think that could really happen, Mr. Pollard?

Mr. Pollard: Well, it was certainly sensational, but if you recall from the movie, there are several degrees of severity for tornadoes and that may have been an especially fierce one.

Kendra: There was a fierce tornado in *The Wizard of Oz* that picked up their house.

Hoa: Oh, yeah, I saw that and my little sister has the book!

Mr. Pollard: You are exactly right, Hoa; a tornado was an important part in the book. Can anyone tell me how a tornado is different from a hurricane?

Joshua: From what I have seen on the news, it seems like you don't get much warning for a tornado.

Like, there's this funnel cloud that rips through the town real quickly, smashing everything in its path. But when we had the hurricane here, they were telling us on the news to evacuate for a whole day.

Mandy: Yeah, the movie showed the tornado happening really fast, before the guys who were studying it had time to get out of the way! And they were in a car!

Mr. Pollard: So, you think the tornado comes on more suddenly?

Joshua: Oh, yeah—way more suddenly. I guess that would make 'em even scarier than Hurricane Floyd, and that was for sure the most scared that I have ever been! (Others murmur in agreement.)

Raul: They're bigger and black, too. And I don't think you have to have any rain with them. At least what I've seen on the news.

Kendra: And is there an eye with them, the part that is the worst like it was with Floyd? I don't ever remember hearing about it if there is.

Hoa: Do we have tornadoes in North Carolina? I hope not!

Crystal: I'm pretty sure we do! My aunt lives in Greenville and there was one there a long time ago. My cousin told me about it. The roof of their trailer was torn off and a telephone wire came down on it. But it was weird because it was just in some parts of the town and not in others. My aunt was shopping when it happened, so she didn't get hurt.

Mr. Pollard: I am glad to hear your relatives were not hurt! You children seem to know quite a bit about tornadoes. From your comments, it seems that tornadoes have some similarities to and also some differences from a hurricane. Let's find out more. I brought in some photographs that I got from the Internet showing a recent tornado in Oklahoma. (He passes these around.)

Mr. Pollard explains that tornadoes are often called "twisters" because of their funnel shape. He adds that tornadoes usually occur in flat prairie land, so the chances of having one on the North Carolina coast, while not impossible, are not likely. He then asks students if they have any questions about tornadoes. Several students respond and he writes their questions on the board:

What causes tornadoes? What kind of weather makes them happen?

Why do they twist and have a funnel shape?

Why are they found in flat prairie land but not on the coast?

How are they different from hurricanes?

Through discussion, Mr. Pollard has not only assessed the prior knowledge of the students in his class about the upcoming science selection, but he has allowed them to share their experience and knowledge with each other. While doing so, they have set purposes for their subsequent reading and will have a more personal involvement with the reading.

After the reading, Mr. Pollard leads a discussion based on the students' questions. They talk about the new information they have learned and compare the data from the selection with what they remembered from *Twister,* the movie many of them had seen, as well as their other previous associations with the topic. From their comments and questions, Mr. Pollard can evaluate how well the children read and understood the selection, and how they are able to synthesize the new information with their prior knowledge. The last question about how tornadoes are different from hurricanes was not addressed in the text, so Mr. Pollard breaks the class into discussion groups consisting of three or four members and invites them to use a Venn Diagram to come up with a list of similarities and differences between tornadoes and hurricanes using information they find on the World Wide Web and in trade books (see Figure 6.1). Finally, Mr. Pollard helps the groups to consolidate their lists into one, thus deepening their understanding of the two storms through reading and much rich oral discussion.

FIGURE 6.1 The Venn diagram used in Mr. Pollard's class to compare tornadoes and hurricanes.

HURRICANES   TORNADOES

heavy rain

long duration

mostly on coasts

rain clouds

wind

damage

loud

seasonal

short duration

mostly in-land

funnel cloud

INTRODUCTION

The importance, academically, socially, and vocationally, of the ability to speak and listen with ease in contemporary society cannot be emphasized enough. Although we sometimes seem to believe that speaking and listening are learned automatically simply through contact with other people, we must remember that there are so many forms of speaking and listening for which we need to reserve considerable classroom time for work at the oral level and, better yet, to find ways to best integrate the language arts of reading, writing, listening, speaking, viewing, and visually representing with other content areas. Additionally, with the influx of non–native English speakers into our North American schools, it becomes even more critical to create classrooms rich with the spoken word.

In particular, all children need a strong oral language base from which to develop other literacy skills. Through speaking and listening, children develop vocabulary, acquire concepts, and perceive the structure of the English language—the essential building blocks of all learning (Smith, 2001). Moreover, the child who possesses a strong oral language facility has the best chance of becoming a proficient reader and has greater potential for writing well (Heath, 1983; Loban, 1976; Sampson, 1986).

The objectives of an oral language program in the upper grades around which most state standards are based include the following and are addressed at length in the remainder of this chapter. Students need to be taught to

- speak fluently and easily.
- use language as a way to communicate their ideas.
- perceive oral language as a way of learning.
- be familiar with specific skills of effective speaking.
- utilize different modes of expression.
- become strategic and skillful listeners.

To reach these objectives, a teacher in a balanced and comprehensive literacy program can expose students to informal speaking, including conversations, classroom discussions, and informal debates; formal speaking, including speeches, oral reports, and interviews; and drama, including role playing, readers theatre, and simulations. An excellent resource for additional activities that enhance oral communication skills is *Creating Competent Communicators: Activities for Teaching, Speaking, Listening, and Media Literacy in K–6 Classrooms* (Cooper and Morreale, 2003).

INFORMAL SPEAKING

informal speaking ●

Informal speaking, such as that contained in conversation and spontaneous or directed discussions, is the most frequently used expressive language mode. Most native English–speaking children are fluent users of oral language by the time they start school. Because most children have already acquired considerable competence using oral language, teachers often assume that oral language does not need to be emphasized in elementary classrooms, especially as children enter the upper grades. (In fact, some teachers expend considerable energy trying to *prevent* students from talking in class!) A significant body of research has shown, however, that students benefit greatly from participation in both formal and informal oral language activities (Cazden, 1986). Moreover, it has become increasingly important to have a language-rich environment; such a classroom is the best source of language learning for the increasing numbers of students in today's schools who do not speak English or who are in the process of acquiring it (Peregoy and Boyle, 1993).

Conversations

Oral language can and should be a natural and essential part of a balanced and comprehensive literacy program in the upper grades. Older students can converse with peers as they plan and carry out collaborative projects or conduct writing conferences. Teachers, the primary models of standard English in any classroom, can also conduct informal conversations with students at various times during the day. Special time can be set aside for teachers to communicate with shy students, those who are experiencing difficulties in their lives, or those who need extra attention.

The rich context of a personally relevant conversation creates the *schema,* or background, necessary to store new word meanings. Moreover, the definitions students receive through conversations will probably be in terms they are developmentally able to understand. Then, in the context of that same conversation, students will often say the new word or words they have just learned. This immediate application further ensures that these terms will become part of students' permanent speaking, reading, and writing vocabulary.

Conversations, besides increasing vocabulary and helping students crystallize their thoughts on a variety of subjects, provide a way for teachers to make their students feel important and show respect for their ideas. Conversations can also provide teachers with important insights into the possible reading interests of their students as they discuss their likes and dislikes in the context of everyday discourse.

Students with similar interests can form self-initiated **conversation clubs,** to chat about an event, an idea, or an experience they have in common. During these sessions, teachers can learn much about the oral language prowess of students by taking anecdotal notes on which students ● conversation clubs

- extend the conversation without coaxing.
- hold listeners' attention.
- check for accuracy without being told to do so.
- ask questions for clarification.
- add interesting data.
- have adequate grammar and vocal habits.

From these notes teachers can group students for minilessons on informative and interpersonal language uses.

Teachers may find it helpful to have at their command a list of provocative topics to which they can refer when they wish to plan a special conversation time (see Figure 6.2). Additionally, the following activities are sure to provoke even the quietest student to contribute an oral response.

FIGURE 6.2 | Topics for informal conversations.

What movies have you seen that you liked?

What do you do on weekends?

What qualities do you value in a friend?

What music groups do you enjoy?

What is your favorite place to be? Why?

What is your favorite TV show?

What would you do if you had a million dollars?

What things make you happy or sad?

Do you have any pets? Describe your pet(s).

What is your favorite holiday? Why?

If you could go anywhere in the world, where would you go?

Who is your favorite relative? Why?

What do you do to be kind to your brothers and sisters?

ACTIVITY *Just Suppose*

1. Develop a set of cards containing interesting suppositions (see suggestions).
2. Put students in pairs.
3. Give each pair a card with a printed Just Suppose idea.
4. Allow students to talk about their idea for five minutes.
5. Encourage each pair to arrive at a consensus.
6. Invite pairs to share their ideas with the rest of the class.

SUGGESTIONS FOR "JUST SUPPOSE . . ." CARDS

. . . everyone looked exactly alike.

. . . you could talk to animals.

. . . you could become invisible.

. . . you could fly.

. . . you could learn by just taking pills.

. . . you were president of the United States.

. . . you could read people's minds.

. . . there was no money.

Campfire

ACTIVITY

1. Change the seating arrangement for this activity to make it enjoyable and relaxing. One possibility might be to have students sit in a circle and pretend they are around a campfire. Be sure to audiotape or videotape the sharing period so that a tape will be available in a listening center designated for this purpose.

2. Select a topic (see Figure 6.2), or allow students to talk about a favorite object. Ask them to speak loudly enough so everyone can hear.

3. Instruct the class to listen politely as each student takes a turn speaking. Once each speaker has finished, invite students to ask a question of the speaker. The question must begin with one of the five *W*s: Who, why, what, where, when. For example: "Where did you get that skateboard? Why is it so important to you?"

4. Correlate other subjects with this oral sharing time. For example, it might be combined with a current events lesson, where children can share something they have read in the newspaper or heard on the news.

Directed Group Discussions

Discussions are similar to conversations in several ways. Both involve the use of oral language in an informal setting. Both involve an exploration of an issue or a topic and offer children the opportunity to use a variety of speaking skills. A **discussion** can be defined as "problem solving by cooperative thinking." The goal of any discussion or problem resolution should be to consider a question from many angles, allowing all students a voice.

● discussion

As children advance through the elementary grades, teachers may begin to focus less on informal discussions and more on teacher-directed discussions, with a specific learning goal that the teacher has preidentified. Discussions are the principal means through which the conversational skills related to thinking patterns and to interpersonal functioning are developed.

Suggestions for Teacher-Guided Discussions

Plan for the discussion by

- defining the issue to be discussed.
- preparing some leading questions.
- allowing students to research the topic.

Initiate the discussion by

- making a brief statement or offering a pertinent quotation.
- providing a handout with a summary of data about the topic.
- reminding students of guidelines for courteous behavior.

Keep the discussion running smoothly by

- having a recorder write responses on the board.
- discouraging domination of discussion by a vociferous few.
- inviting shy students to contribute.
- allowing gestures from and home language of English language learners.

Bring out all sides of the topic by

- providing informative data from both sides of the issue.
- asking students to consider the opposing viewpoint.
- playing the role of "devil's advocate."

Help students to reach a consensus by

- summarizing points made by students on both sides.
- clarifying problematic issues as they arise.
- offering topics for subsequent discussions.

In the primary grades these skills are taught largely through teacher modeling. The teacher must contribute as well as solicit comments related to the topic under discussion; point out the connection among ideas being discussed; and demonstrate the processes of hypothesizing, summarizing, generalizing, and relating new information to one's own experience. Asking provocative questions that probe students' imagination helps these discussions become one of the richest sources of learning and processing information for students.

Gradually, as students enter the upper elementary grades, they begin to incorporate these conversation skills into their own discussions. For example, in the vignette opening this chapter, the students in Mr. Pollard's class, typical of older students, were able to relate a new concept to their own experiences and make generalizations about hurricanes and hypothesize about how they may be different from tornadoes.

At other times it is helpful to precede discussion periods with time for students to explore a specific content area topic to be addressed, such as "Why are the rain forests diminishing and what can we do about it?" By establishing this precedent, children will have a depth of information to share. One of the benefits of creating such informative and interactive discussions is that—provided the teacher has set up a safe, nonthreatening classroom environment, where no put-downs are allowed—students will appreciate their classmates' oral exchanges even more. They will actually learn from each other in a potent way not always possible from an adult.

For more formal discussions, and to foster a more student-centered classroom, it is sometimes helpful to appoint a discussion leader. The discussion leader has various specific responsibilities. The leader opens the discussion and establishes its goals. The leader may find it necessary to clarify participants' statements and to summarize progress as a basis for continuing productive discussion. Occasionally, the discussion leader will have to handle differences of opinion between participants. The leader also may need to learn to cope diplomatically, at times, with a talkative student who attempts to dominate the discussion and draw in a shy student who needs to be invited to participate. Teachers will find it necessary to model discussion leader behavior for students initially, but then all students should have an opportunity to perform this role, which is so pivotal in developing leadership qualities.

The following guidelines may be helpful to share with students when initiating formal classroom discussions:

- Find out as much as you can about the topic ahead of time.
- Support your opinions with facts.
- Stay on the topic.
- Listen carefully to other speakers.
- Do not repeat what has already been said.
- Ask for clarification when you don't understand what has been said.
- At the end, help the leader summarize the most important points.

Discussions About Literature

Students need many opportunities to discuss books they have read or to hear discussions about books they may not yet be able to read. Smith (1998) cautions that simply asking students a list of questions about text to probe their thinking is rarely productive. Much as adults wish to share their feelings about a book they have recently read that touched them in some way, children's oral response to literature can deepen their appreciation for literature, and hearing their peers' perspectives on what they have read increases critical and evaluative thinking about text (Gambrell and Almasi, 1996; Paratore and McCormack, 1998; Roser and Martinez, 1995).

Literature circles (see Chapter 5) are a wonderful means for encouraging intensive discussion and reflection about books students are reading. When students share their personal responses and interpretations of a book with their peers, they are able to gain a deeper understanding of themselves and their world. Moreover, the discussions lead to enhanced enjoyment of literature (Samway et al., 1991).

These "grand conversations," as they are sometimes called (Eeds and Wells, 1989), can follow a read-aloud or the independent reading of chapters in a novel. In small groups or in pairs, students can respond to story elements such as plot, illustrations, imagery, or specific characters. They can make connections between books, compare works by the same or another author, contrast other versions of the story, or compare some facet of the story to their own lives. These same ruminations about a text can follow the reading of a poem, listening to a story at a listening center, or the guided reading of a difficult piece of literature with finely shaded meaning.

The most common approach to literature circles is for small groups or partners to simply sit together following the reading of a book or a portion of a book to talk about what they have read. They may discuss the same title or different books they have read on a similar theme, perhaps by the same author or illustrator, or from a particular literary genre. The teacher sets up a system that allows students to select books and schedules class time for students to meet. The partners or groups may have rotating, assigned roles, such as "discussion director" or "illustrator" or "vocabulary enhancer" to give individuals accountability for the reading and ensure that each student has a voice in the group discussion (refer back to Figure 5.5). This kind of rich, open-ended literature discussion offers literature experiences to all students regardless of current reading level.

literature double entry journals ●

Another, less structured form of literature discussion groups uses **literature double entry journals** (see Figure 6.3). With this approach, students keep journal entries for every book they read. For each chapter or page assignment they are instructed to jot down quotes that strike them in some way. For example, the quote could remind them of something specific in their own life, or they could find the excerpt to be especially sad, humorous, interesting, or frightening. Students write their selected quotes on one side of the page and then write how the writing resonated with them on the other side. Later, in small share groups, students select some of their favorite excerpts to share with classmates and explain why they selected them. Other students are encouraged to articulate their own reactions to the selected material.

Informal Debates

When a whole-class discussion has revolved around a controversial issue and the class has seemingly taken sides on it, an informal debate can be a perfect avenue for combining critical thinking with informal speaking. First, the teach-

Excerpt from a literature double entry journal.   FIGURE 6.3

Double Entry Journal

Dmitra P.   Out of Nowhere (Scholastic, 1994)   by Ouida Sebestyen

Quote:	Response:
May had put her glasses on and was puzzling over a map when Harley got in. He didn't know what to say about the damage to her jug and food. He couldn't believe she was letting it pass. (p. 36)	That reminds me of last week when I spilled Coke all over the new carpet in the TV room. I expected my father to go ballistic but he just asked me to clean it up. He said the carpet was "stain resistant."
He turned to her. "I don't like you, either. Or your lying and mooching and drifting around and promising us a house." It was coming out for the first time ever, like a blast from a fire hose he couldn't turn off. (p. 91)	Harley <u>finally</u> lost his temper and told Vernie what he really thought. I have been angry like that but I'm always afraid I will destroy the relationship if I say what I really think.
Harley watched them go, amazed that they could walk out of his bad dream and leave him still in it. (p. 136)	When my parents got divorced, I remember my cousin coming over all happy and everything. Then she left and I kind of felt like Harley, like don't leave me in this nightmare!
"Oh, May," Singer breathed, and dropped to her knees. She picked up the kitten gently and gathered it close under her chin. "Oh, sweet baby," she crooned. (pp. 158–159)	I remember feeling just like that when we got our cat, Albert, from the SPCA. He was so tiny and fragile and I was so excited to have a real baby kitten.

er helps students to clarify what the issue is and what the opposing positions are. Then students are asked to move to opposite sides of the room, designated "opposers" and "supporters," depending on the position they have taken, and to appoint a spokesperson. If certain students have not made up their minds, they are asked to take a seat in the middle of the classroom. The opposing sides are then given 10 to 15 minutes to write down several arguments in support of their position. Next the teacher starts the debate by asking the spokesperson who is on the supporting side to make an opening statement. The opposition is then allowed to make a statement. After each of these statements has been made, both the neutral students and the opposing students may ask questions. After the debate, participants render an evaluation of the points made on both sides. No vote is required but some kind of consensus may emerge.

Some possible topics for informal debate are as follows:

- Should there be homework on weekends?
- Should we explore outer space?
- Should scientists be allowed to clone human beings?
- Should a woman become president of the United States?
- Should animals be allowed in restaurants?
- Should 12-year-olds be allowed to drive?

FORMAL SPEAKING

Oral reports, interviews, panel discussions, announcements, and impromptu speeches are some of the formal ways students can learn to organize information and fluently express ideas and information. Through extensive classroom conversations and discussions, students gain confidence from their experience talking in groups, where the responsibility for communication is shared with others. During the intermediate grades, students will be introduced to more formal oral language experiences that require more preparation. Following are instructional practices and activities that provide formal speaking experiences.

Oral Reports

oral reports • **Oral reports** are a way of sharing information and ideas before a group of people. Learning to prepare and deliver oral reports can be an important part of the curriculum, especially for intermediate-age students. It can be a positive, confidence-building event if authentic purposes are honored and adequate guidance in the process is provided. Teachers must remember (and convey to students) that research reports serve genuine language functions—to inform or (less frequently) persuade. When students give reports, they learn in-depth about the chosen topic and develop their communication abilities. Teachers must guide children through the four steps in preparing a report:

1. choosing a topic
2. gathering information
3. organizing the information
4. making the presentation

Choosing a topic. Oral reports are most successful when students are involved in choosing their own topic. Choice allows them to feel ownership of the project, which will often motivate them to invest more time and energy in the preparation. In some cases, students can choose any topic that interests them, but in other cases the teacher may need to limit students to a broad topic within an area of class study. Within this broad area, they are then free to choose their specific topics. For example, the class may be studying the gold rush. Students could choose within that broad area a variety of topics such as cultural groups involved, how to pan for gold, people's reasons for going West, or hardships encountered there.

Gathering information. Students should be guided to gather information from a variety of sources, including the Internet, academic software, encyclopedias, almanacs, books, magazines, and primary sources such as interviews (discussed later). In addition to these print sources, students should learn to use video excerpts and to talk with experts in the area they are studying. For more information on researching, see Chapter 8. Notes in the form of key words or phrases may be recorded on note cards or diagrams.

Organizing the information. Students will need to cull the information they have gathered and decide in what sequence to present it. They should be encouraged and shown how to create visual aids such as posters, graphs, pictures, models, or PowerPoint presentations, which serve to enhance audience interest and understanding. They may also choose an unusual format for presentation if it lends itself to their specific topic. For example, a short skit might help an audience gain insight into the decision-making process a family had to go through in order to make the journey West in the 1840s in their quest for gold.

Making the presentation. The final step in the oral report is the actual presentation. Students should rehearse the presentation several times by reviewing key points and reading over the note cards or diagrams they have prepared. Before the presentations begin, the teacher needs to discuss the critical points that students need to remember. For example, speakers should speak slowly and loudly enough for all to hear, keep to the main points, refer to their note cards as prompts for important information but not read them, and weave in the visuals they have prepared. They should also make eye contact with the audience and speak with expression as opposed to speaking in a monotone.

Students may present their oral reports to the whole class or to small groups of students. For example, have students studying the gold rush give their reports to groups of five or six students at a time. Groups may be spread around the room, listening to each report and asking questions and giving comments, and then rotating on to a different speaker. In this way, students will be giving their first formal report to a small group, which is less intimidating than a large one, and they will each get a chance to give their report four times, affording practice and refinement. When students are more experienced, they can give their oral reports in front of the whole class and perhaps be videotaped. In response to the presentations, the class can offer constructive feedback on the content and effectiveness of the presentation.

For information about assessing oral reports, see Chapter 2 and the scoring rubric for oral presentation in Appendix D.

Interviews

interview ● An **interview** is a form of oral information gathering. Interviewing is an important language tool that can be integrated effectively with almost any area of the curriculum. The interviewer may speak with one or two individuals or a small group of people. Interviewers gather information regarding an individual's life history, a group he or she is involved in (e.g., musical, political, or humanitarian), or a situation that concerns that person (e.g., recycling, crime, terrorism, or the ozone layer). Students may choose to interview local people, such as the principal, a local artist, a teacher, a spelling contest winner, or a person from a culture different from theirs. Students can also interview longtime area residents about local history, or even people who live far away—such as a favorite author or a professional athlete, using a long-distance telephone conference call. The interviewer prepares a set of questions that will obtain the desired information. The questions should be written on note cards, one per question, and consist of open-ended queries, as opposed to questions that could simply be answered "yes" or "no." For example, "Why did your family emigrate from Russia?" The questions should be organized according to related topics and reviewed by the teacher to ensure that they will elicit the information the interviewer is seeking. As they become more experienced, students can ask follow-up questions, such as, "Could you tell me a little bit more about that?"

Interviewers should make an appointment with the person or persons in advance. They should also learn as much as they can about the person prior to the interview. Interviewers often tape interviews (video or audio), but permission should be obtained before taping. If the interviewee does not permit taping, then the interviewer should carefully write down all responses. When the interview is complete, the interviewer should thank the person for his or her time and follow up with a written note to that effect.

To share the results, the interviewer should first carefully read over the notes or listen to the tape of the interview. Then the interviewer should organize the information and decide on a format for presenting it (see Figure 6.4).

Project presentation options.	FIGURE 6.4

Performance	Graphics/Visuals
report	poster
review	collage
panel	PowerPoint slides
debate	video excerpt, or i-movie
skit	time line
role play	map
simulation	mural
expert guest speaker	flow chart
	model
	overheads

Following is an informal interview activity to use early in the year to help the class become acquainted and feel comfortable asking questions, an important precursor to a more formal interview.

Getting to Know You   ACTIVITY

1. Elicit a set of questions about things students may or may not have done. For example:

HAVE YOU EVER . . .	DO YOU . . .	WHO IS . . .
been in a country other than the United States?	have a brother or a sister?	the person you admire most?
flown in an airplane?	have a pet?	your favorite singing group?
had a part in a play?	like to read?	
planted a garden?		your favorite TV star?
baby-sat?		your favorite movie star?
earned money?		

2. Write these questions on the board and ask students to copy them on a sheet of paper.

3. Divide the class in half. Designate half of the class as interviewers and the other half as interviewees.

4. Allow each interviewer to ask a few "off-the-cuff" questions in addition to the listed ones for variety. Instruct each interviewer to record all responses.

5. After the interviews are completed, have students switch roles and repeat the process.

6. Have the whole class compile the results in tallies, maps, or graphs, or use them in a bulletin board display entitled "Who Did What?"

Panel Discussions

A panel discussion is a favorite activity for formally sharing different kinds of information. The panel, usually consisting of three to eight members, conducts a discussion before the rest of the class. The topic, issue, or question is predetermined. The panel format is most effective when the presentation is thoughtful and informative rather than argumentative or spontaneous. When panelists conclude their presentations, class members are invited to ask them questions regarding a specific point that was made.

It is suggested that the teacher or panel members select a moderator. The moderator is responsible for organizing the panel to ensure that various points of view are represented and for monitoring the discussion so that all participants get an opportunity to be involved. A time limit should be placed on individual participation as well as the posing of questions by classmates. With practice, intermediate-age students will gain confidence in presenting information to their peers. Teachers are often surprised at how deeply student panelists will research a topic, given that it is a provocative subject.

The following is a variation on a panel discussion known as controlled participation, or CONPAR. The process was developed by General Motors for use with sales personnel in training sessions, but it is adapted here for use with children in the intermediate grades. CONPAR is one of the best methods to guarantee the participation and involvement of all members of a group, regardless of group size or the age of the participants.

ACTIVITY *Controlled Participation (CONPAR)*

1. Decide on a problem to be solved or a topic to be discussed.

2. Select three to eight panel members.

3. Give the panel members and other class members the assignment to find out everything they can about the topic or problem.

4. Divide the other class members into groups, seat the groups together, and label each group.

5. Select a chairperson, to keep the discussion going, for each group, as well as a recorder.

6. Allow 10 minutes for discussion about the problem or topic. Instruct students in each group to come up with three questions and have the recorder write these on note cards.

7. Have the groups turn in the cards and shuffle them. Then read aloud the questions, one at a time.

8. Invite one or more panel members to respond to each question. Limit each response to two minutes.

9. Read the second card aloud and ask different panel members to respond. Continue in this manner until all the questions have been answered.

10. At the end of the session take a few minutes to summarize key points that have been made.

Announcements

Announcements are common to all classroom situations and to all grade levels. Therefore, announcements are vehicles through which all children can learn how to deliver information clearly and concisely.

Some announcements are ineffectual because they do not express the ideas the speaker is trying to convey. Others are incomplete or simply fail to capture the listener's attention. As with most oral literacy activities, the teacher should first model how to make an effective announcement to offer children an example worth imitating. When preparing an announcement, the speaker should create an introduction that will grab the listener's attention. Then the essential information (what, where, why, when, who, and how) should be shared and restated. The message should be brief without sacrificing accuracy or clarity. Before the announcement is delivered, the speaker should practice saying it aloud in a clear, audible voice.

Children can practice making announcements by reading the lunch menu, participating in the morning routine of opening exercises, or explaining school activities on the public address system. See Figure 6.5 for an example of an effective announcement.

Example of a fifth-grader's announcement. FIGURE 6.5

Hey, kids! Did you hear about the awesome book fair coming to Aerohaven School? Well, this is your chance to buy all of the books you love in science fiction, romance, drama, historical fiction, poetry, and fantasy. Yes—there will even be all the Harry Potter books! And the best part is that they are all 20 percent cheaper than you can buy them in any bookstore! The book fair will be held in the cafeteria on Thursday, October 9, after school from 3 to 5:30. Hurry down there, because the first 30 book buyers will receive a free Kobe Bryant poster. See you there!

Impromptu Speeches

impromptu speech ●

An **impromptu speech** can be defined as a talk that is prepared without extensive planning, thus requiring a modicum of creativity and "thinking on one's feet" for children. The ability to give an impromptu speech is a very important oral language skill to develop because it is perhaps the one that will be used the most often in a child's later life.

To stimulate this type of formal speaking, prepare several 3 × 5 cards with provocative topics for students, such as "The strangest dream I ever had." Have each student select a card and then allow a few moments for the student to think about the topic. In a comfortable and safe small-group setting, invite each student to speak for three minutes on the topic on his or her card. Evaluations of this type of speaking should be supportive and positive. The following are additional examples of topics to use for impromptu speeches:

> My favorite thing to do
>
> If I were stranded on a desert island
>
> Why conservation is important
>
> The best movie I have ever seen
>
> The person I most admire
>
> Things that make me happy
>
> Things I would like to change about the world
>
> Things I do on weekends
>
> A place I have been
>
> If I were an animal

DRAMA

Drama is an integral part of a balanced and comprehensive literacy program for the middle grades. Classroom drama is an incomparable forum for language enjoyment, enriched comprehension, and community building. Additionally, drama can be a powerful way of learning and an alternative way of knowing—the actors become participants in the learning process and not merely passive bystanders (Wagner, 1976). Drama makes especially strong contributions to the growth of the speaking ability of English language learners, because it provides natural comprehensible input: the words that are uttered are provided with an immediate context by the actions accompanying it. Furthermore, drama gives students opportunities to experiment with words, emotions, and social roles and encourages them to make sense out of their world in a multisensory way. Above all, through drama, students become more sensitive, confident communicators.

In this section, we explore three types of drama well suited to children in the middle grades: role plays, simulations, and dramatic productions.

Role Plays

The term *role playing* is used to refer to a type of playacting in the classroom. By definition, **role playing** is a dramatic oral language activity in which children explore, in the most intimate way, the relationships of human living for the purpose of acquiring needed understandings and intrapersonal communication skills. But unlike the dramatic play common to most primary classrooms, role playing can be structured for older children to be imbued with clear goals and desired outcomes. And unlike more formally structured theatrical presentations, in which set lines are read or memorized, role playing unfolds rather spontaneously, without a predetermined script. It uses the dramatic elements of characterization and dialogue. Empathy for another's point of view is usually heightened because the actor is attempting to take on the internal characteristics of the person who is being emulated.

● role playing

In the intermediate grades, role plays can grow out of current daily situations, problems, past episodes, or dilemmas students may soon face, such as moving to a new grade. At times, the situation itself is the point of departure; at other times, the teacher sets the scene for the role play. Still another approach to role playing is to bring to life a favorite piece of children's literature in which there are complex relationships to be understood and rich opportunities for characterization, as will be discussed later. Lee Galda (1982) conducted a study in which a teacher read a familiar folktale to the class and then divided the students into three groups. The first group drew a picture about the story, the second group discussed the story, and the third group did a role play of the story. According to scores on a subsequent comprehension test and a retelling of the story, the dramatic activity was significantly more beneficial in deepening the students' understanding of the text.

Whether the situation enacted is a real-life experience that just took place, a story, an important concept, or a hypothetical event, the process through which language and literacy learning can evolve the most dynamically is through role play. Allow children to reflectively reenact an argument and they will develop insight and communication skills; let them simulate concepts through drama and what is unclear will be made clear and what is remote will become near and alive (Cecil, 1994).

Problem Solving/Conflict Management Through Role Plays

Consider the following scenario from a fifth-grade playground, typical of what occurs daily on playgrounds all across the country, at recess:

Vlade: I'm getting tired of playing kickball every day. Today, why don't we play soccer instead?

Jason: Nah, let's not play soccer. I don't know how to. Besides, soccer's a sissy game. Let's just play kickball like we always do, or baseball.

Raúl: Uh uh. I like Vlade's idea. Let's play soccer for a change. I'll be the captain and Vlade can be the other captain. Let's choose up sides!

Jason: *No way!* I have the ball and you can't have it if you're going to play soccer.

Vlade: You are such a loser! I'm telling the teacher!

Jason: Go ahead! She'll take my side—she likes me!

Raúl: All right, Jason, just give me the ball right now or I'm gonna beat you up.

Jason: Oh, yeah? You and what army?

Role Play can be used to resolve conflicts

In the next few moments, of course, the argument escalates. Normally, this type of situation ends with angry feelings all around, as the teacher on recess duty reprimands all three boys and/or sends them to the principal's office.

Role playing is the vehicle through which such a commonplace scenario might be transformed into a dynamic oral language/social studies lesson, not only for the students directly involved, but for the rest of the class as well. Because a variety of solutions are available for dealing with any conflict, role playing and discussing these options can provide insights into what causes conflicts and what effects can be expected with varying solutions.

ACTIVITY   *Role Play*

To help students gain insight from the previously mentioned scenario, or another you create, guide students through the following activity:

1. Have a neutral observer from the class give his or her version of what took place.

2. Select students to play the roles of each person involved.

3. Ask the actors to take a few moments to prepare two role plays: the first a reenactment of the situation as it actually occurred, and a second that changes the outcome to a more positive solution to the conflict.

4. As the actors are preparing their role plays, instruct the other students as follows: "Watch what the actors do and say. Try to put yourself in their shoes and feel what they must be feeling. As you watch, be thinking of other ways the conflict could have been resolved."

5. Have the actors present their role plays in the center of the classroom, surrounded by other class members.

6. Discuss the differences in the outcomes of the two role plays. Invite other class members to contribute their alternative solutions to the problem. Write these on the board without evaluation.

7. Discuss the "cause" and "effect" patterns in the two role plays in terms of words or actions and resultant feelings and events.

For the particular actual playground scenario with Jason, Raúl, and Vlade, the three students might be asked to play themselves in the reenactment; or, to develop more insight into each other's point of view, they could be asked to switch roles. The three boys' alternative solution to the conflict might take the form of Vlade conceding that they will play kickball again as they always do. Other class members who have watched both role plays dispassionately may have some different suggestions for them; for example, since Jason has admitted that he doesn't know how to play soccer, might Vlade and Raúl teach him how to play? Could they set up a rotating schedule of playing soccer one day, kickball the next, and baseball the following day? What if they agreed to toss a coin each day to decide which game would be played?

Subsequently, through a teacher-guided reflective discussion, all the students in the class can begin to see exactly which turn of events caused the buildup of bad feelings that resulted in three friends arguing instead of communicating effectively to solve their conflict. Moreover, the entire class has orally problem solved ways for such an unfortunate event not to be repeated, while second language learners have been provided with a rich context—the role play—for the ensuing discussion. To further reinforce the concept of role play, a relevant children's literature selection could be read and discussed as a follow-up activity.

Role Playing Characters in Children's Literature

When reading a book with many complex characters with a group of students in the intermediate grades, role playing can help make the characters come alive and enable children to discover the relationship between what they are reading and their own lives.

Role playing of literature can be used with many favorite children's stories, but those with many characters are best suited. For this activity, children can be assigned to partners, with shy children paired with more outgoing ones. The names of all the characters in the book are written on the board and then each pair is assigned to one character, or to the author or illustrator of the book. The characters assigned for a Harry Potter novel, for example, might be these:

J. K. Rowling	Harry Potter	Ron Weasly
Hermione Granger	Professor Dumbledore	Lord Voldemort
Draco Malfoy	Hagrid	Uncle Vernon Dursley
Neville Longbottom	Crookshanks	Nearly Headless Nick

After reading the book, students are asked to reread it in order to study their own character's contribution to the text. Each pair discusses their character's personality, behaviors, and motivation. Then they create a list of at least three questions that their character might wish to ask another character in the book, including questions that go beyond the scope of the book. For example, Hagrid might ask: "Draco, what happened in your early childhood that made you such an awful little boy?" Similarly, Neville Longbottom might ask Harry, "How do you steer and control the speed of your broomstick during a quidditch match?" Or Hermione Granger might ask, "Lord Voldemort, what would you do to defeat Professor Dumbledore in a duel?"

After the preparation phase is completed, students are ready for the role playing. Students should be seated in a circle. Simple costumes can add to the characterization, or character name tags may be used so other class members will be able to recognize the characters they wish to question. Members of each pair take turns answering the questions, although they are free to consult.

The teacher opens the session by asking the character on his or her left the first question. For example, "Professor Dumbledore, are there any Muggles who can perform real magic?" Then pair by pair students ask a question of a different character until each pair gets a turn to role play, although students should be encouraged to ask follow-up questions related to previous ones, such as, "You said, J. K. Rowling, that you have three more books to write about Harry Potter. What do you think Harry will discover in the next book?"

Similar role plays can be created with any number of children's books that contain a large cast of three-dimensional characters that in some way reflect real life. Children not only gain a deeper appreciation of the characters and new insights into themselves, but they can actually bring the characters to life, investigating another's feelings and motives, enlightened by the characters who have become infinitely more memorable.

Mock Interviews

Some years ago, the late Steve Allen hosted a program called "Meeting of the Minds" on which he would question, or do a "mock interview," of noted historical figures of the past who were played by actors. A fascinating discussion would ensue as Mr. Allen asked his pretend guests—often such interesting pairings as Marie Curie and Sigmund Freud—probing questions relating to their thoughts on current problems in the world today.

Upper elementary children will thoroughly enjoy similar role plays in the classroom. Such an oral language activity becomes a self-motivating reason to do historical research, because such labor will, in this situation, lead to a chance to become, for a short while, a very famous person.

To prepare for the mock interview, a pair of students must decide on a historical figure, preferably one who has been studied in class or is familiar to the rest of the class. The pair must then research the person thoroughly—

using the Internet, videos, books, magazine articles, and other resources—so that they can become intimately acquainted with the significant events of the person's life, his or her personality, style of dress, opinions or political stances, mannerisms, style of speech, and perhaps even memorize some of the particular quotations for which the person is best known. Among the historical figures who will work well for intermediate grade students are the following:

Nelson Mandela	Will Rogers	Mahatma Gandhi
Golda Meir	Jesse Owens	Albert Schweitzer
Wilt Chamberlain	John F. Kennedy	Abraham Lincoln
Martin Luther King, Jr.	Clara Barton	Amelia Earhart
Harriet Tubman	Arthur Ashe	Ludwig von
Mother Teresa	Jacques Cousteau	Beethoven

Next, from the research the pair draws up a list of questions that would ask their historical figure to project how he or she would respond to current world issues or events. For example, Abraham Lincoln might be asked, "What are your thoughts on apartheid?" or "How do you feel about civil rights?" The actor's response would be largely based on what the two researchers have discovered about Lincoln's contributions to the abolition of slavery, as well as their general understanding of the man's core values.

For the presentation, the pair decides who will play the part of the historical figure and who will be the interviewer and ask the prearranged questions. After the interview session, the rest of the class, who have been taking notes, are encouraged to ask their own questions of the historical figure, while the actor playing that part tries to "think in character" and respond as the person might actually have responded.

The follow-up discussion is a time for the teacher and the students to try to clear up any inconsistencies between what they know about the historical figure and the actor's responses, providing documented reasons for their objections to what was said by the actor. For example, if a student playing the role of Mahatma Gandhi has stated that he would support a war in the Mideast, an audience member could remind the actor about the implications of Gandhi's credo of passive resistance. Most important, during the reflective discussion there must be ample time to share new insights and appreciation for the historical figure in his or her now human, multidimensional form and to explore any new questions or concerns that were raised.

Simulations

Sometimes, in the course of working with intermediate-age students, it becomes clear that all the verbalization in the world is failing to get across an important concept or idea. In such a situation, it is sometimes advisable to preplan an experience where the students can actually simulate—or vicariously play out—the concept. Although many excellent computer programs are now available to provide simulations of everything from creating an entire city to avoiding a war, oral simulations provide the ideal vehicle through which to enhance oral language as well as include second language learners.

Acting out an idea brings about a sense of discovery of the concept being introduced and also offers, in many cases, a visceral response that is not soon forgotten. Setting the stage for such discovery through simulation is often time consuming, and therefore not feasible for every concept that is addressed. Some concepts, however, such as the two prototypical activities described next, are worth the time and effort involved.

ACTIVITY *Haves and Have Nots*

It is hoped that most of the students we teach will never go to bed hungry, but it is important for them to understand the concept of "poverty" and all that it entails, in order for them to empathize fully with two-thirds of the world's population. Children, particularly in middle-class culture, take it for granted that their basic needs will be met, and therefore grow up quite insulated from, and apathetic to, the desperate concerns of those who are less fortunate. To launch a thematic unit featuring a novel set in the Holocaust or to give students a brief glimpse of how inequitable it is to have the world's wealth so unevenly distributed, do the following:

1. Arrange with the school cafeteria to provide lunch for only one-third of your students for one day. For another third, bring in small amounts of white rice and small bowls. The remaining third will receive no lunch. (Note: Letters must be sent to parents well in advance, explaining the educational objectives of this temporary change in routine.)

2. Explain to students that they will be taking part in a very important social experiment and that you will discuss the reasons later. Encourage them to write down all their questions, feelings, and complaints about the event, which will be addressed during the later discussion.

3. To begin the simulation, assign students to groups, at random, based on receipt of a blue (full lunch), red (bowl of rice), or yellow (no lunch) card that will determine what their lunch fare will be. There will, of course, be much moaning and groaning from those students who received only a bowl of rice, more so from students who were given no lunch. Make it clear to these particular students that they may not buy any other food, but that they are free to ask the other students to share their food, although they are not obligated to do so.

4. The next day, when hunger and anger have abated, encourage the three groups of students to vent their feelings and share their written records. As the yellow group complains that being given nothing to eat was unfair, they are now ready to hear that one-third of the people in the world have nothing to eat on a daily basis.

5. Poll the red and yellow groups to see how many received something to eat from the blue group. They are now ready to understand the concept of "charity" and explain how important it can be for those who are destitute.

6. Discuss the analogy of the simulation to the real world and conduct a brainstorming session so students can think of ways to ease world poverty.

Prejudice

Much has been written about some very intense simulations of prejudice that were carried to such an extreme that students were psychologically damaged when the teacher and students apparently began to lose touch with what was simulation and what was reality. Rest assured that a more reasoned simulation can have the desired effect without causing lasting harm.

The following simulation can enhance a multicultural unit in social studies. Because of the anger and frustration that this simulation quite naturally produces, the activity should not continue for more than a morning or afternoon, at most, and, of course, parents should be advised of the intentions of the simulation in advance.

1. Categorize students, artificially, as "good" or "bad" according to some trait over which they have no control, such as the color of their eyes or their gender. If eye color is chosen, for example, tell students that those with brown eyes will now have special privileges, such as being the first to go to lunch and extra computer time. Throughout the simulation period, they will receive many other special privileges, simply because of the color of their eyes.

Brown Eyed vs. Blue Eyed.

2. When students question this favoritism, tell them that brown-eyed students are receiving special privileges because some people might believe that brown-eyed children are superior to children with other eye color.

3. When the time for the simulation is up, conduct an oral debriefing. Divide the chalkboard into two columns. Have the brown-eyed children share their feelings and reactions to the special treatment, and then the children with other eye color. Summarize the student's contributions on the board.

4. Explain that, although this was a rather unfair exercise, many people really do judge people merely on the basis of the color of their skin, their gender, or other traits they can do nothing about.

5. Lead a reflective discussion on how this activity might change the way participants behave toward others in the future.

Dramatic Productions

The ultimate goal of the drama component in a balanced and comprehensive literacy program for students in the intermediate grades is to have students eventually create and put on their own plays, thus bringing to life words, feelings, and ideas that have personal significance to them. Writing plays, however, demands some experience with the play as a unique form of expression, and many teachers today feel so pressured to teach skills that will be measured in annual testing that they tend to devalue this critical oral language activity, even though such language activities can actually help prepare students to do well on standardized tests.

It is often helpful to "work students up" to the goal of actually writing their own plays, especially if they have had little or no previous experience with formal drama. To minimize frustration, dramatic productions can be introduced in two phases: First, stories and books shared in literature circles or through guided reading (see Chapter 5) are read dramatically in readers theatre, or are recalled, blocked, and turned into plays by students. Particular conventions of scripts are pointed out to students through minilessons. With this background of script reading and the creating of characters, settings, and actions, students are ready to write and take part in their own original plays.

Readers Theatre: Turning Stories into Plays

Readers theatre is an oral interpretation strategy that provides an excellent opportunity for creative thinking, oral expression, practicing fluency skills, developing self-confidence, and teamwork to achieve common goals. It becomes a means to reinforce narrative structure through the language arts of reading, writing, listening, speaking, and viewing. Perhaps the most important benefit of readers theatre, however, is the satisfying practice it affords of speaking informally before an audience and having an enjoyable experience with literature. See Chapter 3 for a detailed description of this activity.

Creating Original Drama

Many intermediate-age students will enjoy writing their own original scripts for puppet shows, skits, and formal productions. Such activities offer teachers an excellent opportunity to integrate the language arts because in order to write scripts, students will be discussing, writing, and then producing their work. Frequently, students enjoy working together to write the scripts, providing a remarkably natural vehicle for focused conversations.

Students can study existing play scripts to learn the layout and specific conventions used in preparing scripts. After students have read some plays in readers theatre format, looked at commercial scripts, and minilessons have reinforced the conventions used in script writing, they can write an original script using their own creativity. Students have become sufficiently adept at utilizing commercial scripts when they can memorize or paraphrase their lines, speak them on cue, and create appropriate characterizations. As students go from reading and acting out the words of others to bringing

Structure for creating original drama (adapted from Block, 2000). FIGURE 6.6

To help students create an original script, ask them to consider the following four strands that constitute a complete drama:

(1) ROLES (OR IDENTITY)	(2) PLACE (OR SITUATION)	(3) FOCUS (OR ISSUE)	(4) CONFLICT (OR PROBLEM)
Who are you?	Where are you?	What is the play about?	What is the problem that needs solving?
Examples:	Examples:	Examples:	Examples:
a compassionate nurse	a hospital	saving lives and caring	nurse gets a disease
a sad soldier	a barracks	missing loved ones	soldier can't kill
a benevolent alien	a corn field	accepting differences	alien is feared

their own words to life, they are given an enormous sense of pride and ownership from the cooperative undertaking. Figure 6.6 identifies a structure students can follow to create their own scripts.

To ensure the success of play writing, the most ambitious phase of the drama component in a balanced and comprehensive literacy program, the following suggestions may be helpful:

- Begin with simple one-act skits.
- Divide students into small, cooperative groups.
- Provide each group with a "plot" or structure from which to build.
- Eliminate makeup, which is distracting.
- Do not use prompters, thus encouraging students to learn each other's lines.
- Allow "spontaneous paraphrasing" of the script.

Although all dramatic enterprises fare best with an audience, the first skits do not necessarily require a stage or extensive props and scenery; in fact, a "propless playlet" has the advantage of increasing student's ability to imagine and can easily move from classroom to classroom. This way, children are not overwhelmed by large crowds, nor must they shout to be heard for their first efforts.

LISTENING INSTRUCTION

Research suggests that children who receive direct practice in listening comprehend better than children who have not received this instruction; listening plays a crucial, although often ignored, role in the literacy development of children,

especially those for whom English is a second language (Au, 1993; Devine, 1982). Research conducted by Pearson (1985) with students in the intermediate grades produced especially positive results. These researchers reached the following conclusions based on their synthesis of research on listening instruction:

1. Listening practice in the same skills typically taught in reading instruction (i.e., getting the main idea, comparing and contrasting) tends to improve comprehension in both listening and reading.

2. Listening comprehension is enhanced through students offering personal verbal reactions during and after listening.

3. Reading literature aloud to students tends to improve listening comprehension.

4. All the language arts tend to reinforce one another; in other words, instruction in either reading, writing, listening, or speaking is correlated with gains in the other three.

5. Direct teaching of listening strategies seems to help students become more conscious of their listening habits than less explicit approaches do.

Designing Listening Instruction

Listening instruction must be a major part of the curriculum if it is to improve students' listening ability. To increase listening comprehension, it should be integrated into daily lesson plans rather than a "one-shot," infrequent activity. Five to 10 minutes a day of listening instruction or practice is generally more effective than longer, less frequent lessons.

Listening comprehension should focus on teaching students strategies they can use to listen, while listening activities can be included to give students an opportunity to practice these skills in various settings. Above all, listening instruction should provide for transfer of listening skills from practice situations to actual use in the classroom and beyond. Ideally, listening comprehension should be an integral piece of content area instruction through reading to children, modeling one's thinking, and asking thought-provoking questions; listening for the main idea in practice material should be quickly transferred to social studies or science content material.

Successful listening instruction encourages students to listen to meet their own needs, interests, and desires. For instance, students who are listening to complete an assignment, create an argument for escaping punishment, find out how to build a project, or simply listening to a story for pleasure have differing purposes for attending, yet each situation is authentic and very important to them. The suggested teaching guidelines that follow develop both active listening and oral responses, because research shows that such responses result in optimal listening skill development:

1. Always set a purpose for listening by asking questions that will focus thought and encourage students to predict what will be included in the content.

Effective Listening Skills

When attempting to list skills needed for effective listening, it is important to understand that the needed skills vary depending on the *purpose* for listening. We use different skills when we listen to learn than we do when we need to make critical decisions or when we are simply listening for enjoyment. Here are a few of the many purposes for listening and some of the related skills:

- *Listening for learning:* Skills include using memory techniques (e.g., rhyming, acronyms, and acrostics), listening for main ideas (have students paraphrase a message to assess their understanding of it), and taking notes.

- *Empathetic listening:* Skills include focusing attention on the speaker (including looking at the speaker and resisting distractions) and reacting with appropriate verbal and nonverbal clues (including nodding one's head and displaying appropriate facial expressions).

- *Critical listening:* Skills include learning to make informed decisions or judgments based on what is heard (such as when students must evaluate requests made of them by peers and adults) and learning to understand, judge, and evaluate information (such as when we question what we read and see and evaluate sources). Critical listening is very important in student interactions with media.

Teachers and their students must learn to distinguish among different types of listening so that the appropriate skills can be learned and applied.

From P. Cooper and S. Morreale (Eds.), 2003. *Creating competent communicators: Activities for teaching speaking, listening, and media literacy in K–6 classrooms* (p. 44). Scottsdale, AZ: Holcomb Hathaway.

2. Look for the structure of the content of expository material. Has the author organized the passage through comparison, contrast, sequentially, or simple enumeration? Brain researchers tell us that human beings naturally seek patterns in their experience. Use this tendency to point out to students the patterns in the text they are listening to.

3. When reading to students, categorize, relate, and associate ideas with those that are already familiar to them. Give students guided practice, doing this as well by encouraging them to ask questions such as: How does this concern me? How does this relate to what I already know? What does this remind me of in my own life? How can I apply this information?

4. Summarize periodically as you are reading to students. In summarizing, the main ideas are identified and related briefly. Stop occasionally and encourage students to summarize also, in their minds, orally, or on paper.

5. Make oral or written responses to content and invite students to add their ideas to yours. This, as much as any other strategy, helps students to become active listeners and thinkers. Moreover, encourage students to listen with pencil in hand. This offers them a minimal structure for response, allows for physical involvement, and is a link to note taking.

6. Provide a structure for responding to a presentation, such as the following:
   - What was the speaker's purpose (persuading, informing, sharing, etc.)?
   - List five ideas the speaker had.
   - Write a three-sentence summary of the presentation.
   - Write down two things that you would now like to know more about.

ACTIVITY *Listening Comprehension* (Adapted from Block, 2000)

The following activity can be used to help students practice the skills of listening comprehension. (See Cooper and Morreale [2003] for additional activities that teach listening skills.) This activity can also be used to help teachers diagnose problems individual students have with listening comprehension.

1. Pair students and provide each pair with an unfamiliar short story on their instructional level.

2. For each pair, select one student to be the reader and the other to be the listener.

3. Have the reader read two pages silently and then "tell" the two pages to the listener.

4. Once the story has been read and retold in this way, have the listener summarize the entire story to the reader.

5. Have the reader write down everything the listener has said.

6. Have the pair look at the book together and compare it to the written retelling.

7. Have the pair discuss why certain parts were not included in the original retellings or the final summary (e.g., "not important," "didn't hear it," "didn't remember that part").

8. Have the pair note the parts omitted on the back of the story summary sheet, along with the listener's explanation for each part's absence.

9. Have partners switch roles and repeat the process.

10. Analyze each student's listening comprehension strengths and needs. Students can also be encouraged to assess their own listening skills by using the checklist provided in Appendix D.

TROUBLESHOOTING

The oral language skills—and confidence—of every learner can be enhanced through ample practice speaking and performing before a group of caring and supportive peers. However, there are several universal oral language concerns that may need to be addressed in the intermediate-grade classroom when they occur.

Dominating a Discussion

Students who tend to dominate conversations and discussions and do not listen to others can cause other students to withdraw entirely in any oral language situation. Teachers can help such students by providing them with specific listening purposes and then discussing these purposes with students after the oral language event. Another alternative is to advise such students that every student will have one turn to share ideas in the particular oral language event to ensure that everyone gets a chance to speak. Finally, a successful concentration strategy that some teachers use is to teach all students to stop, listen, and think before they hold

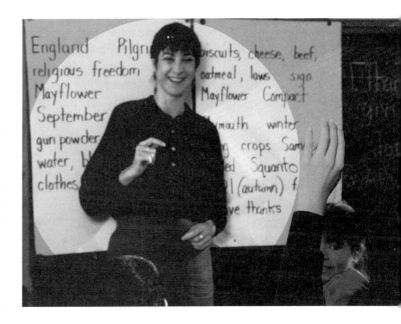

up their hand. Making individual stop signs also helps them to remember the three steps of stop, listen, and think before participating in any discussion. After every student is cognizant of this strategy, students begin to monitor each other to be sure that everyone listens and thinks before they speak.

Lack of Verbal Skills in English

If students are in the initial stages of learning to speak English, the best course of action is to allow those students the time they need to emerge from their "silent period," before they say their first words in a new language.

code switching ●

Concentrate on building students' receptive language and allow gestures and other nonverbal cues to communicate with them. Make certain the classroom environment is supportive and safe to the degree that other classmates are rooting for these students to say their first English words. Additionally, in any oral or written language venture, encourage **code switching,** or having students speak some words in English and other words they do not know in their home language. Finally, totally disregard grammar and accent concerns whenever these students do speak. Concentrate only on understanding what they are attempting to communicate. Then, paraphrase their contribution in standard English while expressing appreciation for their participation.

Lack of Participation

In many teacher-controlled classrooms, it appears that a student who rarely speaks is a blessing, but it seems axiomatic that students must be allowed plenty of opportunity to talk in order to process their ideas and learn on a deeper level; moreover, in our society the ability to speak fluently is arguably even more of an asset than the ability to read and write.

Some students who will not participate in large- or even small-group oral language events can practice speaking and become more comfortable doing it by conducting a series of speaking activities using a tape recorder. This has the added benefit of affording the teacher an opportunity to assess oral language development to determine whether there is an underlying language problem that is causing the student to refrain from speaking out, or if the student is simply shy. Additionally, some shy students will speak fluently with the aid of a prop such as a puppet or a model that turns attention away from them; similarly, shy students can often be coaxed to take part in a dramatic activity, and many even seem to "bloom" when they are able to don a different persona. In addition to shyness, some children may experience higher levels of nervousness and anxiety than their peers when speaking in front of others. Communication specialists refer to this as **communication apprehension.** The Personal Report of Communication Fear (PRCF) provided in Appendix D will help you to determine if a child is communication apprehensive. These children will benefit from the same type of oral activities as shy children and should be encouraged to speak as often as possible to reduce their fears.

communication apprehension ●

Limited Voice Projection

A commonly reported problem with oral language activities in the intermediate grades is that many students speak so softly that they cannot be heard. This becomes a distinct problem when other classmates have been urged to listen politely. After a few minutes of straining their ears, even the most courteous of youngsters will begin to turn their attention elsewhere.

Students must learn to lift their heads up and project their voice. One way to achieve this is to have children stand at their desks and project (not shout) the phrase, "How now brown cow!" and to tell them to "throw their words across the room and make them bounce off the opposite wall of the classroom." Additionally, choral reading, singing camp songs, and readers theatre provide opportunities to practice projecting one's voice.

SUMMARY

It is easy, but erroneous, to assume that students, especially if they are native English speakers, have already developed their oral language abilities. With such an assumption, we can often overlook the importance of helping students further their ability to speak confidently in many different situations. The basic curriculum cornerstones of reading and math take precedence over most other parts of the curriculum, and talk is not often interwoven effectively into content areas. However, oral language must be continually nurtured in a balanced and comprehensive literacy program for upper elementary grade school students, for speech is the most widely used of the expressive forms of discourse. Moreover, proficiency in speaking enhances ability in all the other language arts.

The foundation for a sound oral language program is the variety of spontaneous and planned speaking situations that occur every day in most classrooms. Opportunities for instruction in oral language occur frequently in the intermediate grade classroom. They include informal speaking, as in casual conversations and discussions, and more formal speaking, as in oral reports, interviews, panel discussions, and debates.

Finally, there is no better avenue than drama to channel the boundless energy and emotions of students in the intermediate grades. Drama is a way of learning as well as a communication mode. Students thrive on a medium that allows them to create with their minds and bodies using expressive movements as well as their words. In addition, drama may be the prime vehicle to attach words with concepts in authentic context for the benefit of English language learners. Finally, used on a routine basis, the recognition and community building afforded by drama can enhance the self-esteem of all learners. One budding fifth-grade actor summed it up this way: "I helped to write this play and put it on with my class. I got to be the biker dude and I also sang a song that had 'em rolling in the aisles. I also helped everybody else remember their lines. I usually hate writing and talking in front of the class, but this was more fun than summer camp!"

Questions

1. Of the four interrelated literacy skills of reading, writing, listening, and speaking, which, if any, do you believe to be the most important? Why? Defend your answer.

2. Recall a time in the intermediate grades when you were in a skit or a play. What was your role and how did you prepare for it? What else do you remember about this event? How do you feel such activities can be conducive to confident oral speaking for native English speakers in a classroom? For second language learners?

3. Respond to the following statement that an uninformed parent might make: "An oral language program in the intermediate grades is a waste of time, because children spend plenty of time talking on the playground and at home." How would your argument change if there were several second language learners in your classroom?

Suggestions

1. Find a teacher in the intermediate grades who is currently preparing a dramatic production with students. Discuss with the teacher his or her reasons for using this instructional activity. Observe the students as they practice their roles. Are all the students involved? In what capacities? What are the major oral language goals that you believe are being achieved through this activity?

2. Observe a class giving oral reports. In what ways, if any, are students encouraged to use technology and other multimedia materials to enhance their presentations? How has the delivery of oral presentations changed since you were in school?

3. After carefully reviewing the guidelines on p. 166, lead a discussion with a small group of intermediate-age students on a controversial topic, such as "Is homework a necessary evil?" Reflect afterward and share your reflections with the rest of the class. What went well? What was difficult? What would you do differently next time?

References

Au, K. H. (1993). *Literacy instruction in multicultural settings*. Fort Worth, TX: Harcourt Brace Jovanovich.

Block, C. C. (2000). *Teaching the language arts: Expanding thinking through student-centered instruction* (3rd ed.). Needham Heights, MA: Allyn & Bacon.

Cazden, C. (1986). Classroom discourse. In M. C. Whitrock (Ed.), *Handbook of research on teaching* (3rd ed., pp. 432–463). New York: Macmillan.

Cecil, N. L. (1994). Role playing: Trying life on for size. In N. L. Cecil (Ed.), *Freedom fighters: Affective teaching of the language arts*. Salem, WI: Sheffield.

Cooper, P. & Morreale, S. (Eds.). *Creating competent communicators: Activities for teaching speaking, listening, and media literacy in K–6 classrooms* (p. 44). Scottsdale, AZ: Holcomb Hathaway.

Daniels, H. (1994). *Literature circles: Voice and choice in the student-centered classroom*. York, ME: Stenhouse.

Devine, T. T. G. (1982). *Listening skills schoolwide: Activities and progress*. Urbana, IL: National Council of Teachers of English.

Eeds, M., & Wells, D. (1989). Grand conversations: An exploration of meaning construction in literature study groups. *Research in the Teaching of English, 23*(1), 4–29.

Galda, L. (1982). Playing about a story: Its impact on comprehension. *The Reading Teacher, 36,* 52–56.

Gambrell, L. B., & Almasi, J. F. (1996). *Lively discussions! Fostering engaged reading*. Newark, DE: International Reading Association.

Heath, S. (1983). *Ways with words*. London: Cambridge University Press.

Loban, W. (1976). *The complete book of language development: Kindergarten through grade twelve*. Urbana, IL: National Council of Teachers of English.

Martinez, M., Roser, N. L., & Strecker, S. (1998/1999). I never thought I could be a star: A reader's theatre ticket to fluency. *The Reading Teacher, 52,* 326–334.

McMahon, S. I., & Raphael, T. E. (Eds.). (1997). *The book club connection: Literacy learning and classroom talk*. Newark, DE: The International Reading Association.

Paratore, J. R., & McCormack, R. L. (1998). *Peer talk in the classroom: Learning from research*. Newark, DE: International Reading Association.

Pearson, P. D. (1985). Changing the face of reading comprehension instruction. *The Reading Teacher, 38*(8), 724–738.

Peregoy, S. F., & Boyle, O. F. (1993). *Reading, writing, & learning in ESL*. White Plains, NY: Longman.

Roser, N. L., & Martinez, M. G. (Eds.). (1995). *Book talk and beyond: Children and teachers respond to literature*. Newark, DE: International Reading Association.

Sampson, M. R. (1986). *The pursuit of literacy: Early reading and writing*. Dubuque, IA: Kendall/Hunt.

Samway, K. D., Whang, G., Cade, C., Gamil, M., Lubandina, M. A., & Phom Machanh, K. (1991). Reading the skeleton, the heart, and the brain of a book: Students' perspectives on literature study circles. *The Reading Teacher, 45,* 196–205.

Smith, K. (1998). Entertaining a text: A reciprocal process. In K. G. Short & K. M. Pierce (Eds.), *Talking about books: Literature discussion groups in K–8 classrooms* (pp. 17–31). Portsmouth, NH: Heinemann.

Smith, P. G. (2001). *Talking classrooms: Shaping children's learning through oral language instruction*. Newark, DE: International Reading Association.

Wagner, B. J. (1976). *Dorothy Heathcole: Drama as a learning medium*. Washington, DC: National Education Association.

CHAPTER 7
Reading and Writing Connections

- What are the components for an effective writing program in the intermediate grades?

- What is writer's workshop and how can it help students to become skilled and motivated writers?

- How can teaching the six traits of effective writing provide a common vocabulary for both narrative and expository writing?

In the Classroom

The students in Mrs. McCray's fifth-grade class have just returned from lunch. They eagerly head for the file full of individually decorated writing folders in the back of the classroom. Each student has his or her own folder in which papers are kept related to the writing projects he or she is working on. As the students retrieve their folders, they quickly sit down at their desks, arranged in small groups. Three students are sitting at computers, using a word-processing program to neatly print out their final draft of pieces they have been working on all week. Some students are quietly discussing new writing ideas with a classmate. Other students are writing intently, while still others are sharing their drafts with their classmates—or "peer editors"—who offer suggestions about content or writing conventions, as requested by the author. Everyone is focused and clearly on task, yet working at their own pace.

At her desk, Mrs. McCray conferences briefly with several students: the rest of the students will be engaged in such encounters over the remainder of the week. During these one- to two-minute sessions, Mrs. McCray asks individual students to quietly talk about what they are writing, listens to them read a paragraph or two of their work, and questions them about what they are planning to do next. Hoa, for example, explains that yesterday she received valuable input from her peer editor, so she is now going to correct spelling mistakes and add a more exciting opening idea that will better "grab" her audience.

Other students are at the revising stage of writing. Jessie and Alyce sign up to meet with Mrs. McCray so that she can offer feedback about the strengths of the current work each is doing and ask questions about ideas that may be unclear. Sometimes Mrs. McCray also offers suggestions for improvement and the two collaborators—the teacher and the author—decide if the suggestions are compatible with what the writer is trying to say.

After a half hour, Mrs. McCray calls the whole class together in a circle in a large section of the room. Brianne and Raúl, who have just finished the writing they have been working on, are ready to sit in the "author's chair" to read their finished pieces to the rest of the class. Although a couple of classmates propose specific suggestions to each student, the rest of the class offers mostly praise and celebratory comments for the two completed writing projects—a detailed description of Harriet Tubman's house that was visited recently on a field trip for Brianne, and an amusing autobiographical incident for Raúl.

When all who wish to have shared their writing with the whole class, the students return to their desks and Mrs. McCray conducts a 10-minute mini-lesson. She usually focuses such lessons on writing strategies and skills that, from her charted observation of students' writing, she feels most students will find helpful to allow them to move forward in their writing. Today, Mrs. McCray shows the students how to use quotation marks to express dialogue in conversation. She shows them a transparency of a student's writing on an overhead projector (examples are usually obtained from the preceding year's class to avoid embarrassment). The writing is a conversation that is told secondhand, without the benefit of direct quotes. She guides students to see how much richer and more personal the writing seems with the addition of dialogue and quotation marks. For similar lessons, Mrs. McCray often copies excerpts from books the students are reading to show how published authors use the writing skills and strategies she is trying to portray.

HOW INSTRUCTION IN WRITING HAS CHANGED

In the past 30 years, our attitude toward the teaching of writing has changed dramatically. Many older adults recall writing homework compositions that were essentially a "one-shot deal." In those days, students would write a draft; turn it in to the teacher; and receive a grade, usually based primarily on spelling, grammar, and handwriting. In the 1970s, researchers began to stop focusing solely on the writing product in such a simplistic manner and started to study how the entire process of writing can impact thinking. Among their most consistent findings was that students truly needed direct teaching at every stage of the writing process—to enable them to generate better ideas, to elaborate on those ideas, to organize their writing for a specific purpose or audience, to edit their work so that it was communicated effectively, and to develop their own style of writing (Block, 2000).

In the 1980s and 1990s, our knowledge expanded so that instruction went beyond assisting students to select topics, compose, and edit to eliminate errors. In that era children were instructed to adjust to new purposes and audiences, and to revise their thoughts and ideas. Researchers of the time noted that "the problem with writing is not poor spelling, punctuation, grammar, and handwriting. The problem with students' writing is NO writing" (Stuart and Graves, 1987, p. 12).

In this new millennium, instruction continues to move toward increasing student's abilities to generate thoughts and ideas and then, as a second but equally important concern, to strive to communicate these ideas in written form, and to do so often. Moreover, for the student, writing requires specific kinds of critical thinking: questioning, citing evidence, evaluating content, and using one's own personal schema (Langer and Applebee, 1987). Today's teachers, more than ever before, consider the thinking processes that go into forming a final product and use the writing process as a vehicle to help students to think through the problems that all writers encounter. As Laib (1989) stated,

> Good writing cannot be understood or taught effectively as an empty and unsystematic collection of rules . . . The real objective of a writing course is literacy in the highest sense: to be knowledgeable and observant, inventive in thought but careful in method, respectful of one's sources, impressive in reason and wit, appropriate in style, graceful in expression, and effective in result. (p. 22)

Mrs. McCray is informed about the current theories and research in the teaching of writing. She is also acquainted with the language arts framework and the standards set for the fifth-graders of the state where she teaches. But what makes her students passionate about the hard work of drafting, revising, and editing a piece of writing is simply this: Mrs. McCray has created a literacy-centered classroom where reading and writing are not only connected, but viewed as important life skills. This teacher allows plenty of opportunities for her students to experience what it is like to share a writing topic one is engrossed in with someone else. She is well aware that each student in her class will be engaged with writing if that student is allowed to explore a variety of topics in which he or she is interested. Above all, this teacher knows that it is all but impossible to resist the appreciation of a sincere and respectful audience (Cohle and Towle, 2001).

An Effective Writing Program in the Intermediate Grades

Mrs. McCray, and many other teachers across the country, have found that it is possible to get students to become enthusiastic and capable writers with a writing program that is characterized by the following five elements, which we elaborate upon throughout the remainder of this chapter:

1. Schedule plenty of time for writing. Students need ample time to draft, share, and think about their writing. Donald Graves (1994) suggests that students write at least four days a week; less writing than that encourages poor habits, which often leads to the dislike of writing. Moreover, the time set aside should be predictable. When students know when they will be writing, they begin to anticipate and plan mentally for what they will write. They are able to "mull over the possibilities" when they are away from the task (Calkins, 1994).

2. Teach the writing process as a way to write. The focus on the writing process is what writers think and do as they write. The process consists of prewriting, drafting, editing, revising, and sharing as a series of recursive cycles as students think through a piece of writing.

3. Use writer's workshop as a structure for writing. Writer's workshop encourages students to become a community of writers who write and share. The teacher becomes a facilitator in the process.

4. Provide feedback on students' writing through peer and teacher conferences. Through teaching students to provide critical feedback on each other's work, they are better able to evaluate their own writing. When students write for peers, even those at a distant school through e-mail correspondence, the quality of their work has been shown to be significantly better than if they write solely for their teachers (Cohen and Riel, 1989). The teacher, too, provides information about each student's writing strengths and needs.

5. Use the "Six Traits" to explain good writing in ways students can understand. The important aspects of writing can be narrowed down to six essential traits— ideas, organization, voice, word choice, sentence fluency, and conventions—that can be taught to students so that they know exactly what good writing is and how to reproduce it themselves. Each trait can be discussed in minilessons and then practiced through authentic writing situations. Examples of students' writing or the writing of published authors can be used to point out how the examples exemplify or do not exemplify any one of the six traits.

THE WRITING PROCESS

The writing process is a series of experiences that a writer engages in to solve certain problems unique to a certain stage of writing. It is exactly this problem-solving approach that makes the writing process more effective in creating thoughtful writers than more traditional approaches that focus solely on the finished product. In traditional writing programs, the finished product is usually a second draft consisting of copying the teacher's corrections made in red ink. Through the writing process, with continuous and scaffolded support from a competent teacher/facilitator, students go through the stages published authors do and, thus, begin to think of themselves as authors, a process that furthers their ability to construct meaning.

The writing process consists of five recurring stages, each of which should be explained and modeled for students. The stages are these:

1. planning/prewriting
2. composing/drafting
3. revising
4. editing
5. publishing

Although students will often follow the steps through to the final reward of publication, all writing need not progress through these steps. There will be times when students will not be making progress with a piece of writing or lose interest and decide to go in an entirely different direction with it. This may occur at any point in the writing process, and the teacher should make it clear that all writing does not have to be published. The student together with the teacher should make the decision after considering both the quality of the piece and how the student feels about it.

Planning/Prewriting

The first stage of any writing effort is a "planning/prewriting" stage in which writers explore and then organize ideas that they feel passionate enough about to sustain all the hard work that will follow. This stage often includes a kind of mental rehearsal. In most writer's workshops, much time is spent allowing students in this stage to select their own topics. Although this may seem easy because it is so wide open, it often initially leaves many students wondering what to write about. Peha (1996) suggests having students take out a sheet of paper and divide it into two columns. In one column, students should make a list of all the things they really like; in the other, all the things they really detest. These topics can then lead to a whole-class discussion in which the teacher supports topic selection by making comments such as, "That sounds like a good topic to write about!" It is also a good idea for students to keep a list of topics (which can continue to grow) attached to the inside corner of their writing folder. Peha (1996) further suggests discussing with students exactly what makes an idea good enough to explore in written form. The idea is worth pursuing if it is:

- *something you have strong feelings about.* What do you feel about the subject? Can you communicate those feelings to readers? How?
- *something you know a lot about.* What can you share with readers that they would be interested in knowing? What is the most important part to tell readers?
- *something you are able to describe in great detail.* Why are these details important? Will they help readers see what you see and feel how you feel?
- *something your audience will be interested in.* Who is your audience? What could you tell them that will interest them most?
- *something your audience will feel was worth reading.* Will your audience learn something new from your piece? What will keep them reading all the way to the end?

Brainstorming

Another way to help students select ideas for writing is through brainstorming with a partner. This oral prewriting activity helps students, especially reluctant writers, to bounce their ideas off another person and gain confidence that their idea is worth pursuing. Similarly, oral discussions on a topic before a writer's workshop session can help students come up with their own intriguing ideas. For example, a teacher writes a provocative question on the board such as, "What would it be like if everyone looked exactly the same?" Students then consider the pros and cons of such a scenario: some muse that prejudice would disappear and people would be judged for their character rather than their looks; others suggest that such a world would be as boring as a garden with only one variety of flower. After such a discussion, students are able to write a three-paragraph expository piece, with the first paragraph containing advantages of such a situation; the second, negatives; and the third, their own personal opinion.

I-Search Process

Planning to write a report is a unique mode of preparation that requires a student to search for information and relate the details of that search to others. Bay Area Writing project teachers (Olson, 1986) attest to the effectiveness of the I-Search Strategy, or "hunting story," for teaching the skills students will need throughout their lives for reading and writing research reports.

Freedman (1986) teaches the *I-Search process* in three stages: (1) identifying the topic to be studied, (2) searching for information, and (3) writing the report. She advises teachers who are introducing the I-Search technique in the classroom (usually starting in third grade) to begin with a prewriting exercise in which students write statements about topics of interest to them and then generate a list of things they would like to know about the topic. For example, one topic might be dinosaurs. Students might pose questions, such as,

"When did dinosaurs live?"

"Did they kill people?"

"What caused them to become extinct?"

"Where did they live and what did they eat?"

After several ideas have been generated, students select one topic of special interest from their lists to explore. This brainstorming activity helps to stimulate thinking and ensures that all students will have a topic that they care enough about to spend time gathering information about it.

The second step is to show students how to obtain information through the use of various resources available to them, such as the World Wide Web, encyclopedias and other reference materials, trade books, interviews, and resource people.

Finally, a structure is given to students to help them plan and organize their information so that they can share it with others. The I-Search reporting format is as follows:

1. *Statement of the problem*: What do I want to know? (establish key questions)

   When did dinosaurs live?

   Why did they die out?

2. *The hunting process*: Where will I find information about my topic? (list possible resources)

   The Internet

   Encyclopedias in the library

   Books in the classroom

3. *Summary of findings*: What did I learn about my topic? (compose written summary)

   Dinosaurs lived many millions of years before the first human being appeared on earth. Although many cartoons show humans and dinosaurs together, that never really happened. Most dinosaurs were plant eaters, although some others were meat-eaters and hunted other, smaller dinosaurs. No one really knows for sure why dinosaurs became extinct. Some scientists think it was because of disease, while others believe an ice age, which caused the world to become very cold, killed them. Though we often imagine that they were ferocious and that we would fear them, we will never know, because no human EVER saw a live dinosaur!

4. *Conclusion*: How can I best share my information? (create multimedia presentation)

   I will use a PowerPoint presentation of the information and include some clip art of dinosaurs.

Clustering

Students may sketch a map of their ideas, or "cluster" them, to form a kind of a graphic outline that can then be filled in with details that flesh it out. Using the clustering technique, students start with their idea, which forms the nucleus of the cluster. Then, using a process akin to free association, they write down everything they can think of that relates to their topic. Many teachers report that this technique is very helpful in assisting second language learners and reluctant writers to plan their compositions effectively (Martinez, 1986). Figure 7.1 shows a cluster created by a fifth-grader, as she prepared to write her first draft of a four-paragraph essay on her sister, and the resultant essay.

Composing/Drafting

Composing, or drafting, is the stage where writers develop their topic and actually translate their ideas into written form. If computers are available, a word-processing program is perfect for this stage, because later revisions can be accomplished easily. If computers are not available, it is often helpful to ask students to write drafts on lined paper, using every other line, so that there is ample room for later revisions. Students should also be instructed not to erase, but to draw one line through words or sentences they wish to change or delete; many times, in retrospect, their original ideas seem better than later ones, so it is important for students to still have access to those ideas.

Revising

Revising is the step in the writing process that requires the most difficult work and generally encounters the most resistance. Revision requires reexamining content, word choice, and organization and rethinking the writing style with an emphasis on how effectively it communicates its intention to the audience.

Response Guides

response guide ●

Revision can be initially introduced by showing students how to use a response guide to examine pieces of writing. A **response guide** offers specific compliments to and asks specific questions of the writer concerning the effectiveness of the writing. A sample response guide is shown in Figure 7.2.

Using this or a similar response guide, the teacher can show students examples of bland or ineffective writing (decodable text is perfect for this purpose) on the overhead projector and have students practice commenting on the writing by selecting phrases appropriate to the piece from the response guide. To extend this activity further, the teacher can invite small groups of students to rewrite the piece and discuss with the class exactly how the writing has been made more effective.

Cluster for "My Sister" and the resultant essay.

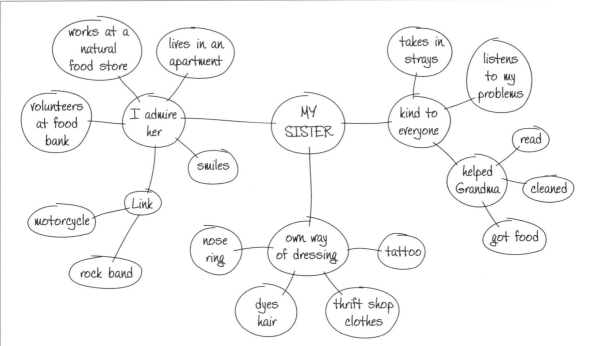

My Sister

The person I most admire in my family is my sister. My oldest sister, Jenna, is 20 years old and lives in an apartment with two other girls. She works at a natural food store and helps out at the food bank on weekends. She has a boyfriend named Link who rides a motorcycle and is in a rock band. When Jenna smiles, she lights up the room.

Jenna is always kind to everyone. When my grandma was sick, Jenna took time off from work to help her get groceries and clean her house. She read to her every single night. Also, Jenna takes in every stray animal that comes around and has always listened to my problems when I ask her to.

My oldest sister has her own way of dressing. Some people say she looks like a punk, but I think she looks more like a rocker. She has a nose ring and a little wrist tattoo that looks like poison ivy. Even though she has a job, she wears old clothes that she buys at thrift shops. She changes her hair color about every month. It has been red, blue, and black. This month it is brown with red streaks.

When people first meet my sister they sometimes think she is weird. At times, they even call her names because she looks so different. Just because she looks different they should not judge her; they should take the time to get to know her. Her outside appearance may be strange, but inside she has a heart of gold. To know my oldest sister Jenna is to love her. If you met her you would see what I mean.

Use for Peer Editing.

FIGURE 7.2   Response guide.

COMPLIMENTS

I liked the part where . . .

You used some great words like . . .

The imagery was effective in the sentence(s) . . .

I like the way you explained . . .

Your writing made me feel . . .

I like the order you used in the piece because . . .

The dialogue was realistic when [the character] said . . .

Your writing made me more interested in this topic because . . .

QUESTIONS

Could you write an opening sentence to "grab" the reader?

Could you throw away these tired words . . . ?

Is this paragraph all on one topic?

Do you need an ending that summarizes better?

Are your paragraphs in the right order?

Could you add more details to this part?

I got confused in the part where . . .

Could you combine these sentences?

Can you make this part clearer?

Can you tell me more about . . . ?

Could you leave this part out because . . . ?

Peer Editing

When students are adept at offering suggestions that are both helpful to the writer and appropriate to the piece of writing, they are ready to become peer editors. **Peer editors** are selected by a writer who has written a draft and is seeking constructive feedback in order to make the piece communicate its intent more effectively. By taking on the role of author as well as peer editor, students not only get the benefit of an audience with whom to share their work, but also begin to learn how to evaluate a piece of writing objectively.

peer editors •

Cecil (2003) suggests that peer editors give their feedback to the authors in written form using a format known as *PQP*, which stands for praise, question, and polish. Multiple copies can be available for students so that when they are ready to share a draft and get revision suggestions from a peer editor, this template makes the work easier. An example of a PQP form is in Figure 7.3.

Author ___Rachel___ Title of Piece ___Grandfather's watch___

Peer Editor ___John___ Date ___3/12/03___

PRAISE: I particularly like these things about your piece of writing.

The beginning sentence made me really want to read on. I could really relate to what Nellie was feeling when she lost her watch. That happened to me once. I was actually worried she would get into trouble. By leaving the outcome until the end, you had me dying to find out what kind of punishment she would get.

QUESTION: These things were unclear to me.

Why didn't she just go back to the park and look for the watch? Wouldn't she have tried to do something about it? I also don't understand who Martin is. Is he her brother or just a friend?

POLISH: I have these suggestions to help make your piece even better.

Your dialogue is realistic but could you use another word besides said all the time. Maybe a word that explains more how Nellie is feeling. It might be helpful, also, to describe what Nellie looks like. You described other things about her so well that I care about her and would like to know if my mental image is correct.

Editing

The editing stage of the writing process is where the writer "cleans up" the spelling, punctuation, and other mechanics of the language that make the writing more accessible to the reader. This step should only take place after the writer has made all the content changes he or she feels are necessary. During a minilesson, the teacher and students should make a list of age-appropriate factors to look for in the editing stage, and the list should be prominently displayed in the classroom so that students can refer to it as they write and edit their work.

FIGURE 7.4   Editing checklist.

Author _____   Peer Editor _____

Author	Peer Editor	
☐	☐	1. I have circled the words I am not sure how to spell.
☐	☐	2. I have checked the spelling for each homonym (e.g., their, there; its, it's).
☐	☐	3. I have checked that all sentences end with appropriate punctuation.
☐	☐	4. I have checked that all paragraphs are indented.
☐	☐	5. I have checked that all sentences begin with capital letters.
☐	☐	6. I have checked that all proper nouns have capital letters.

An example of a generic checklist is provided in Figure 7.4. Such a checklist can be used by the writer to edit his or her own writing as well as by the peer editor, who may be specifically requested to look for problems with the conventions of the language. The items on the checklist can be adjusted as needed to meet students' levels of writing sophistication.

Publishing

Publishing is the celebratory step in the writing process where the teacher helps students find many ways to share and disseminate their writing. This public phase of the writing process creates a sense of the real purpose of writing and allows students to feel genuine pride in their completed product. The more students publish their writing, the more they will develop a true sense of themselves as "authors," and the cycle begins to perpetuate itself. Soon, even reluctant writers become prolific.

Allowing students to illustrate their efforts and provide attractive covers is part of the reward for the writer's accomplishment. Though the format may vary according to the type of piece written, book form is the most common way for children to physically publish their work. A laminated or cloth cover is appealing and sturdy enough to allow the book to be read many times by classmates. There are also commercially made hard-cover blank books that can be decorated by students.

Besides sharing their final product with the class while reading it in a special "author' s chair," there are other avenues for publication that make students feel that all the hard work was worthwhile. Work can be displayed on classroom bulletin boards as well as on special showcases around the school. Class or school newspapers are another way to highlight the work of individual students. In addition, there are several children's magazines, such as *Merlyn's Pen* and *Young World,* that solicit the creative work of students from the intermediate grades.

WRITER'S WORKSHOP

Writer's workshop has been recommended by numerous researchers as well as practicing writing teachers (Atwell, 1998; Calkins, 1994; Hansen, 1987). Descriptions of writer's workshops appear in several full-length books (see, e.g., Calkins, 1991; Calkins and Huron, 1987; Stuart and Graves, 1987). The workshop itself is a very flexible plan that places students and teacher in a partnership for learning. Managing writer's workshop cannot be reduced to a simple how-to formula; it is an ongoing, complex set of tasks that develop differently within the context of different classrooms (Peha, 1996).

Writer's workshops that buzz with the activity of students working on a variety of tasks may, to an outsider, appear to be disorganized and chaotic. However, most of these classrooms are built on a firm, underlying structure (Muschla, 1998a). In most classrooms, writer's workshop takes place two or three times a week, often alternating with reader's workshop or literature circles. The writer's workshop approach to organizing a writing program can be conducted in three or four centers, or writing stations, through which students rotate to complete the writing stages discussed in the previous section in this chapter. In smaller classrooms, as in the opening vignette, students can be completing all stages of writing at their desks. The writing workshop consists of four basic parts: minilessons, state-of-the-class conferences, writing and conferencing, and group sharing.

Minilessons

4 Parts of Writers Workshop.

The minilesson is a focused lesson done with the whole class that usually lasts no more than 5 to 10 minutes. The content of this brief lesson is determined by what the teacher has observed to be a mutual writing need of most members of the class. To model the topic being addressed, the teacher usually prepares a good example of the skill and/or a poor example of the skill procured from literature with which the students are familiar or from writing saved from former students. Such lessons do not focus exclusively on isolated skills but on a range of topics based on student needs. The only absolute topics addressed in these sessions are the six traits of effective writing, discussed later in this chapter. Although there is no end to the possible topics for minilessons, following are some common topics that can be addressed:

- appropriate vocabulary and strategies for finding words
- how to determine when a paragraph is needed
- how to select specific mood words to convey fear or sadness
- the conventions for a business letter
- procedures for writer's workshop
- how to select a topic that has relevance to the writer
- examples of imagery from familiar literature

② State-of-the-Class Conferences

For means of assessment and accountability, a teacher may choose to build in a five-minute state-of-the-class conference once or twice a week to make sure he or she knows exactly what each student is going to be doing during writer's workshop. By examining a chart such as the one in Figure 7.5, the teacher can determine who is at what stage in the writing process and who might benefit from a teacher conference, or a discussion about how to become "unstuck" from a certain stage, such as getting an idea. Additionally, although the stages in the writer's workshop are not necessarily linear but recursive, the teacher may feel a student is leaving out a certain step that would be beneficial with a particularly problematic piece.

③ Writing and Conferencing

Sign up for conference times.

The majority of students' time in writer's workshop—30 to 40 minutes, depending on grade level—is spent in actual writing and talking about that writing in peer-editing conferences and/or teacher conferences.

Students may select a peer editor and schedule a peer conference with an individual or a small group at any time when informal feedback is needed about formulating and planning an idea, the need for revisions, or for specific proofreading for the purpose of editing.

The teacher in a writer's workshop is not the "authority," but a co-collaborator who also writes and shares pieces of work as well as ideas. During the writing time, the teacher may be holding individual or small group conferences that have been scheduled by previous sign-ups on a special place on the bulletin board. Writing conferences with the teacher should be brief (usually between one and four minutes) and concentrate on a piece the writer is doing or finishing. During the conference, the teacher can answer

State-of-the-class chart.

FIGURE 7.5

NAMES:	MON.	TUES.	WED.	THURS.	FRI.
José	1stD	S	R	2ndD	(3)
Brianne	1stD	S	2ndD	(2)	T
Jennifer	P	1stD	(2)	P	2ndD
Hoa	T	R	2ndD	S	(1)
Svetlana	(1)	(1)	1stD	P	2ndD
Garrett	P	2ndD	R	(3)	S

	CODE		CODE
Prewriting	(1)	Drafting	D
Peer editing	P	Proofreading	(2)
Sharing with group	S	Revising	R
Teacher conference	T	Illustrating	(3)

questions and help solve writing problems. In addition, the teacher can offer the following:

1. ask for more information about the content of the piece.
2. restate or mirror the student's ideas.
3. share similar writing experiences he or she has had.

Comments during the conferences should take a positive, encouraging tone, focusing on particularly effective writing and pointing out to the student what has made it effective (Graves, 1983). When there are significant problems, the teacher should concentrate on only one or two concerns in any one session, making a note to check on progress in those areas in the next conference. Finally, students should take an active role in the conference by asking their own questions about the pieces they are working on.

also carry note book to take Notes

If no conferences are scheduled, the teacher walks around the room, engaging in "writer's talk" (e.g., "What an interesting observation" or "The way you described the monster made me just shudder!"), prompting, encouraging, and lending support. The teacher also carries a notebook to jot down anecdotal records (see Chapter 2) on the progress of students, which will provide information as to what to address in future minilessons.

There is no one correct organizational scenario for writer's workshop, because each day tends to be different from the day before. Some days most students will be conferencing with each other or with the teacher in an attempt to bounce their ideas off others; other days students will be at work drafting or revising their ideas and the teacher will be busy talking to individual students at their desks. The key concepts to remember are flexibility and decision making based not on curriculum but on the demonstrated needs of the students.

[handwritten note: - Flexibility - Decision making based on students needs.]

4 Group Sharing

Group sharing is an oral activity, as compared with publishing, and is usually done in front of the whole class (often in a special "author's chair"). The purpose is not to obtain feedback to create a better piece, but to get group appreciation, suggestions for future pieces, and celebratory comments for the completed piece and all the hard work that it necessarily entailed. Though the time allotted for this sharing is ordinarily brief—five minutes or so—it is incredibly important and should never be omitted because

- sharing their work gives students a real reason to write—to impress an audience.
- sharing work allows peer editors to see how their ideas had an effect on a piece.
- sharing work in a safe environment builds a sense of community.
- sharing work makes literacy public.
- reading one's own writing shows the interconnectedness between the two processes. (Graves, 1983)

USING TECHNOLOGY IN CLASSROOM WRITING

The writing process is a valuable approach for teaching students how to write, but often students who lack the skills of good handwriting and appropriate spelling can allow these conventions to interfere with bringing their thoughts and ideas to publication. Technology can help in each stage of the writing process.

In the planning stage, students can use the Internet to further their understanding of the topic. Then, through the use of the word processor, they can generate ideas and explore the topic they are writing about. They can prewrite, web, brainstorm, or do free association without worrying about hurriedly producing pages so rough they are unreadable even to the author.

The word processor can help students avoid frustration by allowing them to explore their ideas while composing without fear of mistakes, which lead to extra effort. Students can easily make deletions and move sentences and paragraphs without erasing or starting all over again.

Revising easier w/ peer Editor

Revising, perhaps the hardest stage to "sell" to any student, is far more manageable when students can easily incorporate suggested word changes, add or delete paragraphs, or even do more extensive rewriting of certain parts of the piece. Because revising is more easily done with a word-processing program, students are more open to the constructive feedback of the teacher and peer editors.

Editing also becomes easier with a word-processing program. The spellchecker and thesaurus built in to most word-processing programs can be valuable tools to students, helping them to find misspellings as well as choose among many synonyms to express their ideas in more powerful ways. In addition, some programs contain a grammar check that can help students, especially those for whom English is a second language, structure their sentences more effectively.

Finally, the wide variety of fonts available on most word-processing programs allows all students—even those with the poorest handwriting—to produce neat, professional-looking pieces of writing.

TEACHING THE SIX TRAITS OF EFFECTIVE WRITING

The **Six Traits approach** to writing was developed in the Northwest Regional Laboratory (Northwest Regional Educational Laboratory, 1998/1999) to create an easy-to-understand language that helps teachers describe to students just what it is that makes good writing effective. Six Traits is not a writing program but, rather, a common vocabulary for describing quality in writing, both narrative and expository. As discussed earlier, the traditional approaches to writing instruction tended to focus solely on the teaching of isolated subskills of writing, such as grammar, spelling, and punctuation. The "rules" taught in such programs often amounted to little more than dutifully memorized tricks for achieving the correct mechanics of writing. Such instruction tends to spend too much time and effort on having students write "correctly," without really addressing what they are attempting to say; moreover, such instruction rarely motivates students to want to write beyond their minimum classroom assignments.

With the Six Traits, students do not simply learn tricks; they learn the traits that make quality writing work. They come to know exactly what good writing is and how to produce it themselves. They do this by comparing their own efforts as writers with those set forth in the high standards of the Six Traits criteria. Thus, they are encouraged to become steeped in the real purpose of writing as a medium for communication, rather than the

● Six Traits approach

various subskills that have no purpose at all if not used in the context of written communication. Moreover, since virtually every state now has some criteria-based writing standards, the Six-Trait approach more than covers what is required in the sets of standards the authors have surveyed.

The Six Traits represent the most basic knowledge we need to impart to students about what good writing—in all genres—is and how they may go about producing it. The traits are as follows:

- ideas
- organization
- voice
- word choice
- sentence fluency
- conventions

See Figure 7.6 for the Six-Trait guide to revision.

FIGURE 7.6   Six-Trait guide to revision.

IDEAS

☐ Does my paper have a clear, focused idea?

☐ Did I use details to elaborate?

ORGANIZATION

☐ Does my piece have a clear beginning, middle, and end?

VOICE

☐ Does my piece have a spark, a mood, a personality, a specific tone—formal or informal—that expresses what I want the reader to feel?

WORD CHOICE

☐ Did I use any interesting words?

SENTENCE FLUENCY

☐ Do my sentences sound smooth?

CONVENTIONS

☐ Did I check my capitals, periods, and spelling (editing for conventions)?

Based on the Six-Trait writing assessment model from the Northwest Regional Educational Laboratory. Copyright © 1998 Christopher-Gordon Publishers.

Ideas

In order to be effective writers, students need to understand that the *ideas* they come up with are the most important element of their writing. The ideas are the fundamental core of the writer's message, the content of the piece, or the theme that, together with the supporting details and images, enriches and develops the writing by building new insight in a way that holds the reader's attention.

Evidence of the writer's ideas can be found dispersed throughout the piece. However, the general "idea" is more than simply the main idea or topic sentence; it also consists of the careful fleshing out, or elaboration of the topic; the quality and quantity of the details; and how these supporting sentences help convey and clarify the writer's message.

The best ideas come from our own lives, from the unusual as well as the mundane aspects of our lives. But just writing about our lives does not guarantee an effective piece of writing. There also has to be a specific purpose for the writing that makes readers so aware of its significance that they want to continue reading.

The teacher can facilitate the free flow of ideas by holding brainstorming sessions with students, or by offering provocative prompts, such as "What is one thing you have done that you will never regret?" or "What would the world be like if everyone looked exactly alike?" (See the section "The Writing Process" for additional suggestions.) Teachers can also help students grasp the importance of ideas and what they should look like by posting the following questions, which will help them analyze their own ideas as well as others':

- Does the writing make sense?
- Do I know the topic well?
- Have I included interesting details?
- Does the writing have a clear purpose?
- Does the writing make you want to continue reading?

Organization

Students need to understand that good writing constitutes much more than just an endless flow of freely associated thoughts. For writing to be truly effective, it must demonstrate strong organization, or a logical sequence of ideas, which means that it begins with a purposeful, enticing lead sentence and terminates with a satisfying, thought-provoking ending. In between, the writer carefully links each new detail or development with the larger picture, building to a turning point or key revelation. Strong transitions are provided, so that the reader never feels lost.

Some adults may remember being given a writing assignment in which they were instructed to produce a specified number of words. This preconceived way to write promotes form over function, the opposite of how real authors write. In other words, a piece should be as long as it takes to express the author's ideas in such a way that the reader is not left with questions at the end. Similarly, a section or paragraph of the piece should only exist if it has a specific function to perform such as stating the theme, advancing the plot, or providing more information about a character.

Teachers can introduce the idea of structure by initially introducing expository frames for expository writing (see Chapter 8) and story grammars for narrative writing. Teachers can also help students see how the internal structure of a piece is important by posting the following questions, which will help them analyze the organizational structure of their own and others' work:

- Will my beginning grab the reader's attention?
- Do all of the sections or paragraphs hang together?
- Does the writing build up to a key part?
- Is the writing in a logical sequence that is easy to follow?
- Does the piece feel finished at the end?
- After reading the piece, will it make the reader think?

Voice

voice ●

Students need to understand that the heart and soul of a piece of writing is its voice. That "voice," or life force, is the writer's personality emerging through words. When a writer has especially strong feelings for the chosen topic, the result is a piece that explodes with energy and the reader feels close to not only the writing but the writer.

All writing has voice. Even a dreary encyclopedia entry has voice, in that the person who wrote it had to determine what facts to include and those to overlook. What determines a person's likelihood of including certain facts over others is a person's unique personality, or voice.

Voice is perhaps the most fundamental of the Six Traits because all the others flow from it. From the writer's own voice come the ideas that are chosen and a unique way of organizing those ideas. Word choice flows from voice, for the words we select are part of who we are. Sentence fluency, especially, emanates from a complex interaction of the words and phrases we choose. And even conventions, such as the way a writer decides to use an exclamation point to show emphasis, are part of the exclusivity that is voice.

If students never find their voice, they will never really discover who they are as writers. Without this trait, they will be forever guessing when it comes to selecting topics, organizing ideas, choosing words, and revising for clarity and style. Confusion will lead to frustration and frustration will lead to fear. When students fear writing—because they think they have nothing to say or they are afraid to say what they think in a way that makes them feel comfortable—they do less of it and decrease their chances of ever becoming good at writing.

Students can find their voice when a teacher values their unique perspective and urges them to tell their own stories—stories that all students have to tell. For students to find their voice, the teacher must expect, and actually require, a diversity of opinions within the class. Students must hear that even if they start with the same topic, no two pieces of writing should be the same because no two writers are exactly the same. A strong voice, however, usually develops over time with much practice, reflection, and feedback from a knowledgeable writing coach.

Teachers can introduce the idea of voice by closely examining each student's writing to find the part that is unique and personal to the student who wrote it and hold that up as an example of "voice." Students can be invited to reflect on why the writing works and what was done to make it sound just like the person who wrote it. Teachers can also help students use their own voice in a piece of writing by posting the following questions, which will help them analyze the use of voice in their own writing as well as others':

- Does this writing sound like me?
- Is this what I really think and feel?
- Could a reader feel my commitment to the topic?
- Do I know why I am writing and who my audience is?
- Do I want to share this writing with someone?

Word Choice

Appropriate **word choice** is the artistic element of writing that involves using fresh and colorful language to fascinate the reader and make certain passages memorable and worthy of reading aloud. Word choice emanates from a true love of language and a desire to select words to express the exact image, impression, or mood in the reader's mind's eye.

● word choice

Word choice becomes apparent to the reader when a writer's language describes an event or feeling in such a manner that the reader feels he or she has received new insights into the mundane; with such writing, it seems clear that no other words or phrases would have worked as perfectly. Word choice is much more than simply effective adjectives or phrases; it entails many factors, such as unusually vivid descriptions and sensory impressions ("a white carpet of fresh snow"), strong and specific verbs ("enveloped by the gloom"), effective use of colloquial language ("He hogtied the critter and threw him into the truck"), and even the occasional use of invented words ("He went shrooming down the slide") when they add to the image needed.

In the intermediate grades, effective use of words is often confused with using large, grandiose-sounding words. When introduced to the thesaurus, students often delight in finding unfamiliar words because they sound, to them, astute and therefore better. Instead, they need to be shown that clarity is the goal and that this often entails using fewer words to get the reader to see clearly what is in the writer's head. For example: "There were multitudinous tomes creating a disarray underneath the man's bed" versus "The books littered the carpet under Joe's bed."

Perhaps the most effective way for teachers to help students become aware of subtleties in language choice is to give them plenty of experiences with good literature. As the teacher conducts a guided reading lesson or reads aloud to students, he or she should point out excellent word choice as it is encountered: "Oh, I can really see that sunset!" or "Wow! I feel as though I were there, don't you?" or "Gosh, I never thought of it that way!" Teachers can also help students practice word choice by having them transform simple sentences, orally or in written form, into ones that vividly depict a situation. For example, they could transform the simple sentence "The boy ran." into "The tiny, freckle-faced boy ran swiftly through the field, fearing the angry bull would make a meal of him." Teachers can also help students choose appropriate words and phrases by posting the following questions, which will help them analyze their own word choices as well as others':

- Is this the best way I can say this?
- Do my words and phrases create mind pictures?
- Have I tried new ways to say everyday things?
- Are my verbs powerful?
- Do any of my words and phrases linger in my mind?
- Would any of my phrases be interesting to read aloud?

Sentence Fluency

sentence fluency ●

Writing fluency is that intangible essence that separates excellent writing from the ordinary. It is the careful crafting of sentence structures into graceful sentences so that paragraphs flow smoothly and effortlessly. While effective word choice is part of this trait, **sentence fluency** is more than just the individual words chosen. It is the entire effect of the way the sentences sound when read aloud, including such features as parallel construction, easy transitions between paragraphs, alliteration, and the variety of lengths and constructions of the sentences—all of which add a sense of aesthetic satisfaction to the reader.

Sentence fluency takes time and practice for students to develop because, more than any of the other traits, it depends heavily on their ability to hear the difference between awkward writing that is hard to understand and follow, and crisp, smooth writing that communicates the writer's intent with an efficiency of words.

As with attuning student's ears to effective word choice, sentence fluency can best be fostered by reading aloud often to them with expression and gusto, and pointing out examples of excellent writing when they appear. Point out the use of alliteration ("pink poppies"), conversational style ("Aaaahhh, I wish I weren't so tired!"), similes ("as brown as the tired desert"), as well as pleasing and consistent rhythm in pieces of writing. Teachers can also demonstrate how *they* write, modeling how they think through the process. In addition, with the overhead projector, students can practice rewriting awkward sentences so they more clearly and concisely convey intended ideas. Finally, teachers can help students write fluent sentences by posting the following questions, which will help them analyze their sentence fluency and that of others:

- Are my sentences a variety of lengths?
- Do my sentences "flow" as I read them aloud?
- Do I use alliteration and/or similes to make my sentences interesting?
- Does the writing flow easily from sentence to sentence?
- Do the sentences begin in different ways?
- Are the sentences powerful and memorable?

Conventions

The most important traits of writing are, arguably, the ones just covered because they concern the core of what the writer has to say. They all concern the composing part of writing. Conventional correctness, however, should not be overlooked because it constitutes the tools of the trade that help bring the writing to others in a uniform manner that readers expect. **Conventions** include grammar, spelling, paragraphing, capitalization, punctuation, and all the mechanics of the language that are often corrected in the editing process.

● conventions

Conventions are more than the window dressing used to make our writing correct, or a list of simple rules to be obeyed. They should be presented as "tools," not "rules." Combined, they are a systematic set of symbols to facilitate communication between writer and reader. Conventions have meaning just as words do, and it is a skillful writer who takes advantage of a full range of these meaning-making tools and situations to communicate most effectively with the reader.

While more materials exist for the teaching of conventions than for all the other traits combined, there is much evidence that assigning worksheet after worksheet on grammar usage, punctuation, and the like out of context is ineffective in teaching students to write; such undue focus often interferes with what the writer has to say (Weaver, 1996). Individual conventions, such as the proper use of capital letters, should be taught in short mini-lessons but be reinforced continually by showing writers how important it is for their writing to be readable and telling them how much we appreciate being able to clearly understand what they have written. Appropriate use of conventions should be pointed out as they occur, rather than negative ones. Students also need to hear that the more they read and write, the more proficient they will become at using conventions appropriately. Teachers can help students use the proper conventions by posting the following questions, which will help them proofread their writing and that of others:

- Have I used capital letters correctly?
- Is all the punctuation in the right place?
- Are all the words spelled correctly?
- Have I used a resource to help spell unfamiliar words?
- Did I indent each paragraph?
- Are my sentences logical and grammatically correct?

INSPIRING STUDENTS TO WRITE

Writer's workshop and the Six Traits are highly effective tools to help students become proficient writers; however, writing, like any other skill, requires continual practice to hone and refine its many nuances. The crafting necessary for good writing can be developed through daily writing for real purposes, with continual feedback from caring peers and adult coaches. The following section concerns two daily practices that can help students become engaged writers who write for authentic purposes. The first is the use of dialogue journals, to offer a vehicle through which students can use writing in much the same way as they use conversation with friends. The second is the use of the novelette, to offer students the opportunity to write a narrative piece that is both longer and more in-depth than the ordinary classroom writing assignment.

Dialogue Journals

Of the variety of journal-writing formats used in elementary classrooms, the one that provides the most helpful feedback about writing for students is the
dialogue journal ●   **dialogue journal,** also known as the interactive journal (Cecil, 1994a). The "dialogue" part simply means that in this journal, a running dialogue is carried on between the teacher and each individual student. The student begins the dialogue by writing down anything that is of interest to him or her, and the teacher simply responds, in the margins, to what the student has expressed. The teacher may comment on the student's ideas, use thoughtful questions to ask for elaboration, or paraphrase what the student has said to validate and affirm the student's ideas. The teacher and no one else (unless the student initiates sharing with someone else) reads what the student has written.

    To initially launch the idea of dialogue journals in the intermediate classroom, it is often helpful to write two or three questions on the board to inspire students, such as, "What are your favorite things to do on a Saturday morning?" or "Who is one famous sports figure you admire and why?" Advising students that these topics are only possibilities for writing and not mandates frees those who already have their own diary-like writing agenda, which can be problems, goals, fears, or just a recording of the things they have recently been doing.

    Gradually in the course of dialogue journal writing, a writing stimulus becomes less and less important as the written conversation, or dialogue, between the teacher and student follows its own natural path. Most teachers find that, while the first dialogue topics are cautiously neutral to begin with, their positive feedback leads to a more trusting and caring relationship. At that point, the student will look forward to the writing as a chance to complain, share successes, express undying love for the teacher, confess to wrongdoing, or reveal many other personal feelings that make the writing rewarding. Ideally, students should have some time set aside for journal writing every day, beginning with a few minutes and graduating to 15 or 20 as they find more and more to say in their dialogue.

Justification for adding dialogue journal writing to an already overcrowded literacy curriculum is compelling, and in this age of teacher accountability, it is worth examining. First, students who participate in such a program develop a much more positive attitude toward writing. If sessions are frequent; endure for most of the school year; and include caring, nonjudgmental feedback from the teacher, even reluctant writers will be more favorably inclined toward writing and will write much more (Danielson, 1988).

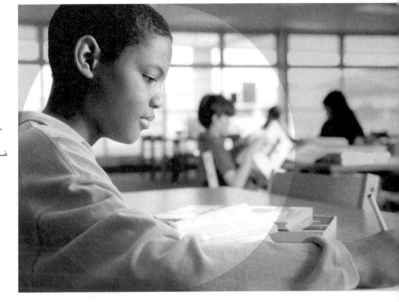

Second, students become more confident as they begin to believe in the power of their writing ability and look forward to the teacher's comments, rather than dreading the proverbial "sea of red marks" common in traditional writing programs. As they realize their thoughts and ideas have merit, their self-perception as writers will increase. In addition, the nonthreatening nature of dialogue journals makes them particularly appropriate for students for whom English is a second language. They can write in their home language or "code switch," by using words from their native language and their newly acquired language. Such learners are too often fearful of being publicly ridiculed for their lack of oral and written fluency (Peyton and Reed, 1990).

Third, students receive important writing practice through journal writing and, as a result, they become more fluent writers. As in any activity—skiing, typing, riding a bicycle—writing improves with continual practice. Moreover, through the teacher's modeling and questioning (see Figure 7.7), students begin to recognize just what details to include to make their writing more effective. Additionally, through modeling, student's use of conventions such as spelling, grammar, and punctuation improve markedly (Cecil, 1994a). The teacher is actually able to be there for certain "teachable moments" when students need to use an unaccustomed grammatical construct or to spell an unfamiliar word, as in the word *Hawaii* in Figure 7.7.

FIGURE 7.7 Dialogue journal entry.

No, I have never been to Hawaii, Kim, but I have always wanted to go there. Did you get to do any snorkeling? Yes, I noticed your lovely tan!

We had such a fun time in ~~Hawiiy~~ Hawie Mrs. Cecil. Were you ever thare? I got sun bruned like a ~~lob~~ lobstor. Did you notis Mrs. Cecil. I can't wait to go back thare.

Snorkeling is fun, isn't it, Kim? How did you learn? Did your mother teach you? Was it difficult? What else did you do in Hawaii?

Yes we got to ~~snk~~ snorkel when we were in Hawaii. It was so neat! There were so many fish with all difrint colors. I never saw anything like that befor.

I'm sorry you are being bothered, Kim. I will change your seat and speak with Meg. No, I am not angry with you! ☺

You know, Mrs. Cecil. You were telling me to stop talking today in math class. but it wasn't me. Meg was talking. Meg keeps bothing me. Please move her seat. Dont be mad at me please, Mrs. Cecil??

I have one daughter, Kim. Like you, I am sure she thinks I am mean sometimes. It is hard being a Mommy!

Mrs. Cecil, do you have any children? I wish I was your child. Instead of your student. My mother is to mene. I think you are probly never mene to your children?

Kim, the important thing is that you have now told the truth. Sometimes it's hard to tell the truth. No, I am not angry, but please don't do it again, okay? ☺

Now I want to tell you something o.k. Last weak when I was absint I was'nt sick. I ~~wut~~ just made that up becuase I wanted to stay home and watch Scuby Do. Im sorry, Mrs. Cecil. Are you angry now???? Do'nt be.

Finally, students begin to see an authentic use for writing for their own purposes rather than to fulfill a teacher-directed assignment. In the informal venue of their own private journals, many students find that writing can be a most cathartic experience—especially when they are using it to vent strong feelings and emotions. As students get older, they find, too, that writing can be a positive outlet to diffuse potentially explosive situations ahead of time because they can examine their written feelings before they act on them. In this age of school violence, the importance of such a constructive outlet should not be underestimated.

Novelettes

Students who have had the experience of writing an original episodic novel, or a multichaptered novelette, come away with a tremendous feeling of accomplishment and a sense of pride at having produced a complex set of characters who have evolved with time and effort. These characters actually become real to them in much the same way as any characters do to adults who have just finished reading a satisfying novel. Indeed, students who write novelettes are understandably quite impressed that their creation more closely resembles an adult novel in scope and size than the typical shorter pieces they traditionally pen (Cecil, 1994a).

To initiate the writing of a novelette, it is often helpful to provide an extensive outline of what possible chapters could look like. Outlines might focus on themes related to a certain emotion, such as greed, jealousy, love, or hope. Or, after reading with students a variety of Greek and Roman myths, teachers can create an outline of the adventures of a similar hero or heroine. After reviewing the basic elements of narrative structure, the teacher can invite students to write chapters telling about their main character and his or her struggles and resolutions, or use the longer format to explain one of our natural phenomena, such as tornadoes or hurricanes.

After distributing guidelines to students, such as the ones offered in Figure 7.8, have them brainstorm a list of possible ideas for the first chapter. For example, in the first chapter in Figure 7.8, the characters brainstormed may range from a telepathic Martian to a young woman living out on the prairie with eight children. Students will thus be inspired to select an idea to work up for their own chapter, or choose another that comes to their mind. It is crucial for the teacher to remind students that there are no right or wrong characters, only many ideas, each of which can be an interesting beginning for a novel.

After the class brainstorming session, each student selects a character and then fleshes out the chapter with class ideas as well as his or her own. Students can then be paired with a peer editor during writer's workshop to share their chapter and receive praise, questions, and suggestions for improvement. New chapters are usually written weekly or biweekly, with revisions and teacher and peer editor conferences occurring in between. However, by the second or third chapter, the class brainstorming, and even the outline, become less and

FIGURE 7.8 Writing a novelette.

1. Invent and describe a character; physical characteristics, habits, likes, dislikes, traits. (characterization)

2. Provide your character with a history: What has his or her life been like up to now? Who were his or her parents? What sort of childhood did he or she have? What were his or her friends like? (background)

3. Describe where your character lives. (setting)

4. Describe a typical day in the life of your character.

5. Your character is going to leave town; describe what led to this decision.

6. Just before leaving town, your character receives advice from someone; re-create this scene in dialogue.

7. The first day out of town your character meets someone strange; describe this person and what makes him or her strange.

8. This person asks your character to do something, but your character is not sure if he or she should. What was your character asked to do and what goes through his or her mind?

9. Your character decides to do what has been asked; describe the decision and its consequences.

10. Some time later, your character turns up in a large city with very little money. Your character decides to find a job. Describe the search for a job and the job he or she finally secures.

11. Describe a typical day on the job.

12. Despite the fact that your character likes the job, he or she is fired. Describe this scene, making clear why he or she was fired.

13. Your character is depressed and inattentive. As a result, he or she has an accident. Describe it.

14. Your character is taken to a hospital and learns that he or she is not expected to live. Describe this scene and your character's feelings about the imminence of death.

15. Despite the doctor's predictions, your character recovers and decides the city is not for him or her. Your character moves to a small town where he or she lives for a year. Describe this period.

16. While living in this small town, your character sees a number of things he or she believes ought to he changed. What are they?

17. In order to bring about changes in the town, your character decides to run for mayor. Describe the campaign.

18. Your character wins the campaign and begins to inaugurate changes; however, he or she encounters difficulties. What are they? How are they resolved? How will you end the novelette? (Cecil, 1994a)

less important as students become very close to their characters and look forward to expanding them wherever the characters decide to go.

By the fourth or fifth chapter, the characters in most novelettes have usually evolved to the point where they seem to have minds of their own. Therefore, as the teacher presents the next chapter in the outline, he or she can encourage students to deviate from the outline if they feel their character(s) is heading in other directions. As more and more chapters are written, the outline lessens in importance and the excitement of the deepening development of the character and plot becomes a unique source of motivation.

When the last chapter is completed, through the joint efforts of the author, the teacher, and the author's editorial partners, which can take anywhere from a few weeks to several months, students are eager to do the final editing and illustrating. A minilesson can address the fact that a title should be chosen with great care, not only to catch the reader's attention but also to capture the essence of the novelette. Completed novelettes can then be word processed and professionally bound. Finally, the authors can read them aloud to the entire class and receive appreciative comments, and the teacher can explore other venues to share students' accomplishments, such as reading the novelettes to another class or taking a field trip to a convalescent home to read to the residents.

High-quality children's literature can be the inspiration for writing these novelettes in particular styles and genres. Teachers can foster this inspiration by calling attention to interesting phrases, word choice, dialogue, character development, and foreshadowing in books that are read aloud to students, or those that are read by students in their literature circles (see Chapter 5). If the books are wisely chosen, students will have excellent models from which to draw for their own writing. Some high-quality novels for children can be found through recommendations from the school librarian, or from professional organizations such as the International Reading Association or the American Library Association. An additional source is the Newbery medal books, presented each year by the American Library Association to the author of the most distinguished contribution to literature for children published during the preceding year.

Some titles that we have found to be particularly useful for modeling the traits of a well-crafted novelette are the following:

Blume, J. (1972). *Tales of a fourth grade nothing.* New York: Dutton.

Howe, D., & Howe, J. (1979). *Bunnicula: A rabbit tale of mystery.* New York: Atheneum.

McAfee, A. (1987). *Kirsty knows best.* New York: Knopf.

Naylor, P. R. (1991). *Shiloh.* New York: Atheneum.

O'Dell, S. (1960). *Island of the blue dolphin.* Boston: Houghton Mifflin.

Patterson, K. (1977). *Bridge to Terabithia.* New York: Harper & Row.

Wilder, L. I. (1953). *Little house in the big woods.* New York: Harper & Row (and others in the series).

Poetry

The entire spectrum of writers in today's intermediate classrooms—from gifted to second-language learners to hard-to-motivate writers—can be encouraged to create poetry through the use of literacy scaffolds. The **literacy scaffold** is a kind of formula for writing a poem by imitating, to a greater or lesser degree, an existing poem. By simplifying the process of writing a poem—a process that can seem threatening and esoteric to many—students can see that once they are given the structure, they are freed to fill in their own creative thoughts and ideas. The following eight steps guide the teacher and children through the process (Cecil, 1994b).

literacy scaffold

ACTIVITY   *Writing Poetry Using a Literacy Scaffold*

1. Provide a literacy scaffold, or temporary writing framework, created from the work of a poet students admire, such as Shel Silverstein, Jack Prelutsky, or another selection (see Figure 7.9).

2. Read examples of other student's work, or your own, that contain the structure (save these from previous classes).

3. On an overhead projector, show students a poem using the structure and guide them to identify the structure, as well as the particular conventions (punctuation, spacing, capital letters, and so forth) that the poem employs.

4. As a group, brainstorm some topics for a poem that the whole class can contribute to using the scaffold.

5. Brainstorm some words or phrases that could be used in the poem.

6. Using the overhead, write a group poem on the chosen topic, using the scaffold and brainstormed words and phrases.

7. Individually, or in pairs for the reluctant, invite students to write their own poems using the literacy scaffold. (*Note:* More "seasoned" poets should feel free to deviate from the literacy scaffold.)

8. Have students follow the remaining steps in the writing process to revise, edit, share, and publish their work.

An example of how this process can be used was demonstrated recently by a class of fourth-graders. To achieve the objective of having students write a group poem, they were first read a poem about words, using a particular pattern, or literacy scaffold. Then they were shown the poem on the overhead projector and were able to discover the pattern of adjectives used in the poem, all beginning with the same letter sound. The teacher added that the adjectives in the first and last two lines are called *predicate*

Snakes are sneaky,
Snakes are slim.
    Slithery, slimy.
    Somber, slinky.
    Scaly, sneaky.
    Simple, sassy.
Snakes are slim.
Snakes are sneaky.

adjectives, because they come after the verb *are,* and describe the noun. On further investigation, the students pointed out that the first two lines and the last two lines are the same, but in reverse. Finally, the students observed that all lines begin with a capital letter and noted the use of commas and periods. After brainstorming some topics for their group poem, the students settled on "bees," and then, with help from student dictionaries, brainstormed some words and phrases that would be associated with bees that also started with the letter *b*. Figure 7.10 shows the students' final product.

Bees

Bees are buzzy,
Bees are bold.
    Boisterous, bashful.
    Belligerent, bold.
    Beautiful, bellicose,
    Bewildering, bright.
Bees are bold,
Bees are buzzy.

TROUBLESHOOTING

Nothing is more satisfying to most students than sharing a piece that they have successfully drafted, revised, edited, and illustrated with a trusted audience and then receiving celebratory comments. However, a variety of factors can make writing a dreaded chore for many students. Following are some suggestions for this common dilemma.

No Confidence

Reluctant writers with little or no confidence in their ability to write—especially English language learners just coming to terms with a new language—may initially prefer to draw pictures of their ideas in the prewriting stage. They can be invited to share these pictures orally with trusted peers or the teacher. Additionally, after using the writing process as discussed in this chapter, such students can be shown specific sentences that illustrate the strengths and limitations in their own writing and be told how to correct or avoid specific problems. Diederich (1991) suggests that writers lacking confidence generally respond better to praise of what they have done well than to any specific type or amount of correction. Further, Johnston (1992) offers that instead of asking reluctant writers questions about a weak part of their writing, it is more helpful to give a specific reason for your confusion. For example, instead of asking, "Why was the boy so sad at the end of your story?" it might be more helpful to state, "I really liked the way you ended your story, but I was confused about why the boy would have been sad when it appeared he had gotten his wish."

No Ideas

Often in the writer's workshop, when students are given free rein to choose their own topics, some will complain that they do not know what to write about. Providing specific prompts ("What would you do with a million dollars?") as well as story starters (see Figure 7.11), provocative lead-in sentences that pique a student's imagination, can sometimes be helpful. When a student is "stuck" on a piece of writing and complains that he or she doesn't know what comes next, a helpful technique is to read the student's work and then offer a snippet of an idea that can lead the student to a new set of possibilities. For example, a student writing about a mirror in an attic may imagine a picnic area on the other side of the mirror but be unable to come up with an idea about what could happen there. The teacher might suggest, "I see a little squirrel scurrying away in the woods and . . .," and then walk away, promising to check back later to see how the student is doing. Often, a tiny nudge of this sort will remove the block. Finally, teachers should not hesitate to tell students an important truth about writing: More often than not, inspiration occurs during writing rather than before it. In other words, as they simply take the leap and begin to write something, most students find that the fear dissipates as the ideas generated beget more ideas.

1. It was the most hideous, monstrous thing I had ever seen.

2. Who would think a tree branch could let go so suddenly?

3. Bringing a Martian home for dinner was something I never thought I'd be doing.

4. I don't suppose you ever spied on someone, at least not for weeks at a time, but I did.

5. I had always hated school until that day when . . .

6. Haunted house stories are a dime a dozen but, I promise you, this one will top them all.

7. The best friend I ever had was not a human but a . . .

8. We had always made fun of her.

9. Moving to the ranch had seemed like such a good idea until that morning when we all had our assigned chores to do.

10. There was blood all over the doorstep that morning when I went out to start my paper route.

11. A helium-filled balloon—especially a very large one—is not an easy thing to carry on a very windy day.

12. He was the tiniest little man (horse, dog, etc.) you ever saw and he was sitting right on my desk.

13. It looked like a very ordinary lamp—a little crooked perhaps, and rather dirty.

14. It was way too big to be a hen's egg, so what was it doing in the chicken coop?

15. I always thought jumping rope was a silly thing to do until my little sister challenged me to try it.

16. Roller blades can get you places in a hurry, as I found out that day.

17. It had been raining for a week and now the road had disappeared.

18. Making someone come back to life after being dead for years is a very scary thing to do.

19. The map was very old, and the paper cracked as I opened it.

20. Stowing away on a cruise ship is not easy but well worth the hassle.

21. "There's no such thing as a werewolf," I said as I watched the hairs on my hands grow longer.

22. "Of course I'll be all right!" I told my parents as they went off on vacation.

23. Summer camp is not all it's cracked up to be. Especially Camp Gitchigumi . . .

24. The little puppy sat by the window looking in at the warm fire.

25. "Three wishes," said the strange old lady, "and use them with great care!"

26. "Zap!!!" There was that annoying sound again. What *was* it???

27. There was no one there when I answered the doorbell, but there sat a very large package with a huge bow.

28. I have always loved to play jokes on people.

29. It had arms like a monkey, fur like a leopard, and a very human face.

30. "Of course I'm not afraid!" I told my friends as we ventured into the rain forest.

Too Many Ideas

Though it may not seem like much of a problem, certain students will have so many ideas that they will become overwhelmed, or even paralyzed, by indecision. In this case, an early idea mental rehearsal conference with a peer editor or the teacher can be helpful in assisting the child in picking a topic. For example, the student would talk about some of his or her ideas and the peer editor or teacher might ask questions or encourage the student to write about a particular idea. Also of help can be a discussion with the student about his or her experiences and resources. Most writers suggest that the best topics to write about are those about which one has the most information and personal experience. Therefore, although a student may wish to write about wild Shetland ponies, space flight, or getting lost in the zoo, the latter may be the better suited topic.

No Interest in Writing

Often students enter a classroom with a decided aversion for writing—especially those children who have not been through the confidence-building adventure of a writer's workshop. Such students need to be encouraged to write and to experience the rewards of writing. Very often the reluctance also emanates from a history of having received numerous discouraging corrections on the mechanics of writing, including the writer's spelling, grammar, and punctuation, as well as marks for poor penmanship. If this is where the problem lies, the teacher can intervene by recording the student's ideas and first draft, emphasizing the difference between the mere physical act of writing and the actual composing, for which the student is still being held responsible. A similar strategy is to allow the student to dictate ideas into a tape recorder and then write the first draft on a word processor, utilizing the spell check and grammar aids, if available. Finally, pairing social students who prefer oral activities over solitary ones for brainstorming discussions and writing the initial draft is a collaborative way to lessen their feelings of isolation and spur interest in writing.

SUMMARY

In a balanced and comprehensive literacy program, writing is not seen as merely the prosaic sum of its parts. Writing, like reading, is viewed as a tool for considering the world, or as a vehicle for sorting out and clarifying one's thinking. The more students reformulate content, the more their thinking and writing abilities grow. In the process, students play with words, organize their ideas into sentences and paragraphs, and express their innermost thoughts to increase their personal significance and self-awareness. Moreover, through a well-constructed writing program, students learn to harness skills that will enable them to examine their ideas and determine whether they can stand up to analysis by their peers.

The writing process, employed in the self-directed setting of the writer's workshop, shifts the emphasis in students' writing from the finished product to the problem-solving stages all writers go through as they gather and organize their ideas, draft them, and refine and polish their pieces with the help of others. Because the teacher is not the only person evaluating the final product, the students, as peer editors, become astute at discerning what does and does not constitute good writing. Reading and writing become reciprocal partners as students write and then read their own writing, and that of other students.

To further help students understand what good writing is, the Six Traits are used in a balanced and comprehensive literacy program for the intermediate grades. In a child-friendly language, students of this age are ready to learn about the important six components of ideas, organization, voice, word choice, sentence fluency, and conventions. Writing is chosen that either exemplifies the trait the teacher is focusing on or fails to be effective because it lacks the desired trait. In either case, students receive valuable information as to what makes writing work. They extend this information to their own writing and to that of their peers.

Arguably, a large majority of the problems experienced by writers can be alleviated by actually having them write often because active young authors become increasingly more engaged in the desire to communicate more clearly their idea. Daily dialogue journals and frequent writing of novelettes are but two means to supplement the ample writing practice offered by writer's workshop.

Finally, teachers utilizing a balanced and comprehensive literacy program must convey the fundamental axiom to students that was proffered by Robert Frost: *"There is no art to writing but having something to say."*

To be sure, the writing process takes much effort and concentration; therefore, students must be gently guided through the process and encouraged to continue when they become discouraged or frustrated with the many revisions that every writer encounters. With the assistance of a teacher who truly believes Frost's claim that everyone has something to say, a writing revolution can occur in every classroom. Eventually, all students will have the confidence to produce a worthwhile piece of writing that they are proud of and eager to share with the world.

Questions

1. Write a specific piece of fiction, nonfiction, or poetry for a specific group of intermediate-age students. Note the process you went through to arrive at the finished product. How might you use your piece of writing in a writer's workshop to teach writing more effectively?

2. Reflect on your own experiences with learning to write in school. Describe any positive experiences that helped you to become a better writer. Also describe any negative experiences that may have hindered your development and/or your motivation to write. How do your experiences relate in terms of the ideas presented in this chapter?

3. Observe writing instruction taking place in an intermediate classroom, and write down your observations. Was the teacher following the process approach to writing or a different approach? How did the students feel about the writing they were doing? What did you think about the quality of their writing? What long-term effects do you think the approach will have on their future as writers?

Suggestions

1. Arrange to visit an intermediate classroom during writer's workshop. Listen to the conversation that accompanies the composing process. Take notes on what you hear. How did "talk" facilitate prewriting, writing, rewriting, and editing in the situation you observed?

2. Ask a small group of intermediate-age students what they prefer to read and what they prefer to write about: fiction (stories, novels), nonfiction (informational texts, biographies, expository prose), or poetry. Is there a difference in form between what students choose to read and write about? Why might this be so?

3. Survey a small group of intermediate-age students about their knowledge of computers. Characterize the computer literacy of these students. How comfortable are they with using the computer's word-processing capabilities? How accessible are computers to these students when they are writing? How often do they actually publish their work on the computer?

References

Atwell, N. (1998). *In the middle: New understandings about reading and writing with adolescents* (2nd ed.). Upper Montclair, NJ: Boynton/Cook.

Avery, C., & Graves, D. (1993). *And with a light touch: Learning about reading, writing and teaching with first graders.* Portsmouth, NH: Heinemann.

Block, C. C. (2000). *Teaching the language arts: Expanding thinking through student-centered instruction* (3rd ed.). Needham Heights, MA: Allyn & Bacon.

Calkins, L., & Huron, S. (1987). *The writing workshop: A world of difference.* Portsmouth, NH: Heinemann.

Calkins, L. M. (1991). *Living between the lines.* Portsmouth, NH: Heinemann.

Calkins, L. M. (1994). *The art of teaching writing.* Portsmouth, NH: Heinemann.

Cecil, N. L. (1994a). *Freedom fighters: Affective teaching of the language arts.* Salem, WI: Sheffield.

Cecil, N. L. (1994b). *For the love of language: Poetry for ALL learners.* Winnipeg, Manitoba: Peguis.

Cecil, N. L. (2003). *Striking a balance: Best practices for early literacy* (2nd ed.). Scottsdale, AZ: Holcomb Hathaway.

Cohen, S., & Riel, B. (1989). The effect of distant audiences on students' writing. *American Educational Research Journal, 26,* 143–159.

Cohle, D. M., & Towle, W. (2001). *Connecting reading and writing in the intermediate grades.* Newark, DE: International Reading Association.

Danielson, K. E. (1988). *Dialogue journals: Writing as conversation.* Bloomington, IN: Phi Delta Kappa Educational Foundation.

Diederich, P. (1991). *Writing inservice guide for English language arts and TAAS.* Austin: Texas Education Agency.

Freedman, A. (1986). Adapting the I-Search paper for the elementary classroom. In C. B. Olson (Ed.), *Practical ideas for teaching writing as a process.* Sacramento: California State Department of Education.

Graves, D. H. (1983). *Writing: Teachers and children at work.* Exeter, NH: Heinemann.

Graves, D. H. (1994). *A fresh look at writing.* Portsmouth, NH: Heinemann.

Hansen, J. (1987). *When writers read.* Portsmouth, NH: Heinemann.

Johnston, P. (1992). *Constructive evaluation in literacy.* White Plains, NY: Longman.

Laib, N. K. (1989, July 5). Good writing cannot be taught effectively as an empty collection of rules. *The Chronicle of Higher Education, 36.*

Langer, J. A., & Applebee, A. N. (1987). *How writing shapes thinking: A study of teaching and learning.* Urbana, IL: National Council of Teachers of English.

Martinez, E. B. (1986). It works! In C. B. Olson (Ed.), *Practical ideas for teaching writing as a process.* Sacramento: California State Department of Education.

Muschla, G. R. (1998a). *Reading workshop survival kit.* Center for Applied Research in Education.

Muschla, G. R. (1998b). *Writing workshop survival kit.* Center for Applied Research in Education.

Northwest Regional Educational Laboratory. (1998/1999). *Assessment and accountability program.* Portland, OR.

Olson, C. B. (Ed.). (1986). A sample prompt, scoring guide, and model paper for the I-Search. In *Practical ideas for teaching writing as a process.* Sacramento: California Department of Education.

Peha, S. (1996). *The compleat writing teacher.* Unpublished manuscript.

Peyton, J. K., & Reed, L. (1990). *Dialogue journal writing with nonnative English speakers: A handbook for teachers.* Alexandria, VA: Teachers of English to Speakers of Other Languages.

Spandel, V. (2000). *Creating writers through 6-trait writing assessment and instruction.* New York: Addison-Wesley/Longman.

Stuart, V., & Graves, D. (1987). *How to teach writing.* Urbana, IL: National Council of Teachers of English.

Weaver, C. (1996). *Teaching grammar in context.* Upper Montclair, NJ: Boynton/Cook.

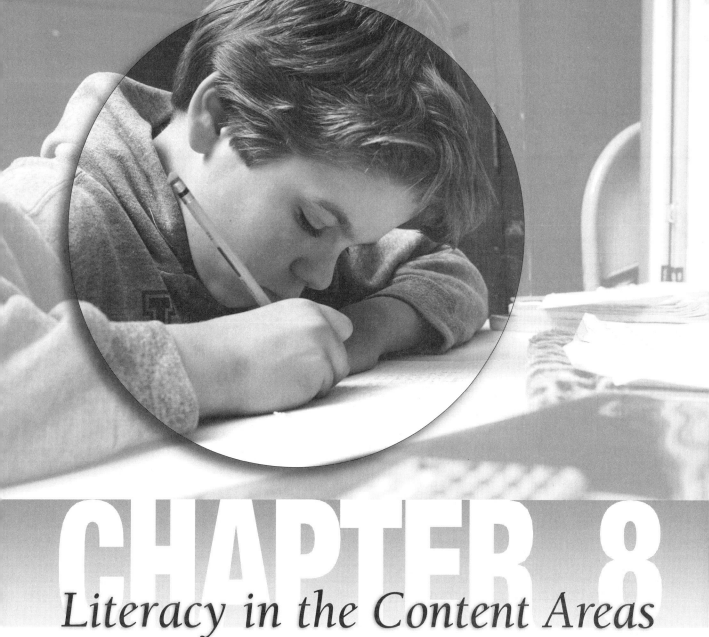

CHAPTER 8
Literacy in the Content Areas
LEARNING FROM INFORMATIONAL TEXT

Focus Questions

- Why is it important to use expository material to teach content area literacy strategies?
- How is content area text different from narrative text?
- What are some effective techniques for expository reading and writing?

WHAT IS CONTENT AREA LITERACY?

Content area literacy refers to the use of reading, writing, speaking, listening, viewing, and visually representing as tools for learning subject matter. Often students in the intermediate grades are expected to learn subject matter through reading; taking notes and outlining; listening to lectures; or viewing, for example, a documentary, but are never taught *how* to learn in these ways. Learning informational material is different from reading or writing stories. A major part of the difference lies in the fact that stories are narrative material and informational text is expository material, each with its own distinctive structure. When teaching students to learn from informational, or content area, text, it is necessary to use expository material for modeling, demonstration, and practice to ensure students can apply appropriate strategies to other informational text. While most of the literacy strategies already introduced in this book are also applicable for use in the content areas—and should be integrated into content area instruction—these strategies need to be taught with expository material. In addition, there are strategies that are most effective for content area literacy, and these will be introduced in this chapter.

LITERACY STANDARDS AND CONTENT AREA STANDARDS OVERLAP

All teachers are literacy teachers. In all the content areas there are standards that incorporate and overlap with literacy standards. For example, note the terminology used in the following content area standards:

- National Social Studies Standards—"identify and give examples," "identify, research, and clarify," "document information from print or electronic sources," and "distinguish facts from opinions."
- National Science Education Standards for Science as Inquiry—"begin with a question, design an investigation, gather evidence, formulate answers, communicate the process and results . . . by producing oral and written reports, writing, labeling

In the Classroom

"Okay, now I will read the passage again, but this time I want you to write down some more key words or phrases to add to those you just wrote," Mrs. Martinez explains.

She then proceeds to read the same section of the sixth-grade social studies text she just read, this being the third time. The first time she read it, she directed students to just listen. The second time, she directed them to listen for key words or phrases, those words or phrases they thought were most important to the material. This time they will listen for some words or phrases they may have missed during the second reading. Mrs. Martinez is using a strategy called *dictoglos* (Wajnryb, 1990) to help her students, especially her second language learners, both understand the structure and language of expository text, and collaborate with others to learn specific content area knowledge.

After she finishes reading, Mrs. Martinez walks around the room looking at students' papers and asks, "Did everyone write more key words and phrases? All right. Now take your paper and pencil and get with your assigned partner." She waits while quietly counting to 30—she knows it takes her students about 30 seconds to move their chairs in order to work with their partners.

Mrs. Martinez continues, "Discuss your notes with your partner and try to re-create the text you just heard me read. Expand your notes and try to rewrite the text just as you heard me read it. You have 15 minutes to work on this."

Mrs. Martinez again moves around the classroom making sure each partnership is clear about what they are doing. After 15 minutes she says, "Okay, now join together with one other pair of students near you so that there are four of you working together."

After another quiet count of 30 seconds, Mrs. Martinez continues with her directions: "Combine all of your notes and try to re-create the text you heard me read. Try to make what you write as close to what I read as you can. After about 10 minutes I will ask you if you need an additional 5 minutes. If not, I will ask for volunteers to read what you have come up with and we will then discuss your work. Be thinking about what parts of the text are hard to re-create. We will analyze why some parts are harder than others to recall, and ways we might be able to remember those parts better."

drawings, completing concept maps, designing computer graphics."

- National Council of Teachers of Mathematics (NCTM) Standards—"interpret and comprehend word problems," "develop, record, explain, critique strategies for solving computational problems," "understand patterns and describe verbally"; and for data analysis and probability, "formulate questions and collect data, organize and display relevant data to answer questions."

This is the same terminology found in national literacy standards. The aspects of critical thinking, formulating questions, and communicating results are very directly literacy tasks that are also expectations in all the content area standards (see NCTE/IRA Standards for the English Language Arts #1, 2, 4, 5, 6, 7, 8, 11, and 12 in Figure 2.4). Furthermore, as Kane (2003) notes, "Wide and varied opportunities for reading, writing, listening, speaking, and viewing can help students meet national content knowledge standards and benchmarks . . . a standards-based curriculum can use literacy strategies not as add-ons, but as integral to content teaching itself" (p. ix).

Themed units are an effective way to integrate literacy instruction and to use the inquiry tools necessary for learning in the content areas. One possible set of inquiry tools for intermediate-grade students follows (Sierra-Perry et al., 1996, p. 37):

- identifying interesting and meaningful topics and questions to pursue;
- gathering quality source materials appropriate to their questions, interests, and abilities;
- gleaning information from these sources;
- organizing this information;
- responding to this information;
- sharing what they've learned; and
- pacing themselves for success.

READING IN THE CONTENT AREAS

We often assume that once students learn to read they can read just about anything. However, we must realize that all reading tasks are not alike. For example, the cognitive demands placed on readers by expository text differ from those placed by narrative text—they are not necessarily more difficult, but they are different. Readers must be taught how to recognize these differences and how to actively engage with expository text.

Narrative Versus Expository Material

narrative text ●

expository text ●

The structure of expository text differs from the structure of narrative text. Stories represent the structure of **narrative text**. Stories have characters, settings, problems, key events, and resolutions. These elements work together to impart a message or theme, and sometimes to present a moral, or lesson. The purpose of **expository text** is to explain, describe, or persuade. Expository material has a content focus and provides information and ideas. Representative examples of expository writing include news stories, reports, case studies, comparison/contrast papers, and historical accounts. Expository writing is organized according to a variety of structures. The seven most common structures are: description, cause/effect, comparison/contrast, time/order, problem/solution, enumeration, and persuasion.

- *Description,* as commonly found in informational text, provides characteristic features of the topic: "Eels are characterized by their snakelike shape, lack of spines in the fins, and the absence of ventral fins."

- *Cause/effect* tells of events and what happens as a result: "The Pilgrims were not used to such long, hard winters. Many Pilgrims became sick—so many that by spring about half were dead."

- *Comparison/contrast* directly discusses two related topics, giving their essential characteristics, and often employs similes to help readers make connections to more familiar concepts: "Hurricanes usually form over warm, tropical water, whereas tornadoes usually form over land. When tornadoes approach, people often say the sound is like that of a fast-moving train."

- *Time/order* (also called sequence) presents a chronological, historical accounting of events: "Archaeologists have learned that the evolution of man began with . . . then . . . followed by . . ."

- *Problem/solution* presents real-life events that require research in seeking a solution: "Apples cost 99 cents per pound. Jack needed three pounds to make the applesauce. How much money will he need?" or "Wetlands are valuable nursery areas for aquatic and land animals. They can even filter out some kinds of pollution . . . but developers are planning to build on these wetlands."

- *Enumeration* (can also include sequence) presents listings, step-by-step directions, or stages of development: "Amphibians first lay their eggs in clumps in quiet water or on moist leaf mold. Then the eggs hatch into larvae, or tadpoles. The tadpoles develop legs and grow into frogs."

• *Persuasion* offers a statement that is a proposition—a statement that can be argued as accurate—and support for that proposition: "The school bond referendum should be passed, and this is why . . ." Examples of persuasive writing are reviews of books, plays and films; editorials; letters to the editor; and position papers.

It is important to locate these structures within the expository materials that students will be using, which includes textbooks, trade books, and electronic text. A teacher should provide modeling and have small groups work together to find other examples within their classroom materials. Just as retellings are done for narrative comprehension, retellings of expository text can also be done by using the following guiding questions (Hoyt, 1999, p. 125):

- What is the topic?
- What are the most important ideas to remember?
- What did you learn that you did not already know?
- What is the setting for this information?
- What did you notice about the organization and text structure?
- What did you notice about the visuals such as graphs, charts, and pictures?
- Can you summarize what you learned?
- What do you think was the author's purpose for writing this [material]?

use these guidelines in order to write about what you read.

Literature Across the Curriculum

Textbooks are certainly not the only materials appropriately used in the content areas. Nonfiction trade books, or nonfiction children's literature, as well as electronic text provide useful tools for learning content and learning to read critically; they also can motivate and enrich content area teaching and learning. The nonfiction trade books available today are beautifully illustrative and cover a wide range of content area topics. Resources such as *Celebrating Children's Choices: 25 Years of Children's Favorite Books* (Post et al., 2000), *Nonfiction Matters: Reading, Writing, and Research in Grades 3–8* (Harvey, 1998), and *Using Literature in the Middle Grades: A Thematic Approach* (Moss, 1994) provide a wealth of information about specific book titles for use in the content areas.

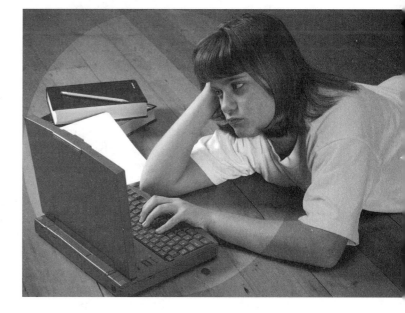

In addition, several valuable websites offer listings of materials, activities, supplies, and lesson plans, as well as links to extensive electronic text material for content area themes. Here are a few of these websites:

- **http://scholastic.com/MagicSchoolBus/theme/index.htm** lists materials, supplies, and activities related to popular science themes. For example, the Wetlands theme provides information and activities that are geared to help students persuade a town council to protect wetlands from being developed into a shopping mall—an all too real situation in many communities.

- **http://school.discovery.com/schrockguide** is one of the best sites for curriculum ideas in all content areas. This is a very thorough and well-maintained site. Visit the content-rich award-winning page for links to sites that are full of curriculum content organized by content areas. For example, under Science there is a link to "Secrets of the Ocean Realm" that would relate to a thematic unit on oceans. This site is a PBS-developed site and provides extensive information, photos, and activities for a wide variety of ocean-related topics. It would also be a wonderful source for helping students locate the different structures found in expository text.

- **www.sunburst.com/resources/game** provides free web-based activities accessed simply by signing in and receiving a user name; the user name enables students to gain an ad-free entrance (since Sunburst is also a software company). Students can enter the Classroom Challenges activities available for the content areas of social studies (e.g., geography), science (e.g., Journey Through Space), and mathematics (e.g., Venn diagrams). Each activity comes with an instructional plan for the teacher.

- **www.carolhurst.com** includes a collection of reviews of great books for kids; appropriate grade-level usages; ways to use these books in the classroom; and collections of books and activities on particular topics, curriculum areas, and themes.

Many content area teachers use both fiction and nonfiction literature as a way to introduce challenging subject area content. For example, historical fiction can be used to introduce and clarify a unit on World War II. A book such as *Friedrich* (Richter, 1970), a novel written from the perspective of a non-Jewish boy about the persecution and destruction of his Jewish neighbors and best friend in Nazi Germany, may be read aloud to students and their responses to the characters and events may be written in journals and referred to at relevant points in the study of World War II.

Teachers may choose to use several books across a wide range of reading ability levels and genres on a particular topic (e.g., ocean life, rain forests, the Holocaust, the stars, shapes). These books are made available for students to search for answers to questions they have about the particular topic (see the discussion of data charts later in this chapter). The use of literature has the potential for enhancing the interest students have for a topic and also helps teachers address curriculum standards related to providing students with a variety of genres for individual content areas such as social studies, science, and mathematics. See Appendix A; also Kane (2003) for extensive bibliographies of children's literature appropriate to the content areas.

WRITING IN THE CONTENT AREAS

We often assume that if we teach students to write about their experiences or to write stories, they will then be able to transfer those abilities to writing in the content areas. But students must have opportunities to write in response to expository text, to use writing as a tool for learning, and to write in expository modes (i.e., to inform, describe, persuade, or explain) in order to develop these skills. As indicated by many states' content standards, we now expect students to be able to write in a variety of genres (see Chapter 2). The techniques described in the following sections can help guide teachers in planning instruction for writing in the content areas. In addition, scoring rubrics for assessing expository writing, like those found in Appendix D and in Chapter 2, are valuable tools.

Using Expository Text Structures

As students experience the variety of structures used in expository material through their reading (see earlier discussion of expository text structures), they should be asked to write using these various structures. A strategy such as **ROW,** or Read/Organize/Write (Stephens and Brown, 2000), is useful as a framework for helping students move from locating each of the various text structures in their reading—one at a time, to identifying the characteristics of that structure, to writing their own selection for each of the text structures as they learn them.

● ROW

Read/Organize/Write (ROW)

ACTIVITY

The steps for using ROW are as follows:

1. Present a short, clear example of one of the expository text structures for the class to read. (**R**ead)

2. Guide students in developing a working definition of the text structure (see preceding definitions in the section "Narrative Versus Expository Material"), and perhaps a graphic organizer that represents that structure (see the section on "Organizational Techniques That Assist Expository Writing"). (**O**rganize)

3. Using a current topic, have students write an expository piece using a particular expository text structure. (**W**rite)

Writing Summaries

It is quite common for students in the intermediate grades to be asked to write summaries of what they have read as a way of demonstrating comprehension of their content area material. It is expected that a summary will provide only the main points from the material without interpretation or commentary. These summaries may be kept in a notebook or used as a way to prepare for unit tests. However, writing a summary is not an easy task for most students. Summaries are not retellings. In a retelling the student tries to include as much information as possible, whereas in a summary the goal is to be concise.

When asked to write a summary of what they have read, students often use personal criteria for deciding what is important to include, or they use a "copy and delete" method (Friend, 2000/2001), which means they copy or paraphrase some sentences and leave out others, again for personal reasons. Strategy instruction is needed to teach students how to determine the most important information and to concisely summarize that information. The best way to determine what is most important is to look for repeated information. When an argument is repeated often, or when reference is made to the same topic or idea even if different words or phrases are used, that is a clue that the information is important. Students should first ask themselves, "What does the author keep talking about?" A second question that will help lead students to a summary thesis statement is, "What is the author trying to say about (the idea identified in the first question)?"

Depending on the length of the material read, the summary might range from one sentence to a paragraph, or several paragraphs. A good summary should be concise, with a minimum of details, and with nothing repeated. Only the most central ideas are included, and these are written in the student's own words. For example, consider a lengthy section of a social studies text discussing Native Americans and how their life changed after Europeans arrived. This text provides detail about these people's differing views of the land, the clashes they had about land rights, the ensuing battles, and the emergence of reservations. It goes on to discuss joblessness among Native Americans and how several tribes (e.g., Choctaw, Navajo, Seminole, Cherokee, Passamaquoddy) began businesses to provide jobs for those living on the reservations. It continues with a discussion of powwows and what they mean to Native Americans. Friend (2000/2001) provides a model summary for this text:

> Native Americans are adjusting to mainstream American practices and strengthening tribal economies and culture. When the Europeans came to America, they took over most of the land and forced the Native Americans onto reservations. Recently many Native American tribes have opened businesses on their reservations to reduce unemployment. Their schools now teach their traditions along with modern American ideas. Powwows have become a social and cultural force to hold Native American people together. (p. 323)

Writing a Summary

ACTIVITY

Have students practice writing an effective summary using the sample passage below:

1. Have students preview, think, and read. Ask students to preview the entire passage and think about what they expect to learn. Then have them read the passage.

2. Have students ask themselves, "What does the author keep talking about? What is the author trying to say about this topic?" This will be the main idea, or the thesis, of the material.

3. Have students ask the same two questions in step 2 about each paragraph, or group of paragraphs. Ask them to write that idea in their own words in one sentence but leave out details, examples, or stories, giving only the important idea.

4. Have students continue this process for the entire reading selection.

5. Have students check their sentences against the passage, ensuring that they tell the most important ideas, not the details. Have them make sure that nothing is repeated; that the sentences are their own words; and that their first sentence gives the overall main idea, or thesis, of the entire selection, with the following sentences supporting the meaning of the first sentence.

Sample passage for "Writing a Summary" Activity

Animals' Body Coverings

Every animal's body covering is an adaptation that helps the animal survive. Feathers protect birds and help them fly. The fur or hair that covers most mammals helps keep them warm. Some mammals have sharp hairs that are used for protection. Others have whiskers that they use as sense organs. Many fish are covered with scales that protect them from disease and other animals that live in the water. A reptile's scales protect it from injury and from drying out.

Many animals have body coverings that are camouflage to help them hide. For example, a tiger's fur is striped. The stripes help the tiger blend in with the light and shadows of the tall grass in its environment. Toads—with their bumpy, brownish skin—look like pebbles on the forest floor. A chameleon's color changes to match its surroundings. The dark skin on an alligator's back makes it blend into the swamps where it lives. (Adapted from Lesson 2, How Do Animals' Body Parts Help Them Meet Their Needs? A16–A18 in *Science*, Grade 4.)

The following statements are intended as example student responses to the numbered steps above, for writing a summary.

1. I expect to learn about the different body coverings of animals.

2. The author keeps talking about the body coverings of animals, and how they help the animal survive.

3. The author is telling how body coverings can help animals blend in with their environment.

4. Animals have body coverings that help them survive by keeping them warm, and protecting them from other animals, from injury, or from weather. Body coverings also help animals blend in with their environment so they can hide from their enemies.

Proposition/Support Writing

One of the purposes of expository writing is to persuade. Persuasive writing has its own style, one that makes a proposal that is discussed and supported. There are many opportunities for authentic persuasive writing in the classroom. The school needs new playground equipment, or any number of other school needs; the neighborhood around the school faces environmental or safety issues that students recognize and want to do something about; state or federal budget discussions are threatening to cut education budgets—these are only a few examples of the types of issues that students can rally around and for which they can be taught to write persuasive essays or letters to the editor.

ACTIVITY   *Proposition/Support Outline*

A strategy developed by Buehl (2001, p. 101) called Proposition/Support Outlines helps students to write persuasively and also to read more critically material of an editorial nature. Engaging in this strategy also helps build analytical thinking skills so important for functioning in the world at large.

Five steps are involved in the strategy:

1. Discuss the difference between facts and opinions with students. Brainstorm examples of each and have students define the terms in their own words. Some examples might be the following:
   - The temperature today is 78 degrees. (Fact)
   - It feels warm today. (Opinion)
   - Everybody enjoys eating pizza. (Opinion)
   - There are 13 boys and 11 girls in our class. (Fact)
   - Dogs are the best pets. (Opinion)
   - Ten students in our room have a dog for a pet. (Fact)

2. For students, define the term *proposition* as "an opinion represented by a statement that is put forth as being true, or accurate." Give an example, such as, "Wearing school uniforms increases student achievement." Have students brainstorm other examples of possible

propositions. Then, in small groups, ask students to think of arguments they could make to support one of these propositions. Introduce the Proposition/Support Outline and model the five ways used to support propositions: facts, statistics, examples, expert authority, and logic and reasoning (see Figure 8.1).

3. Practice analyzing an author's persuasive piece using the outline from step 2. (Carefully choose a piece of writing that very clearly features the elements in the outline.) For example, students might work in pairs to analyze an editorial that details how the loss of a local wetland area will cause flooding in surrounding communities. They should be prepared to share the clues in the writing that helped them determine the facts, statistics, examples, expert authority, and logic and reasoning elements of the outline.

4. Discuss the quality of the support presented in the material read with the students. Is it convincing? Is only one means of support (e.g., logic and reasoning) relied on? Are the statistics reliable? Are the examples far-fetched? Is more than one expert authority cited?

5. Use the outline to critique editorials, prepare for a class debate, guide independent research, or write a position paper.

Organizational Techniques That Assist Expository Writing

Content standards usually include an expectation that students be able to write in a variety of genres and for a variety of purposes. At the intermediate-grade levels, students are generally expected to be able to write research reports and persuasive letters or compositions. (See Figure 8.2 for some suggested resources for such writing.) Organizational techniques similar to those used to aid in reading comprehension (e.g., maps, webs, charts) also work for expository writing. Use of these techniques will result in better reports and research papers. The following are effective ways to assist students in expository writing.

Cubing

Cubing (Neeld, 1986) is a strategy that requires students to explore a topic from six viewpoints: describe, compare, associate, analyze, apply, and argue. Typically, cubes are created to show what has been learned about a topic studied or to review a topic being studied. However, they can also be used to help students respond in writing to expository text, and thus to learn forms of expository writing.

Using the six sides of a cube, students answer key questions, some that may represent the structure of expository text, and write their answers on

● cubing

FIGURE 8.1   Example of a proposition/support outline.

PROPOSITION/SUPPORT OUTLINE FOR RAIN FORESTS

Proposition: The loss of rain forests will lead to an environmental disaster.

Support: 1. Facts

- Rain forests use carbon dioxide.
- There is increased carbon dioxide in the earth's atmosphere.
- The rain forests contain many endangered plant and animal species.
- Deforestation leads to widespread soil erosion in many areas.
- The burning of fossil fuels puts carbon dioxide into the environment.

2. Statistics

- The 1990s were the "hottest" decade in the last 100 years.
- One acre of rain forest disappears every second.
- Four million acres (larger than the state of Connecticut) disappear every year.
- Fifty to 100 species are destroyed with each acre of forest cleared.
- If present trends continue, half the rain forests of Honduras and Nicaragua will disappear by year 2000.

3. Examples

- India has almost no remaining rain forest.
- Current plans target eliminating much of the Congo's rain forest.
- Run-off from deforestation in Indonesia threatens their coral reefs and diminishes the fish population.
- Cutting of rain forests in Bangladesh and the Philippines has led to killer floods.

4. Expert Authority

- Computers predict doubling of carbon dioxide in the 21st century, raising temperatures by 3 to 9 degrees.
- National Center for Atmospheric Research believes increased carbon dioxide will lead to the Greenhouse Effect and global warming.
- Environmentalist leader Al Gore calls the Greenhouse Effect our most serious threat ever.

5. Logic and Reasoning

- Warmer temperatures will harm crops and increase energy costs.
- More people will starve because of less food and increased population growth.
- The polar glaciers will melt and raise the sea level, flooding coastlines.
- Many species useful to humans will disappear.
- More sections of the world will become uninhabitable deserts due to soil loss, erosion, overgrazing, and overcultivation.

Source: From Buehl, D. (2001), *Classroom Strategies for Interactive Learning* (2nd ed., p. 102). Reprinted with permission of Doug Buehl and the International Reading Association.

"How-to" resources on writing in the various content areas and in different genres.

FIGURE 8.2

Bentley, N., & Guthrie, D. W. (1995). *The young producer's video book: How to write, direct and shoot your own video.* Brookfield, CT: Millbrook.

Bentley, N., & Guthrie, D. W. (1998). *The young journalist's book: How to write and produce your own newspaper.* Brookfield, CT: Millbrook.

Day, R. A. (1998). *How to write and publish a scientific paper.* Phoenix, AZ: Oryx.

Dragisic, P. (1998). *How to write a letter.* New York: Franklin Watts.

Geffner, A. B. (1995). *How to write better business letters* (2nd ed.). Hauppauge, NY: Barron's.

Giblin, J. C. (1990). *Writing books for young people.* Boston: The Writer.

Goldberg, N. (1986). *Writing down the bones.* Boston: Shambala.

Hand, B., Prain, V., Lawrence, C., & Yore, L. D. (1999). A writing in science framework designed to enhance science literacy. *International Journal of Science Education, 21*(10), 1021–1035.

Ledoux, D. (1993). *Turning memories into memoirs: A handbook for writing lifestories.* Lisbon Falls, ME: Soleil Press.

Phillips, E. H. (1999). *Shocked, appalled, and dismayed! How to write letters of complaint that get results.* New York: Vintage Books.

Sheffield, C. (1999). *Borderlands of science: How to think like a scientist and write science fiction.* Riverdale, NY: Baen.

Wilson, E. O., & Bilger, B. (2001). *The best American science and nature writing 2001.* Boston: Houghton Mifflin.

Zinsser, W. (1998). *On writing well* (6th ed.). New York: HarperPerennial.

From S. Kane (2003). *Literacy and learning in the content areas.* Scottsdale, AZ: Holcomb Hathaway, p. 206.

each side of the cube for a content area topic they have chosen or that the teacher has assigned, taking about three to five minutes. (See Figure 8.3 for a sample cube for writing about the topic of statistics.) Sample questions are as follows:

- What is it like [describe]?
- What is it similar to or different from [compare/contrast]?
- What does it make you think of [associate]?
- How is it made or what is it composed of [analysis]?
- How is it used [application]?
- What are arguments for or against it [persuasion].

Students can use these cubes as springboards for longer writing assignments. Small groups can also work together compiling their information into a group paper. Additionally, these cubes can be used to jigsaw (see Chapter 5) content area information and can be shared so all students have access to the information for review purposes.

FIGURE 8.3   Cubing for expository writing about the topic statistics.

ASSOCIATE
doing research

APPLY	**DESCRIBE**	**COMPARE**	**ANALYZE**
In our class 10 people have dogs for pets, 5 have cats, 3 have fish, 1 has a bird. We did a bar graph.	Statistics—the collection and organizing of data	Portfolio—a collection of work organized to showcase abilities	We can use our data to say dogs are the most popular pet.

**ARGUE
(FOR OR AGAINST)**
Statistics: important b/c it helps us describe things we can use to persuade others.

Graphic Organizers

As discussed in Chapter 5, graphic organizers are a visual aid for constructing meaning. As such, they help both reading comprehension if constructed during and after reading, and writing as a prewriting exercise to organize thoughts. Also referred to as maps, clusters, webs, Venn diagrams, T-charts, think-links, sequence charts, or outlines, graphic organizers provide a visible structure that can assist the writer with expository forms. By appropriately using symbols and/or arrows, graphic organizers can be constructed to correspond to the patterns found in expository text. As the examples in Figure 8.4 show, a student wishing to write about Abraham Lincoln's life might use a **time/order** or **sequence chart,** to indicate chronological order. Another student who is going to write about the causes of the Civil War would use a cause/effect web. Someone writing to compare or contrast two events or concepts could use a **T-chart** (a two-column chart that resembles a lower-case t)

time/order or
sequence chart ●

T-chart ●

Examples of graphic organizers for expository text patterns. FIGURE 8.4

TIME/ORDER CHART

| Lincoln born | → | Lincoln moves | → | Lincoln teenager | → | Lincoln works | → | Lincoln adult | → | Lincoln President |

CAUSE/EFFECT WEB

TOPIC AND DETAILS MAP

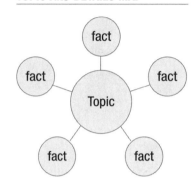

COMPARISON/CONTRAST T-CHART

TRIANGLE	SQUARE
3 sides	4 sides
3 angles	4 angles
	4 right angles
Sides can be different lengths	Sides are the same length

VENN DIAGRAM

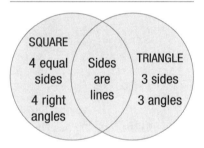

ENUMERATION CHART

How to Solve Multiplying Fractions

1. Multiply the numerators.
2. Multiply the denominators.
3. Whole numbers act as numerators with a denominator of 1.

CONCEPT AND EXAMPLES WEB

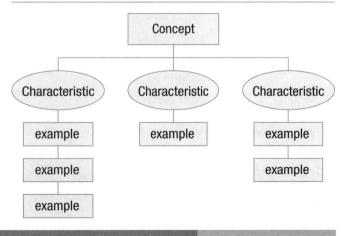

Venn diagram ●
topic and
details map ●

or a **Venn diagram** (two overlapping ovals to show both similarities and differences) to organize their thoughts. Simple **topic and details maps** are a way to organize paragraphs about a single topic. A student writing to describe a science concept might use a more weblike organizer to present characteristics of the concept with examples. A student explaining the steps to follow for solving a math problem could use a *listing (enumeration)* (an ordered category of elements) or a *flowchart* format (a visual description of a process).

✗ K-W-L Plus

K-W-L Plus strategy ●

A widely used strategy called a K-W-L chart has been expanded to include developing a concept map that helps a student convert information learned through reading into an expository piece of writing. This expansion, the **K-W-L Plus strategy** (Carr and Ogle, 1987), which maintains the "Know," "Want to know," and "Learned" columns, has one added step: using the categories of information developed during the "know" phase to categorize (or organize) the information listed in the "Learned" column. That information is then arranged in a concept map that students can use for writing a summary of the information, or an expository paper (see Figure 8.5).

FIGURE 8.5 K-W-L Plus for science writing, and the concept map generated.

TOPIC: SPIDERS

K (KNOW)	W (WANT TO KNOW)	L (LEARNED)
They have 8 legs.	How many kinds are there?	D—there are 30,000 species of spider.
Some are poisonous.		P—only a few are poisonous enough to harm a person.
They make webs.	How many are poisonous?	D—all have venom to paralyze their food.
They eat insects.		D—they eat insects, their 6-legged relatives.
	What do the poisonous spiders look like?	D—they have 2 breathing systems (tubes called tracheae, like insects, and the other called a book lung—looks like a stack of pages from a book).
Categories of Information We Expect to Use:	Where do the poisonous spiders live?	L—they are found everywhere.
1. What they are like (D = Description)		A—they can make silk to weave a web, or tie up insects, or wrap their eggs.
	Can the poisonous spiders kill a person?	A—they have knees so legs can curve, keeping them low to the ground for speed and stability.
2. Where they live (L = Location)	How do spiders make their webs?	A—they have gripping feet to help with web building and repair.
3. How they live (A = Abilities)	Where are their eyes?	P—they help keep down the population of disease-spreading insects.
4. How they affect people (P = People)		D—they have 2 eyes on top of their head, 1 on each side, and 4 across their forehead—a total of 8 eyes.
		D—they are also called arachnids.

Continued.   FIGURE 8.5

The data are then organized into a concept map in preparation for writing an expository passage about spiders where the writer can indicate possible order of presenting information, and what information is still lacking for further search.

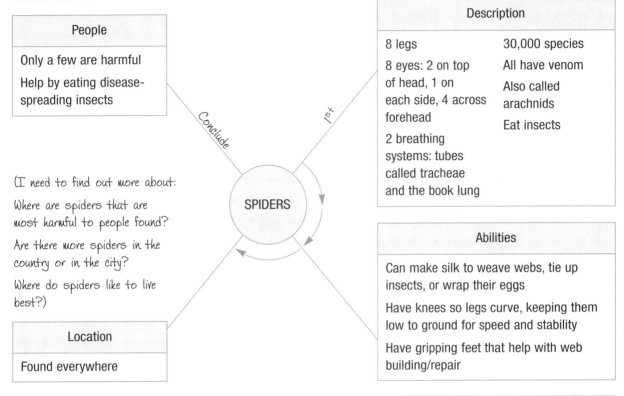

People

Only a few are harmful

Help by eating disease-spreading insects

(I need to find out more about:

Where are spiders that are most harmful to people found?

Are there more spiders in the country or in the city?

Where do spiders like to live best?)

Conclude

SPIDERS

1st

Description

8 legs	30,000 species
8 eyes: 2 on top of head, 1 on each side, 4 across forehead	All have venom
	Also called arachnids
	Eat insects
2 breathing systems: tubes called tracheae and the book lung	

Abilities

Can make silk to weave webs, tie up insects, or wrap their eggs

Have knees so legs curve, keeping them low to ground for speed and stability

Have gripping feet that help with web building/repair

Location

Found everywhere

Other variations of the original K-W-L chart include KNL (*N* = What do I *need* to know?), KWHL (*H* = *How* am I going to learn this, or research this, or investigate this, or report this?), KWLL (the second *L* = What do I *still* need to learn?), and KWLU (*U* = How can I *use* this information?) (Stephens and Brown, 2000).

Scaffolds for Content Area Writing

Even with teacher modeling and organizational frameworks, some students will experience difficulty with expository writing. **Paragraph frames** (Cudd and Roberts, 1989) can provide the kind of support needed for students who struggle in this area. This instructional tool helps students write about what they learn in content area material following their reading. A modified cloze format is used that provides sentence starters concentrating on the various organizational structures for expository text; however, the sequence or time order structure is the easiest one to use to introduce this

● paragraph frames

FIGURE 8.6

Example key words and phrases that indicate an expository structure.

EXPOSITORY STRUCTURE	KEY WORDS
Sequence or time/order	first, next, then, now, finally, before, after
Cause/effect	because, since, for, hence, so, as a result, if . . . then
Enumeration	one, two, three, another, more, to begin with, to continue, also
Comparison/contrast	but, however, although, yet, similar to, in contrast
Description	for example, in fact, characteristics are, for instance, like
Problem/solution	how, when, where, what, why, the problem is, one answer is
Persuasion	important, experts agree, percentage, statistics show, should

strategy. For example, the teacher writes a paragraph based on a content area topic currently being studied, being careful to use key words and phrases that will clearly reveal the expository structure. (See Figure 8.6 for examples of these key words.)

Next, the teacher puts the individual sentences on separate pieces of paper, or sentence strips. As a group, students are asked to think about the topic they are studying, and then arrange the sentences into a paragraph. With practice students can learn to order these sentences on their own, and eventually to complete paragraph frames independently (see Figure 8.7). After working with paragraph frames, students will have many models for their own independent expository writing.

FIGURE 8.7

A completed paragraph frame for adding fractions (enumeration structure).

These are the directions for adding fractions. First, look at the denominator of the fractions to see if they are the same. Second, change all the numbers, even the whole numbers, so they have the same denominator. Third, add the numerators. The denominator does not change. Last, if the fraction is more than a whole, change it to a mixed number.

Probable Passages   ACTIVITY

An adaptation of probable passages (Wood, 1984), a strategy more commonly used to assist in the writing of narrative material, can also provide support for students who struggle when writing expository text. The steps in this adaptation are as follows:

1. Identify the most significant concepts or terms that appear in the content area material currently being studied. Place these terms on the board or an overhead transparency (see Figure 8.8).

2. Supply an incomplete writing frame, similar to a paragraph frame, representing one of the various expository writing structures. (Model use of this strategy with each of the structures over a series of days.) For example, see the writing frame in Figure 8.8.

FIGURE 8.8 Probable passage: sample terms/vocabulary, writing frame, and passage.

KEY CONCEPT: Blue Whale (terms/vocabulary)

Characteristics and Features:

breathing hole, or nostril	dorsal fin	100 feet
up and down strokes	blowhole	arm bones
flukes	blubber	flipper bones
mammal	30 elephants	two hours
largest creature	stringy plates of	four-ton tongue
baleen	whalebone	few minutes
krill, a shrimplike creature		

Probable Passage (writing frame)

This selection tells us about the blue whale. The blue whale is the
_____ ever to live on Earth, weighing more than
_____ and becoming _____ long. It is not a fish
but a _____. It breathes through a _____, which is the same
thing as a _____. The blue whale eats four tons of
_____ every day in summer. When it eats, about 400
_____, called baleen, hang down from the upper lip.
The _____ traps anything the blue whale catches. Then the whale's
_____ forces water in and out of the mouth, making
the food go down the throat. In winter the blue whale survives on its own
body fat. A thick layer of _____ under the skin helps to keep in
body heat.

FIGURE 8.8 Continued.

As the whale roams the oceans it uses its _____, the muscular tail flippers, in _____ to propel itself through the water at about 20 miles per hour. The whale also has a boneless _____, _____, and _____ to help it move and stay in an upright position. Because it is a mammal and needs air to breathe, the whale must come to the surface every _____, although it can hold its breath for up to _____.

The Blue Whale (actual passage)

This selection tells us about the blue whale. The blue whale is the largest creature ever to live on earth, weighing more than 30 elephants and becoming 100 feet long. It is not a fish but a mammal. It breathes through a blowhole, which is the same thing as a breathing hole, or nostril. The blue whale eats four tons of krill, a shrimplike creature, every day in summer. When it eats, about 400 stringy plates of whalebone, called baleen, hang down from the upper lip. The baleen traps anything the blue whale catches. Then the whale's four-ton tongue forces water in and out of the mouth, making the food go down the throat. In winter the blue whale survives on its own body fat. A thick layer of blubber under the skin helps to keep in body heat.

As the whale roams the oceans it uses its flukes, the muscular tail flippers, in up and down strokes to propel itself through the water at about 20 miles per hour. The whale also has a boneless dorsal fin, arm bones, and flipper bones to help it move and stay in an upright position. Because it is a mammal and needs air to breathe, the whale must come to the surface every few minutes, although it can hold its breath for up to two hours.

3. Prior to their reading of the material, present to students the writing frame and the key vocabulary from the content area topic. Tell students this strategy is intended to help them learn the content area vocabulary and better comprehend the material they are about to read, as well as to help them write about the topic in the expository style.

4. Read and discuss the words with students. Invite students to think about where and how these words might be used in the writing frame. They may also use words not listed to complete the writing frame.

5. Work with students to develop a probable passage. They write in words and phrases to complete the writing frame.

6. Have students read a section of the related content area material.

7. After reading and discussing the material, have students look back at the probable passage and modify it to accurately reflect the information presented in the content area material (see the actual passage in Figure 8.8). After several teacher-directed sessions, students can work on their own, in pairs, or in small groups, to develop and share probable passages.

RESEARCHING IN THE CONTENT AREAS

Another important aspect of content area literacy is learning how to find out what you want to know. As all the content area standards indicate, students need to learn

- to be problem solvers.
- to ask questions.
- how to find out the answers.
- to communicate their findings.

In essence, this is what research is all about.

Brainstorming

Brainstorming is a structured way to activate learners' prior knowledge about and create interest in a topic. Students are asked to share their knowledge and experiences related to a set of words or concepts the teacher has identified from the content area materials. For example, before beginning a unit on Egypt, the teacher lists words such as pyramids, mummies, and pharaohs and asks students to share (either orally or in writing) what they know about these terms. As this information is shared, the teacher adds information that will assist the students in their understanding of these concepts (Sadler, 2001). Following this discussion, the teacher asks students what they want to find out about these concepts. Questions from students are compiled and posted for all to see, providing purpose for upcoming readings.

Locating Information

To assist students in locating information that helps to answer their questions about particular content area topics, several underlying skills need to be present. In addition to basic alphabetizing skills and knowledge of how

[handwritten margin note: learn how to categorize Data]

to use book parts such as a table of contents, the index, glossaries, or appendices, students need to be able to categorize information in a variety of ways. For example, if students are trying to learn more about the habitat of the polar bear, they need to recognize that information about weather can also be found under the category heading of climate. Recognizing potentially useful category headings and "key words" is critical when using online resources such as www.google.com for Internet searches, or CD-ROM encyclopedias.

As a first step before beginning research, teachers can list possible sources of information for answering a research question. These sources, however, should only include the ones for which the teacher has modeled the use. Possible sources for research are many, including almanacs, atlases, biographies, dictionaries, encyclopedias, magazines, maps, museum exhibits, newspapers, nonfiction books, photographs, published interviews, records, tapes, television programs, thesauri, and video productions. As online access has become common in classrooms, the Internet also has become a powerful research tool at the intermediate level. Teachers, however, need to be aware that the amount of information available can be overwhelming to students. A single key word search can result in thousands of websites, which can vary substantially in the quality and accuracy of the information they provide. One of the best resources for classroom teachers who are using the Internet as part of their teaching is Kathy Schrock's website at http://school.discovery.com/schrockguide/. She provides a wealth of information for educators, including suggested websites. She has also developed a set of relevant questions in both English and Spanish for elementary, middle, and secondary students to use in evaluating websites. For a set of questions for use by the classroom teacher in evaluating websites, see Figure 8.9, a compilation of several checklists. In addition, a teacher might consider a field trip to a public or university library for further instruction in using the Internet as well as the multitude of other resources available (Gipe, 2002).

Data Charts

data chart ● A **data chart** serves as an organizational structure for keeping track of research questions, notes, and information from several sources. These charts can be kept by individual students, small cooperative study groups, or posted for whole-class contributions. They can also be used as listening or viewing guides for students who are gathering information from resources such as a television documentary or a taped interview. An example using the questions generated from brainstorming the topic of ocean life is presented in Figure 8.10. The completed data chart can reveal relationships among concepts and help students get an overall picture of the topic being studied. As such, these charts serve students well as study guides before exams, or as guides for writing informational papers or project web pages, or preparing a speech or oral presentation.

The set of questions that follows is a compilation of several checklists developed for evaluating websites and is intended to be used by the classroom teacher.

AUTHOR CREDIBILITY

- Who is the author/source or producer?
- What is the authority or expertise of the individual or group that created this site? With what organization is the author of the website affiliated?
- Is there a way to contact the author or supply feedback?

  Tips: Check the header and footer information to determine the author and source.

  In the URL, a tilde (~) usually indicates a personal web directory rather than being part of the organization's official website.

  To verify an author's credentials, you may need to consult some printed sources such as *Who's Who in America* or the *Biography Index*.

ACCURACY AND RELIABILITY

- Is the information accurate?
- How current is the information? Is a date of publication provided? When was the website last revised? How frequently is the resource updated?
- Is the information presented in an objective, balanced manner?
- Is the information well written? Does the text follow basic rules of grammar, spelling, and composition?
- Are the sources of information stated? Can the information be verified?
- Does the information contradict something already known or learned from another source?
- Has the site been reviewed or ranked by an online reviewing agency?

SCOPE

- What is the primary purpose of the site (e.g., advertising, information)? Is the purpose of the resource clearly stated? Does it fulfill its purpose?
- Does the site contribute something unique on the subject?
- Is the material covered adequately?
- Is the site appropriate for the intended audience? Is it interactive enough to make students think?
- Are excerpts from texts provided or are entire texts available?
- Is the information available in other formats?
- Is the information factual or opinion?
- Does the site contain original information or simply links?
- Is a bibliography of print or web resources included?　　*(continued)*

FIGURE 8.9 Continued.

FORMAT AND NAVIGATION

- Can you find your way around and easily locate a particular page from any other page?
- Is response time fast?
- How many links does it take to get to something useful?
- Is the arrangement of links uncluttered?
- If there are links to other sites, do they work? How up-to-date are the links?
- How many links lead to a dead end?
- How stable is the connection to the site?
- Do parts of it take too long to load?
- Does the site require additional software or hardware?
- Is the site open to everyone on the Internet, or do parts require fees?
- Can nonmembers still have access to part of the site?
- Must a name and password be registered before using the site?
- Is there a text alternative? Text only? Can the graphics be turned off?
- Do illustrations, video, or audio add value to the site?
- Is the site conceptually exciting? Does it do more than can be done with print?
- Do the multimedia, graphics, and art serve a function or are they decorative?
- What is the quality of the multimedia, or graphic images? Do these images enhance the resource or distract from the content?
- Are the individual web pages concise, or does one have to scroll extensively?
- Does the site have its own search engine?
- Is the site easily browsable or searchable?

SOURCES

www.unc.edu/cit/guides/irg-49.html

www.lib.vt.edu/research/evaluate/evalbiblio.html

http://trochim.human.cornell.edu/WebEval/webeval.htm

www2.widener.edu/Wolfgram-Memorial-Library/webevaluation/inform.htm

www.hu.mtu.edu/teachtech/search2.htm

http://library.usm.maine.edu/guides/webeval.html

| Sample data chart for ocean features. | FIGURE 8.10 |

Research Group: <u>Ocean Features</u> (other groups are Ocean Plants and Ocean Animals)

Source	How many oceans are there?	How deep are the oceans?	What is on the ocean floor?	How much water is in the ocean?	Why is ocean water salty?	What causes waves?	What are tides?
1.							
2.							
3.							

EFFECTIVE INSTRUCTIONAL PRACTICES IN CONTENT AREA LITERACY

Before presenting strategies that are especially effective for literacy instruction in content areas, this section provides a general instructional approach to content area literacy as well as a summary of the research on best practices in content area instruction.

Instructional Approach—The FLIP Strategy

FLIP is a prereading strategy the reader uses to determine the friendliness (F), language (L), interest (I), and prior knowledge (P) of a reading selection (Schumm and Mangrum, 1991). The **FLIP strategy** can also be used effectively by the teacher in preparing content area lessons. In addition, students can be taught to use this strategy before they attempt their content area reading. The steps for this strategy as presented by Sadler (2001) are based on the following questions:

● FLIP strategy

- F (Friendliness): Which features of the content area material are easy to understand and which ones need further explanation (e.g., use of headings, sidebars, graphics)?
- L (Language): What terms might students have difficulty understanding?
- I (Interest): How much interest will my students have in this topic and how might that affect their level of involvement? How might I enhance their interest?
- P (Prior knowledge): Do I know what my students already know about this topic? If not, I need to find out.

For example, students are about to start a new science unit on light. The related chapter in their science textbook is called "The Nature of Light." The teacher examines this material and applies the FLIP strategy (Sadler, 2001, p. 38):

F   The text is divided into sections with questions.

L   Go over words such as *opaque, translucent,* and *transparent.*

I   Think how fast light moves!

P   Ask what students already know about light.

Best Practices

We know more today than we did 10 years ago about what instructional practices are effective. Zemelman et al. (1998) present a summary of research on best practices in content area instruction, and a brief synopsis of their findings can be seen in the accompanying box.

Synopsis of Research on Best Practices

**THE BEST CLASSROOM STRUCTURES
FOR CONTENT AREA INSTRUCTION:**

- Integrative units: multiweek chunks of curriculum organized around topics (e.g., whales) or themes (e.g., perseverance)

- Small group activities: less teacher talk; more active student involvement within continually shifting groupings (e.g., pairs, threes, study teams, group investigations) organized around skill needs, interests, or random assignment

- Representing-to-learn: a broadening of writing as a way to show what has been learned to include sketch books, maps, and other artistic and graphic representations

- Classroom workshop: a long, regularly scheduled chunk of time during which the focus is on doing the subject, such as doing writing, doing reading, doing math, doing history, doing science, rather than just hearing or reading about it. Student choice about what books to read, projects to complete, or topics to pursue, and frequent conferences between teacher and students are the two major elements of workshops with a typical time breakdown of 5 minutes for each student to share what will be worked on during the workshop, 30 minutes of workshop time to include conferences, and 10 minutes of each student sharing what was done that day. *(continued)*

Continued

- Authentic experiences: genuine real-world issues that are addressed much like in a service-learning (see Chapter 10) way that begins with student interest or natural curiosity for solving a problem or answering questions (e.g., homelessness—reasons for it and ways to help)

- Reflective assessment: use of observation, interviews, questionnaires, artifacts, portfolios, and rubrics with the goals of monitoring growth and helping students set goals, keep track of their own work, and evaluate their efforts (see Chapter 2)

BEST PRACTICES FOR MATH

use of manipulatives	connecting to other subjects
cooperative groups	understanding key concepts
discussion	estimation
questioning	spatial sense
justification	collecting/organizing data
writing about math	tables, graphs
problem solving	use of multiple assessment techniques (written, oral, demonstration)
word problems with everyday problems and applications	

BEST PRACTICES FOR SOCIAL STUDIES

provision of choices about what to study in depth	cooperative groups
inquiry and problem solving	integration of other curriculum areas
student decision making	getting to know cultures
participation in community/school affairs	open expression of ideas (e.g., class meetings)

BEST PRACTICES FOR SCIENCE

hands-on activities	in-depth study of a few important thematic topics
observation	integration of reading, writing, and math
hypothesizing	
reflection	collaborative, small group work
questioning	use of literature circles
thinking	
problem solving	

Strategies for Instruction in Content Area Literacy

Most of the strategies that follow are appropriately used for prereading, during reading, and postreading. Those that are best used differently are so indicated.

The Two-Minute Preview (prereading)
(Stephens and Brown, 2000)

Time spent previewing a content area selection prior to reading it helps students prepare adequately for what might be difficult, complex, or technical material. Previewing the material places the student in an active role right from the start. A checklist such as the one in Figure 8.11 can be used to guide the previewing. The actual items might change depending on the purpose of reading and the nature of the material itself. Students can work alone, or in pairs, for two minutes, jotting down their responses on the preview form. Following this, the teacher might suggest a strategy for reading the selection, based on the structure of the material.

FIGURE 8.11 Two-minute preview checklist.

☐ **Introduction.** What is the selection about?
_____
_____

☐ **Headings.** What are the topics in this selection?
_____
_____

☐ **Graphics and other visuals.** Can I interpret this information?
_____
_____

☐ **Margin notes.** Are there notes in the margins? What kind of information do they contain?
_____
_____

☐ **Summary.** Is it a clear and concise overview of the selection? What is one key idea in the summary?
_____
_____

Anticipation Guides (prereading, during reading, postreading)

A simple anticipation guide, a prereading tool, may provide from three to five statements and require students to indicate whether they agree or disagree with the statement. Students then read the text and either confirm or deny their choices.

1. There are about 1,500 active volcanoes. ___*disagree*___
2. Mt. St. Helens is a dormant volcano. ___*agree*___
3. Mauna Loa is the world's most active volcano. ___*agree*___
4. Once a volcano is dormant it can never erupt again. ___*agree*___

Anticipation guides can be more extensive and include an additional part that is completed during or after the reading. In the extended anticipation guide (Duffelmeyer and Baum, 1992), students determine whether or not there is support in the text for their agree/disagree choices, indicating yes or no and stating why. For the preceding example, students asked to extend their thinking during or after reading might provide the following information:

1. No support. I disagreed, but the article says there are about 1,500 active volcanoes.

2. Support. I agreed, and the article says that when a volcano is between eruptions it is dormant. Since Mt. St. Helens is not erupting now, it is dormant.

3. No support. I agreed that Mauna Loa is the most active volcano, but it is actually Kilauea, in Hawaii.

4. No support. I agreed that a dormant volcano never erupts again, but a volcano that never erupts again would be called extinct. Mt. St. Helens erupted in 1980 after being dormant for about 120 years.

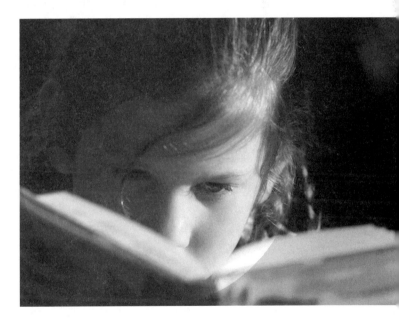

See Figure 8.12 for an anticipation guide for mathematics that goes beyond asking for agree/disagree responses. Students are asked to formulate/predict answers before reading.

Beyond Survey, Question, Read, Recite, Review (SQ3R)

Having a study system helps students develop an awareness of their own abilities to understand and learn information from expository material. Several systems are available to explore and perhaps modify to suit one's

FIGURE 8.12

An anticipation guide for mathematics prepared by an education student.

DIRECTIONS: Before reading Chapter One of *The Broken Dice: And Other Mathematical Tales of Chance* by I. Ekeland, answer the following questions.

1. How many possible outcomes are there if two dice are rolled? How did you arrive at your answer?

2. To the best of your ability, draw a tree diagram that would represent the possible outcomes of rolling two dice, along with their probabilities. If you're not sure, draw something anyway to see if you discover anything.

3. What are some uses of dice?

4. For what purposes do you, personally, use dice?

5. What is meant by the phrase *loading the dice*? What is the effect of loading the dice?

6. What would happen if a die broke while in use? For example, if two faces of a die are facing up, should both numbers count?

Now you're ready to read the chapter. After the reading, we'll have a class discussion of the story, and we'll solve a problem that involves issues of the accuracy of the methods discussed in the story. Then, we'll look at different ways to represent the use of dice to solve problems.

From S. Kane (2003). *Literacy and Learning in the Content Areas.* Scottsdale, AZ: Holcomb Hathaway, p. 103.

SQ3R—Survey, Question, Read, Recite, Review ●

personal preferences. Most of these systems stem from, or are modifications of, the classic study strategy of SQ3R—Survey, Question, Read, Recite, Review (Robinson, 1946). Briefly, to *survey,* the student reads the title, introductory paragraph, main headings, and chapter summary and examines any illustrations. To *question,* the student rephrases the main headings into questions to be answered during reading. The student then proceeds to *read,* with the purpose of answering the questions. To *recite,* the student simply recites the answers to the questions out loud. Finally, to *review,* the student will try to recall answers to questions as well as the general structure of the material, from memory. As students are introduced to a study strategy, they may find that a variation of that strategy works better for them. Students might be more willing to use a study system if they have participated in creating a personalized system. The many acronyms for study systems and a brief description of their characteristics follows:

SQ3R = Survey, Question, Read, Recite, Review (Robinson, 1946)

PORPE = Predict, Organize, Rehearse, Practice, Evaluate (Simpson, 1986)

STAR = Skim and set purpose, Think, Anticipate and adjust, Review and retell (Stephens and Brown, 2000)

PLAE = Preplan, List, Activate, Evaluate (Simpson and Nist, 1984)

PLAN = Predict, Locate, Add, Note (Caverly et al., 1995)

PQRST = Preview, Question, Read, Summarize, Test (Spache, 1963)

REAP = Read, Encode, Annotate, Ponder (Eanet and Manzo, 1976)

SCAIT = Select key words, Complete sentences, Accept final statements, Infer, Think (Wiesendanger and Bader, 1992)

SQRQCQ = Survey, Question, Read, Question, Compute, Question (Fay, 1965)

Study Strategy Tryout   ACTIVITY

The steps in this activity are as follows:

1. Model the use of several of the previously listed systems.

2. Discuss with students what they seem to have in common, and invite students to use these strategies when reading informational text.

3. After students have had an opportunity to try various strategies, discuss which ones seemed most helpful.

4. Encourage students to create their own combinations of study systems that seem most helpful to them. Some systems created by students might look like these (Stephens and Brown, 2000, p. 113):

    GOAL = Glance through, Order information, Adjust, Learn by retelling

    LAFF = Look over, Ask questions, Find answers, Follow through by reviewing and retelling

Find Someone Who . . . (postreading)   ACTIVITY

(Stephens, and Brown, 2000, p. 60)

This strategy is a fun and motivating way for students to clarify their comprehension of expository material by interacting with classmates.

1. Explain to students that their goal is to locate a classmate who can respond to a particular prompt related to a specific content area topic.

2. Using a teacher-prepared form (see Figure 8.13), students should seek individuals who can provide the needed information. Give students sufficient time to interact with each other and find someone to sign each box.

3. Have students write comments about what they have learned.

4. Encourage students to use the material read as a resource if needed. This reminds students that their materials, as well as other people, are resources and that it is sometimes necessary to reread material that is complex or technical.

FIGURE 8.13 Find Someone Who . . .

Find Someone Who . . . (Use your math textbook if you need to.)

can tell the difference between a triangle and a quadrilateral. Page Number: Answer: Signature:	can give an example of a parallelogram. Page Number: Answer: Signature:
can define polygon. Page Number: Answer: Signature:	can list the kinds of quadri-laterals. Page Number: Answer: Signature:
knows what type of polygon has nine sides. Page Number: Answer: Signature:	can compare an equilateral tri-angle with an isosceles triangle. Page Number: Answer: Signature:

Important Words—The Top Five (postreading) ACTIVITY

To ensure that students come away from their expository reading with an awareness of important subject matter terminology, this strategy focuses on helping students connect particular vocabulary with a particular topic of study.

1. Following the reading of some informational text, ask students to look back over the material and choose about 10 words that they think are the most important words in the selection.

2. Have students work in pairs or small groups to develop a Top Five list of words for this material. (*Note:* The number of words to settle on can certainly be something other than five.) To do this, they will need to discuss the words' meanings and their relative importance to the topic, as well as learn to compromise.

3. Ask each pair, or group, to present their list and reasons to the whole class.

4. Follow with further discussion to develop a whole-class Top Five list of words for the selection.

5. Use a graphic organizer to show the relationship of certain words that could in turn help students see that some words are subsumed within others.

TROUBLESHOOTING

It is very common for students who have made good progress in their literacy development up to the fourth grade to then start to show signs of difficulty. The increased attention to subject matter knowledge as opposed to narrative materials does cause some students to struggle. Use of the content reading interview might help initially to identify students who need extra attention in this area (Figure 8.14). However, it is the lack of familiarity with expository text structure that is generally the basis for difficulty. Following are some suggestions for dealing with this common difficulty.

Lack of Familiarity with Expository Text Structures

Students who have sufficient abilities in reading narrative material need to recognize that these same abilities are applicable to the more unfamiliar structures of expository material. In some ways, developing these new skills in reading expository material is like learning a new language—the language of expository text. Providing opportunities to use the patterns of content area language through all the language arts areas will accelerate both learn-

FIGURE 8.14   Content reading interview.

1. How much do you read in _____ (content area) _____
   What do you read? Why?

2. When you are reading in _____ (content area) _____ and come to something you don't know, what do you do?
   Do you ever do anything else?

3. Who is the best reader you know in _____ (content area) _____ ?
   What makes him or her a good reader in _____ (content area) _____ ?

4. How good are you at reading your _____ (content area) _____ book(s)?
   How do you know?

5. What is the hardest part about answering the questions in the book(s) used in _____ (content area) _____ ?

6. If you needed to study a chapter in _____ (content area) _____ so you could remember the information, how would you do it?

7. Have you ever tried _____ (name a study strategy) _____ ?
   Tell about it.

8. What do you have to do to get a good grade in _____ (content area) _____ class?

Source: Adapted from Wixson et al., 1984.

ing the content knowledge and learning the structure of expository text language. Students need to become comfortable with the unfamiliar language patterns and structures associated with various subject areas.

Because we know that English-speaking students begin to have difficulty in their literacy development when content area material is the focus, it is no surprise that nonnative speakers might experience difficulty. As the "In the Classroom" example of the dictoglos strategy demonstrates, it is especially valuable when working with second language learners to integrate the four language arts areas of reading, writing, listening, and speaking.

Dictoglos

1. Select an expository passage from a textbook or nonfiction trade book and read aloud to class.

2. While reading, have students write down key words and phrases.

3. Have students work in pairs to rewrite the text as they heard it from their notes.

4. Have the pairs join together to form groups of four and repeat step 3.

5. Ask for volunteers to read their re-created passages.

6. Lead a discussion about the material in the passage that is hard to re-create and ways to make this material easier to remember.

As indicated earlier in this chapter, graphic organizers can be especially helpful to readers struggling in content area literacy. The use of such visuals can help second language learners and native speakers alike understand expository text structures and comprehend organization patterns. When students are asked to read large quantities of material, some may have difficulty and feel they are overwhelmed with information. The **herringbone** **strategy**, a graphic, structured outlining technique, helps readers organize the most important information from expository material. The herringbone structure (see Figure 8.15) reminds them of what information to look for while they are reading. Six basic questions are asked: Who? What? When? Where? How? and Why? In addition, readers are asked to determine the main idea. Students can easily reproduce the herringbone form in their notebooks and record their answers there while they read their informational texts. After several sessions involving teacher modeling, students are ready to begin completing their own herringbone forms. Students may notice that all the questions may not be answered within the selection they are reading. This situation leads to the recognition that a variety of sources is needed to learn as much about a topic as possible.

● herringbone strategy

FIGURE **8.15** Example of herringbone strategy for chapter on Bass Reeves.

Who? Bass Reeves law enforcement officer

When? 1875

How? Often captured outlaws through use of disguises and undercover operations.

Main Idea: Bass Reeves was a legendary U.S. marshal of uncompromising principles and courage.

(Did) What? Became the first Black deputy U.S. marshal— not just an honorary post (like Frederick Douglass)

Where? West of the Mississippi River in Indian territory

Why? Bass Reeves wished to avoid shoot-outs and unnecessary violence.

Source: Abdul-Jabbar and Steinberg, 1996.

SUMMARY

This chapter has presented a wealth of information about the nature of content area literacy, the relationship of literacy standards and content area standards, as well as many examples for instruction in content area reading and writing. The most important aspect of content area literacy instruction is to use expository material to teach the strategies that will help students most with informational text. Recognizing that expository text is different from narrative text, and how it is different, will help students understand that they will need to adjust their typical reading behaviors, such as reading fast, and do more stopping, thinking, and reviewing of informational material.

Questions
FOR JOURNAL WRITING AND DISCUSSION

1. Identify key concepts that students need to know in a math, science, or social studies text being used in a local school district. What kind of activities could you design that would enhance students' comprehension of these concepts?

2. Discuss the value of metacomprehension or comprehension monitoring abilities for reading in the content areas.

3. You have a friend whose child was given an open-ended homework assignment that requires the child to demonstrate his or her knowledge about the topic, ocean animals. Your friend and the child have no idea what to do or where to start. How could you help?

Suggestions
FOR PROJECTS AND FIELD ACTIVITIES

1. Model the K-W-L Plus strategy with a small group of intermediate-grade students. Then, with new material, let the students try the technique. Question them regarding the effectiveness of the technique. Did they feel the strategy was helpful? Why or why not?

2. Prepare a paragraph frame based on a content area selection read by a student. Discuss the detail sentences with a student who typically has difficulty with expository text material. Have the student sequence the detail sentences and then complete the paragraph frame. Reflect with the student on the effectiveness of this technique. Did the student find this strategy helpful? Why or why not?

3. Choose a topic or theme that is widely used in your local school districts (e.g., rain forests, exploration, the planets, geometry in our daily lives), and prepare an annotated bibliography of fiction and nonfiction materials (not just text materials) that span a wide range of reading ability levels for this topic/theme.

References

Abdul-Jabbar, K., & Steinberg, A. (1996). Bass Reeves. In *Black profiles in courage: A legacy of African American achievement* (pp. 112–139). New York: William Morrow and Company.

Buehl, D. (2001). *Classroom strategies for interactive learning* (2nd ed.). Newark, DE: International Reading Association.

Carr, E., & Ogle, D. (1987). K-W-L plus: A strategy for comprehension and summarization. *Journal of Reading, 30*(7), 626–631.

Carr, K. S., Buchanan, D. L., Wentz, J. B., Weiss, M. L., & Brant, K. J. (2001). Not just for the primary grades: A bibliography of picture books for secondary content teachers. *Journal of Adolescent & Adult Literacy, 45*(2), 146–153.

Caverly, D., Mandeville, T., & Nicholson, S. (1995). PLAN: A study-reading strategy for informational text. *Journal of Adolescent & Adult Literacy, 39,* 190–199.

Cudd, E. T., & Roberts, L. L. (1989). Using writing to enhance content area learning in the primary grades. *The Reading Teacher, 42,* 392–404.

Duffelmeyer, F. A., & Baum, D. D. (1992). The extended anticipation guide revisited. *Journal of Reading, 35,* 654–656.

Eanet, M. G., & Manzo, A. V. (1976). REAP—a strategy for improving reading/writing study skills. *Journal of Reading, 19,* 647–652.

Fay, L. (1965). Reading study skills: Math and science. In J. A. Figurel (Ed.), *Reading and inquiry.* Newark, DE: International Reading Association.

Friend, R. (2000/2001). Teaching summarization as a content area reading strategy. *Journal of Adolescent & Adult Literacy, 44*(4), 320–329.

Gipe, J. P. (2002). *Multiple paths to literacy: Classroom techniques for struggling readers* (5th ed.). Upper Saddle River, NJ: Merrill/Prentice Hall.

Harvey, S. (1998). *Nonfiction matters: Reading, writing, and research in grades 3–8.* York, ME: Stenhouse.

Hoyt, L. (1999). *Revisit, reflect, retell: Strategies for improving reading comprehension.* Portsmouth, NH: Heinemann.

Kane, S. (2003). *Literacy and learning in the content areas.* Scottsdale, AZ: Holcomb Hathaway.

Moss, J. G. (1994). *Using literature in the middle grades: A thematic approach.* Norwood, MA: Christopher-Gordon.

Neeld, E. C. (1986). *Writing* (2nd ed.). Glenview, IL: Scott Foresman.

Post, A. D., with Scott, M., & Theberge, M. (2000). *Celebrating children's choices: 25 years of children's favorite books.* Newark, DE: International Reading Association.

Richter, H. P. (1970). *Friedrich.* Translated from the German by Edite Kroll. New York: Holt, Rinehart & Winston.

Robinson, F. P. (1946). *Effective study.* New York: Harper and Bros. (Also 1970, 4th ed. New York: Harper & Row.)

Sadler, C. R. (2001). *Comprehension strategies for middle grade learners: A handbook for content area teachers.* Newark, DE: International Reading Association.

Schumm, J. S., & Mangrum, C. T. (1991). FLIP: A framework for content area reading. *Journal of Reading, 35,* 120–124.

Sierra-Perry, M., with Ewing, J., Foertsch, D., & Sierra, S. (1996). *Standards in practice grades 3–5.* Urbana, IL: National Council of Teachers of English.

Simpson, M. L. (1986). PORPE: A writing strategy for studying and learning in the content areas. *Journal of Reading, 29,* 407–414.

Simpson, M. L., & Nist, S. L. (1984). PLAE: A model for planning successful independent learning. *Journal of Reading, 29,* 218–223.

Spache, G. (1963). *Toward better reading.* Champaign, IL: Garrard.

Stephens, E. C., & Brown, J. E. (2000). *A handbook of content literacy strategies: 75 practical reading and writing ideas.* Norwood, MA: Christopher-Gordon.

Wajnryb, R. (1990). *Grammar dictation.* Oxford, England: Oxford University Press.

Wiesendanger, K. D., & Bader, L. (1992). SCAIT: A study technique to develop students' higher comprehension skills when reading content area material. *Journal of Reading, 35,* 399–400.

Wixson, K. K., Bosky, A. B., Yochum, M. N., & Alvermann, D. E. (1984). An interview for assessing students' perceptions of classroom reading tasks. *The Reading Teacher, 37*(4), 346–352.

Wood, K. D. (1984). Probable passages: A writing strategy. *The Reading Teacher, 37,* 496–499.

Wood, K. D. (2001). *Literacy strategies across the subject areas: Process-oriented blackline masters for the K–12 classroom.* Boston: Allyn & Bacon.

Zemelman, S., Daniels, H., & Hyde, A. (1998). *Best practice: New standards for teaching and learning in America's schools* (2nd ed.). Portsmouth, NH: Heinemann.

CHAPTER 9

Differentiating Instruction for Students with Special Needs

- What are the major groups of diverse learners for which differentiated instruction is important?
- What are some specific adaptations for these diverse learner groups?
- When differentiating instruction to meet the needs of diverse learners, what curricular components could be modified?

WHY DIFFERENTIATE INSTRUCTION?

It is common knowledge that today's classrooms are places of great diversity. All classrooms are academically diverse, but, in addition, there are other ways in which classrooms are diverse. Students come to school speaking a variety of first languages other than English. Some come with academic giftedness, and some with learning disabilities. Others are physically or neurologically challenged by a variety of impairments, such as speech, hearing, or vision deficits (communication disorders); cerebral palsy; dyslexia; autism; and attention deficit hyperactivity disorder (ADHD). Still others demonstrate social/emotional maladjustments or health and environmental issues associated with extreme poverty. Nearly all of these students will have academic, behavioral, physical, or social needs, or combinations of these, that will require instructional adaptations within the classroom setting (Lewis and Doorlag, 1999).

Unfortunately, most teachers are not well prepared to meet the needs of these diverse learners. There are two main goals for this chapter: (1) to provide information about the important characteristics and special adaptations for several diverse learner groups, and (2) to provide information about how to differentiate instruction in ways that help all students learn and grow. Recognition of who these diverse learners are and the importance of their perceptions of themselves as learners to their self-esteem is necessary for guiding their learning (Glazer, 1998). Therefore, it is also important to explain to the entire class that we all learn differently, but that we are all capable of learning. Students may be doing different assignments on occasion, but these assignments are differentiated based on particular learning needs.

DIVERSE LEARNER GROUPS

Students Who Are Linguistically Diverse (English Language Learners)

Characteristics. Linguistic diversity is a reality in today's public schools. As many as 8 million children in the United States have a non-English background (Grossman, 1995). Among the school-age population,

In the Classroom

Marcia, a special education student, and Jason, an advanced learner, both in fifth grade, are working together researching the Tasmanian devil—its habitat, eating habits, and physical characteristics. Their teacher, Mrs. Hooper, liked Mr. Perez's study of exotic animals so much (see Chapter 3) that she gave her fifth-grade students the choice of studying one particular animal that is real, but that is also considered "exotic." Both Marcia and Jason wished to study the Tasmanian devil, so they are working together on this research project, which will culminate with a creative presentation of the information they have learned. During computer searches for information, Jason does most of the reading, while Marcia's strengths are more apparent in the creative areas of art and designing. Marcia also likes food and cooking, so she suggests creating recipes for a restaurant serving Tasmanian devils that she and Jason are working on for their culminating presentation. During a brief sharing time, Marcia and Jason solicit feedback from their classmates on their ideas so far.

Marcia shares some recipes she has created for Tas's Cave Café, which is only open for dinner since Tasmanian devils are nocturnal creatures. She tells classmates that she has created a poultry item for the menu that includes fried grubs as a side dish because Tasmanian devils eat grubs, small mammals, and birds. Jason tells how he realized their menu needed prices, and since Tasmanian devils live on Tasmania, an island south of Australia, he needed to figure out what the food costs would be in Tasmanian currency. He says he enjoyed converting American dollars and cents to Tasmanian money, giving as an example the poultry dish Marcia created, which is listed at $6.95 US or $13.75 AUD (Australian currency). Peer feedback comes in the form of both a compliment and a suggestion: classmates say that they really like Jason and Marcia's project idea of the restaurant and suggest that including on their menu more specific information about what Tasmanian devils look like will improve the presentation.

1.9 million students in California, almost 1 million in Texas, and about 700,000 in New York speak a non-English language at home (Hernandez, 1997). Spanish speakers are currently the largest group of bilingual individuals in the United States, with other large groups being German, French, Chinese, and Italian (Hernandez, 1997; Lewis and Doorlag, 1999). But there are many other languages represented in classrooms today: Arabic, Asian Indian, Filipino, Greek, Hmong, Hungarian, Japanese, Korean, Polish, Portuguese, Russian, Spanish, Ukranian, Vietnamese, Yiddish, and others, as well as a decreasing number of tribal languages of Native Americans. And linguistic diversity is not limited to foreign languages. There are dialects of English, such as African American vernacular English (AAVE), that are also represented in many classrooms.

When students acquire English as a second language, their speech still may sound different from that of native English speakers. They may speak with an accent as a result of the nonequivalence of speech sounds that exist between their native language and English. For example, a student whose native language is Spanish might say "chip" for "ship," or "sip" for "zip." A student who speaks AAVE might say "sick" for "six," or "birfday" for "birthday." Other sound differences for some of the many languages in today's schools are presented in Figure 9.1.

Adaptations. There are general principles that teachers need to keep in mind in order to be supportive of their English language learners. As condensed from Gipe (2002, pp. 59–62), these are as follows:

- Respect differences in languages and dialects as natural.
- Use methods that bridge cultural background knowledge and whatever texts are being read.
- Contextualize instruction on language structures and skills within the composing and comprehending process.
- Use authentic materials from the learner's community.
- Design literature-based instruction for developing language competence.
- Use technological and other communicative arts to facilitate oral and written language acquisition.

273

FIGURE 9.1 Problematic sounds for English language learners.

LANGUAGE	SOUNDS EITHER NOT PART OF THE LANGUAGE OR PROBLEMATIC
Chinese	b ch d dg g oa sh s th v z f j l m n ng l-clusters r-clusters
French	ch ee j ng oo th a h oy s schwa
Greek	aw ee i oo schwa
Italian	a ar dg h i ng th schwa v l-clusters end clusters
Japanese	dg f i th oo v schwa h l r sh s w l-clusters r-clusters
Korean	b l oa ow p r sh t th l-clusters r-clusters
Spanish	dg j sh th z b d h m n ng r t v w y s-clusters

- Facilitate authentic, functional communication.
- Base literacy assessment on authentic language and literacy tasks and events.
- In interpreting assessment data, be sensitive to cultural and linguistic variation.

General approaches for adapting instruction to better meet the needs of the English language learner include cooperative learning and sheltered English. **Cooperative learning** is an approach in which students work together to achieve a common goal. It is useful for English language learners to work cooperatively with native English speakers because they will need to communicate orally with each other. Through cooperative learning, English language learners can acquire competence in oral language because of the increased opportunities for "comprehensible input" from their peers (Krashen, 1987).

cooperative learning ●

sheltered English ●

The goal of **sheltered English** is to teach English language skills at the same time students are learning specific subject matter knowledge (California Teachers of English to Speakers of Other Languages, 1992). The teacher must examine the content of the lesson to identify and select key concepts, or terms, that are critical to the lesson. These are taught systematically in ways that maximize students' abilities to comprehend—that is, ways that use Krashen's (1987) notion of "comprehensible input." For example, the use of graphic organizers, as discussed in several chapters throughout this book, would be very appropriate. These structures provide for visible and manipulable input. Hernandez (1997) shares several types especially useful for English language learners: realia organizers, verb organizers, noun organizers, concept organizers, and episodic organizers (see Figure 9.2 for an example of a concept organizer). These organizers can also be posted to pro-

Example of a concept organizer for the concepts bulb and sprout. FIGURE 9.2

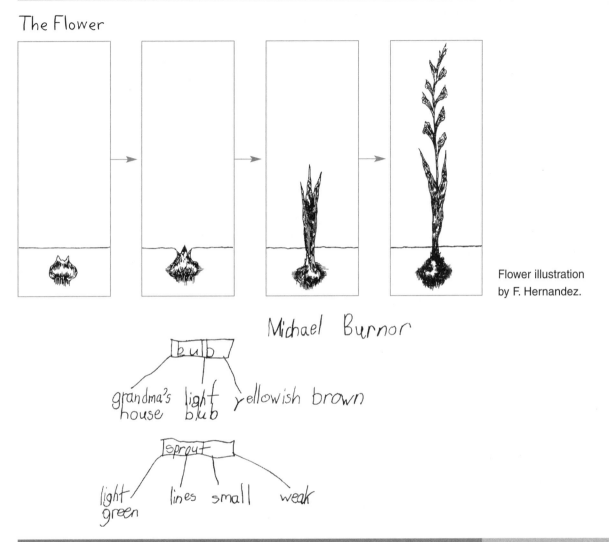

The Flower

Flower illustration by F. Hernandez.

Source: Teaching in Multilingual Classrooms: A Teacher's Guide to Context, Process, and Content, by Hilda Hernandez. © 1997. Reprinted by permission of Pearson Education, Inc., Upper Saddle River, NJ.

vide a visual reference for students. Anything and everything should be used to create a context for the content information to make it understandable. In addition to **realia,** or real objects, pictures, sketches, gestures, body language, demonstrations, and dramatic enactments will all provide for "comprehensible input." For example, for the sentence "Her facial expression was as sour as a lemon," students can be given a bit of lemon to taste as they look at their face in front of a mirror. Examples from the students' own backgrounds should be included. Helping students personally identify with the topic will make the learning more meaningful to them.

● realia

Students Who Are Gifted and Talented

Characteristics. Gifted and talented students have extraordinary intellectual abilities or they demonstrate exceptionally high achievement in particular academic areas or in the visual or performing arts compared with their peer group. These students represent all cultural, ethnic, and socioeconomic backgrounds. However, there is variability in the way individual states identify, classify, and implement programs for gifted and talented students. Frequently, intellectually gifted students are identified by very high scores on standardized tests and their high achievement levels in school. Their linguistic abilities are usually highly developed compared with their peers. Hyperactivity may also be a sign of giftedness; students who are gifted often have high levels of activity in the classroom as a result of boredom or intense interest in an activity. See Figure 9.3 for characteristics of intellectually gifted children.

FIGURE 9.3 Characteristics of intellectually gifted children.

Few children will display all of the characteristics in a given list; however, when clusters of these characteristics are present, they do serve as fairly reliable indicators. These characteristics are best used as signals to indicate that a particular child might warrant closer observation and could require specialized educational attention, pending a more comprehensive assessment by a qualified specialist.

GENERAL BEHAVIORAL CHARACTERISTICS

☐ Many typically learn to read earlier with a better comprehension of the nuances of the language. As many as half of the gifted and talented population have learned to read before entering school. They often read widely, quickly, and intensely and have large vocabularies.

☐ They commonly learn basic skills better, more quickly, and with less practice.

☐ They are frequently able to pick up and interpret nonverbal cues and can draw inferences which other children have to have spelled out for them.

☐ They take less for granted, seeking the "hows" and "whys."

☐ They display a better ability to work independently at an earlier age and for longer periods of time than other children.

☐ They can sustain longer periods of concentration and attention.

☐ Their interests are often both widely eclectic and intensely focused.

☐ They frequently have seemingly boundless energy, which sometimes leads to a misdiagnosis of "hyperactive."

☐ They are usually able to respond and relate well to parents, teachers, and other adults. They may prefer the company of older children and adults to that of their peers.

☐ They are willing to examine the unusual and are highly inquisitive.

☐ Their behavior is often well organized, goal directed, and efficient with respect to tasks and problems.

☐ They exhibit an intrinsic motivation to learn, find out, or explore and are often very persistent. "I'd rather do it myself" is a common attitude.

☐ They enjoy learning new things and new ways of doing things.

Continued.

FIGURE 9.3

LEARNING CHARACTERISTICS

☐ They may show keen powers of observation, exhibit a sense of the significant, and have an eye for important details.

☐ They may read a great deal on their own, preferring books and magazines written for youngsters older than themselves.

☐ They often take great pleasure in intellectual activity.

☐ They have well developed powers of abstraction, conceptualization, and synthesizing abilities.

☐ They generally have rapid insight into cause-effect relationships.

☐ They often display a questioning attitude and seek information for the sake of having it as much as for its instrumental value.

☐ They are often skeptical, critical, and evaluative. They are quick to spot inconsistencies.

☐ They often have a large storehouse of information regarding a variety of topics which they can recall quickly.

☐ They show a ready grasp of underlying principles and can often make valid generalizations about events, people, and objects.

☐ They readily perceive similarities, differences, and anomalies.

☐ They often attack complicated material by separating it into its components and analyzing it systematically.

CREATIVE CHARACTERISTICS

☐ They are fluent thinkers, able to produce a large quantity of possibilities, consequences, or related ideas.

☐ They are flexible thinkers able to use many different alternatives and approaches to problem solving.

☐ They are original thinkers, seeking new, unusual, or unconventional associations and combinations among items of information. They also have an ability to see relationships among seemingly unrelated objects, ideas, or facts.

☐ They are elaborative thinkers, producing new steps, ideas, responses, or other embellishments to a basic idea, situation, or problem.

☐ They show a willingness to entertain complexity and seem to thrive in problem situations.

☐ They are good guessers and can construct hypotheses or "what if" questions readily.

☐ They are often aware of their own impulsiveness and the irrationality within themselves and show emotional sensitivity.

☐ They have a high level of curiosity about objects, ideas, situations, or events.

☐ They often display intellectual playfulness, fantasize, and imagine readily.

☐ They can be less intellectually inhibited than their peers in expressing opinions and ideas and often exhibit spirited disagreement.

☐ They have a sensitivity to beauty and are attracted to aesthetic dimensions.

Source: Whitmore, J. R. (1985). Characteristics of intellectually gifted children (Digest 344). *Digests on the gifted* (pp. 1–2). Reston, VA: The Council for Exceptional Children.

Students are also classified as creatively gifted and talented if they excel in the visual or performing arts. These talents usually become apparent when a student is relatively young. Davis (1995) lists 12 categories as representative of creative individuals: "original, independent, risk taking, aware of creativeness, energetic, curious, has a sense of humor, attracted to complexity, artistic, open-minded, needs time alone, and intuitive" (Mastropieri and Scruggs, 2000, p. 148). Further information about recognizing giftedness in students can be found on websites for national organizations (e.g., www.nagc.org or www.gtworld.org).

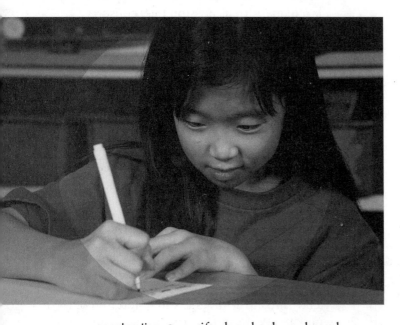

Adaptations. Just because a student may have exceptional abilities does not mean that student can realize his or her full potential without specially adapted educational programs. Gifted and talented students "often have special learning needs that are not fully met by the general education program" (Lewis and Doorlag, 1999, p. 394). The most common educational approaches for

acceleration ● gifted and talented students are acceleration and enrichment. **Acceleration** simply means moving students through the curriculum at a faster pace than general education students. This could mean beginning school early, skipping grades, testing out of classes, or providing more ability-appropriate curriculum. Acceleration often means students do not remain with their age

enrichment ● peers. **Enrichment** simply means expanding on the curriculum. The same subjects may be studied in greater depth, or after-school programs may provide instruction in additional subjects or content not typically found in the curriculum (e.g., chess, finance policies in state government). More often enrichment programs keep gifted students in their general education classrooms with their age peers. Both accelerated and enrichment programs can be provided within the regular classroom, in resource classes, in university classes, or through flexible scheduling or mentoring programs. General classroom teachers would do well to heed the advice of Kennedy (1995, pp. 233–234) when they find gifted students within their classrooms:

- Resist policies requiring more work of those who finish assignments quickly and easily. Instead explore ways to assign different work.
- Seek out supplemental materials and ideas that extend, not merely reinforce, the curriculum.
- Deemphasize grades and other extrinsic rewards.
- Encourage intellectual and academic risk taking.
- Help all students develop social skills to relate well to one another.

- Take time to listen to responses that may at first appear to be off target.
- Provide opportunities for independent investigations in areas of interest.
- Be aware of the special needs of gifted girls (i.e., they can achieve high-level career goals and succeed in math and science).

Students Who Are Learning Disabled

Characteristics. Students with learning disabilities are also referred to as neurologically impaired, or perceptually handicapped. They are often unfairly labeled and described in negative terms. However, students with learning disabilities are average and bright learners who do *not* necessarily have hearing or visual impairments, physical or health issues, emotional disturbances, or environmental, cultural, or economic disadvantages, yet they perform poorly in school. They are quite puzzling to their teachers.

A widely accepted definition of **learning disability** is that provided by the National Advisory Committee on Handicapped Children (1968):

● learning disability

> A disorder in one or more of the basic psychological processes involved in understanding or in using language, spoken or written, which may manifest itself in an imperfect ability to listen, think, speak, read, write, spell, or to do mathematical calculations. . . . The term does not include children who have learning problems which are primarily the result of visual, hearing, or motor handicaps, of mental retardation, or of environmental, cultural, or economic disadvantage.

Students with learning disabilities have difficulty processing information. These processing problems may be in the area of perception, attention, memory, or expressive language. They often have poor strategies for learning. In addition to poor performance in school subjects, they often have a high activity level and difficulty paying attention. And they can lack the skill to communicate appropriate social messages, making group work difficult.

Adaptations. Because their difficulties are unique, students with learning disabilities present a special challenge to classroom teachers. Teachers will need to use their collaboration, creative thinking, and problem-solving strategies to best help these students. Mastropieri and Scruggs (2000, pp. 83–84) provide an extensive list of adaptations to consider when teaching students with learning disabilities; an abbreviated version appears here:

- Adapt the physical environment to provide a distraction-free workplace that will help students focus their attention (e.g., rearrange seating positions, provide quiet space within the classroom, keep desks away from potentially troublesome stimulation).
- Model organization (e.g., a place for everything and everything in its place; show what an organized desk or notebook looks like).
- Structure daily routines and schedules (e.g., make a list of what to do first, second, etc.).

- Adapt instructional materials (e.g., make assignments more compatible with literacy skills and organizational abilities—see section on differentiated instruction later in this chapter).

- Teach study skills (e.g., how to schedule time, keep an assignment calendar, and use study strategies).

- Adapt instruction (e.g., use of SCREAM variables: structure, clarity, redundancy, enthusiasm, appropriate pace, maximized engagement).

- Vary presentation formats (e.g., verbal, visual aids, realia, field trips, computers, audio- and videotapes).

- Question students frequently (e.g., ask students to rephrase information in their own words, checking for understanding).

- Provide clear directions and accessible goals (e.g., use short, concise sentences, reminders for long-term assignments, regular monitoring).

- Teach students how to learn (e.g., model how to use learning strategies).

- Use peer tutors (e.g., classmates can provide assistance or additional practice).

- Conduct periodic reviews (e.g., recall previously taught content and relate to new information being learned).

- Adapt evaluation procedures (e.g., use alternatives to standard paper-and-pencil tests, such as drawings, sketches, or dramatic enactments).

The majority of students with learning disabilities are not placed in special classes but remain in the regular classroom with some part-time help from a resource teacher. It is imperative for classroom teachers to recognize these students and do their best to help them learn.

Students Who Have Communication Disorders

Characteristics. Communication disorders are those that affect students' ability to interact with teachers and peers. Generally communication disorders involve language and speech disorders. **Language disorders** are characterized by the inability to use the oral and/or written symbols of language. Students have trouble expressing themselves either orally or in writing. Grammatical patterns are not used appropriately. Students' vocabulary is limited, and they have difficulty following directions. **Speech disorders** are characterized by frequent and severe difficulty in pronouncing certain sounds (articulation), or speaking fluently (stuttering). In addition, autism is a condition that affects communication skills. **Autism** is defined in the 1990 Individuals with Disabilities Education Act as "a developmental disability significantly affecting verbal and nonverbal communication and social interaction, generally evident before age 3. . . ." Some children with autism do not speak at all, while others simply repeat back what they hear (echolalic speech). Students with **Asperger's syndrome,** a milder form of autism, have more developed communication ability and are often highly

language disorders

speech disorders

autism

Asperger's syndrome

intelligent but have difficulty interacting socially. For obvious reasons, students with communication disorders will have difficulty becoming fully functioning members of the classroom community.

Adaptations. With the possible exception of students with autism, students with communication disorders will remain in regular classroom settings for their instructional needs. They are generally able to participate in most aspects of the curriculum. For severe speech impairments a specialist will help the student develop speech skills. The classroom teacher will need to reinforce the work of the specialist by providing opportunities for these students to practice their new skills in a safe, risk-free environment. Through modeling appropriate grammar, providing language models through quality children's literature, and emphasizing vocabulary development, the teacher will be assisting the student with communication disorders.

More specifically, teachers cannot allow peers to tease or ridicule students who make speech errors. Building a classroom atmosphere that is respectful of all learners, and recognizes that everyone has strengths and areas that need to be developed, is crucial not just for students with communication disorders, but for all members of the classroom community. When students with communication disorders do speak, they need to be listened to carefully. The teacher need not correct their speech but can model the appropriate articulation or word order in responding to the student. Attention to the content of what was said is most important. For those students with more severe disorders, there are special devices, called **augmentative communication systems,** that may be used to help them communicate. One such device is the *communication board.* The board (which can also be just a piece of paper with pictures pasted on) contains pictures of common objects or representative pictures for common activities that the student can simply point to in order to convey his or her ideas. Pictures could be faces that show the emotions of happiness or sadness; clothing items; food and beverage items; buildings such as school, home, or church, or rooms in the home; as well as the words *yes* and *no.* More sophisticated electronic communication boards, more commonly referred to as **assistive technology** (see www.asel.udel.edu/at-online), are also available. These devices may have larger than normal keys, or keys with larger spaces between them so the desired keys are easier to locate and hit. Letter keys might appear in alphabetical order, or the keys may feature pictures or words rather than letters. For those with communication disorders, the most sophisticated devices actually "talk" by using prerecorded speech when a particular key is pressed.

For working with students with autism in the regular classroom setting, Wood et al. (1993, p. 115) provide some suggestions:

- Structure the learning environment so that it is predictable and consistent. This includes the physical structure of the classroom as well as routines, schedules, and teacher behavior.

● augmentative communication systems

● assistive technology

- Design instructional programs to provide ways to help children learn to communicate. Remember that verbal communication is but one way to communicate; provide students with alternatives such as signing, writing, [or] using the computer.

- Since students with autism have difficulty managing their own behavior without structure, develop individual and group behavior plans that stress positive behavior management and set forth clear instructions, rules, and consequences.

- Work closely with the family to ensure consistency between school and home and other settings in approaches, methods of interaction, and response to students.

Students Who Are Physically Challenged

Characteristics. Students with physical challenges represent a large group of students. In addition to the obvious challenges of a visual or hearing impairment, other physical challenges include AIDS, allergies, arthritis, asthma, cerebral palsy, congenital anomalies (e.g., albinism, cleft lip, spina bifida), diabetes, epilepsy, hemophilia, leukemia, muscular dystrophy, poliomyelitis, rheumatic fever, Tourette's syndrome, as well as impairments resulting from a traumatic injury. (For more detailed explanations of these conditions visit www.navh.org, www.nad.org, www.aap.org, or www.seals.com.) Because there is such a wide variety of conditions that cause physical challenges—the preceding list names only a few—there is not a concise list of characteristics; however, in general, these physical challenges are just that—physical. Students with one or some combination of physical disability are quite capable of performing well intellectually. For example, some individuals who have cerebral palsy with severe motor impairments are intellectually gifted. There is no relationship between the degree of physical impairment and intellectual ability. What can happen is that students may experience excessive absences or fatigue as a result of certain physical impairments, and learning problems can begin in this way. Students who are more "medically fragile"—that is, their participation in school requires heart monitors, oxygen tanks, suctioning units, or special medical support—are now being placed in regular classroom settings and **individualized education programs** (IEPs) are developed. IEPs help the teacher, support personnel, parents, and the student understand their respective responsibilities toward meeting educational and medical needs.

individualized education program (IEP) ●

Adaptations. For students with visual or hearing impairments, special arrangements within the learning environment can be made. For example, the use of technology, visuals, and special seating will allow for maximum visual access to information for those with hearing impairments. And for those with visual impairments, three-dimensional models, oral presentations, and wide, clear aisles will be helpful. In addition, the structure of certain teaching procedures may need to be adapted, such as directly facing a student who is deaf to allow for lipreading or using American Sign Language, or for a student with a visual impairment, providing printed materials in a large print or Braille format, and the extra time it will take to read these materials. There are technological devices that can also be used such as amplification devices for those with hearing impairments and Braillewriters for students who are blind.

For most physical impairments, the teacher will first need to learn more about the particular condition. (See Figure 9.4 for a listing of websites related to many physical impairments.) Again, as with visual and hearing impairments, the physical arrangement of the classroom may need to be adapted to provide students with mobility difficulties easy access to all classroom areas and activities. Other areas of the school should be checked for accessibility as well (e.g., curb cuts in the sidewalks, handrails at the appropriate height, wide door openings, nonslip surfaces on the floors, toilet accessibility, and water fountains at a variety of heights). Students needing wheelchairs may also need a lapboard for writing. Crutch holders can be attached to the sides or backs of chairs. For students with muscular impairments, papers can be taped to their desk, or pencils attached to the desk by a string and thumbtacks. Some students may need to record their responses orally rather than write them. A plastic ruler serves the student with poor muscle control better than a paper bookmark (Glazzard, 1982). Sometimes simple modifications are all that is necessary.

Students Who Have Behavioral Disorders

Characteristics. There is no one definition of behavioral disorder, nor is there a pattern of behaviors that identifies a student as having a behavioral disorder. Behaviors range from extreme withdrawal to extreme aggression. However, it is common for classroom teachers, especially upper-grade and middle school teachers, to be the first to recognize the atypical behaviors

---

Websites for learning more about physical impairments.   FIGURE 9.4

Cerebral palsy: www.ucpa.org

Muscular dystrophy: www.mdausa.org

Spina bifida: www.sbaa.org

Brain injury: www.biausa.org

Epilepsy: www.efa.org/index.ctm

Diabetes: www.diabetes.org/main/application/commercewf

AIDS: www.aids.org/index.html

Others: www.cmcresearch.com

behavioral
disorder ●

and begin the referral process (Lewis and Doorlag, 1999). A **behavioral disorder** is generally indicated when a student's behavior deviates significantly from what is recognized as normal, occurs often and/or intensely, and occurs over time (Nelson, 1993). It is common for behavioral disorders to negatively impact the student's academic achievement, and there is the possibility that the student also has a learning disability. In fact, the behavioral disorder could be the result of poor academic performance brought about by the learning disability. Students with behavioral disorders are often described as hyperactive, distractible, or impulsive. Students with behavioral disorders experience difficulty because they do not have appropriate social and study skills. Instruction focused on these two areas should improve their chances of success in the classroom.

Adaptations. Because study skills are discussed elsewhere in this book, suggestions for improving social skills (also called life skills) and classroom conduct are presented here. The classroom teacher will need to enlist the help of the school counselor or psychologist to help students with behavioral disorders. Additionally, the student's parents need to be informed of the types of interventions being implemented at school so they can respond to their child in ways that are consistent with what the school is trying to achieve. General suggestions for helping students with behavioral disorders include

- establish an open, accepting classroom environment;
- clearly state class rules and consequences;
- stress positive behaviors and focus on student successes;
- reward positive behaviors and state the behavior that is being rewarded;
- provide extra opportunities for student success;
- use good judgment, be patient and tolerant;
- teach self-control, self-monitoring, and conflict resolution using role playing and examples;
- select partners to work with carefully;
- have alternative activities available;
- allow groups of "one";
- use behavioral contracts. (Mastropieri and Scruggs, 2000, p. 98)

It is important to have a consistent approach when reacting to students' inappropriate behavior. For example, rather than immediately reprimand negative behavior, say to the student in a normal tone of voice, "Stop and think about what you just did. What should you have done? Now, try to do this more appropriately." By using these same words each time students behave inappropriately, students will begin to take responsibility for their actions and to "learn that making good choices about their behavior is in their own best interest" (Mastropieri and Scruggs, 2000, p. 221).

Some students will benefit from more formalized procedures. In potentially volatile situations, students may be asked to go to **time-out** as a way

time-out ●

of providing a chance for cooling down and thinking about their behavior. Time-out can be a location in the classroom, or a designated location within the school. Occasionally, the student may need to be escorted to a time-out location. Most schools have policies and procedures in place for such situations. Debriefing activities need to occur following these cool-down periods. For many students this can be a verbal conversation such as that seen in Figure 9.5. Or students can be asked to complete a **think sheet** like the one seen in Figure 9.6, which can serve as a way of documenting behaviors and any positive changes that occur over time.

● think sheet

Debriefing following time-out. FIGURE 9.5

Teacher: Raul, your time-out is over. But before you join the class, I want you to tell me what happened. Why were you sent to time-out?

Raúl: (Raul shrugs his shoulders, indicating he doesn't know.)

Teacher: Okay, well, just tell me what happened.

Raúl: Luis and Mike were pointing at me and laughing. I said, "What are you laughing at?" and they just kept laughing. So I threw my pencil at them and told them to stop it.

Teacher: Did you have to go to time-out because Luis and Mike were laughing at you?

Raúl: No.

Teacher: No, you were sent to time-out because you threw the pencil.

Raúl: Yes.

Teacher: Do you know why it is not okay to throw pencils at other people?

Raúl: The point could hit them in the eye and hurt them.

Teacher: That's right. Our classroom needs to be a safe place for all of us, so we cannot throw things at other people. Tell me what you can do the next time someone points at you or laughs at you.

Raúl: Ignore them.

Teacher: That's a good idea. If you ignore them they will probably just get bored and stop. What else could you do, if you think you will not be able to ignore them?

Raúl: Tell you.

Teacher: Okay, you could tell me and then I could try to help you not get into trouble, and also stop the people who are teasing you. Can you remember to try these ideas the next time something like this happens?

Raúl: Yeah.

Teacher: You don't have to throw things at people. Ignore them or come tell me if you are having a problem with somebody. You need to control your own behavior. I really like you, Raul, and I want you to do well in school. Can you try these ideas?

Raúl: Yeah.

Teacher: Great! Okay, let's go back to class now. I know you will do better.

FIGURE 9.6 | Think sheet for use with students behaving inappropriately.

THINK SHEET

Name of student: _____

Teacher: _____ Date: _____

This is what I did:

_____

_____

This is the rule I broke:

_____

_____

I behaved this way because:

_____

_____

This is who I bothered when I behaved this way:

_____

_____

This is what I could have done instead:

_____

_____

Student signature: _____ Date: _____

Students with behavioral disorders often lack basic knowledge of social skills. For example, they may not understand the components of a conversation—knowing how to join, interrupt, start, maintain, or end the conversation. Or, they may not know how to ask for clarification, make a request, or exhibit politeness. "Play" skills are social skills that include being able to share with others, encourage and praise others, or invite others to join in the activity. Classroom skills include being on task, completing tasks, following directions, and trying to do the best one can. Self-help skills are good grooming (being clean and neat), and good table manners and eating behaviors. Commonly, students with behavior disorders lack knowledge of problem-solving, or coping, skills such as staying calm, thinking of possible solutions, choosing best solutions, taking responsibility for their actions, handling name calling and teasing, and avoiding trouble.

Social skills instruction begins with the teacher explaining and discussing the targeted social skill. Then the teacher needs to operationalize the targeted social skill (e.g., sharing, being a "good sport," handling name calling) by demonstrating both appropriate and inappropriate behavior while students observe and identify the skill.

> **Teacher:** This is an example of how to get the crayons you need to draw your picture. "Please may I have the red and blue crayons." This is *not* the way to get the crayons. "Give me those crayons!" or just grabbing the crayons.

The teacher then describes a situation for students to role play, with the teacher's guidance, and during which students can offer suggestions or give examples of appropriate behavior:

> **Teacher:** Pretend you are on the playground and you kicked the soccer ball into a group of students by mistake, but they grab the ball and won't give it back to you. How should you act?
>
> **Students:** We could say, "Please give the ball back to me" or "I'm sorry I kicked the ball too hard—it was my mistake. Could I please have the ball back?"
>
> **Teacher:** Good suggestions! These ideas are examples of appropriate behavior.

As actual situations occur in the classroom, students can be reminded of the role plays and their behavior rewarded when they act in socially appropriate ways without being reminded.

THE CONCEPT OF DIFFERENTIATED INSTRUCTION

At the beginning of this chapter we asked, Why differentiate instruction? It should be very clear that there is no one approach or learning activity that will meet the needs of all the students in one classroom. Yet, the classroom teacher is responsible for providing a learning environment in which all students can achieve their full potential.

According to Tomlinson (1999, p. 12), a teacher who differentiates instruction embraces the following four beliefs:

- Respect the readiness level of each student.
- Expect all students to grow, and support their continual growth.
- Offer all students the opportunity to explore essential understandings and skills at degrees of difficulty that escalate consistently as they develop their understanding and skill.
- Offer all students tasks that look—and are—equally interesting, equally important, and equally engaging.

differentiated
instruction ●

Figure 9.7 presents an overall look at the concept of **differentiated instruction,** in which the nature of all students' needs is taken into account. Notice that several of the strategies mentioned throughout this book are also strategies employed by teachers who use differentiated instruction. Most of the strategies presented throughout this book can be implemented with a wide variety of students.

Differentiated instruction is a way to meet the needs of all students, including those with special needs, because different tasks can take into account the nature of their needs. It is not necessary to differentiate every lesson; however, there are particular points within an instructional unit or topic of study that can be differentiated based on students' readiness for the topic, materials, or skills needed; their interests; and/or their learning profiles.

FIGURE 9.7 Concept definition word map for differentiated instruction.

What Is It?

A way of adjusting instruction that takes into account students' readiness for particular learning topics, their interests, and their individual learning profiles in order to help them achieve.

What Is It Like?

The teacher responds to learners' needs in the planning process.

Grouping is flexible.

Instructional tasks are respectful of students' readiness, interests, and learning profiles.

Assessment is ongoing.

Individual growth is the measurement of concern.

NOT every lesson is differentiated every day for everyone.

A wide variety of instructional arrangements, materials, and tasks are used.

Multiple forms of assessment are used.

DIFFERENTIATED INSTRUCTION

Examples of Strategies Used

Independent study

Literature circles

Taped materials

Jigsaw (see "Read a Book in an Hour," Ch. 5)

Interest groups

Tiered lessons

Graphic organizers

Comparison

Whole-class instruction

In any classroom there will be students who are capable of reading materials at or above their grade level, and those who struggle with reading and need easier materials. There may be a few nonreaders in the class as well. Likewise, not all students are interested in the same topics. Finally, students have different learning profiles. In addition to notations regarding particular special needs as described earlier in this chapter, these profiles include personality traits (e.g., shy, gregarious, sensitive); learning styles (visual learner, auditory learner, kinesthetic learner); and students' personal profiles of intelligences, or degrees to which they reflect linguistic, spatial, bodily-kinesthetic, logical-mathematical, musical, intrapersonal, interpersonal, or naturalist intelligences (Gardner, 1983, 1999). Attempts to match students' learning profiles with school tasks may help students initially with those tasks that are completely new and unfamiliar, but to match perfectly the learning environment on a regular basis to a student's developmental level will likely arrest the student at that level (Hunt, 1971). In other words, a certain amount of discomfort is a good thing and leads to growth. Joyce et al. (2000) make this point clear:

> For example, gregarious students are initially the most comfortable with social models and can profit from them quickly. However, the less-gregarious students were in the greatest need of the models least comfortable for them. Hence, the challenge is not to select the most comfortable models but to enable the students to develop the skills to relate to a wider variety of models, many of which appear, at least superficially, to be mismatched with their learning styles. . . . If environment and the student are too much in harmony, the student is permitted to operate at a level of comfort that does not require the challenge of growth. (p. 401)

Thus, it is important for the teacher to know the learning profiles of students in order to sometimes match instruction with those profiles, but also to know where students need to expand their ways of knowing.

Planning and Implementing a Differentiated Lesson

The most important aspect of planning a differentiated lesson is to clearly establish goals for students. According to Tomlinson (1999) "During planning, a teacher should generate specific lists of what students should know (facts), understand (concepts and principles), and be able to do (skills) by the time the unit ends" (p. 40). Then, using what is known about the students' specific readiness levels, interests, and learning profiles, the teacher develops a set of engaging activities that provide for the varied opportunities for learning needed by the students. Finally, the teacher identifies several options for how the students can demonstrate what they have come to know, understand, and are able to do at the conclusion of the unit.

However, all these components need not be differentiated for every single lesson. In fact, it may be easier to think about differentiating instruction by looking at just one curricular component that can be modified to meet students' needs. Thus, we can look at

- differentiating the content, or what students will learn and the materials they will use.
- differentiating the process, or the activities students will engage in to understand key ideas and use essential skills.
- differentiating the product, or how students will demonstrate what they understand and can do as a result of the lesson.

Differentiating the content. One example of differentiating content would be varying the spelling words that students need to learn. Based on a pretest, some students may show they need to work with third-grade words

while others top out with a ninth-grade word list. The teacher could use the same procedures for presenting and practicing spelling words with the students, but the words themselves would be appropriate for their readiness levels. In other words, the students would not all be learning the same words, but learning words appropriate to their needs, and they would be practicing and being tested on them in the same way.

Differentiating the process. This same teacher could also differentiate the process, or the activities students use to learn the spelling of their words. For example, based on their learning profiles some students will best learn their words by writing each word with a crayon and then tracing it while spelling it out loud to get a sensory impression of the word. Other students may simply need to look at the whole word and then practice saying and writing it in order to learn the spelling.

Differentiating the product. Finally, the product could differ as well. In addition to the written spelling test, students with a particularly strong bodily-kinesthetic intelligence could literally use their bodies to spell out their words. Or they could perform a "cheerleader spelling" of the words and lead a small group of students in spelling out their words (Rogers, 1999).

Achieving Differentiation Through Tiered Activities

A teacher can design and adapt a single lesson plan to meet the varied needs of the class as well as provide specific instructional aid to individual students through the use of **tiered activities;** that is, versions of activities that

tiered activities ●

are designed to provide the same essential understandings but that address a variety of learning needs. "Tiered activities are very important when a teacher wants to ensure that students with different learning needs work with the same essential ideas and use the same key skills. For example, a student who struggles with reading or has a difficult time with abstract thinking nonetheless needs to make sense of the pivotal concepts and principles in a given chapter or story" (Tomlinson, 1999, p. 83). The following teacher guidelines are useful for developing tiered activities:

- Identify the concept that will be the focus of the lesson.

- Think about your students. Know their talents, interests, and learning profiles.

- Create one activity that is interesting, requires high-level thought, and clearly focuses on elements that require students to use a key skill to understand a key idea.

- Draw a ladder, with the top rung representing a very high skill level and understanding and the bottom rung a low skill level and understanding. Decide where the activity you created fits on this ladder. Is it too challenging for the advanced students, or will it challenge the less advanced students? In this way you will see who needs another version of the activity.

- "Clone" the activity to provide versions that will work to meet the needs of all your students. This might mean varying the material students use, or varying the ways in which students will express their learning.

- Match a version of the activity to each student based on their needs.

Sixth-Grade Science Example: The Biosphere

Mr. Caday's sixth-grade students are studying the biosphere. They have read a text chapter and understand the meanings of words such as *organism* and *environment*. In the text chapter they were introduced to new vocabulary, including *atmosphere, energy, environmental factors,* and *biosphere*. The essential understanding that Mr. Caday wants his students to have is to be able to name and describe the four conditions necessary for most life on Earth—presence of water, an atmosphere, light, and temperature.

Mr. Caday knows his students well. Of the 30 students in his class, 10 are reading at grade level, 10 above grade level, 7 two years below grade level, and 3 well below grade level. Of the 3 reading below grade level, two are non-English speakers. One student in the class is learning disabled and has been diagnosed with ADHD. Another student has cerebral palsy, but he is in the group who reads above grade level. He does use a wheelchair and a special communication device for reading and writing. Through observation, Mr. Caday notes those students who learn better through visual means (the majority), and those who prefer auditory and kinesthetic activities. Mr. Caday also administers a survey to his students to help him identify their multiple intelligences profile (see www.surfaquarium.com/MIinvent.htm). All of Mr. Caday's students can use context clues to determine word meanings, and they all enjoy word puzzles. They are a close group, and while there is the occasional misunderstanding, everyone gets along well.

Mr. Caday works at an urban school in a high-poverty location, so his students are unfamiliar with agricultural land uses. He has developed a small experiment as his "ladder" activity. On Friday, he plans to give each student four sandwich bags, some rye grass seed, four cotton balls—two wet and two dry—and some masking tape. He will then have each student "plant" the seeds inside the sandwich bag. Students will write their name on a piece of tape to identify their bags. Then Mr. Caday will collect one wet bag and one dry bag from each student and place these in a dark cabinet. The other bags will be taped to the windows in his classroom. Mr. Caday will ask the students to predict what will happen over the weekend to the seeds in both bags. Then, as some seeds sprout, Mr. Caday will ask students to predict what will happen to these sprouts under a variety of other conditions.

Mr. Caday places this activity in the middle of his ladder. He feels it is not challenging enough for his advanced students, but too physically challenging for the student with cerebral palsy (this student will not be able to plant his seeds). Mr. Caday likes the use of realia for his non-English speakers but will need to think about how he will help them understand the directions for planting and predicting. He will have his advanced students identify as many permutations of the experiment as they can to test the four conditions for life. He will create a poster that uses pictures and symbols to direct the non-English speakers but will encourage them to give short oral explanations of what happened to the seeds. Finally, he will ask for a volunteer to help the student with cerebral palsy complete the physical aspects of the experiment.

Mr. Caday also wants to assess what his students learn from their tiered activity. Since he differentiated the process for his students with these tiered activities, Mr. Caday realizes that tiered assessment will also be needed, allowing students to adequately show their understanding of the four conditions necessary for life as demonstrated in the rye grass seed experiment. Therefore, Mr. Caday wants to differentiate the product, or how his students will demonstrate what they learned.

Mr. Caday will ask his advanced students to analyze their data on the permutations they set up, prepare charts to show the results of these permutations, and write a summary report on their findings. The majority of the students will prepare timelines showing each day the seeds were "planted" within the sandwich bags and what happened for each of the four bags. They will then write a summary report discussing their findings as related to the four conditions of life. The non–English speakers will draw their results to share and orally explain these results. The student with cerebral palsy will orally dictate the daily observations and explain these findings in writing using his assistive communication device for both oral dictation and for writing.

Figure 9.8 shows the "ladder" of Mr. Caday's differentiated activity. Figure 9.9 shows the poster Mr. Caday used to represent the grass seed experiment.

Differentiated lessons may be thought of as "ladder" activities.   FIGURE 9.8

PROCESS

Identify permutations to test the four conditions

Max, Luis, Hoa, Lisa, David, Cathy, Mike, Adam, Kelly

Plant seeds in bag

Predict what will happen

Anne, James, Grace, Chris, Jeremy, Maria, Ramon, Lydia, Gina

LESSON FOCUS CONCEPT

Name and describe the four conditions necessary for life on Earth: water, atmosphere, light, and temperature

Use of realia (non-English speakers)

Follow poster that uses symbols and pictures

Give oral explanations

Mika, Sam, Emilio, Lin, Robert, Michelle, Arthur, Brad, Marla, Randy

Volunteers help with physical tasks

PRODUCT

Analyze data on permutations

Write a summary report

Prepare timelines to chart growth

Write a summary report

Draw results of plantings

Orally explain results

Use assistive device to explain results orally and in writing

FIGURE 9.9

Visual representation of the grass seed experiment, which might be used to clarify steps for non-English speakers.

Grass Seed Experiment

SUMMARY

All students, including those with special needs, deserve the best education that teachers can provide. There is no one best method that will meet the needs of the wide variety of students found in today's classrooms. If anything, the diversity is increasing. Teachers really need to view this diversity as a positive development in the history of schooling, and accept the challenge that comes with it in terms of helping all students move forward in their development.

In this chapter, we provided brief descriptions of various categories of learners as they are classified by the educational system. We also presented information related to instructional adaptations appropriate to each learner type. Finally, we provided some guidelines for implementing instruction that is differentiated in an attempt to meet all learners' needs, along with an example to illustrate these guidelines.

Questions
FOR JOURNAL WRITING AND DISCUSSION

1. Design an instructional program to address the needs of linguistically diverse students. What materials would be appropriate? What techniques would you use and why? How will your program enhance the emotional needs of the students?

2. Divide a piece of paper into two columns. Label one column "Lead" and the other "Gold." Brainstorm a list of negative labels that are used to describe students who seem to learn differently from the norm (e.g., dyslexic, lazy) and list them in the "Lead" column. Then try to think of a positive word or phrase for each negative label and list these in the "Gold" column (e.g., hyperactive = a kinesthetic learner). Discuss your list with your classmates.

3. Write about a time when you had difficulty learning something. What were your feelings? How were you finally able to learn? How might this experience impact your teaching?

Suggestions
FOR PROJECTS AND FIELD ACTIVITIES

1. Interview a student whose first language is not English. Ask the student how he or she came to speak English. Ask about the student's attitudes toward both English and his or her native language. Try to learn from the student some of the problems involved in translating from one language to another. Then take the data from this interview

and identify the unique features of the student's language (phonology, syntax/structural/lexical/semantic). What differences and similarities of language do you share with this student?

2. Observe, over a period of three to five days, a student with one of the special needs discussed in this chapter. What can this student do well, and what seems to be difficult for this student? Summarize your observations, and make suggestions about how you could differentiate instruction to meet the needs of this particular student.

3. Begin to develop an annotated bibliography of books, poems, videos, or other materials that deal with students who have overcome adversity due to learning disabilities, physical challenges, language diversity, behavioral issues, or social problems caused by giftedness, or by conditions of poverty. Sharing such books with students in similar situations can be a form of bibliotherapy. (See the article by Landrum [2001] to help you get started.)

References

California Teachers of English to Speakers of Other Languages. (1992). Catesol position statement on specially-designed academic instruction in English (sheltered instruction). Retrieved 12/16/97 from www.catesol.org/shelter.html.

Davis, G. A. (1995). Identifying the creatively gifted. In J. L. Genshaft, M. Bireley, & C. L. Hollinger (Eds.), *Serving gifted and talented students: A resource for school personnel* (pp. 67–82). Austin, TX: Pro-Ed.

Gardner, H. (1983). *Frames of mind: The theory of multiple intelligences.* New York: Basic Books.

Gardner, H. (1999). *Intelligence reframed: Multiple intelligences for the 21st century.* New York: Basic Books.

Gipe, J. P. (2002). *Multiple paths to literacy: Classroom techniques for struggling readers* (5th ed.). Upper Saddle River, NJ: Merrill/Prentice Hall.

Glazer, S. M. (1998). *Assessment IS instruction: Reading, writing, spelling, and phonics for ALL learners.* Norwood, MA: Christopher-Gordon.

Glazzard, P. (1982). *Learning activities and teaching ideas for the special child in the regular classroom.* Englewood Cliffs, NJ: Prentice Hall.

Grossman, H. (1995). *Teaching in a diverse society.* Boston: Allyn & Bacon.

Hernandez, H. (1997). *Teaching in multilingual classrooms: A teacher's guide to context, process, and content.* Upper Saddle River, NJ: Merrill/Prentice Hall.

Hunt, D. E. (1971). *Matching models in education.* Toronto: Ontario Institute for Studies in Education.

Joyce, B., Weil, M., with Calhoun, E. (2000). *Models of teaching* (6th ed.). Boston: Allyn & Bacon.

Kennedy, D. M. (1995). Plain talk about creating a gifted-friendly classroom. *Roeper Review, 17,* 232–234.

Krashen, S. D. (1987). *Principles and practices in second language acquisition.* Upper Saddle River, NJ: Prentice Hall.

Landrum, J. (2001). Selecting intermediate novels that feature characters with disabilities. *The Reading Teacher, 55*(3), 252–258.

Lewis, R. B., & Doorlag, D. H. (1999). *Teaching special students in general education classrooms* (5th ed.). Upper Saddle River, NJ: Merrill/Prentice Hall.

Mastropieri, M. A., & Scruggs, T. E. (2000). *The inclusive classroom: Strategies for effective instruction.* Upper Saddle River, NJ: Merrill/Prentice Hall.

National Advisory Committee on Handicapped Children. (1968). *Special education for handicapped children* (First annual report). Washington, DC: U.S. Department of Health, Education, and Welfare.

Nelson, C. M. (1993). Students with behavioral disorders. In A. E. Blackhurst & W. H. Berdine (Eds.), *An introduction to special education* (3rd ed., pp. 528–561). New York: HarperCollins.

Rogers, L. K. (1999). Spelling cheerleading. *The Reading Teacher, 53,* 110–111.

Tomlinson, C. A. (1999). *The differentiated classroom: Responding to the needs of all learners.* Alexandria, VA: Association for Supervision and Curriculum Development.

Wood, J. W., Lazzari, A., & Reeves, C. K. (1993). Educational characteristics and implications. In J. W. Wood (Ed.), *Mainstreaming* (2nd ed., pp. 78–120). New York: Merrill/Macmillan.

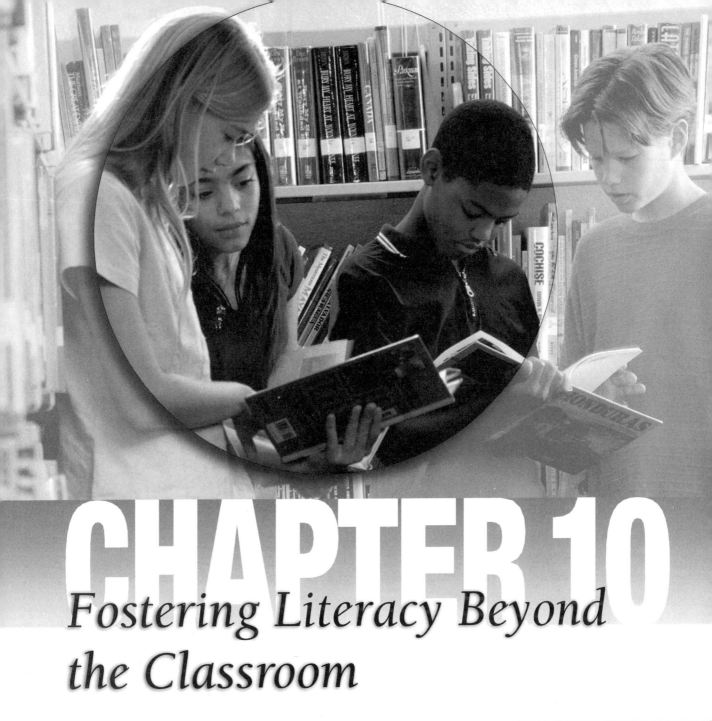

CHAPTER 10
Fostering Literacy Beyond the Classroom

- What are ways we engage in literacy outside the classroom?
- How can we develop motivation for engaging in reading and writing?
- Why is service learning a valuable organizational/curricular element for the intermediate-grade levels?

In the Classroom

"Let me share with you the ways I used literacy this weekend," Mr. Fortier begins. "Then I will ask you to think about your weekend and how you engaged in literacy outside the classroom." Mr. Fortier proceeds to give his sixth-graders a detailed account:

"I rose on Saturday morning and looked at the clock, which read 7:46. Then I read the newspaper while having breakfast. Later, I checked the TV listings to see if there was a sports program on that I wanted to watch. Seeing I had plenty of time before the game started, I decided to put together a chest of drawers I had purchased. The directions were clearly written and I finished the project in about an hour. Next I made a grocery list for the week and went to the store. I am careful about what I eat, so I first checked the labels before buying several new items I've been wanting to try. When I returned home, I put the groceries away, and watched the Sacramento Kings basketball game on TV. After the game, I paid a few bills with checks. I then turned on my computer to check for e-mail and corresponded with some of my friends who live far away. While online, I searched for a website on kitchen appliances. I need to buy a new refrigerator, so I decided to gather information from the Internet so I can make a wise purchase. For dinner, I wanted to try a new recipe, so I read the list of ingredients, gathered them, and began to prepare the meal. After dinner, I checked the TV listings again but didn't see anything appealing, so I decided to read a mystery novel instead. On Sunday, I attend religious services, so when I awoke I first looked at the clock to determine which service I would be able to attend and then got dressed. At the service I read through the weekly bulletin and used the hymnal to sing along with the choir. After services, I like to eat breakfast out, so I drove to one of my favorite breakfast places. At the restaurant I studied the menu and chose a pancake breakfast. On the way home, I bought the Sunday newspaper, which kept me busy for the next few hours. After a light lunch, I began to grade some papers and prepare lessons for Monday. A new friend had invited me for Sunday dinner so I checked my road map to find the best route to my friend's house. On the way there, I watched the street signs closely so I wouldn't miss my turns. After dinner, I returned home and read my mystery novel some more before watching the nightly news and going to bed."

Mr. Fortier then makes a chart on the board that has four column headings: "Informational," "Recreational," "Occupational," and "Environmental" (Goodman, 1996). He and his students begin to classify the ways he used literacy during the weekend.

Mr. Fortier then directs his students to think back to their weekend and list all the literacy activities they can remember, and to create a similar chart of their own, considering their current occupation as "student."

INFORMATIONAL	RECREATIONAL	OCCUPATIONAL	ENVIRONMENTAL
• read newspaper • read directions for chest of drawers • wrote grocery list • read food labels • found and read web site for kitchen appliances • read recipe • read bulletin • read menu • read road map • watched TV news	• read TV listings • read e-mail • sent e-mail to friends • read mystery novel • used hymnal	• wrote checks to pay bills • graded papers • prepared lessons	• read clock • read scores, etc. while watching Kings on TV • gathered ingredients for recipe • read restaurant sign • read street signs to friend's house

EXPANDED GOALS FOR LITERACY INSTRUCTION

As discussed in Chapter 1, literacy is a continuum of skills, including reading, writing, speaking, listening, viewing, visually representing, and critical thinking, applied in a social context to enable a person to function effectively in his or her group and community (Harris and Hodges, 1995). In this sense, literacy goes far beyond the classroom walls.

As students progress through the grades, the goals of literacy instruction change from ones that focus on learning to read, to ones that include reading to learn. But we not only want students to be able to read and to read to learn, we also want them to *want* to read. To continue developing their competencies in literacy, students must continue to engage in literate activities once they are beyond the classroom setting. Elsewhere in this book we have presented information on strategies for a variety of literacy competency areas such as word recognition, vocabulary, comprehension, and content area literacy. In this chapter, the emphasis is on two areas: the affective aspects of literacy, or developing positive attitudes and interests for reading and writing; and authentic literacy experiences, or recognizing the value of literacy in our daily lives. The goals of literacy instruction in the intermediate grades must expand to include

- developing motivated readers and writers.
- establishing lifelong habits of reading and writing.

Each of these goals is now discussed in detail.

Developing Motivated Readers and Writers

Creating and enriching reading interests and positive attitudes will certainly go a long way in developing motivated readers and writers. As adults, we do not often engage in activities for which we have negative feelings or no interest. Attitudes toward reading and writing refer to how an individual feels about reading and writing. These feelings can be positive or negative toward reading or writing in general or can vary depending on the subject area (Mathewson, 1985). In other words, an individual might really like reading about historical events but have very negative feelings about reading science material. This aspect of attitudes seems closely related to interests; in fact, Schiefele (1991) describes *individual interests* as relatively stable feelings (i.e., attitudes) about different areas such as reading. He distinguishes between individual interests (stable) and situational or text-based interests that are less stable because this type of interest might be sparked by a particular activity or text. There is support in the literature that individual feelings about reading relate to motivation and that reading interest positively impacts comprehension (Alexander et al., 1994; Mathewson, 1994; McKenna, 1994). Thus, it is important for teachers to help students develop both positive attitudes and reading interests in order for them to become motivated readers and writers.

Unfortunately, researchers have shown that reading motivation decreases as students advance in grade level (Eccles et al., 1993; Marsh, 1989). However, this same body of research also concludes that this decline results from changes in school and classroom environments. In reality, then, this is a hopeful finding because school and classroom environments are something that educators do have control over. Following are several techniques for increasing student motivation.

Responsive Classroom Culture

Oldfather (2001) suggests a responsive classroom culture as an effective environment for increasing motivation. A *responsive classroom culture* is one that honors student voices in the following ways:

1. It develops a community of learners that promotes the maintenance and enhancement of caring.
2. It gives teachers access to important insights for meeting student's educational needs.
3. It alleviates motivational struggles and promotes students' perceptions of self-determination, and thus their ownership of their own learning agenda. (Oldfather, 2001, p. 14)

Common characteristics of responsive classrooms include the following:

✓ Teachers explain to their students reasons for particular activities or topics of study.

✓ The environment is one in which learning is more important than getting the right answer.

✓ Teachers discuss with students the value of what is being learned (e.g., How might this skill be useful to you in the future?).

✓ The atmosphere encourages risk taking.

✓ Each student's contribution of ideas is expected and responded to.

✓ Teacher and students participate together as learners.

✓ Desks are arranged to support group work.

✓ Samples of student work fill the room.

✓ The curriculum is developed thematically, incorporating students' interests and suggestions.

✓ Topics often relate to large issues, current events, or environmental concerns.

✓ Students read self-selected books as well as books from the core curriculum.

✓ Writing is a daily activity and often a favored activity.

Several techniques already discussed in Chapter 5, such as literature circles and book clubs, would likely be found in a responsive classroom. These activities provide ways for teachers to lead students to read quality literature.

Concept-Oriented Reading Instruction (CORI)

Guthrie and McCann (1997) researched an integrated curriculum plan they call **concept-oriented reading instruction (CORI)** with third- and fifth-grade classrooms as an instructional context to support the development of motivation. In this context, one containing many responsive classroom characteristics, students were encouraged to direct their own work, collaborate with classmates, develop new metacognitive strategies, and express their knowledge in innovative ways. After three years of CORI, Guthrie and McCann concluded that in this learning context, students exhibit strong intrinsic motivation and use effective strategies for finding books, managing time, locating places to read, and avoiding distractions to a greater extent than students receiving traditionally organized curriculum.

● concept-oriented reading instruction (CORI)

Where in the World Are You Reading?

In January 2002, we read about a fourth-grader who is hooked on reading because "it takes me to different places" (Petrillo, 2002). This student's school invented a schoolwide reading program called "Where in the World Are You Reading?" The program combines literacy with geography. Students cross the seven continents by logging hours spent reading at home. After 12 hours they have crossed a continent. Every time they cross a continent they win a prize and recognition at the school's weekly assembly. The prizes are geography-related treats (e.g., when crossing Asia students win edible chopsticks, actually French fries; Antarctica's prize is ice cream).

While the prizes might be necessary to spur some students to read at home, many students need no enticement.

Incentives

Several studies demonstrate that the use of tangible incentives, such as prizes, under certain conditions can enhance intrinsic motivation. If a valued reward is offered (1) when the level of initial interest is low, or (2) when the attractiveness of the activity will become apparent after engaging in it over time, or (3) when a certain level of mastery needs to be attained, then the reward will lead to intrinsic motivation (Lepper et al., 1973; McLoyd, 1979). Thus, programs such as the All American Reading Challenge (sponsored by McDonald's; the American Library Association; and Scholastic, Inc.), Book-It! (sponsored by Pizza Hut), Bucks for Books (sponsored by the Earning by Learning Foundation), and RUNNING START (sponsored by Reading Is Fundamental) can be effective for increasing intrinsic motivation. Verbal praise and positive feedback increase intrinsic motivation because of their informational value. Student choice is also a powerful incentive and is likely the reason that the sponsored reading programs and approaches such as book clubs and literature circles are successful—students like to be in charge of choosing what they read. In fact, the research is most clear on the strong positive correlation between choice and the development of intrinsic motivation (Paris and Oka, 1986; Rodin et al., 1980; Turner, 1995).

Working with Differing Levels of Motivation

Even within responsive classrooms there will be students who are not motivated intrinsically but will choose to be positive about the learning activity, maintain openmindedness, search for the worthwhileness of the activity, observe other classmates' interest in the activity, plunge ahead into the activity, and in doing so become motivated and fully participate. Then there are those who will do the activities but are only motivated by some type of reward system to complete their work. This situation is probably true for all students at some time or another. Finally, there are those students who are not motivated and who do not participate. This situation involves avoidance or perceived helplessness. Avoidance occurs when the student finds other reasons for not getting around to the work, perhaps after several attempted starts. The more serious situation, perceived helplessness, often involves physical symptoms such as feeling ill, or an excessive need to move. These students feel anxious and less than competent and need special accommodations for completing tasks, such as being offered a choice of tasks, or freedom to move in order to complete a task, or use of hands-on activities. Timed tests are usually a disaster for students in this category. Teachers who respond to these students with care and empathy and take actions that attempt to alleviate anxiety levels will best serve this group.

Establishing Lifelong Habits of Reading and Writing

Teachers can begin the effort to establish lifelong literacy habits by helping students learn how to choose books, estimate the difficulty of reading material, and read and write for authentic reasons. Reading material that is at an appropriate level of difficulty is important for several reasons. First, teachers want students to read easy material in order to practice their reading skills. Second, they want students to read somewhat challenging material in order to expand their reading skills. Finally, they want students to be able to independently recognize when text material is too easy, just right, or too hard for them, and then to decide to stay with that material or look for something else.

Choosing Books and Estimating Reading Difficulty

Teachers must first locate material at a variety of readability levels to ensure that they will have sufficient examples for modeling appropriate difficulty levels with their students. Use of Fry's Readability Graph (http://school. discovery.com/schrockguide/fry/fry.html) (see Appendix E) can assist the

teacher in identifying the grade-level readability for text. Using a variety of genres, print media (e.g., books, magazines, newspapers), and topics, teachers can develop a series of activities that are designed to show students how to locate material on a particular topic and then how to look at this material to decide if it is "readable." For example, the teacher might provide students with a list of titles that will actually be available to them and another list of topics and ask students to match those titles with the topics they are likely to address. Once students complete this matching activity, the group can discuss their reasons for matching. Following this discussion the actual materials should be made available so students can look at them to see if they indeed provide information on the topic they thought was a match.

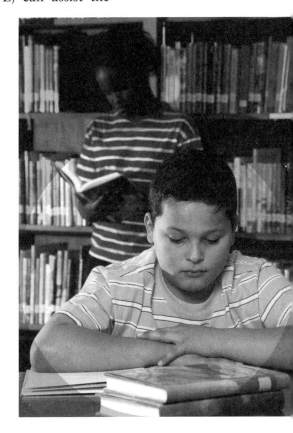

Using the "leveled" materials, teachers can model a process for locating material that is "too easy," "just right," or "too hard" for reading. Known as the **Goldilocks strategy** (Ohlhausen and Jepsen, 1992), this strategy is based on group discussion about what makes a book too easy, too hard, or just right. Easy books are books in which students can read every word and understand every idea. Hard books are books in which there are many words students cannot read and many ideas they cannot understand. Books that are just right are books in

● Goldilocks strategy

which students can read most of the words and can understand most of the ideas. Using actual examples, the teacher can think out loud about a "too easy" book using phrases such as "there are not many words on each page," or "I know all the words on the page," or "there are lots of illustrations in this book." A book that is "just right" represents material that is at a student's instructional reading level, or 95 percent word recognition accuracy. Thus, out of approximately 100 words, there should be no more than 5 words that are unknown. Keeping this in mind, the teacher might describe the book using phrases such as "there are a few words on each page that seem new to me," "there are no more than five words on a page that are new to me," "I think I will not have trouble with the number of words on each page," "I can figure out the words myself," "I know something about this topic already and that will help me read this," or "the pictures (or headings) look interesting." A "too hard" book is described using phrases such as "there are too many new words on each page," "the print is too small," "there are many words on each page," or "I would have to ask for lots of help reading this." Finally, the teacher needs to remind students that sometimes it is necessary to work with material that is really too hard in order to locate a particular piece of information, but most of the time, when the material seems too difficult, students and the teacher should look for something else, something that is "just right."

The school library would be a great place for each student to practice locating material on a particular topic, and then to decide whether the material is appropriate for him or her. In this way students receive guided practice and also have access to a librarian who can assist them in finding something that is appropriate. This step will show students that they can independently seek information if they know what they are looking for. A field trip to the public library might also be arranged to further expand this practice.

Reading and Writing for Authentic Reasons

Once students can identify appropriate materials, they are well on their way to becoming lifelong learners. An additional aspect of helping students develop lifelong habits of reading and writing is to provide classroom experiences that relate to the types of real-world reading and writing they will engage in as adults and citizens living within a community. Shelley Harwayne (2000) shares a letter that she wrote to the families of students in the Manhattan New School. Relevant portions of that letter appear here:

Dear families,

. . . *[I responded by suggesting that literacy needs to be long lasting.]* Your children will not only know how to read and write, but more importantly they will choose to read and write.

[I went on to explain how this heartfelt promise.] Your children will choose to read and write—has implications for classroom practice. It is no longer enough in the reading classroom for students to be able to answer questions at the end of a chapter or fill in the blanks on a worksheet. . . . Instead, we have much higher expectations. Students throughout the grades are being asked to read a wide range of beautifully crafted authentic materials and to read them deeply and critically, discovering new meanings, making personal interpretations, connecting one text to another, and even reading as a writer intent on borrowing techniques for their own writing.

. . . Writing no longer means simply following a teacher's specific instructions. We are no longer asking for 250 words on "Your Summer Vacation." Instead, students throughout the grades are working much harder and learning a great deal more. Students are filling journals, discovering important and original ideas, shaping and revising those ideas into appropriate forms, and editing those drafts into publishable finished works that do real work in the real world. Students are sending letters, crafting picture books for younger students, performing original plays for their peers, publishing non-fiction texts for their class libraries, etc. . . . (pp. A-11–A-12)

SERVICE-LEARNING: TAKING LITERACY BEYOND THE CLASSROOM

It is the "real work in the real world" part of Shelley Harwayne's (2000) letter that brings us to the next focus of this chapter. Referred to as service-learning, more and more teachers and students are becoming involved in doing real literacy work within their communities. **Service-learning** is generally defined as "a teaching strategy that combines classroom curriculum with community service, to enrich learning, teach civic responsibility, and strengthen communities" (National Commission on Service-Learning, 2002). Students of all ages, from all backgrounds, and from all over the world have become involved in service-learning projects (visit www.servicelearning.org). Of course, service-oriented organizations, such as Boys and Girls Clubs, have been doing this kind of community service work for many years; but, more recently, there has been a groundswell of interest in viewing service-learning as part of what school is, or should be, about. Research also supports the inclusion of service learning by revealing many benefits for students, schools, and communities. Participation in effective service-learning programs is linked to such benefits as

● service-learning

- higher scores on state achievement tests (Anderson et al., 1991).
- improved grades and increased attendance (Follman, 1998).
- increased classroom participation (Loesch-Griffin et al., 1995).
- improved problem-solving skills (Stephens, 1995).
- more positive and respectful relationships with peers and teachers (Weiler et al., 1998).
- fewer behavioral problems (Stephens, 1995; Switzer et al., 1995).
- greater acceptance of cultural differences (Berkas, 1997; Melchior, 1999).
- greater empathy and cognitive complexity than comparison groups (Courneya, 1994).

Important to this chapter is the potential that service-learning has to motivate disengaged students. For students who see little relevance between the school curriculum and their own lives, service-learning highlights the relevance. Projects weave together such curricular areas as literacy, math, social studies, science, and health and nutrition. "Service learning puts academics into action because it puts learning into an authentic context. It engages young people in addressing real problems in their communities, not just fictitious problems in a textbook" (Glenn, 2002, p. 1). What follows are some examples of service-learning projects that demonstrate the interweaving of several academic curricular areas, to include literacy.

Garden Project: Westfield Elementary School

Situated in an area of many Mexican and Southeast Asian families, Westfield Elementary School allocated a half acre of its property as a community garden. Forty families who were eager to receive a garden plot for family use were given their own plot in exchange for agreeing to help maintain the

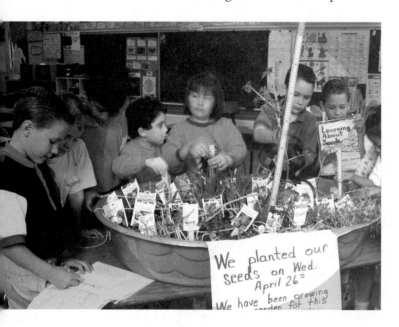

school garden. Students, teachers, student teachers, and parents all helped plant fruit trees and grapes around the perimeter of the garden and then planned an ornamental garden and flower beds. Mexican parents also planted corn and beans to share with the school. Gardening activities were connected to the curricular areas of science, language arts, math, and social studies. Writing became a favorite tie-in to the garden project for language-building activities. Students wrote poetry and stories about the garden and kept field notes by recording and drawing what they saw happening in the garden. Sixth-graders connected to their social studies curriculum by planting ancient-world perennials such as grapes, olives, and pomegranates.

As vegetables were harvested from the garden, recipes were published in a multicultural cookbook. This activity reinforced lessons on fractions as well as other units of measurement (Hammond and Heredia, 2002).

Garden Project: Chenowith Elementary School

Another garden project is tended by all students at Chenowith Elementary School, a school where 80 percent of the 370 students are on free or reduced lunch. To begin the project, parents, teachers, and students all worked together to create six raised flower beds. The art teacher and his fourth- and fifth-grade students painted over graffiti-filled walls to create beautiful, butterfly-filled murals surrounding the garden. The school secretary, a master gardener, shared how to take care of the soil and the plants with the students. The students are the ones who grow the plants from seeds, water and weed the garden, harvest the flowers and vegetables, and make compost to fertilize the soil. Keeping careful records of when things are planted, where, and how often they have been watered; counting days until plants are ready to harvest; and measuring for location of seeds and amount of fertilizer all involve doing literacy and math. The students harvest the vegetables and flowers and deliver them to senior citizens. They also lead tours of the garden and can describe the elements of the butterfly garden, an herb garden, and a garden of plants native to their area. The teachers note that this project is particularly beneficial for their limited-English students (Fredericks et al., 2001).

Gardens are very popular service-learning projects. One such project led to the publication of *The Edible Schoolyard* (Learning in the Real World, 1999), for those who are interested in pursuing the curricular possibilities of such projects.

History of the Community Project: Horace Mann Academic Middle School

As the sixth-graders began a language arts assignment to write a paper on the history of their community (the Mission District in San Francisco), they found there was little information available on a specific stage of development, called the "fifth stage" by historians. It was this stage of development that was most important to the students in understanding their community. The students and their teacher decided to address this shortage of information by talking with the people who were a part of the community's development. And in so doing an impressive list of academic skills was addressed. The students began by identifying the things they would need to do and the supplies they would need. They proceeded to write a project budget and develop a grant proposal to acquire what they needed. They then began to create a "living history" by talking with individuals identified as "community heroes." To prepare for this, students developed interview questions and interviewing skills. After hearing the stories of the heroes and compiling their biographies, the students created a mural to document the period, the missing fifth stage, and to celebrate the accomplishments of everyday heroes. Throughout the project, students needed to engage in multiple writing tasks such as writing biographies of the heroes, letters to community members, as well as the grant proposal. They also learned good telephone skills through the numerous calls they made to invite speakers and gather information. The mural covers almost four city blocks; depicts 28 community heroes of the Mission District, and required much planning, measuring, and artistic designing (Learning In Deed, 2002).

REAL-WORLD CLASSROOM ACTIVITIES

Service-learning is not the only way to add relevance to the curriculum in order to motivate and engage students. Other types of authentic, or real-world, activities can be used in the classroom to demonstrate that what students are learning in school has direct application in their own lives. Following is a sampling of these activities.

ACTIVITY *Bike Repair*

Most students either own or are familiar with bicycles. A number of bike-related activities can be accomplished within the classroom that allow students to practice the skills of reading comprehension, following directions, reasoning, and descriptive writing. Bike repair is one such activity.

1. Gather some bike repair manuals.
2. Ask a local dealer or a student if he or she has a used or broken bike he or she is willing to donate to the class for disassembling.
3. Gather a few simple tools: vise grips, adjustable wrench, screwdrivers, pliers, hammer, steel wool, oil can, Liquid Wrench, rags, oil.
4. Have students work on the bike during several class meetings and keep a log of what they did and why. This provides a record of the repair effort and requires students to write an explicit account.

Additional bike-related activities include obtaining bike registration (writing to local police or to the official trade association of the bicycle industry for information on how to set up a bike registration one-day drive); seeking information on local and national biking groups; and locating, reading, and sharing contents of bicycling magazines.

ACTIVITY *Job Market*

The local business community is a great resource for materials that can provide relevant and exciting learning experiences for students.

1. Ask local businesses for sample job application forms and hints for interviewing techniques. Fast-food restaurants, supermarkets, and discount stores will be the most likely businesses where students will find their "first" part-time jobs.
2. Ask managers to come speak to classes about the importance of following directions when filling out job applications and interviewing techniques.
3. Have students fill out job application forms as neatly and accurately as possible.
4. Go over the forms with them as they work and then again when they finish to check spelling and accuracy.

Medical Practice

Medical subject matter has technical, humanistic, and ethical dimensions that are a valuable resource for teachers to use in strengthening students' critical-thinking, decision-making, and reading skills. Using case histories (real or created) and role playing add to the activity. The steps in this activity include

1. Prepare a fact sheet regarding a particular medical condition and, if possible, include relevant photographs obtained from discarded medical magazines (ask a local physician for old copies). An example fact sheet and case histories related to kidney failure are provided in Figure 10.1.

2. Have students read the fact sheet and discuss it.

3. Have students study the case histories and decide on a treatment plan.

4. Try to find medical students who are willing to come to class and discuss the physical, moral, and ethical implications of each suggested treatment.

FIGURE 10.1   Fact sheet and case histories for kidney failure.

FACT SHEET

1. Your body has two kidneys.

2. The function of the kidneys is to purify the blood and excrete the waste products of metabolism.

3. If one kidney fails, the other can still do the job.

4. If both kidneys fail, death from metabolic poisoning results because the body can no longer eliminate waste products.

5. There are two techniques used when both kidneys fail: dialysis and kidney transplantation.

Dialysis is the process of filtering the blood through an artificial device outside the body. It often involves four sessions per week of several hours each in the hospital or at a special dialysis center. The patient is hooked up to a machine that purifies the blood and does the work of the diseased or nonexistent kidneys. Under such treatment, the patient's general health often suffers, and the treatment process may cause the person to become depressed. The body will tolerate this treatment for only about seven or eight years.

A successful **kidney transplant** restores normal kidney function for life. However, the surgical and medical treatment involved can be extremely dangerous, especially to older people. The biggest medical

(continued)

FIGURE 10.1 Continued.

problem in kidney transplants is the body's tendency to reject implanted organs. The body has mechanisms by which it can kill "intruders" such as germs and transplanted organs. After transplant, doctors prescribe powerful drugs to suppress these normal bodily defense mechanisms so that the transplanted organ will not be destroyed. During this time the patient is more vulnerable than normal to other diseases. For instance, the transplant patient is far more likely to die of an illness such as pneumonia than a healthy person.

It is best if the kidney for transplant comes from someone closely related to the patient. The best donors are a brother or sister or parent. Remember, it is possible for a person to live with just one kidney, so the second kidney could be offered to someone else. If no close relative is available to donate a kidney, then a kidney may be taken from a person who recently died. However, the odds for success are better if the kidney comes from a relative than from an unrelated individual (about 50 percent versus 27 percent).

If the patient's body rejects the transplanted kidney, a dialysis machine can be used to sustain life until another kidney becomes available. However, only really healthy people can survive several such operations.

CASE HISTORIES

Directions: Read each of the three case histories (names have been changed to protect the privacy of the individuals). Three courses of treatment are possible: (1) kidney transplant, (2) kidney dialysis, or (3) no treatment at all. Your task is to arrive at a reasonable decision as to the best treatment for each individual using current medical understanding and the particular circumstances of the patient's life.

1. **Mabel Prouty** is 93 years old. She is a widow with 4 children, 31 grandchildren, and 70 great-grandchildren. She had never been sick a day in her life until three years ago. Then, at age 90, she developed progressive kidney failure. Her youngest son, a wealthy bachelor who lives at home with her, is extremely worried about her and is pressing for a kidney transplant. The patient herself accepts the disease as a normal part of old age. She has never been in a hospital and does not wish to go now.

2. **Harold Clarence** is 57 years old. He is married and has no children. On December 3, 1997, he was admitted to Mercy Hospital for multiple fractures and bleeding due to an automobile accident in which his only brother and sister were killed. Since then, he has suffered generally poor health. He is financially secure. His poor health led him to retire partially from his engineering job in 1998. On August 3, 2002, he suffered serious kidney failure and was put on dialysis. The hospital psychiatrist reports that he is a very cheerful patient who reacts calmly to dialysis.

FIGURE *10.1* Continued.

3. **Georgia Fox** is 18 years old. She is not married, a high school senior, and the sixth of seven children. She wants to be a physical education teacher. On January 6, 2001, she was admitted to Mercy Hospital for chronic kidney infection. She was treated for three weeks and released as an outpatient to be treated with drugs at home. On July 14, 2002, she was readmitted for massive kidney failure and put on dialysis. Her siblings are willing to act as donors.

Complete the following:*

1. **Mabel Prouty**

    Course of treatment recommended:

    Reason for decision:

2. **Harold Clarence**

    Course of treatment recommended:

    Reason for decision:

3. **Georgia Fox**

    Course of treatment recommended:

    Reason for decision:

*Mabel Prouty's real doctor recommended no treatment; Harold Clarence's real doctor recommended continuing dialysis; Georgia Fox's real doctor recommended a kidney transplant.

ACTIVITY *Reading Can Save You Money*

Students in the intermediate grades are already full participants in the consumer culture. It is a service to them to teach critical-reading and thinking skills as they relate to reading and responding to advertisements and making wise purchases. Constructing a lesson such as the following helps students to become smart consumers.

1. Browse for misleading advertisements in popular magazines. Depending on the student population, these could be related to weight reduction, skin problems, astrology, or hobbies.

2. Collect and laminate about 50 advertisements.

3. Choose from this group a few to be mounted on poster board for all to see.

4. As a readiness activity, have students share their own experiences related to misleading or deceptive mail-away offers, or other responses to advertisements that they, or a family member, have personally experienced.

5. Using the mounted advertisements, discuss the misleading ads.

6. With students working in pairs, have each pair choose two additional ads from the 50 that were laminated. Have each pair read these aloud to each other, discuss them, and analyze them using a set of prepared questions (Figure 10.2).

7. Have students share their ad analyses in a whole-class discussion.

FIGURE 10.2 Questions for analyzing misleading advertisements.

1. What is the product being advertised?

2. What is the eye-catching line? Write it down exactly so you can read it to the class.

3. What does the advertiser want you to believe you will get?

4. What do you think you really will get for your money?

5. What is the total amount of money that this product will actually cost?

6. What do you think are the outright lies, if any, in this advertisement?

The World When You Were Born

ACTIVITY

An activity that integrates history with reading comprehension, skimming, and reference skills, The World When You Were Born fosters personal interest in a particular time period of history. The more general point to conclude from this activity is that history is being made each and every day. As students will learn from this activity, we are either making history or reacting to past history.

1. Find a resource such as *Our American Century* (Time Life) that provides excellent photographs and enough text to give an idea of what life was like during a particular decade.

2. Design a set of questions for students to answer that helps them to understand what life was like when they were born and when they were growing up (see Figure 10.3).

3. To provide more depth, have students do further research on their decade, or research on what the world was like when their parents were born.

4. After the research, share memories with students and discuss the part of their lives that is already a part of history.

FIGURE 10.3   History questions for the 1990s.

1. What significance did the Internet have?

2. Why was Colin Powell called the "Reluctant Warrior?"

3. What happened on April 19, 1995?

4. Who are Generation Xers?

5. Who is the sports idol known as "His Airness?"

6. What was the subculture "extreme sports?"

7. Who was Boris Yeltsin?

8. What is meant by "video game warfare?"

9. What happened on August 2, 1990?

10. What was the most successful sitcom of the 1990s?

ANSWER KEY:

1. The Internet has been a democratizing force giving ordinary people the same access to a wealth of information whether they live in a well-to-do suburb or a remote rural area, or the inner city. It has changed the way we communicate, learn, and work.

2. Because of his deliberate hesitation to use force until necessary in the Vietnam War.

(continued)

FIGURE **10.3** Continued.

3. Car bomb exploded at the Alfred P. Murrah Federal Building in Oklahoma City.

4. Label attached to upstart men and women in their 20s, who immersed themselves in retro fashion and grunge.

5. Michael Jordan.

6. A new breed of athlete on the lookout for novel, exciting, often dangerous physical challenges, e.g., snowboarding, street luge, sky surfing.

7. Russian president from 1991–1999.

8. Warfare that featured a new type of hi-tech weaponry, e.g., stealth bombers, night vision equipment.

9. Saddam Hussein's Iraqi army invaded Kuwait.

10. Seinfeld.

Source: Time Life (2000). The Digital Decade: The '90s, from the *Our American Century* series. Alexandria, VA: Time Life.

Some of these activities only simulate real-world experiences. It is also important for students to conduct assignments that are real in terms of interest, choice, doing what real workers do (e.g., scientists, teachers, or any other particular career), responsibility, and teamwork. For example, while on the playground a class of students noticed the earthworms living in the vacant lot next door. They were totally fascinated with these worms, so their teacher took advantage of this high level of interest and suggested that they find out more about the kind of habitat earthworms require. This led to an extended study of earthworms both within and outside the classroom walls. The experience was authentic scientific inquiry and students acted as true researchers: asking questions, gathering data, manipulating variables, discovering answers, and asking more questions.

GUIDELINES FOR CREATING AUTHENTIC LEARNING EXPERIENCES

Zemelman et al. (1998) provide ideas for authentic learning that can occur both inside and outside the classroom.

INSIDE SCHOOL

- Let kids in on curriculum planning, choosing topics and readings, making schedules, keeping records.

- Develop broad, interdisciplinary, thematic units based on student concerns.
- Use tangible, tactile materials, artifacts, and live demonstrations where possible.
- Favor learn-by-doing over learn-by-sitting-there-quietly-and-listening.
- Follow news and current events, connecting them with curriculum.
- Include activities that connect with students' multiple intelligences and cognitive styles.
- Let students subdivide content, form groups, and conduct team projects.
- Use primary source documents, not just textbooks, to teach history, science, etc.
- Invite in speakers, experts, and interview subjects from the community.
- Bring in parents to give presentations, conference with kids, create materials.
- Mix children through multiage grouping, cross-age projects, buddy programs, and mainstreamed special education.
- Schedule time in flexible blocks that match the curriculum.
- Stress student goal setting and self-assessment.

BEYOND SCHOOL

- Give homework assignments that require interaction with family and community.
- Share student work through parent and community newsletters, displays, and events.
- Display student artwork or research projects in off-campus settings.
- Plan regular field trips and attend arts performances that support the curriculum.
- Visit, study, and investigate local government, services, and businesses.
- Get involved in community issues: recycling, safety, programs for kids.
- Launch family and community history projects.
- Join in a community beautification or art project.
- Take children on outdoor education, wilderness, ecology, and adventure programs.
- In conjunction with integrative units, have fact-finding tours; students take notes, make observations, or conduct interviews.
- Conduct survey or opinion research, by mail or in person. (pp. 203–204)

Maehr (1976) discusses the concept of continuing motivation and describes this to mean "individuals' engagement in a learned activity outside the context in which it was learned" (p. 443). He argues that "schools focus too much on learning in school and not enough on promoting children's continuing motivation to learn outside the school setting" (Wigfield, 1997,

p. 17). Perhaps by using the listed inside and beyond school practices, schools can promote continuing motivation. For example, using popular cultural texts such as those found in music lyrics as a way to explore multiple meanings can provide a way to engage students in school literacy practices and, at the same time, help teachers gain valuable insight into students' lives (Alvermann and Hagood, 2000, p. 445). Similarly, using a readers' workshop approach, Taylor and Nesheim (2000/2001) helped their students appreciate the value of reading aloud to young children, so as parents they would more likely engage in shared reading activities.

INTO THE REAL WORLD: INFORMATION LITERACY

"Book- and print-based literacies, and the industrial model of schooling built around book culture, are no longer wholly adequate in a changing information, social, and cultural environment" (Luke, 2000, p. 424). In our world today, information is expanding at an exponential rate along with enormous strides being made in technological advancements. We are truly in the Information Age, and now knowledge, not agriculture or manufactured goods, is this country's most precious natural resource. Thus, people

information literate ●

who are **information literate**—who know how to locate, acquire, and use information—are America's greatest resources.

The American Library Association Presidential Committee Report on Information Literacy (ALA, 1989) describes what we need to do as educators.

> To be information literate, a person must be able to recognize when information is needed and have the ability to locate, evaluate, and use effectively the needed information. Producing such a citizenry will require that schools and colleges appreciate and integrate the concept of information literacy into their learning programs and that they play a leadership role in equipping individuals and institutions to take advantage of the opportunities inherent within the information society. Ultimately, information literate people are those who have learned how to learn. They know how to learn because they know how knowledge is organized, how to find information, and how to use information in such a way that others can learn from them. They are people prepared for lifelong learning, because they can always find the information needed for any task or decision at hand. (p. 1 of 13)

Educators realize that the people who most need to be information literate, such as minority groups, at-risk students, illiterate adults, people for whom English is a second language, and those who are economically disadvantaged, are the least likely to have the learning experiences or the access to information that will enable them to improve their situations. For example, these individuals are most vulnerable when they need to make decisions about health care for their children; find affordable insurance; locate and select nursing care for an elderly parent; or purchase, finance, or insure a car. The emphasis placed in school on textbooks, workbooks, and lectures is not sufficient to provide the learning experiences needed for the Information Age. At the very least, providing students with a lifelong habit of library use should be an additional focus in the intermediate grades. Such a focus would actively involve students in

- knowing when they have a need for information;
- identifying information needed to address a given problem or issue;
- finding needed information and evaluating the information;
- organizing the information; and
- using the information effectively to address the problem or issue at hand. (ALA, 1989, p. 6 of 13)

In addition to the activities already described in this chapter and the chapter on literacy in the content areas (see Chapter 8), the following items describe what education might be like if information literacy were a central focus, rather than a peripheral focus.

1. **The school would be more interactive in these ways:**

- Students interact with teachers, other students, multiple information resources, and their community in pursuit of questions that interest them personally.
- Students engage in long-term quests for answers to at least one real and serious social, scientific, aesthetic, or political problem.
- Quests involve searching print, electronic, and video data; interviewing people in and outside of school; reading original sources; and doing extended writing.
- Learning is more self-initiated and more intellectually and emotionally demanding when asking important questions; gathering data; reducing and synthesizing data; and analyzing, interpreting, and reporting information in a variety of forms.
- The results of student projects are prominently displayed.
- Discussion and debate about substantive, relevant issues pervade the halls, playgrounds, and cafeteria, as well as the classroom.
- Questions such as "How do you know that?" "What evidence do you have for saying that?" and "How can we find out?" are commonplace.

2. **Teachers would be team members, coaches, and guides:**

- Not capable of being repositories of all information that is found in libraries and databases worldwide and that can be accessed by classroom computers, teachers focus on arousing curiosity, asking the right questions, leading serious debate and discussion, and modeling inquiry.

- Together with librarians, media resource people, and instructional designers, teachers ensure that student projects are challenging, interesting, and productive learning experiences.
- There is less lecturing and more coaching and guiding.

3. Evaluation would reflect the interactive nature of the school:

- Interactive tutoring software provides useful diagnostic information to help teachers and students understand student needs.
- A broad range of literacy indicators, to include knowing appropriate information sources and the ability to perform information searches, are assessed.
- Assessments would relate specifically to ways students use their minds and achieve success as information consumers, analyzers, interpreters, evaluators, and communicators of ideas.

In general, most schools are far from placing an emphasis on students being information literate. Those who are engaging in the service-learning projects discussed earlier in this chapter probably come closest. However, as the strategies and activities presented throughout this book demonstrate, it is possible to develop literacy in ways that are compatible with the new demands of our world. Cooperative learning, comprehension skills, research skills, and writing in a variety of genres are all necessary skills in the Information Age.

SUMMARY

Motivation, lifelong literacy habits, involvement in real-world aspects of literacy, and information literacy were discussed in this chapter. There is no one way to develop motivation for literacy activities, and motivation can vary depending on the task. However, by engaging students in meaningful and relevant work, such as service-learning projects, or real-world applications that require the need for literate activity, chances improve of developing motivation and a lifelong habit of reading and writing, two major goals of intermediate-grade literacy instruction. Addressing the importance of becoming information literate will also motivate students to engage in literacy activities. Techniques for encouraging students to read quality literature, to select their own books, and to become involved in literate activities within their own communities serve to move students from needing extrinsic rewards for doing literate work, to being more intrinsically motivated. Teachers must do whatever it takes to help students become literate individuals, *especially* beyond the classroom.

Questions
FOR JOURNAL WRITING AND DISCUSSION

1. Recall a time when you were highly motivated to complete a task. Write about your feelings and try to explain why you were so motivated. Share your reasons with a small group of your classmates and compile a list of common characteristics for what motivates.

2. How do you choose a book to read for pleasure? How do you choose a book to read for information? How would you direct a student to locate a book to read for pleasure?

3. Develop a list of activities you could use in the classroom, or potential service-learning projects, that would involve students in doing real literacy work.

Suggestions
FOR PROJECTS AND FIELD ACTIVITIES

1. Interview an intermediate-grade student using one of the reading attitude or interest surveys found in Appendix D (or develop your own set of questions to ask). Analyze the results to draw some conclusions about the student's level of motivation. Then, if possible, observe this student within the classroom setting. Do the survey results match the student's actions?

2. Complete for yourself a chart similar to the one Mr. Fortier made with his students in the chapter's opening scenario. Then try to do the same with a group of intermediate-grade students. Have a discussion with them on why it is important to be literate in today's world.

3. Choose several representative printed materials that students are expected to read from an intermediate-grade classroom. Determine the readability levels of these materials using Fry's Readability Graph (see Appendix E). Discuss this information with the classroom teacher. What other possible factors would make these materials more or less readable than the graph indicates?

References

Alexander, P. A., Kulikowich, J. M., & Jetton, T. L. (1994). The role of subject-matter knowledge and interest in the processing of linear and non-linear texts. *Review of Educational Research, 64*, 201–252.

Alvermann, D. E., & Hagood, M. C. (2000). Fandom and critical media literacy. *Journal of Adolescent & Adult Literacy, 43*, 436–446.

American Library Association. (1989). *Presidential Committee on Information Literacy Report*

[Online] Available: www.ala.org/acrl/nili/ilit1st.html.

Anderson, V., Kinsley, C., Negroni, P., & Price, C. (1991, June). Community service-learning and school improvement in Springfield, Massachusetts. *Phi Delta Kappan, 72,* 761–764.

Berkas, T. (1997). *Strategic review of the W. K. Kellogg Foundation's service-learning projects, 1990–1996.* Battle Creek, MI: W. K. Kellogg Foundation.

Courneya, J. (1994). An evaluation of the Native American school's water quality testing program. In M. Neal, R. Shumer, & K. Gorak (Eds.), *Evaluation: The key to improving service-learning programs* (pp. 163–182). Minneapolis: Minnesota Department of Education and the University of Minnesota.

Eccles, J. S., Wigfield, A., Harold, R., & Blumenfeld, P. S. (1993). Age and gender differences in children's self- and task perceptions during elementary school. *Child Development, 64,* 830–847.

Follman, J. (1998). *Florida learn and serve: 1996–97 outcomes and correlations with 1994–95 and 1995–96.* Tallahassee: Florida State University, Center for Civic Education and Service.

Fredericks, L., Kaplan, F., & Zeisler, J. (2001). *Integrating youth voice in service-learning.* Learning In Deed issue paper produced by Education Commission of the States' Initiative and Learning in Deed, the W. K. Kellogg Foundation's Service Learning Initiative [Online] Available: www.ecs.org.

Glenn, J. (2002, June). Service learning puts academics into action. *Education Update, 44*(4), 1, 3.

Goodman, K. S. (1996). *On reading.* Portsmouth, NH: Heinemann.

Guthrie, J. T., & McCann, A. D. (1997). Characteristics of classrooms that promote motivations and strategies for learning. In J. T. Guthrie & A. Wigfield (Eds.), *Reading engagement: Motivating readers through integrated instruction* (pp. 128–148). Newark, DE: International Reading Association.

Hammond, L., & Heredia, S. (2002, Spring). Fostering diversity through community service learning. *Service Learning Network, 9*(1), 2–4.

Harris, T. L., & Hodges, R. E. (Eds.) (1995). *The literacy dictionary: The vocabulary of reading and writing.* Newark, DE: International Reading Association.

Harwayne, S. (2000). *Lifetime guarantees: Toward ambitious literacy teaching.* Portsmouth, NH: Heinemann.

Learning In Deed. (2002). *Service-learning profiles* [On-line] Available: www.learningindeed.org/slcommission/horace.html.

Learning in the Real World. (1999). *The edible schoolyard.* Berkeley, CA: Center for Ecoliteracy, 2522 San Pablo Avenue, 94702. E-mail: info@ecoliteracy.org; website: www.ecoliteracy.org.

Lepper, M. R., Greene, D., & Nisbett, R. E. (1973). Undermining children's intrinsic interest with extrinsic reward. *Journal of Personality and Social Psychology, 28,* 124–137.

Loesch-Griffin, D., Petrides, L. A., & Pratt, C. (1995). *A comprehensive study of project YES—rethinking classrooms and communities: Service-learning as educational reform.* San Francisco: East Bay Conservation Corps.

Luke, C. (2000). New literacies in teacher education. *Journal of Adolescent & Adult Literacy, 43,* 424–435.

Maehr, M. L. (1976). Continuing motivation: An analysis of a seldom considered educational outcome. *Review of Educational Research, 46,* 443–462.

Marsh, H. W. (1989). Age and sex effects in multiple dimensions of self-concept: Preadolescence to early adulthood. *Journal of Educational Psychology, 81,* 417–430.

Mathewson, G. C. (1985). Toward a comprehensive model of affect in the reading process. In H. Singer & R. B. Ruddell (Eds.), *Theoretical models and processes of reading* (3rd ed., pp. 841–856). Newark, DE: International Reading Association.

Mathewson, G. C. (1994). Model of attitude influence upon reading and learning to read. In R. B. Ruddell, M. R. Ruddell, & H. Singer (Eds.), *Theoretical models and processes of reading* (4th ed., pp. 1131–1161). Newark, DE: International Reading Association.

McKenna, M. C. (1994). Toward a model of reading attitude acquisition. In E. H. Cramer & M. Castle (Eds.), *Fostering the love of reading: The affective domain in reading education* (pp. 18–40). Newark, DE: International Reading Association.

McLoyd, V. C. (1979). The effects of extrinsic rewards of differential value on high and low intrinsic interest. *Child Development, 50,* 1010–1019.

Melchior, A. (1999). *Summary report: National evaluation of learn and serve America.* Waltham, MA: Center for Human Resources, Brandeis University.

National Commission on Service-Learning. (2002). *Learning in deed: The power of service-learning for American schools,* Final Report [Online] Available: http://learningindeed.org/slcommission/report.html.

Ohlhausen, M., & Jepsen, M. (1992). Lessons from Goldilocks: "Someone has been choosing my books but I can make my own choices now!" *The New Advocate, 5,* 31–46.

Oldfather, P. (2001). *When students do not feel motivated for literacy learning: How a responsive classroom culture helps* [Online]. Available: http://curry.edschool.virginia.edu/go/clic/nrrc/respon_r8.html.

Paris, S. G., & Oka, E. R. (1986). Self-regulated learning among exceptional children. *Exceptional Children, 53,* 103–108.

Petrillo, L. (2002, January 4). *Grade school globetrotters: Reading program has students*

'crossing continents' for books [Online]. Available: www.uniontrib.com/news/uniontrib/fri/metro/news_1mi4read.html.

Rodin, J., Rennert, K., & Solomon, S. (1980). Intrinsic motivation for control: Fact or fiction. In A. Baum, J. E. Singer, & S. Valios (Eds.), *Advances in environmental psychology II* (pp. 64–86). Hillsdale, NJ: Erlbaum.

Schiefele, U. (1991). Interest, learning, and motivation. *Educational Psychologist, 26,* 299–323.

Stephens, L. (1995). *The complete guide to learning through community-service, grades K–9.* Boston, MA: Allyn & Bacon.

Switzer, G., Simmons, R., Dew, M., Regalski, J., & Wang, C. (1995). The effect of a school-based helper program on adolescent self-image, attitudes and behavior. *Journal of Early Adolescence, 15,* 429–455.

Taylor, S. V., & Nesheim, D. W. (2000/2001). Making literacy real for "high-risk" adolescent emerging readers: An innovative application of readers' workshop. *Journal of Adolescent & Adult Literacy, 44,* 308–318.

Turner, J. (1995). The influence of classroom contexts on young children's motivation for literacy. *Reading Research Quarterly, 30,* 410–441.

Weiler, D., LaGoy, A., Crane, E., & Rovner, A. (1998). *An evaluation of K–12 service-learning in California: Phase II final report.* Emeryville, CA: RPP International with the Search Institute.

Wigfield, A. (1997). Children's motivations for reading and reading engagement. In J. T. Guthrie & A. Wigfield (Eds.), *Reading engagement: Motivating readers through integrated instruction* (pp. 14–33). Newark, DE: International Reading Association.

Zemelman, S., Daniels, H., & Hyde, A. (1998). *Best practice: New standards for teaching and learning in America's schools* (2nd ed.). Portsmouth, NH: Heinemann.

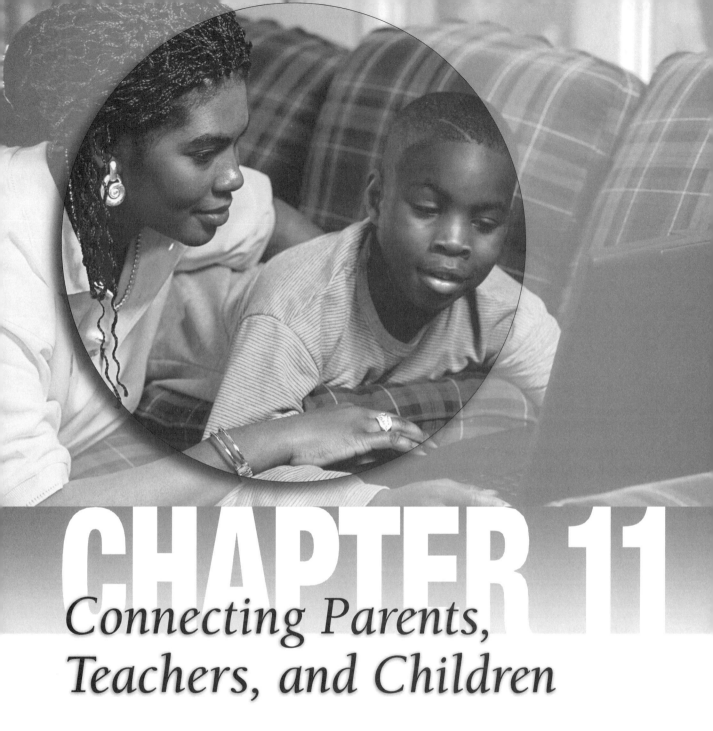

CHAPTER 11
Connecting Parents, Teachers, and Children

Focus Questions

- What should teachers know about the home backgrounds of their learners?

- How can teachers forge a relationship with parents or caretakers that facilitates the literacy development of their children?

- What should parents be told about literacy development in the intermediate grades?

In the beginning of the school year, Ms. Janos has little success getting nine-year-old Lydia's mother, a single parent from the Caribbean, to come to parent–teacher conferences. Mrs. Baptiste, a vivacious woman from St. Croix, U.S. Virgin Islands who speaks a lilting Cruzan dialect, shares with Ms. Janos that she had to drop out of school at age 16 to care for younger siblings. She feels intimidated by the thought of going to an educational institution so different physically and culturally from that with which she is familiar. Mrs. Baptiste returns neither Ms. Janos's phone calls nor notes sent home with Lydia. Unperturbed, Ms. Janos quickly decides to make a home visit. She asks Lydia to arrange a time, at her mother's convenience, when she can pay a social visit. The two women meet one Friday afternoon and, over tea and Johnny cakes graciously offered by Lydia's mother, discuss nothing about school; instead, they chat about their shared affection for the little girl. The next time Mrs. Baptiste is summoned, she is less fearful, having fond memories of the respectful human connection that Ms. Janos has forged.

This evening, Ms. Janos smiles warmly as she greets Lydia's mother at the door of her classroom. She asks Mrs. Baptiste to sit down and the two briefly exchange pleasantries. Then Ms. Janos shares Lydia's progress reports and discusses her improvement in reading and writing. She shows Mrs. Baptiste a portfolio of Lydia's writing at the beginning of the year, comparing it with a sample piece that she recently wrote and had asked to be included in her portfolio. Mrs. Baptiste is impressed. Ms. Janos explains, in simple terms, exactly what literacy skills Lydia has mastered thus far and explains her plans for continuing to meet her instructional needs.

The conference ends, as such conferences often do, with Mrs. Baptiste asking what she can do to help her child to become a successful student. However, she frowns and puts her head down as she reveals that she herself is barely able to read. Ms. Janos assures Mrs. Baptiste that there is much she can do to further her daughter's academic career. First, she acknowledges the fact that Mrs. Baptiste and her daughter have an enviable, close relationship and talk so easily together in such an animated fashion. She explains that such "talk" is crucial to literacy development. Second, she suggests that Mrs. Baptiste have Lydia read to *her* whenever it is convenient and that both of them discuss what was read in an enjoyable, pleasant atmosphere. Finally, she tells her that in later meetings, she will offer a few specific "tips" of learning activities for selective objectives and instruct her in their use. But, for today, enough has been accomplished. Lydia's mother leaves the classroom beaming, reassured that her lack of a formal education will in no way impede her precious daughter's progress. Indeed, she has heard that she is already doing much "right," and she has been amazed to learn that simply by listening to Lydia read she will be furthering her growth. A true partnership has been formed.

LITERACY GROWTH AT HOME

Every teacher hopes for a class full of students whose parents, or caretakers, care about and support their literacy growth at home. Teachers know, intuitively and through research, that such students will have a much easier road to becoming readers and writers. Indeed, research from the 1970s and 1980s consistently identifies and reports strong correlations between parents reading to and with their children and the children's later success in literacy (Anderson et al., 1985; Chomsky, 1972; Laosa, 1982; Teale and Sulzby, 1986). More recent research has attempted to identify the essential nature of what transpires during parent–child reading interactions to make them so beneficial. Lancy and Bergin (1992) found that children who are more fluent and positive about reading came from parent–child pairs who viewed reading as fun, kept stories moving with a "meaning-seeking" rather than a purely "decoding" orientation, and encouraged questions and humor while reading together.

Teachers have long been telling parents to simply "read to your child!" but perhaps this exhortation has been misguided in the light of research findings. For example, Lancy et al. (1989) describe the parents of good readers as using *expansionist strategies*, which include adding personal information and explanations, or scaffolding, as their children grapple to understand stories. For example, the parent might start reading a story with the child and then make guesses as to what will happen next, modeling the comprehension strategy of making predictions. Over time, the parent takes a less active role and encourages the child to utilize these strategies when reading. This is especially useful with a story that has been read multiple times. According to Lancy et al. (1989), when a child experiences difficulty, the parent of a good reader tends to make a mild joke of it, thus diffusing anxiety, whereas the parent of a poorer reader treats a decoding error as a serious infraction, sometimes even covering up an illustration in order to prevent "cheating."

UNDERSTANDING DIFFERENCES IN HOME PRACTICES

Because many teachers come from middle-class backgrounds, there is often an unfortunate tendency to view effective home literacy practices to be only those that teachers recall experiencing in their own comfortable homes. The image that most often comes to mind, then, for most teachers is a young child sitting on the lap of a parent—usually a young female—while a large story book is being read. Such an image sets up the notion that parents who do not read books to their child in this manner are somehow to blame for their child's lack of progress in literacy. However, it is important to consider the wide range of literacy practices that may occur in the homes of a variety of diverse children. This approach allows us to build more effectively upon the literacy experiences that children, from a host of backgrounds, bring with them to school (Thomas et al., 1999).

In fact, it appears that literacy in the home and community is very much a part of people's culture. Moreover, each community has its own special literate traditions. Shirley Brice Heath's (1983) seminal investigation of two different African American communities showed how literacy may vary widely depending on the cultural context of children's homes and communities. There were fewer reading materials in the first community she observed, but there seemed to be a collaborative approach to literacy. In the second community, a higher value was placed on literacy in terms of the people's statements, but not necessarily their actions. Both communities hold differing beliefs about how their children will learn to read and write; however, neither community's literacy concepts and practices matches well with the concepts and practices of the formal literacy that is taught in school.

It is critical for teachers to keep in mind that most parents—regardless of income level or cultural or ethnic background—value education for their children. However, different parents may have differing perceptions of what it means to be literate, and they may not always be aware of the most effective tactics for them to take to foster literacy with their child. Several researchers have reported the high value placed on literacy by many low-income families. For example, Delgado-Gaitan (1987) found that the possibility of a better education for their children was cited as a major reason for Hispanics to immigrate to the United States. Taylor and Dorsey-Gaines (1988), studying low-income parents whose children succeed in school, noted extraordinary sacrifices and efforts being made by the parents in the interest of their children's education, despite the parents' limited educational levels. Finally, Fitzgerald et al. (1991), in a study of low- and high-income parents, reported that the low-income families rate the value of education even higher than the high-income families.

Perhaps a more important difference among parents concerns exactly what they view literacy to be. Baker et al. (1994) found that low-income Hispanic parents help their children to acquire literacy mainly by emphasizing letter names and spelling–sound correspondences. Similarly, Baker et al. (1994) reported that low-income parents spend much time explicitly instructing their children in the work and practice elements of reading, whereas middle-income parents use a more playful approach, through stories and play. Literacy is presented and modeled as an enjoyable pastime and an important avenue through which to understand the world. Knowing that this difference might occur, it seems that it would be helpful to emphasize to all parents that children who find literacy learning painful tend to avoid books and reading, whereas those who learn to enjoy reading for its own sake are more likely to ask for books and read recreationally, thus becoming more successful (Baker et al., 1995).

Teachers should be aware that every parent participates in some sort of literacy activities with their children. True, some parents may have problems reading and writing, or English may not be their first language, but nearly all still engage in a wide range of literacy activities in the course of their daily lives. In his research, Barton (1997) found many examples of parents experiencing difficulties with written communication who nonetheless kept diaries, maintained household accounts, wrote poetry, took phone messages, and sent letters. These parents dealt with shopping lists, bills, forms to fill out, recipes, junk mail, and TV schedules. Such parents should not be perceived as unintelligent people living in barren homes "waiting to be filled up by literacy," as the media would often lead us to believe. For the most part, adults who admit to problems with reading and writing are ordinary people leading ordinary lives and, if they have children, like other parents, they are deeply concerned about their child's education.

Educators are beginning to move beyond thinking of just the mother in a family as the key partner in literacy with the schools and are now including the father, siblings, and the cadre of relations and family friends whom children often cite as important in their literacy lives. Additionally, focusing exclusively on parent–child relations excludes important social agencies and community resources that may enhance literacy behaviors. Educators are also moving beyond the notion that parents should read only to young children and recognize that homes are significant places for a myriad of literacy practices to occur from infancy all the way up to the teenage years, and that parents can often learn from their children too. Literacy learning can be a symbiotic event within families. Finally, rather then asking parents to replicate what teachers do in schools, teachers are now trying to support the practices parents are already doing, in their homes, to promote literacy (Barton, 1997).

COMMUNICATING WITH PARENTS

In this section, we first provide important information that should be communicated to parents about their child's literacy learning in the intermediate grades. Then we discuss the many ways teachers can communicate with the home.

What Parents Should Know About Literacy in the Intermediate Grades

There are certain basic understandings about the nature of literacy that, if understood by parents, will positively influence any assistance they offer their children at home. They must recognize that the simple naming of words, or "word calling," is not true reading and that until a meaningful communication is taking place between the author and the reader, there is no real reading by an acceptable definition of that process. Parents can be informed of the factors that influence that communication and lead to what we call reading comprehension.

First, comprehension is affected by decoding skills. Children who fail to obtain meaning from the printed page may fail to do so because their attention is so intently focused on trying to recognize individual words. It is difficult to maintain the gist of a passage while spending an inordinate amount of time struggling to identify its components. It is essential that children develop fluency in word recognition if maximum comprehension is to be attained. Parents need to be told, therefore, that both decoding and comprehension lead to proficient reading.

Second, comprehension is affected by experience. Essentially, what the reader will get from the printed page will only be in proportion to the experiences that the reader brings to it. Both comprehension and interpretation are based on past as well as present experiences, and the wider and deeper the past experiences the child has had, the more basis that reader has for making judgments; thus, the better will be the reader's comprehension and interpretation. No amount of teaching in school can offset a lack of experience, so it is important for parents to provide a wide range of experiences for their children and to discuss them at length, providing an expansion of vocabulary. A simple maxim can be shared with parents: *The more a child brings to a book, the more that child will take from it.*

Finally, comprehension is affected by fluency of language development in the language of instruction. Comprehension is dependent on the ease with which the reader decodes printed symbols into already mastered oral language patterns. If oral language is inadequate, there will be no fluency. Underlying reading is a spoken language in which written words must be translated. Inadequacy in language fluency in general, and in knowledge of the meaning of English words specifically, will limit comprehension. However, knowledge of reading strategies and meaning-getting techniques in one language transfers to another. Linguistically diverse parents who do not speak English but who are literate in their native language, therefore, can still help their children with reading comprehension through modeling and discussions of how they think through the reading process.

Parent–Teacher Conferences

Good communication right from the start of the new school year is essential between the home and the school in any balanced and comprehensive literacy program for the intermediate grades. Because most educators are aware of this need, many schools provide several parent–teacher conference days when teachers are free to talk with the parents about the progress of their child. The parent–teacher conference can be a fruitful time for the teacher to explain to the parents, or caretakers, in clear terms the literacy program and how their child is progressing within the program. Moreover, it is the ideal time to let the parents know how much their partnership is needed to reinforce the notion upon which a balanced and comprehensive literacy program is based: that literacy activities are important in the world and enjoyable. After teachers have explained the literacy program, many parents will want to know how they can help their child at home. It is axiomatic that parents are concerned about their children and they often need reassurance that their concern is appropriate and that they possess the ability to take part in the partnership. The following points are helpful to consider in this regard:

1. Set up the conference with the comfort of the parents in mind. Rather than sitting behind a desk, as an authority figure, choose a setting in which all adults can sit side by side to create a friendlier tone.

2. Understand that parents have a right to their anxiety. It is quite normal for them to wonder how well their child compares with his or her peers.

3. Inform parents about their child's strengths and instructional needs while sympathizing with their concerns. "Don't worry" is a phrase that has little value and should be avoided.

4. Refrain from being judgmental; instead, actively listen to parents, always seeking common ground. Instead of blaming them for what may not have occurred in the home, praise them for their concern and desire to help, engendering a feeling of true partnership.

5. Focus on specific constructive suggestions rather than vague generalities. "Your child needs help breaking down words into syllables" is much more helpful than "Your child is not reading well."

6. Discuss the child's progress using examples such as actual progress forms, test results, or samples of the child's work.

7. Accept parents' questions and provide clear, honest responses.

8. Thank parents for attending and let them know that you are available for additional conferences if there are further concerns.

What brings parents to school? When both the school district and individual schools make a concerted effort to let parents, and caretakers, know that they want them, that they need them, and that they have valuable information to share with them about their child's literacy needs, they will come, if flexible scheduling makes attendance possible. Therefore, schools must take a positive approach and work with the strengths and needs of the families involved. Local radio and television stations as well as newspapers can help publicize the need for caring adults to meet with their children's teachers. In addition, the chamber of commerce can be asked to send letters to all area employers requesting that they release parents, and caretakers, from work to attend partnership conferences.

Conference scheduling is vitally important. A variety of times should be scheduled for teachers to conduct the conferences because some parents cannot come to school during the regular school day. In order for this arrangement to be successful, the district's administrative unit must be fully committed to the partnership concept and arrange for teachers to receive compensation for their efforts.

Conferences can be productive and pleasant for both teachers and parents if teachers follow a few simple procedures. Begin the conference with a friendly and relaxed greeting. Adopt the tone of a friendly acquaintance with the parents, reinforcing the idea, in every way possible, that you are all on the same team. If the parents speak little or no English, arrange to have an aide or community member to translate or invite an older English-speaking sibling to perform this important task. In advance, ask the child to teach you a few polite phrases (e.g., "How are you?" or "I am very pleased to meet you.") in his or her home language to make the parents feel welcomed. Begin and end the conference on a positive note, addressing what is positive and unique about the child. Focus on specific constructive suggestions (e.g., "Your child needs to concentrate on following written directions in sequence") rather than vague generalities ("Your child is not reading as well as her peers"). Discussing the child's progress using actual progress forms or work samples can help in this regard. Finally, offer the parents specific activities they can do at home, such as those offered in the next section, to help the child with any deficiencies or to enhance reading interest and proficiency.

Helping Parents to Help Their Children

The most commonly heard query during parent conferences crosses all ethnic, cultural, and socioeconomic levels. It is, "What can I do to help my child become a better reader?" While this chapter offers parents a general idea of what kinds of practices are helpful, parents are also asking for some very specific activities that they can do with their children to help them succeed at literacy. Many teachers tell the parents of youngsters in the intermediate grades simply, "Turn off the TV and have your child read for 15 minutes every day." This is excellent advice and if every parent did this there would no doubt be fewer reading failures; however, for parents capable and willing, several other activities may be undertaken with their children that will go even further to help them comprehend well and enjoy reading. Many teachers have had great success conducting two or three workshops each academic year, each focusing on one activity. Three such activities are discussed next. Having refreshments or a parent potluck draws many parents, and a format of simple instructions for the activity followed by practicing the activity in small groups ensures that parents will have the confidence to try the activity at home with their own child.

Home Literacy Activity: Questioning

Encourage parents to follow up the critical-thinking strategies introduced in class by exploring at home with their children the kinds of questions that extend and provoke critical and creative thinking. Instruct parents to follow every paragraph or so with a thought-provoking question that can *not* be answered by a simple yes or no. Tell them that questions such as "Why do you think . . . ?" and "What if . . . ?" almost always fulfill this purpose. Begin the workshop by brainstorming a list of the kinds of questions that will be the most useful for expanding comprehension and discuss the kind of responses they will likely generate. Then follow the instruction by giving every attendee a short story containing several paragraphs. Have parents contribute appropriate questions for each paragraph and praise correct responses. If a contributed response is not appropriate, accept it and then rework it into a useful question. Example: A parent offers, "Did the boy go into the woods?" (the answer is given in the paragraph). This response can be accepted and then slightly modified into, "Why do you think the boy went into the woods?" The reader must then consider the data, compare it with what he or she knows of the world, and create an answer.

Home Literacy Activity: Parent Think Aloud

Parents who already read with their children can learn to extend the activity into a comprehension-modeling practice by utilizing think alouds. Explain to parents that as its name implies, this activity is one in which the parent shares aloud everything he or she is thinking as a paragraph is read, including these mental processes:

- *Making predictions:* "I bet Jerry will ask for his dog back."
- *Imaging:* "Ooh—that meadow reminds me of the field behind Mr. Darrow's farm where we used to hike, remember?"
- *Generalizing:* "So I guess these polar bears hibernate like the grizzlies we were reading about."
- *Using the context to figure out the meaning of unknown words:* "It says an Alaskan lifestyle is the *antithesis* of a Californian lifestyle. Since it seems they are way different, I'll bet *antithesis* means the opposite."

Using adult passages, model how parents might do a think aloud by slowing their thinking way down and offering a window to the brain for the benefit of the child. Invite parents to add their observations about the passage to yours, praising comments that would be particularly helpful for children to have modeled. Pass out a passage to each attendee and have pairs of parents practice reading a paragraph out loud, sharing their meaning-gaining thought processes as they do so. Have them switch roles after each paragraph so that both parents get a chance to practice the technique. Finally, encourage parents to try this activity at home as they are doing shared reading. Explain that children can be invited to share their thoughts with their parents as they get the gist of the activity.

Home Literacy Activity: Dyad Reading

A third activity for parents is one that is especially effective for expository text and, thus, will help parents to be of assistance when their child has reading to do in the content areas of science and social studies. Explain to parents that dyad reading is a way to have their child read aloud and be sure they are understanding what they are reading. Instruct them that if only one text is available, as is often the case with content area textbooks, the parent and child will sit side by side and take turns reading aloud, rotating after every paragraph. When the reader has finished the paragraph, the reader will summarize it for the listener, who will then add any material that may have been overlooked by the reader. They will then switch roles. To introduce this activity, explain the steps as you model them with a partner or attendee who has been briefed in advance. It is helpful to model the activity using one text, because this is the way it will be used at home, but for the purpose of the demonstration, the passage may be reproduced for the attendees. Additionally, explain to parents that an effective summary is a shortened version of the original—no more than a third in length—that contains the main idea as well as important details. Answer any questions parents may have about the steps of the procedure. Hand out new expository passages to pairs of parents and have them practice doing dyad reading, rotating roles after each paragraph. Encourage them to use this technique at home whenever their child has homework in the content areas that requires reading.

Other Communication with Parents

Besides the regularly scheduled conferences and workshops, teachers can keep parents informed in a variety of ways. One way is through a monthly newsletter. An attractive, simply written flyer sent to parents can help explain the child's literacy program and help avoid misunderstandings and confusion. The newsletter can also be a vehicle through which to convey or reiterate the suggestions for home reading previously discussed. Additionally, any questions that parents have been asking, or those that frequently come up every year, can he addressed in the letter.

Progress notes are a more personal way to keep parents informed about their child. At frequent intervals, short notes can be written about a child in a positive, congratulatory tone when the child has completed a book, asked an incisive question, or written an especially interesting piece. Such notes might also include a few open-ended questions for parents to ask their child about a story that has been read in class, or some vocabulary to discuss with their child. Parents might also be asked to listen to their child read a passage from a book recently finished so they can share in the enjoyable experience of completing a book and celebrating success.

A special idea to bring parents to the school for an occasion other than the formal parent–teacher conference is the reading festival. Any number of activities can be planned that have the parents, children, and invited community members coming together to share favorite books, articles, and stories. Parents can be asked to bring in their favorite children's book to read with the class, if they wish. Community members—especially those role models whom upper elementary youngsters do not ordinarily associate with reading, such as firefighters, sports figures, and police officers—can be invited to read with small groups of children, or choral reading can be done with adults and children taking appropriate, or reverse, roles. Art activities can be planned, such as creating and playing reading games, or constructing dioramas or murals in connection with a favorite book. Such a festival works well in collaboration with a book fair or a book swap. The book fair can be organized with the help of a local bookstore or a children's paperback book company such as Scholastic. A book swap, on the other hand, requires less advance planning and can be arranged simply by asking children to bring in old books and magazines from home. They can then take turns reading the blurbs on the back covers and auction them, while teachers help parents match books to readers by interest and reading levels.

FAMILY LITERACY PROGRAMS

The ways in which parents interact with their child is paramount to the child's burgeoning literacy abilities, but some parents may require more assistance than teachers can offer in a traditional school-based workshop. Research is increasingly supporting the notion that parent–child interactions are often more complex than just reading to children and providing them with literacy materials. In fact, there is evidence that simply telling a parent to read to a child may even be counterproductive and lead to quite different behavior than the teacher intended, depending on the parent's background (Mikulecky, 1996).

To address this growing concern, the federal government has begun to set up a series of family literacy programs, such as Even Start, designed both to increase the literacy skills of the parents and to provide positive strategies and attitudes for interacting with their child's literacy at home. Projects are targeted for speakers of English as a first or second language and are located in a variety of settings, such as libraries, schools, universities, or family centers. A wide variety of activities take place in these programs, ranging from discussion groups to activities for parent–child interactions, as well as direct teaching of literacy skills for the parent leading to the attainment of a high school diploma.

In literacy programs aimed at both children and adults, there are various perspectives on what family literacy should be. Most initiatives act directly on the need most adult participants feel to help their children become literate while many also stress the vital role of community in education. Additionally, family literacy, in general, provides the possibility of assisting adults in a way that need not be constrained by intimidating traditions of formal education but, instead, actually draws upon the funds of knowledge that each family already possesses. Most educators working with families realize that there is no single road to becoming literate and that they must seek the help of the parents to ascertain what positive practices are already occurring in the home.

Mikulecky and Lloyd (1995) evaluated the impact of family literacy programs in five cities on parent–child literacy-related interactions. After approximately six months in such programs, significant gains were reported in such activities as parent–child home reading, visits to local libraries, quantity of literacy materials found in the home, and the children's independent literacy activities. For example, children's avowed reading of books and magazines increased by 60 percent, to more than once a day. Morrow et al. (1995) summarized the results of more than 30 family literacy programs and found similar positive results. Their results supported a conclusion that such programs are correlated with more parental participation in school events and appear to help children not only have a more positive attitude toward school but actually experience more academic success.

It appears that long-term, community-based family literacy programs can be an important adjunct to the relationship the classroom teacher builds with the parent. The classroom teacher can support such programs by acknowledging that literacy is an issue whose domain is not exclusive to public schools.

TROUBLESHOOTING

Getting parents the help they need for general literacy interactions at home is the focus of family literacy programs. But what about parents with whom the teacher has been totally unable to communicate? Certainly, the value of the parent–teacher conference to discuss specific issues related to the literacy progress of students cannot be underestimated. Therefore, this section addresses several factors that preclude some parents' attendance at any school functions.

Interfering Work Schedules

Most schools have several parent–teacher days when teachers are free to talk with parents, or caretakers, about their child's progress. While this can be an ideal time to talk about the child's literacy, some parents work during the day and for various compelling reasons are not able to take time off to attend these important sessions. Because it is inappropriate—and impossible—for the teacher to evaluate the parents' priorities and work responsibilities, some schools try to rectify the problem with flexible scheduling. Having some conference slots later in the day or in the evening (with the teachers given the morning to prepare) has been helpful in many schools. Teachers who have adopted this flexible plan report being successful in reaching parents who had previously not attended conferences, citing job conflicts.

Reluctance to Attend School Functions

Some parents, and caretakers, may be reluctant to attend any school functions because they feel uncomfortable in the school environment. They themselves may not have done well in school, and for them anything related to school holds unpleasant memories—much as the dentist's office does to those who suffered painful experiences as a child. Furthermore, parents from certain other cultural groups may hold the teacher in such high esteem that they may feel ashamed of being unfamiliar with the language and customs and fear embarrassing themselves in the formal academic environment. These parents are most often the ones teachers usually wish to see in regard to their child's reading habits and attitudes. One suggestion to alleviate this problem is for the teacher to initially go to the family's home environment. A handwritten note or brief telephone call saying the teacher will be in the area on a particular day and requesting to visit for a chat is rarely refused. During this visit, nothing educational need be discussed, but the teacher should look for common ground with the parent; usually the adults' common care and concern for the child is sufficient. A warm and down-to-earth attitude by the teacher often forges an initial rapport that makes the parents' attempt to attend the next conference more likely.

Lack of a Common Language

A third barrier for parents is a tendency on the part of many teachers to use the technical "jargon" of literacy with the parents. Some parents refrain from attending meetings about their child because they hold the perception that they would not be astute enough to understand the teacher's "educated language," and, unfortunately, at times teachers are to blame for this concern. Perhaps in an effort to make the field of education appear as a true profession, educators have acquired a large vocabulary of very specific literacy terminology. *Dyslexia* is one such term (which, to our knowledge, no one has yet adequately defined) that might be better defined for parents more simply as "a problem with the child's reading," followed by a clear explanation of what the problem is, how it is being corrected in class, and how the parents might best help the child at home. Other literacy terms can also be discussed in laymen's terms, with the outcome being that the parents feel they are capable of understanding what the teacher is talking about and able to help. To invite parents to be true partners in the education of their child is to convince them they can communicate as equals.

SUMMARY

To suggest that the relationship among the child, the parents or caretakers, and the school is a "triangle affair" is certainly nothing new. But it is not always appreciated just how much communication and sensitivity are required to make this relationship work optimally so that there is a true synergy between home and the school. Teachers often need to be the prime movers, envisioning innovative ways to get the parents—from all cultural and linguistic backgrounds—to school, or in some cases, even visit them in their homes. They need to make them feel at ease by talking to them in clear terms about the progress of their son or daughter and find ways to explain the most effective ways to reinforce the goals of a balanced and comprehensive literacy program at home. Teachers also must be aware of current research that supports the notion that parents, regardless of income level or educational background, care about their children's success in literacy and only need to be guided to the best practices to augment the school's literacy program. Finally, teachers need to be aware of new family literacy programs in their community that may offer possibilities for parents to not only help their children but also to further their own educational prowess. Such programs add another dimension to the triangle, letting parents and children know that the entire community sees reading as a positive and worthwhile activity, and providing a paraphrase for the popular statement: "It takes a village to *educate* a child."

Questions
FOR JOURNAL WRITING AND DISCUSSION

1. Recall from your childhood any literacy activities that took place in your family. How do you think these activities might have influenced your later academic success?

2. After reading this chapter, why do you think some educators object to labeling the children of poor parents "at risk"? How might you respond to a colleague who claims that "poor parents don't really care about their children's literacy development"?

3. What do you think parents should know about the literacy development of intermediate-age children?

Suggestions
FOR PROJECTS AND FIELD ACTIVITIES

1. Arrange to sit in on a parent–teacher conference in an intermediate classroom in a local school. To what extent were the suggestions in this chapter followed?

2. Read a short story to a small group of intermediate-age children using either the questioning or the think aloud activity. Do you feel sharing such an activity with parents is preferable to telling them to simply "read to your child"?

3. Find out if there are any family literacy programs in your area. If there are, visit a center to determine what its programs offer and how often they are utilized by the parents of schoolchildren in your community. Share your findings with the other students in your class.

References

Anderson, R. C., Hiebert, E. H., Scott, J. A., & Wilkinson, I. (1985). *Becoming a nation of readers: The report of the Commission on Reading.* Washington, DC: The National Institute of Education.

Baker, L., Serpell, R., & Sonnenschein, S. (1995). Opportunities for literacy learning in the homes of urban preschoolers. In L. Morrow (Ed.), *Family literacy: Connections in schools and communities* (pp. 236–252). Newark, DE: International Reading Association.

Baker, L., Sonnenschein, S., Serpell, R., Fernandez-Fein, S., & Scher, D. (1994). *Contexts of emergent literacy: Everyday home experiences of urban prekindergarten children* (Research report). Athens, GA: National Reading Research Center, University of Georgia and University of Maryland.

Barton, D. (1997). Family literacy programmes and home literacy practices. In D. Taylor (Ed.), *Many families, many literacies: An international declaration of principles.* Portsmouth, NH: Heinemann.

Chomsky, C. (1972). Stages in language development and reading exposure. *Harvard Educational Review, 42,* 1–33.

Delgado-Gaitan, C. (1987). Mexican adult literacy: New directions for immigrants. In S. R. Goldman & H. Trueba (Eds.), *Becoming literate in a second language* (pp. 9–32). Norwood, NJ: Ablex.

Fitzgerald, J., Spiegel, D. L., & Cunningham, J. W. (1991). The relationship between parental literacy level and perceptions of emergent literacy. *Journal of Reading Behavior, 13*(2), 191–212.

Heath, S. B. (1983). *Ways with words: Language, life, and work in communities and classrooms.* Cambridge, MA: Cambridge University Press.

Lancy, D. F., & Bergin, C. (1992). *The role of parents in supporting beginning reading.* Paper presented at the annual meeting of the American Educational Research Association, San Francisco.

Lancy, D. F., Draper, K. D., & Boyce, G. (1989). Parental influence on children's acquisition of reading. *Contemporary Issues in Reading, 4*(1), 83–93.

Laosa, L. M. (1982). School, occupation, culture and family: The impact of parental schooling on the parent–child relationship. *Journal of Educational Psychology, 74*(6), 791–827.

Mikulecky, L., & Lloyd, P. (1995). *Parent–child interactions in family literacy programs.* Paper presented at the National Center for Family Literacy conference, Louisville, KY.

Morrow, L. M. (1995). *Family literacy connections in schools and communities.* Newark, DE: International Reading Association.

Morrow, L. M., Tracey, D. H., & Maxwell, C. M. (Eds.). (1995). *A survey of family literacy.* Newark, DE: International Reading Association.

Taylor, D. (Ed.). (1997). *Many families, many literacies: An international declaration of principles.* Portsmouth, NH: Heinemann.

Taylor, D., & Dorsey-Gaines, C. (1988). *Growing up literate: Learning from inner-city families.* Portsmouth, NH: Heinemann.

Teale, W. H., & Sulzby, E. (1986). Home background and young children's literacy development. In *Emergent literacy: Writing and reading.* Norwood, NJ: Ablex.

Thomas, A., Fazio, L., & Stiefelmeyer, B. L. (1999). *Families at school: A guide for educators.* Newark, DE: International Reading Association.

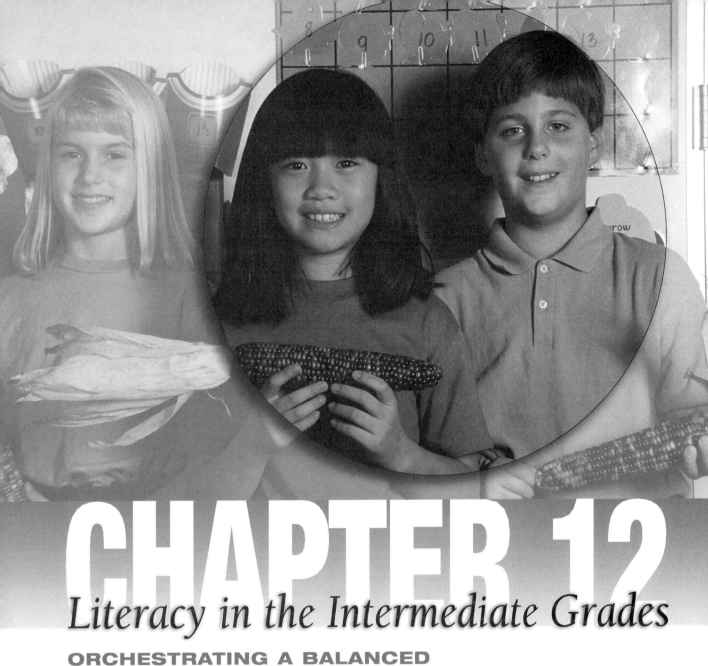

CHAPTER 12

Literacy in the Intermediate Grades

ORCHESTRATING A BALANCED AND COMPREHENSIVE PROGRAM

Focus Questions

- How does a teacher's classroom practice emanate from a philosophy of teaching?

- How does a teacher effectively organize a classroom for literacy instruction?

- What does a typical day in an integrated intermediate classroom look like?

In the Classroom

Mr. Fortney's fifth- and sixth-graders are studying the World War II era in their integrated language arts/social studies class. One group of students is reading and discussing Donna Jo Napoli's award-winning *Stones in Water* (1997), a novel about a young Italian boy who is torn from his family and taken to a Nazi work camp. It is an intense, gripping tale that engages children and allows the teacher to tie in the reading with all other subject areas.

Every day the students meet in small literature circles to discuss the book. Each student in each group reads the assigned chapter at home and is responsible for a specific role. Today, all of the students appear most eager to talk about the chapter they have just read. Dmitra, the summarizer in one of the groups, begins by offering an animated review of the major points in the chapter. Ezran, the investigator, uses a map to explain where in Germany the work camp is located and explains that Germany fought on the same side in the war as Italy. Leann, the vocabulary enricher, shows a set of 3 x 5 cards on which are written words with which she was unfamiliar in the chapter. She teaches the others the words *pummeled, squirmed, throbbed,* and *yelp* by acting them out; for the word *grotesque,* she draws a picture of a hideous monster, and for the word *wrath,* she tells a story of a time her uncle became very angry when someone stole his mail. Leann then adds these vocabulary words to a word wall that is posted in the classroom. The illustrator, a shy Pakistani girl who speaks little English, shows her picture of Roberto giving his food to the hungry little girl, a key incident in the chapter. The discussion director, Carlos, asks the group questions he has designed to get the group thinking and interacting, such as "Do you think you could have given up your food for a friend like Roberto did?" Finally, the literary luminary, Brett, shares his favorite part of the chapter aloud—the part where Enzo calls the guard names, knowing he does not understand his dialect—and tells the group how visualizing the scene made him laugh out loud.

Later, the students use their social studies books to learn more about the World War II era. They work in groups to read the three sections of the chapter. Then they report back to each other and Mr. Fortney helps to direct their focus to the main ideas in each section as he lists them on the overhead. Students in each group make a chart using the main ideas and adding details to their section of the chapter and later present their information to the class, wherever possible connecting this new information to ideas gleaned from the novel.

To exhibit their learning, the students in Mr. Fortney's class create an interactive museum about the Holocaust. Working in small groups, they create displays on the events leading up to World War II, the rise of Adolph Hitler, and what anti-Semitism meant and means today. Students work together to research their chosen topics using the classroom and school libraries as well as the Internet, compiling information on note cards. They engage museum visitors—which include parents, other classes, and community members—through the use of a PowerPoint presentation, a time-line mural, a skit based on the novel, as well as a panel discussion of religious intolerance and how it affects people.

To assess the students' learning, Mr. Fortney and his students developed a five-point rubric to evaluate their contribution to the museum display. By creating and discussing this rubric before initiating the reading and research, the students knew exactly what was expected of them. Knowing what is expected of them, and having many different ways to attain the desired goals, helps all the students in Mr. Fortney's class to succeed.

INTRODUCTION

Mr. Fortney has been teaching a fifth- and sixth-grade combination classroom at Oak Point Intermediate School for 13 years. Oak Point, which includes grades 4–8, is located in the inner city of Sacramento, California. Most of the students at Oak Point come from low-income families, and more than 70 percent qualify for the free lunch program. Seven of the students in Mr. Fortney's class speak English as a second language, although all speak some English. Nine different cultures are represented in the classroom.

Mr. Fortney works in a team with two other teachers, which is fairly typical of most upper-grade classrooms. Before the school year begins, the team meets to make program decisions and to discuss matters such as scheduling or curricular responsibilities. The four classrooms in Mr. Fortney's team are made up of approximately 15 fifth-grade students and 15 sixth-grade students each. When the sixth-graders move on to seventh grade, 15 fifth-grade students take their place, so the children are with the same teachers for two years.

Mr. Fortney has read most of the current literature on literacy, and in describing his program, he frequently refers to topics in that literature. When we asked him to describe the literacy program he and his colleagues have developed, this is what he had to say:

> The literacy program we have developed over the years reflects the unique challenge we encounter as intermediate-level teachers. Our literacy goal for our students is to have them become actively engaged with text. Our students are required to analyze, identify, define, explain, and critique what they read rather than merely understand it, as was expected in earlier grades. But besides the cultural and linguistic differences in our students, the variability in reading ability is extreme in most students by grades 5 and 6. For example, one of my students, a 10-year-old, reads at an eleventh-grade level and typically reads an entire Harry Potter novel over several free reading periods, while another 11 years old struggles with anything higher than second-grade material. He finds it difficult to decode even short articles and displays very little interest at all in reading and writing; his only passion is basketball, so we built on that.
>
> This discrepancy in abilities and motivational levels presents a pressing obstacle for me and my colleagues: How do we meet the needs of all our students, given this formidable range of ability and interest? Given that current thinking in elementary instruction is to move away from traditional heterogeneous grouping of students toward whole-group and flexible group instruction, meeting the needs of the children becomes even more challenging. My colleagues and I are continually honing the methods and resources we use to best address the literacy needs of each of our students while taking into account the state standards we are expected to address.

A CLASSROOM CLIMATE CONDUCIVE TO LITERACY

Despite the challenges facing Mr. Fortney and his colleagues, whatever "methods and resources" this team of teachers is currently using appears to be working. These teachers have experienced success with their literacy program as measured by standardized test scores, which improve and exceed the state average every year, yet also evidenced by the fact that their students appear to have acquired a genuine love for reading and writing. Reading and writing attitude surveys these teachers administer at the beginning and end of every school year suggest that students' attitudes have strongly improved, and reading logs and book circulation attest to the fact that by the end of the school year, most of their students are choosing to read as a favorite free-time activity. How do they manage such success with students at an age when interest in literacy often declines?

The answer to that question lies, in part, in the way Mr. Fortney and his colleagues make decisions about classroom instruction. Any changes in the curriculum that the teachers have developed are usually precipitated by a combination of three factors:

1. Their ongoing assessment of their learners informs them that change is in order.

2. They have read about a strategy or observed an activity that they feel might be beneficial to help them reach their instructional goals.

3. They have reviewed research in a respected journal such as *The Reading Teacher* that provides compelling evidence that a literacy practice they have considered implementing is effective and should be tried.

As an example of their responsiveness to current research, Mr. Fortney explains to us that their philosophy of teaching draws upon four factors taken from current motivational theory (Brophy, 1998):

1. setting objectives
2. providing for differentiated instruction
3. implementing powerful activities and assignments
4. teaching for depth and connections

Setting Objectives

Mr. Fortney and his colleagues plan their curriculum based not on content, but on desired student knowledge and behaviors. When these teachers sit down at the end of a school year to decide what and how they will teach students in the coming year, they think first of how those students will think and behave differently at the end of the school year. Mr. Fortney confesses that when he first started teaching, he planned lessons and units based solely on the content included in the textbook and the activities he found helped students master this content. Essentially, he realized later, he was allowing the authors of the textbook to dictate what goals he would have. Over time, he began to see that his teaching must start with *his* goals—including the attitudes, knowledge, skills, and values he wants his students to come away with—and plan curriculum that will help students to operationalize these goals.

Today, Mr. Fortney and his colleagues plan their curriculum around the most important ideas they want their students to understand. With the help of the State of California Content Standards (California Department of Education, 1999), they determine what their students should know, and then use a variety of resources to help students realize the goals that they set for them.

Providing for Differentiated Instruction

Mr. Fortney and his colleagues organize instruction around the premise that all students can learn but that each student's needs are unique and, therefore, each will need a different amount of time and effort to complete assignments. They also offer multiple ways to access material and a variety of means by which students can complete an assignment. For example, students choose from a number of books to read to complete a book contract. The book contract is a self-contained set of information, through and beyond activities that relate to a particular book (see Chapter 5). The books for each book contract come in a range of reading and interest levels, and a variety of writing, art, and research activities can be chosen in order for students to respond personally to the text. In some cases, the books provided for this assignment all relate to a particular concept or era in the social sciences, such as a unit on China. Books chosen by Mr. Fortney for such a unit range from second- to eighth-grade reading level, yet each book covers the essential information about the Chinese culture and customs that will lead to later whole-class discussion. In addition to the book contract, students sometimes take part in literature circles, where each student assumes a role to help other classmates clarify and deepen their understanding of the chosen text (see Chapter 5).

As another example of differentiated instruction, Mr. Fortney makes wide use of collaboration for research projects, with a variety of ways students can contribute to the final project, from a mural of rural Chinese life to a PowerPoint presentation to a ballad about working in the rice paddies. Such an approach not only ensures the engagement of all learners but taps into the wide range of learning styles and preferences and types of intelligences found in most upper-elementary classrooms.

Finally, Mr. Fortney forms many flexible groups so students who share the need for a reading skill or strategy will be taught as effectively as possible. Groups are deliberately impermanent and, because they exist for a specific purpose, will then be disbanded as soon as the teacher has completed the lessons planned for the group. At times, those students who are having particular difficulty receive individualized instruction—one-on-one sessions with the teacher—as soon as Mr. Fortney, through ongoing assessment, observes that a student is falling behind his or her classmates.

Implementing Powerful Activities and Assignments

Mr. Fortney and his colleagues understand that the most powerful activities and assignments are built around "powerful ideas," such as "freedom" or "oppression." Mr. Fortney shares with us his deep belief that the key to the effectiveness of any activities he chooses is that they get students actively thinking about and applying key ideas, preferably with conscious awareness of the preestablished learning goals mentioned earlier. Contrary to the practice of some teachers, Mr. Fortney believes that an appropriate activity is not one that merely has students all doing something quietly, but one that has them all thinking about what they are doing as they move toward the attainment of an important goal.

Ultimately, Mr. Fortney also believes that the success of any activity depends not only on the quality of the activity itself, but on the teacher–student debriefing that occurs into, through, and beyond the time period in which students are responding to the activity's demands. Mr. Fortney and his colleagues maximize the impact any activity has on their learners by introducing activities in ways that clarify their cognitive and affective goals and create in students the desire to accomplish those goals through constant student buy-in. Then, as students are working on the activity, Mr. Fortney monitors their progress and provides appropriate feedback. Throughout the day of our visit, Mr. Fortney led students through many types of postsharing of and reflection on the insights that had been gained as a result of ongoing activities.

Finally, Mr. Fortney and his colleagues go to great lengths to involve parents in their children's instruction. When they found that few parents were coming to open houses and back-to-school night events, they began to think of more creative ways to reach parents. An early donuts-and-coffee social, for example, allowed parents to drop in before work to chat with the teachers and view the interactive museum and video PowerPoint production their children had constructed. Additionally, the teachers in this team send home brief bulletins containing schedules of classroom activities and suggestions for books that can be read as a family that would also complement current units.

Teaching for Depth and Connections

Mr. Fortney is aware that in recent years, both the findings of research on effective teaching and the instructional guidelines issued by national and state subject-matter specialists have stressed the importance of teaching for thorough understanding, or "mastery." Students who have learned content deeply not only have mastered the content itself but retain it in a form that will make it usable when it is needed. Mr. Fortney provides clear explanations and modeling of new ideas, so students can see how the new content is important, and then helps them see how the new ideas connect with ones with which they are already familiar. He encourages this connection through discussions and debates and helps students apply the new information in problem-solving or decision-making contexts. For example, when his students are studying about immigration in social studies, he makes sure that they have trade books on a variety of cultural groups who have immigrated to the United States from which to choose, in a range of reading levels, for literature circles (see Figure 12.1). Integrated math and social studies lessons center around bar graphs tracking groups of people, and Mr. Fortney finds songs that represent the travails of many of the immigrant groups to further integrate music. Finally, students are encouraged to bring in current newspaper articles concerning immigrants, from which whole-class discussions are followed with personal essays.

Mr. Fortney's books for literature circles.   FIGURE 12.1

CHILDREN'S LITERATURE FOR IMMIGRATION, INTERMEDIATE GRADES

97 Orchard Street, New York: Stories of Immigrant Life, by Linda Granfield, Tundra Books, 2001 (varied cultures)

Becoming Mary Mehan: Two Novels, by Jennifer Armstrong, Laurelleaf, 2002 (Irish immigrants)

Chantrea Conway's Story: A Voyage from Cambodia in 1975, by Clare Pastore, Berkeley, 2001 (Cambodian immigrants)

Coming to America, by Betsy Maestro, Scholastic, 1996 (varied cultures)

Dragonwings: Golden Mountain Memories, 1903, by Laurence Yep, HarperTrophy, 1989 (Chinese immigrants)

The Gift, by Marcia S. Freeman, Maupin House, 2002 (Norwegian immigrants)

Grandfather's Journey, by Allen Say, Houghton Mifflin, 1993 (Japanese immigrants)

Habibi, by Naomi Shihab Nye, Pocket Books, 1999 (Israeli immigrants)

If Your Name Was Changed at Ellis Island, by Ellen Levine, Scholastic, 1994 (varied cultures)

Immigrant Kids, by Russell Freedman, Scott Foresman, 1995 (varied cultures)

In the Year of the Boar and Jackie Robinson, by Bette Bao Lord, HarperTrophy, 1986 (Chinese immigrants)

Letters from Rifka, by Karen Hesse, Puffin, 1993 (Russian immigrants)

ORGANIZING THE CLASSROOM FOR INSTRUCTION

Another challenge facing Mr. Fortney and all other instructors in his over-crowded inner-city school is utilizing classroom space most effectively and comfortably. Mr. Fortney takes time with students at the beginning of the school year, gathering their input so that they feel ownership of the class-room. They also offer suggestions concerning its organization. While all the amenities found in Mr. Fortney's classroom are not in all schools, certain organizational features can be attained in most classrooms.

Materials and Equipment

Mr. Fortney is understandably proud of his extensive classroom library. Two shelves line the periphery of the classroom, and the books from his personal collection are supplemented by books from the school or city library as the subjects being studied necessitate more resources. He claims that he has amassed more than a thousand trade books during his teaching career through commercial book clubs, garage sales, auctions, library sales, and gifts from friends and family. These books range in readability level from low second grade all the way up to high school and include every literary genre; they also reflect the various cultures found in the classroom, the community, and the world at large.

Desks, chairs, and tables are movable so that they can be reorganized based on the demands of a particular activity. The room also contains pillows, an old comfortable couch, and area rugs to further define space and indicate appropriate attitudes for particular projects, such as research, interviewing, illustrating a piece of writing, or simply skimming for information. Students' works are displayed on walls, bulletin boards, hanging mobiles, chart paper, and occasionally on easels. Additional materials and equipment are borrowed or purchased, according to the needs of the subjects being studied and the realities of the school budget.

Centers

Besides bookshelves filled with books and reference materials, Mr. Fortney's classroom has centers (see Figure 12.2). Some centers are permanent, whereas others are temporary according to the units being studied and are dismantled once the unit of study is finished. For example, a recent unit on the rain forest required that tables be moved to certain corners of the room so that students would have access to the science and social studies resources such as maps, globes, a terrarium, and examples of flora and fauna. Permanent centers include the classroom library, the reading area, the art center, the computer corner, and the writing center.

In the writing center are contained many items needed for writing and art activities, ranging from lined paper and perfumed stationery to elaborate

Diagram of Mr. Fortney's classroom.

FIGURE 12.2

computer paper and wallpaper samples. Writing utensils are similarly extensive to invite forays of fancy, including gel pens, ink pens, and even scented
fine-line markers. The classroom library, located in a carpeted corner of the
room containing the comfortable couch and pillows, is the focus of the
classroom. The reading material on the shelves contains a variety of trade
books, both narrative and expository, from different genres, on a wide
range of topics, and at a variety of difficulty levels matching the learners in
the class. Many cultures are represented in these books and some are in languages of the second language learners in the class. Magazines, catalogues,
newspapers, and even comic books find their way onto these shelves, and
students can be seen browsing in the reading area during any free time in
the day, as well as before and after school. The computer corner is another

area where students can access information in a different way through e-mail correspondence and Internet searches. Finally, there is a well-stocked art center. Because the school does not have an art teacher, Mr. Fortney incorporates art activities with the students' language arts and social studies activities. The center is stocked with materials for coloring, painting, drawing, sculpting, and craft making.

DEVISING AN INSTRUCTIONAL PLAN

Three important attributes are evident in Mr. Fortney's and his colleagues' organization—curriculum content, space, time, and students:

- These teachers are committed to the idea of a homeroom, so that students feel one person is mainly responsible for them; moreover, the teachers appreciate this way of sharing the administrative duties.
- The team goes to great lengths to set aside large blocks of time so a topic can be covered in the depth it requires.
- These teachers center their instruction around broad unifying themes containing essential questions that will help drive the investigation. Additional essential questions for the theme in the chapter's opening vignette, for example, are: "Why did the Holocaust happen?" and "How can prejudices such as anti-Semitism be eliminated?"

A typical school day in Mr. Fortney's fifth/sixth grade at Oak Point Intermediate School looks like this:

[9:00–11:15 Homeroom]

9:00 Journal writing/silent reading/computer buddies

9:30 Guided reading/DRTA

10:15 Language arts/social studies/writer's workshop

11:15 Math

12:00 Lunch/recess

12:40 Physical education or library, alternating

1:20 Integrated curriculum block: science, art, music, health, combined with reading, writing, listening, speaking, viewing, and visually representing

2:30 Homeroom: debriefing discussions

2:45 Dismissal

From this schedule, you can see that students remain with their homeroom teacher for more than two hours in the morning and then return in the afternoon. Mr. Fortney's fifth- and sixth-grade students stay with him from 9:00 until 11:15. The team teachers, and the students, like these large blocks in the schedule because they require fewer disruptive "downtimes" between classes and allow for more substantive relationships between teacher and student. The larger blocks also allow teachers to delve into a topic in greater depth, using extended time to make connections with other curricular areas. Finally, the blocks offer time for students to be in small groups in a self-directed manner, allowing the teacher to work closely with those students needing individual assistance.

Students split into grade-level groups for math and physical education. In the afternoon, the integrated curriculum blocks allow the team to teach in their area of greatest expertise; Mr. Fortney's undergraduate minor was in the physical sciences and he has always enjoyed this field, while the other two teachers in the team prefer teaching health and art.

The large amount of time for the language arts and the integrated curriculum block provides an opportunity for the team to illustrate the interconnectedness of reading, writing, listening, speaking, viewing, and visually representing. The literature-based focus of both blocks of time allows for integration of content as well as flexibility in instruction; when more time is needed in science one day, for example, that subject can spill into the health and art time periods, or even the language arts period, without causing a problem. These team teachers are always looking for—and finding—unique opportunities to connect the reading to the other language arts, as well as to state standards and mandated content area material.

This team has found that the literature-based approach is highly motivational for intermediate-grade students. Meeting to discuss what they have read, as described in the opening vignette, helps students develop rich schemata while responding enthusiastically to text in their own words. Mr. Fortney also finds that it is natural for him to model and talk about appropriate literature behavior, because he is able to share his own personal book club experiences with the students. Additionally, literature circles appear to have an advantage with students in the intermediate grades because students are unable to avoid being a participant in the small group discussions, and other group members hold each other accountable for completing their assigned roles. Finally, a clear advantage to the literature circles approach is that students are able to select their own books. While the teacher usually selects all the texts that relate to the broad theme, such as immigration, the students have the freedom to choose which of the four trade books they would like to read, thus increasing the likelihood that they will choose a book that is of interest and at their level of reading ability.

Though unplanned events often interfere with Mr. Fortney's instructional plan (fire drills, assemblies, absences, parties, guest speakers, etc.), one would expect to see a day similar to the one described in the opening vignette. Following is a brief description of his fifth/sixth-grade students' daily routine.

9:00–9:30 Journal Writing/Silent Reading/ Computer Buddies

When students enter the classroom, they immediately take out their "dessert" (self-selected books) and their double-entry journals. Because many of Oak Point's students have extremely chaotic home lives, these intermediate-age students appreciate the predictability of having a certain time of the day that rarely varies. As they read the books they have selected from the classroom library, they very often stop and write down in the first column of their journal a phrase or paragraph that catches their attention because they resonate with the character's feelings or actions. Then they explain, in the second column, how they personally relate to the particular excerpt. Some students have signed up to use the classroom computers to e-mail their computer buddy, a university preservice teacher. Mr. Fortney has set up this arrangement so that his students can have authentic electronic dialogues about the books they are currently reading. Both parties agree to read the same book, and then students enthusiastically "discuss" their reading with their university counterpart, who adds his or her own insights about the text.

9:30–10:15 Guided Reading/DRTA

Mr. Fortney and his team are aware of the importance of direct instruction in reading and study strategies. Therefore, they set aside a time when reading comprehension, vocabulary skills, and comprehension strategies are modeled for students through many of the instructional strategies discussed in earlier chapters of this book. This day, Mr. Fortney prepares students to read a newspaper feature article about a Holocaust survivor who lives in Sacramento and has been reunited with a sister she has not seen since both were in Auschwitz. Mr. Fortney uses several paragraphs to show students how the meaning of the words *corroboration* and *universal* can be gleaned by using the context. The students pair off and use reciprocal questioning to read, summarize, predict, and clarify each paragraph. Then the pairs share their ideas with the whole class as the paragraph is displayed on the overhead projector.

10:15–11:15 Language Arts/Social Studies/ Writer's Workshop

Students get into their groups and quickly attend to the business of sharing their responses to the reading they did the night before. Besides *Stones in Water* (opening vignette), students are reading *The Diary of Anne Frank, The Upstairs Room,* and *Number the Stars.* After doing literature circles, students in one group devise a short readers theatre presentation to share with the rest of the class so that other groups will get a sense of the other books being read. Very often, Mr. Fortney states, students will opt to read all four books being utilized in the literature circles, for recreational reading outside of school. On this day, Mr. Fortney conducts a minilesson on the use of quotation marks in dialogue, the sixth of an ongoing set of lessons designed to teach students to become more effective writers through the use of the Six Traits. Students then incorporate this new learning in an essay about the importance of the Holocaust in today's world, which is assigned for homework. Tomorrow, students may peer edit these essays in writer's workshop, which occurs every other day at this time. On a regular basis, Mr. Fortney returns to the essential questions for a whole-class discussion on the Holocaust and how it has impacted recent events.

11:15–12:00 Math

Mr. Fortney and his team believe in adding an oral language component to all math activities by asking students to articulate their answers to word problems as well as computations and equations. Additionally, Mr. Fortney often checks for understanding by utilizing "quick writes," in which students are asked to paraphrase, in written form, their understanding of a math procedure that has just been taught, providing a check on how effectively the concept has been taught and understood.

12:00–12:40 Lunch and Recess

12:40–1:20 Library/Physical Education

Three days a week, students go to physical education with a specialist; the other two days, they are taken to the library, where the media specialist often provides a lesson on some aspect of study skills such as using a variety of reference materials to augment a report. Because students are allowed to borrow books during a portion of this time, Mr. Fortney is always available to "match books to readers," using his observations and the data from running records to determine reading levels, and the results of his reading interest inventory to get an idea of exactly what books might interest each student.

1:20–2:30 Integrated Curriculum Block

Science. Mr. Fortney and his team decided at the beginning of the year to do a unit on genetics, because it is a topic that can easily be tied into the Nazi's plan to build a "master race" of blue-eyed, blonde-haired people. The unit also provides opportunities to connect with math. For example, students conduct surveys of hair and eye color within the school and use a variety of graphs, using computer software, to chart the results.

Art/Music. Students use the Internet to research many different Jewish artists during the time of World War II. They then select an artist and draw a scene of their choice in the style of their chosen artist. Similarly, students are becoming familiar with Jewish folk music and on this day are gathered in a circle to dance the Hora.

Health. The team admits that, very often, connecting health to themes they are pursuing is often a stretch; however, the team does not believe in forcing a connection where integration does not truly make sense. After much discussion, the team believed that a unit on proper nutrition and, conversely, the effects of malnutrition, would fit well with the rest of the theme, and this unit is launched on this day with a written menu of nutritious food.

2:30–2:45 Homeroom/Debriefing Session

Returning to their homerooms, students have a chance to reflect on what they have learned during the day, through either small-group discussion; quick writes; whole-group share; or question-and-answer sessions, in which individual students ask for clarification concerning a concept or an assignment about which they feel unsure.

SUMMARY

Throughout this book we have explored ways to teach literacy in a comprehensive way that includes direct instruction in the skills of writing conventions, reading comprehension, decoding, and vocabulary enrichment while also focusing on personal response to literature in the most meaningful and joyous way. The skills of literacy, while absolutely necessary, are part and parcel of the more critical task—realizing what reading can mean and how it can make readers feel. To that end, many activities were included in this book that were designed for making text meaningful and using text as a springboard to substantive writing activities.

Yet learning about specific strategies—seeing only individual pieces of the big picture—is not totally satisfactory. Particularly if one has never taught, it is vital to see how a gifted teacher manages to orchestrate all of the elements into a total program. And this program must meet the required state standards while also meeting the needs of the heterogeneous garden of students, with various strengths and needs, who now face teachers in most classrooms.

Though there are many possible ways literacy instruction might be implemented, we chose to showcase one teacher in one team's approach. This team has had success despite major challenges of poverty in homes, limited home support, several home languages, and a wide range of ability levels. Through the substantiation of test scores as well as an impartial observer's examination, the students appear to be learning the skills of literacy and are able to apply them to the content areas in a rich and rewarding way.

Finally, Mr. Fortney's classroom, for us, stood out in another, more fundamental way: it was impossible to miss the zest for teaching and the love for all aspects of literacy, and learning in general, modeled in the classroom of this veteran teacher. He eagerly shared with us his involvement in reading and writing activities outside the classroom. With students, he often refers to books he is reading, or a poem or article he has recently written. Moreover, this teacher is integrally involved in his profession through con-

ducting in-service workshops for colleagues; attending professional conferences; and, on occasion, discussing current journal articles in the teachers'
lounge. His passion for learning is contagious and is clearly "caught" by the
students with whom he works.

A balanced and comprehensive literacy program can be a reality in the
intermediate grades when a competent and caring teacher puts forth the
time and effort it takes to create a program that connects content areas with
the language arts in deep and meaningful ways, and offers important ideas
that students can wrap their minds around through engaging activities. Mr.
Fortney's classroom truly embodies these goals.

Questions
FOR JOURNAL WRITING AND DISCUSSION

1. Reflect on an intermediate-grade teacher you know who appears to be
   highly effective in teaching students to read for knowledge and enjoyment. In light of this chapter, what do you believe makes this teacher
   effective? What do you believe makes Mr. Fortney such an effective
   teacher of intermediate literacy? What are the similarities between the
   two teachers? Differences?

2. Brainstorm a list of ways you can ensure that the students in your
   class will read not only for knowledge but for enjoyment. Share and
   discuss this list with the others in your class. What do you consider
   the most effective methods?

3. Discuss the provisions that must be made so that linguistically and culturally diverse learners may succeed. How do you believe such
   provisions affect the native English speakers in the class?

Suggestions
FOR PROJECTS AND FIELD ACTIVITIES

1. Arrange to observe a fourth-, fifth-, or sixth-grade classroom. Make
   notes about the environment, the classroom climate, and the literacy
   activities in which the students engage. Your observation should be as
   objective as possible. Compare your experience with the other members of your class and include in your discussion your personal
   responses to the classroom you observed.

2. Interview an intermediate-grade teacher. Ask this teacher how decisions are made in his or her classroom about changing instruction.
   Which seems to be the most potent reason for changing a classroom
   practice for this teacher: (a) what research says, (b) what other

teachers say, (c) what the district policy is, or (d) what assessment tells the teacher?

3. Make a sketch of what you consider to be an ideal classroom for the intermediate grades, including furniture, materials, and storage space most suited to what you believe to be a balanced literacy environment. Compare your sketch to Figure 12.2. How is yours different? Why? Share your sketch with others in your class, discussing the benefits and drawbacks of each design.

References

Brophy, J. (1998). *Motivating students to learn.* Boston: McGraw-Hill.

California Department of Education. (1999). *Reading/language arts framework for California public schools.* Sacramento: California Department of Education.

Napoli, D. J. (1997). *Stones in water.* New York: Puffin Books.

APPENDIX A
Children's Literature References

MULTICULTURAL LITERATURE

The following books are suitable for introducing children to other cultures in a respectful and informative way.

Barrie, B. (1990). *Lone star.* New York: Delacorte. (Jewish American)

Bruchac, J. (1997). *Lasting echoes: An oral history of Native American people* (P. Morin, Ill.). San Diego: Harcourt. (Native American)

Delacre, L. (1996). *Golden tales: Myths, legends, and folktales from Latin America.* New York: Scholastic. (Latino American)

Dolphin, L. (1997). *Our journey from Tibet: Based on a true story.* New York: Dutton. (Asian American)

Ekoomiak, N. (1990). *Arctic memories.* New York: Holt. (Native American)

Filipovic, Z. (1993). *Zlata's diary: A child's life in Sarajevo.* New York: Viking. (European American)

Flora, J. (1994). *The fabulous fireworks family.* New York: McElderry. (Latino American)

Hest, A. (1997). *When Jessie came across the sea* (P. J. Lynch, Ill.). Cambridge, MA: Candlewick. (European American)

Hurmence, B. (1982). *A girl called boy.* New York: Clarion. (African American)

Jaffe, N. (1995). *Older brother, younger brother: A Korean folktale* (L. August, Ill.). New York: Penguin. (Asian American)

Jaffe, N. (1996). *The golden flower: A Taino myth from Puerto Rico* (E. O. Sanchez, Ill.). New York: Simon & Schuster. (Latino American)

Lee, M. (1997). *Nim and the war effort.* New York: Farrar, Straus & Giroux. (Asian American)

Mazer, A. (Ed.). (1993). *America street: A multicultural anthology of stories.* New York: Persea. (Many cultures)

Meltzer, M. (1988). *Rescue: The story of how Gentiles saved Jews in the Holocaust.* New York: Harper. (Jewish American)

Mochizuki, K. (1997). *Passage to freedom: The Sugihara story.* (D. Lee, Ill.). New York: Lee and Low. (Asian American)

Myers, W. D. (1991). *Now is your time: The African-American struggle for freedom.* New York: Harper. (African American)

Myers, W. D. (1997). *Harlem* (C. Myers, Ill.). New York: Scholastic. (African American)

Napoli, D. J. (1997). *Stones in water.* New York: Puffin. (Jewish American)

Normandin, C. (Ed.). (1997). *Echoes of the elders: The stories and paintings of Chief Lelooska.* New York: DK. (Native American)

Nye, N. (1997). *Habibi.* New York: Simon & Schuster. (Jewish American)

Orlev, U. (1991). *The man from the other side.* New York: Houghton. (Jewish American)

Spivak, D. (1997). *Grass sandals: The travels of Basho* (Demi, Ill.). New York: Atheneum. (Asian American)

Turner, G. T. (1989). *Take a walk in their shoes*. New York: Cobblehill. (African American)

Vidal, B. (1991). *The legend of El Dorado: A Latin American tale*. New York: Knopf. (Latino American)

Wood, N. (Ed.). (1997). *The serpent's tongue: Prose, poetry, and art of the New Mexico pueblos*. New York: Dutton. (Native American)

LITERATURE ACROSS THE CURRICULUM

The following books can be used as a launching point or as an enhancement for a unit of study in a particular curriculum area.

Arnold, C. (2000). *Easter Island: Giant stone statues tell of a rich and tragic past*. New York: Clarion. (Archaeology)

Blackwood, G. (2000). *Shakespeare's scribe*. New York: Dutton. (Language Arts)

Buettner, D. (1997). *Africatrek: A journey by bicycle through Africa*. Minneapolis: Lerner. (Geography)

Carter, D. A., & Diaz, J. (1999). *The elements of pop-ups: A pop-up book for aspiring paper engineers*. New York: Simon & Schuster. (Art)

Cerullo, M. M. (2000). *The truth about great white sharks* (J. L. Rotman, Ill.). San Francisco: Chronicle. (Science)

Creech, S. (2000). *The wanderer* (D. Diaz, Ill.). New York: Cotler/HarperCollins. (Writing)

Demi. (1997). *One grain of rice: A mathematical folktale*. New York: Scholastic. (Math)

Fradin, D. B. (2000). *Bound for the North Star: True stories of fugitive slaves*. New York: Clarion. (History)

Jackson, D. M. (2000). *The wildlife detectives: How forensic scientists fight crimes against nature*. Boston: Houghton Mifflin. (Science)

Jones, C. F. (1999). *Yukon gold: The story of the Klondike goldrush*. New York: Holiday House. (History)

Matthews, T. L. (1999). *Always inventing: A photobiography of Alexander Graham Bell*. Washington, DC: National Geographic Society. (Science)

Monceau, M. (1994). *Jazz: My music, my people*. New York: Knopf. (Music)

Nagda, A. W., & Bickel, C. (2000). *Tiger math: Learning to graph from a baby tiger*. New York: Holt. (Math)

Rochelle, B. (Ed.). (2001). *Words with wings: A treasury of African-American poetry and art*. New York: HarperCollins. (Poetry/Art)

Stanley, D. (2000). *Roughing it on the Oregon Trail* (H. Berry, Ill.). New York: Cotler/HarperCollins. (History)

Vigna, G. (1999). *Jazz and its history*. New York: Baron's. (Music/History)

LITERATURE TO PROVOKE DISCUSSION

The following books concern relevant, provocative issues that would be useful for engaging older children in lively discussions.

Aylette, J. (1990). *Families: A celebration of diversity, commitment, and love*. New York: Harper & Row. (Diverse Family Configurations)

Fenner, C. (1998). *The king of dragons*. New York: McElderry. (Homelessness)

Fleishman, P. (1991). *The borning room*. New York: HarperCollins. (Intergenerational Relationships)

Krull, K. (1999). *They saw the future: Oracles, psychics, scientists, great thinkers, and pretty good guessers* (K. Brooker, Ill.). New York: Atheneum. (Parapsychology)

Macy, S., & Gottesman, J. (Eds.). (1999). *Play like a girl: A celebration of women in sports.* New York: Holt. (Sexism)

Pettit, J. (1993). *My name is San Ho.* New York: Scholastic. (Stepfamilies)

Rosen, M. J. (1995). *Bonesy and Isabel.* New York: Harcourt Brace. (Death of a Pet)

Strachan, I. (1990). *Flawed glass.* Boston: Little, Brown. (Disabilities)

Woodson, J. (2001). *The other side* (E. B. Lewis, Ill.). New York: Putnam. (Racism)

LITERATURE FOR RECREATIONAL READING

The following books can form a foundation for a classroom library for the purpose of recreational reading in the upper grades. These books were selected by teachers or students for their overall appeal to all readers.

Almond, D. (2000). *Kit's wilderness.* New York: Delacorte.

Ayres, K. (2000). *Silver dollar girl.* New York: Delacorte.

Baker, J. (1987). *Where the forest meets the sea.* New York: Greenwillow.

Blume, J. (1972). *Tales of a fourth grade nothing.* New York: Dutton. (And other books by this author)

Buchanan, J. (2001). *Hank's story.* New York: Farrar, Straus & Giroux.

Curtis, C. P. (1999). *It's Bud, not Buddy.* New York: Delacorte.

Cushman, C. (1995). *Catherine called Birdy.* New York: Clarion.

Henkes, K. (1999). *The birthday room.* New York: Greenwillow.

Hesse, K. (1998). *Out of the dust.* New York: Scholastic.

Howe, D., & Howe, J. (1979). *Bunnicula: A rabbit-tale of mystery.* New York: Atheneum. (And other books in the series)

Kuhn, B. (1999). *The angels of mercy: The army nurses of World War II.* New York: Atheneum.

Lemieux, M. (1999). *Stormy night.* Buffalo, NY: Kids Can Press.

L'Engle, M. (1962). *A wrinkle in time.* New York: Farrar, Straus & Giroux. (And other books by this author)

Lowry, L. (1989). *Number the stars.* Boston: Houghton Mifflin.

Naylor, P. R. (1991). *Shiloh.* New York: Atheneum.

Patterson, K. (1977). *Bridge to Terabithia.* New York: Crowell.

Peck, R. (1999). *A long way from Chicago.* New York: Dial.

Rowling, J. K. (1997). *Harry Potter and the sorcerer's stone.* New York: Scholastic. (And other books in this series)

Spinelli, J. (1998). *Wringer.* New York: HarperCollins.

Wilder, L. I. (1953). *Little house in the big woods.* New York: Harper & Row. (And other books in this series)

Yep, L. (2000). *Dream soul.* New York: HarperCollins.

APPENDIX B
Literacy Websites

The following websites will be especially helpful for teachers of literacy. The sites include lesson plans in the language arts, as well as ideas for curriculum integration with other subject areas. Some of the sites can also be used by children in the classroom and at home. Many of the sites have both teacher and student links.

www.ala.org/parentspage/greatsites/amazing.html   The American Library Association's cybercollection contains more than 700 sites for children of all ages. Topics include "Arts and Entertainment," "Literature and Language," "People Past and Present," and "Science and Technology."

http://a4esl.org   This site includes grammar quizzes, crossword puzzles, and Internet scavenger hunts designed especially for students who speak English as a second language.

www.rockhall.com   This is the Cleveland Rock & Roll Hall of Fame. It offers lesson plans that integrate music with history and literature.

www.adventureonline.com   AdventureOnline is an engaging way for children to practice their reading, writing, math, science, and social studies skills. Aligned with learning standards, it provides teachers and parents with meaningful feedback about children's performance.

http://bookadventure.com   This site provides a child-oriented reading program designed to encourage children in grades K–8 to read more often, for longer periods of time, and with greater understanding, offering stories, contests, quizzes, and awards.

www.ceismc.gatech.edu/busyt   This easy-to-use, award-winning site provides busy teachers with annotated links to source material, lesson plans, and classroom activities.

www.education-world.com   Found on this site are a variety of lesson plans, activities, and current news integrating the language arts with all disciplines.

www.ccclearn.com   A provider of K–12 educational software, services, and assessment tools, this site is focused on curriculum advice and resources.

http://english.unitecnology.ac.nz   Originating in New Zealand, this site is part of a professional development program comprising unit plans created by teachers throughout New Zealand and covering all grade levels.

www.ed.gov/free/kids.html   Sponsored by more than 30 federal agencies, this site provides a host of learning resources such as reading activities, famous paintings, historical documents, web-based tools, and ask-an-expert services.

www.scholastic.com   Teacher lesson plans and classroom activities are provided here. Specific materials for current books, such as the *Harry Potter* series, address the books, the authors, and the stories.

www.kidsplanet.org   This site provides a bibliography of books about specific species of animals and a large database of wolf-related curriculum designed for integrated language arts units, and much more.

www.lightspan.com   This site contains a huge number of ideas for lessons on almost any subject, listed alphabetically with helpful subheadings.

www.rhlschool.com/reading.htm   This site offers weekly worksheets, mostly for upper-elementary and middle school children, for teachers to copy and use at no charge.

http://falcon.jmu.edu/schoollibrary/biochildhome.htm   Offered here is a plethora of information about children's and young adult's authors and illustrators.

www.eduplace.com   This site includes lesson plans and reviews of books by teachers.

www.poetry.com   On this site children can post their poems, enter poetry contests, use the world's most comprehensive rhyming dictionary, and read hundreds of poems by children and accomplished poets.

www.theideabox.com   Online stories for children are offered here. There are also song and craft activities that would be helpful for thematic units.

www.rci.rutgers.edu/~dkbrown/index.html   This site is devoted entirely to young adult and children's literature.

APPENDIX C
Commercial Assessment Tools

INFORMAL READING INVENTORIES

Analytical Reading Inventory (Woods, M. L., & Moe, A. J., 2003. Upper Saddle River, NJ: Merrill-Prentice Hall)

Basic Reading Inventory: Preprimer Through Grade Twelve & Early Literacy Assessments (Johns, J., 1997. Dubuque, IA: Kendall/Hunt)

Classroom Assessment of Reading Processes (Swearingen, R., & Allen, D., 1997. Boston: Houghton Mifflin)

Ekwall/Shanker Reading Inventory (Ekwall, E. E., & Shanker, J. L., 1999. Boston: Allyn & Bacon)

Flynt-Cooter English-Español Reading Inventory for the Classroom (Flynt, E. S., & Cooter, R. B., 1999. Upper Saddle River, NJ: Merrill-Prentice Hall)

Flynt-Cooter Reading Inventory for the Classroom (Flynt, E. S., & Cooter, R. B., 1998. Upper Saddle River, NJ: Merrill-Prentice Hall)

Informal Reading Inventory: Preprimer to Twelfth Grade (Burns, P. C., 1998. St. Charles, IL: Houghton Mifflin)

Qualitative Reading Inventory (Leslie, L., & Caldwell, J., 2000. New York: HarperCollins College)

The Stieglitz Informal Reading Inventory: Assessing Reading Behaviors from Emergent to Advanced Levels (Stieglitz, E., 1997. Boston: Allyn & Bacon)

ATTITUDE SURVEYS

Valid and reliable attitude surveys for reading and writing are available for use or modification by teachers. Here is a partial listing:

Bottomley, D., Henk, W., & Melnick, S. (1997/1998). Assessing children's views about themselves as writers using the Writer Self-Perception Scale. *The Reading Teacher, 51,* 286–296.

Gambrell, L. G., Palmer, B. M., Codling, R. M., & Mazzoni, S. A. (1996). Assessing motivation to read. *The Reading Teacher, 49,* 518–533.

Henk, W. A., & Melnick, S. A. (1995). The Reader Self-Perception Scale (RSPS): A new tool for measuring how children feel about themselves as readers. *The Reading Teacher, 48,* 470–482.

Kear, D. J., Coffman, G. A., McKenna, M. C., & Ambrosio, A. L. (2000). Measuring attitude toward writing: A new tool for teachers. *The Reading Teacher, 54,* 10–23.

McKenna, M. C., & Kear, D. J. (1990). Measuring attitude toward reading: A new tool for teachers. *The Reading Teacher, 43,* 626–639.

Tullock-Rhody, R., & Alexander, J. E. (1980). A scale for assessing attitudes toward reading in secondary schools. *Journal of Reading, 23,* 609–614.

STANDARDIZED TESTS

Stanford Diagnostic Reading Test, Fourth Edition (SDRT 4). This test provides six test levels for more specific information about reading skills. These skills are phonetic analysis, vocabulary, and comprehension at the red (grades 1.5–2.5), orange (grades 2.5–3.5), and green levels (grades 3.5–4.5), and the addition of scanning at the purple, brown, and blue levels. Comprehension is assessed using three types of reading material: recreational, textual, and functional. A review set of materials is available from Harcourt Brace Educational Measurement, 555 Academic Court, San Antonio, TX 78204-2498, 1-800-228-0752.

Estes Attitude Scales: Measures of Attitude Toward School Subjects (Estes, T. H., Estes, J. J., Richards, H. C., & Roettger, D. 1981. Austin, TX: Pro-Ed). This standardized instrument, "is available in both elementary and secondary forms. As reviewed in the *Ninth Mental Measurements Yearbook* (Mitchell, 1985), the *Estes Attitude Scales* measure attitudes toward school subjects. The elementary form for grades 2–6 includes items for math, reading, and science; the secondary form for grades 6–12 includes items for English, math, reading, science, and social studies. The scales take 20–30 minutes to administer. Reliability is reported as .76–.88 for the elementary scale and .76–.93 for the secondary scale, which are quite respectable for measures of this sort. The *Estes Attitude Scales* would be useful for obtaining affective data for comparisons at local levels.

"This instrument is especially valuable in light of research that shows the importance of considering attitudes toward content areas at the middle and secondary levels (Alexander & Cobb, 1992). A positive attitude toward reading in a content area undeniably has an impact on achievement in that subject" (Gipe, 2002, p. 139).

HANDBOOKS

These handbooks contain a variety of assessment tools for both reading and writing.

Bader Reading and Language Inventory (Bader, L. A., 1998. Upper Saddle River, NJ: Merrill Prentice Hall). This instrument not only contains an abbreviated informal reading inventory, but also a test battery for student priorities and interests, English as a Second Language Quick Start, word recognition lists, spelling tests, visual and auditory discrimination tests, preliteracy assessments, phonics tests, cloze tests, oral and written language checklists, and an arithmetic test.

Literacy Assessment: A Handbook of Instruments (Rhodes, L. K., 1993. Portsmouth, NH: Heinemann). This handbook contains many examples of interest and attitude surveys for reading and writing, comprehension checklists, student self-assessment forms for reading and writing, observation checklists for teachers for reading and writing, emergent literacy assessments, interviews for parents, and assessment forms for evaluating the teaching of literacy.

Running Records for Classroom Teachers (Clay, M. M., 2000. Portsmouth, NH: Heinemann). This handbook describes the key ideas for using running records as an assessment tool. Directions and examples are given for how to take a running record, and how to record, score, and interpret the results.

Informal Checklists and Assessment Devices

HOW THE TOOLS IN THIS APPENDIX ARE ORGANIZED

Reading Interest Inventory

Name   Grade   Date

1. What do you like to do most when you have spare time?

   _____

2. What do you usually do after school?

   . . . in the evenings?

   _____

   . . . on weekends?

   _____

   . . . on vacations?

   _____

3. Do you have brothers or sisters? If so, what activities do you like to do with them?

   _____

4. Are your parents/grandparents from a different country? Which one? What language do they speak?

   _____

5. What is the best movie/video you have ever seen? What did you like about it?

   _____

6. What is your favorite television show? What do you like about it?

   _____

7. Do you ever listen to the news on television?

   _____

8. What is your favorite sport/sports figure?

   _____

9. What songs/music do you like?

   _____

10. Do you take any special lessons? Describe them.

    _____

11. Do you have any pets? If not, what kind of animal(s) do you like or wish to own?

    _____

12. If you could meet anyone in the world, who would you choose?

    _____

13. What kind of job would you like to do to earn money?

    _____

14. Which of the following do you enjoy reading? (circle all that apply):

    magazines   newspapers   catalogs
    comic books/strips   books   manuals

15. What kinds of books appeal to you? (circle all that apply):

    fantasy   true stories   action/adventure
    biographies   mysteries   romance
    how to   humor   historical fiction
    autobiography   books in a series   poetry
    books based on TV characters   travel books

16. What book is your all-time favorite? Why?

    _____

17. Do you like to have someone read to you?

    _____

18. Do you prefer to read alone or with someone?

    _____

19. What books would you like to own?

    _____

20. Which of the following describe the kinds of books you most enjoy? (circle as many as apply):

    scary   sad   believable
    adventurous   informative   unbelievable
    insightful   humorous   characters like me
    helpful   historical   characters unlike me

Reading Attitude Survey—Interview Format

Attitude surveys address students' perceptions of reading and writing as processes and perceptions of themselves as readers and writers. An interview format is appropriate for providing the teacher with this information. The interview might include some of the following key questions:

- Do you like to read (write)?
- What is your favorite book (or who is your favorite author)?
- When do you read (write)?
- Do you think you are a good reader (writer)? Why or why not?
- Who is the best reader (writer) you know? Why?
- When you do not understand what you read, what do you do?
- Would you rather read (write) or play sports?
- Would you rather read (write) or watch a movie?
- Would you rather read a story or write a story?
- Would you rather read (write) or do nothing?
- Would you rather read (write) or paint?
- Would you rather read (write) or do math homework?
- Would you rather read (write) or help with the chores?

Open-ended statements are also used to assess attitudes. For example, the student might be asked to complete the following sentences:

What I like most about reading is

_____

I think writing

_____

Most books

_____

My writing

_____

When my teacher reads

_____

Adapted from Gipe, J. P. (2002). *Multiple Paths to Literacy: Classroom Techniques for Struggling Readers* (5th ed, pp. 137–139). Upper Saddle River, NJ: Merrill-Prentice Hall. (See also Appendix C for commercial assessment tools for additional attitude surveys.)

Reading Attitude Survey—Handout Format

Name _____   Date _____

Directions: Make one check for each of your choices.

○ I like reading a lot.

○ Reading is O.K.

○ I'd rather do other things.

What kinds of books do you like to read? Check as many as you like.

○ realistic fiction   ○ picture books

○ poetry   ○ true facts

○ fantasy   ○ folktales and fables

○ myths   ○ mysteries

○ historical fiction   ○ plays

○ biographies (about real people) ○ science fiction

○ (write any other kind you like here)

_____

How do you choose something to read?

○ I listen to a friend   ○ I look to see if it's easy enough

○ I look at the front cover   ○ I look to see if its' hard enough

○ if it's part of a series I like ○ I read the back cover or jacket flap

○ I read the first few pages   ○ follow my teacher's suggestion

○ if I liked other books by that author

When do you prefer to read?

○ in my spare time

○ at home

○ as part of my class work

How do you like to read?

○ with friends

○ with kids who read about the same as I do

○ by myself

○ with my teacher in the group

From *Practical Assessments for Literature-Based Reading Classrooms* by Adele Fiderer.
Copyright © 1995 by Scholastic Inc. Reprinted by permission of Scholastic Inc.

Denver Reading Attitude Survey

Description

The *Denver Reading Attitude Survey* provides an indication of students' engagement in reading activities, their perception of the importance and utility of reading, and their confidence in themselves as readers. The survey includes a few items from the National Assessment of Educational Progress.

Instructions for Administering

So that the results of the survey are not affected by variations in reading ability, read each item aloud. Students respond to each item by circling the letter of their response.

Spanish and English versions are available. Students should complete the survey in the language they are most confident using.

Explain that the purpose of the survey is to learn students' honest feelings about reading in and out of school. Emphasize that this is not a test; there are no right or wrong answers, and the results will have no effect on grades.

As you read the items, clarify them and answer questions as needed. Also draw attention to each change in the response format.

Denver Reading Attitude Survey

Name _____ Grade _____

Teacher _____ Date _____

Make a circle around the answer that is most true for you.

How often do you do each of the following things?

	Almost every day	Once or twice a week	Once or twice a month	A few times a year	Never or hardly ever
1. Get so interested in something you're reading that you don't want to stop.	A	B	C	D	E
2. Read the newspaper.	A	B	C	D	E
3. Tell a friend about a good book.	A	B	C	D	E
4. Read on your own outside of school.	A	B	C	D	E
5. Read about something because you are curious about it.	A	B	C	D	E
6. Read more than one book by an author you like.	A	B	C	D	E

7. What kind of reader do you think you are?
   A. A very good reader.
   B. A good reader.
   C. An average reader.
   D. A poor reader.
   E. A very poor reader.

The following statements are true for some people. They may or may not be true for you, or they may be true for you only part of the time. How often is each of the following sentences true for you?

	Almost always	More than half the time	About half the time	Less than half the time	Never or hardly ever
8. Reading helps me learn about myself.	A	B	C	D	E
9. I feel good about how fast I can read.	A	B	C	D	E
10. Reading helps me understand why people feel or act the way they do.	A	B	C	D	E
11. I believe that reading will help me get ahead when I am no longer in school.	A	B	C	D	E
12. I feel proud about what I can read.	A	B	C	D	E
13. Reading helps me see what it might be like to live in a different place or in a different way.	A	B	C	D	E
14. Being able to read well is important to me.	A	B	C	D	E
15. I can understand what I read in school.	A	B	C	D	E
16. Other people think I read well.	A	B	C	D	E
17. I learn worthwhile things from reading books.	A	B	C	D	E

Encuesta Sobre Lectura de Denver

Nombre _____ Grado _____

Maestro/a _____ Feche _____

Encierre en un círculo la letra de la respuesta que sea mas cierta para usted.

¿Con que frecuencia hace cada una de las siguientes cosas?

	Casi cada día	Una o dos veces por semana	Una o dos veces por mes	Varias veces por año	Nunca o casi nunca
1. Se interesa tanto en la lectura que no puede dejar de leer.	A	B	C	D	E
2. Lee el periódico.	A	B	C	D	E
3. Le plactica a un(a) amigo(a) de un buen libro.	A	B	C	D	E
4. Lee libros de texto (como por ejemplo de ciencias sociales o naturales).	A	B	C	D	E
5. Lee algo por curiosidad.	A	B	C	D	E
6. Lee más de un libro de algún escritor que le guste.	A	B	C	D	E

7. ¿Qué tipo de lector se considera usted?
   A. Excelente lector.
   B. Buen lector.
   C. Lector regular.
   D. Lector con problemas.
   E. Lector con muchos problemas.

Las siguientes declaraciones se refieren a ciertas personas. Estas declaraciones no necesariamente son aplicables a usted, o serán ciertas solo en algunas ocasiones. ¿Con qué frecuencia es cada una de las siguientes declaraciones cierta para usted?

	Casi siempre	Más de la mitad del tiempo	Como la mitad del tiempo	Menos de la mitad del tiempo	Nunca o casi nunca
8. La lectura me ayuda a aprender de mi mismo(a).	A	B	C	D	E
9. Me gusta la rapidez con la que leo.					
10. La lectura me ayuda a entender por qué la gente se siente o actuá de la manera en que lo hace.	A	B	C	D	E
11. Pienso que la lectura me ayudará a salir adelante cuando ya no esté en la escuela.	A	B	C	D	E
12. Me siento orgulloso(a) de lo que puedo leer.	A	B	C	D	E
13. La lectura me ayuda a ver cómo sería vivir de otra manera o en otro lugar.	A	B	C	D	E
14. El poder leer bien es importante para mi.	A	B	C	D	E
15. Entiendo mi lectura escolar.	A	B	C	D	E
16. Otra gente piensa que yo leo bien.	A	B	C	D	E
17. Aprendo cosas que valen la pena a través de libros.	A	B	C	D	E

Spelling Inventory

Directions: Dictate the following words in groups of five. After saying each word, use it in a sentence. Then repeat the word. You may wish to stop your assessment at the end of a set if students seem frustrated with a particular group of words. Possible script: "I want you to spell some words. You have not had the chance to study these words, but I want you to spell them the best that you can. Some might be easy for you, and some might seem hard. If you think you don't know how to spell the word, just listen carefully to the word, say it to yourself, and then write down all the sounds you hear."

SET ONE

1. drawing   Joey was drawing a picture of a dog. *drawing*
2. trapped   The animals were trapped in their cages. *trapped*
3. waving   Mom was waving hello to us from the car. *waving*
4. powerful   The alligator's jaws are powerful. *powerful*
5. battle   The Battle of the Bands is this Saturday. *battle*

SET TWO

6. sailor   Christopher Columbus was a sailor. *sailor*
7. lesson   Pat has a piano lesson every Tuesday. *lesson*
8. pennies   Save your pennies for a rainy day. *pennies*
9. fraction   One-fourth is a fraction. *fraction*
10. distance   The distance for the race is three miles. *distance*

SET THREE

11. visible   The Big Dipper is visible without a telescope. *visible*
12. confusion   There was confusion over who was in charge. *confusion*
13. discovery   The scientists made a great discovery. *discovery*
14. resident   You are a resident of planet Earth. *resident*
15. fortunate   I was fortunate to win the grand prize. *fortunate*

SET FOUR

16. pleasure   Reading a good book brings me pleasure. *pleasure*
17. puncture   He used a sharp pencil to puncture a hole in the balloon. *puncture*
18. confidence   The speaker showed confidence when on stage. *confidence*
19. decorator   They hired a decorator to help them fix up their house. *decorator*
20. opposition   There was too much opposition to the idea and so most people voted against it. *opposition*

Student Record Sheet for Developmental Comparisons

Name _____   Name _____

Date _____   Date _____

Spelling Level _____   Spelling Level _____

		Stage
1.	_____	_____
2.	_____	_____
3.	_____	_____
4.	_____	_____
5.	_____	_____
6.	_____	_____
7.	_____	_____
8.	_____	_____
9.	_____	_____
10.	_____	_____
11.	_____	_____
12.	_____	_____
13.	_____	_____
14.	_____	_____
15.	_____	_____
16.	_____	_____
17.	_____	_____
18.	_____	_____
19.	_____	_____
20.	_____	_____

		Stage
1.	_____	_____
2.	_____	_____
3.	_____	_____
4.	_____	_____
5.	_____	_____
6.	_____	_____
7.	_____	_____
8.	_____	_____
9.	_____	_____
10.	_____	_____
11.	_____	_____
12.	_____	_____
13.	_____	_____
14.	_____	_____
15.	_____	_____
16.	_____	_____
17.	_____	_____
18.	_____	_____
19.	_____	_____
20.	_____	_____

How to Analyze Students' Spellings

1. Look at the student's spelling for each word. Match the spelling with the spelling in the Scoring Chart, or find the spelling that comes closest.

2. Write an abbreviation of the matching spelling stage beside each of the words on the Student Record Sheet for Developmental Comparisons.

3. The stage that appears most often is the label that will be used as the spelling level for that administration date. Administer the same words again three to four months later for a comparison.

References

Bear, D. R., Invernizzi, M., Templeton, S., & Johnston, F. (2000). *Words their way: Word study for phonics, vocabulary, and spelling instruction.* Upper Saddle River, NJ: Merrill.

Fiderer, A. (1995). *Practical assessments for literature-based reading classrooms.* New York: Scholastic Professional Books.

Scoring Chart for Spelling Inventory

Directions: Locate the spelling in the lists below that matches or comes closest to the student's spelling. Look straight up at the heading for the spelling stage represented by that spelling in the developmental continuum. Write that stage on the student record sheet.

Spelling Developmental Continuum for Intermediate Grades

TRANSITIONAL		SYLLABLES AND AFFIXES			DERIVATIONAL RELATIONS		
Middle	Late	Early	Middle	Late	Early	Middle	Late
draing	drauing	drawing					
trapt	traped	trappt	trapped				
waiving	weighving	waveing	waving				
pauerfle	pouerful	powerfle	powerfel	powerful			
batul	batil/batel	batle/battul	battle				
saler	sayler/saylor	sailer	sailor				
lisin	lesen/lesin/leson	lessin/lessen	lesson				
penes/penez	penknees/penees	penys/pennys	pennies				
	frakshun		frackshun	fracktion	fraction		
dizdance	disdance	distanz	distans	distance			
vizabull	vizabel	vizabul	vizable	visable	visible		
confushon	confushun/confution	confustion	conffusion	confusetion	confussion	confusion	
diskuverie	diskkuveree	discuveree	discovere	discoverie	discovery		
resatin	reserdent	rezudint	resadent/resedint	reseadent	resedent	residant	resident
	forhnat/frehnit	foohinit	forchenut/fochininte	fortunet	fortunate		
	plasr/plager/plejer	pleser	plesour	plesher	plesure/pleasur	pleasure	
	pucshr/pungchr/puncur	puncker/punksher	punchure	puncure	punture	puncsure	puncture
	confadents	confadence	confedense	confedence	confidince	confidense	confidence
	dector/decrater	decerator	decarator	decreator	decoratore	decorater	decorator
	opasishan/opozcison	opasitian	opasition	oppisition	oposision	oposition	opposition

Developmental Spelling Test (The "Monster Test")

An easily administered 10-word checklist, such as the following developmental test devised by Gentry (Gentry, 1985), makes it possible for teachers to assess children's developmental spelling level.

WORDS	PRECOMMUNICATIVE SPELLINGS	SEMI-PHONETIC SPELLINGS	PHONETIC SPELLINGS	TRANSITIONAL SPELLINGS	CORRECT SPELLINGS
1. monster	random letters	mtr	mostr	monstur	monster
2. united	random letters	u	unitid	younighted	united
3. dress	random letters	jrs	jras	dres	dress
4. bottom	random letters	bt	bodm	bottum	bottom
5. hiked	random letters	h	hikt	hicked	hiked
6. human	random letters	um	humm	humin	human
7. eagle	random letters	el	egl	egul	eagle
8. closed	random letters	kd	klosd	clossed	closed
9. bumped	random letters	b	bopt	bumpt	bumped
10. type	random letters	tp	tip	tipe	type

From Gentry, J. Richard (1985). You Can Analyze Developmental Spelling. *The Early Years* (9), 44–45. Reprinted with permission.

Checklist for Assessing the Nifty-Thrifty-Fifty

NIFTY-THRIFTY-FIFTY*	TRANSFERABLE	CHUNKS
1. ____ antifreeze	1. ____ anti	
2. ____ beautiful		2. ____ ful (y - i)
3. ____ classify		3. ____ ify
4. ____ communities	4. ____ com	4. ____ es (y - i)
5. ____ community	5. ____ com	5. ____ y
6. ____ composer	6. ____ com	6. ____ er
7. ____ continuous	7. ____ con	7. ____ ous (drop e)
8. ____ conversation	8. ____ con	8. ____ tion
9. ____ deodorize	9. ____ de	9. ____ ize
10. ____ different		10. ____ ent
11. ____ discovery	11. ____ dis	11. ____ y
12. ____ dishonest	12. ____ dis	
13. ____ electricity	13. ____ e	13. ____ ity
14. ____ employee	14. ____ em	14. ____ ee
15. ____ encouragement	15. ____ en	15. ____ ment
16. ____ expensive	16. ____ ex	16. ____ ive
17. ____ forecast	17. ____ fore	
18. ____ forgotten		18. ____ en (double t)
19. ____ governor		19. ____ or
20. ____ happiness		20. ____ ness (y - i)
21. ____ hopeless		21. ____ less
22. ____ illegal	22. ____ il	
23. ____ impossible	23. ____ im	23. ____ ible

*Source: Word list from Cunningham, P. M., & R. L. Allington. *Classrooms That Work: They Can All Read and Write,* 3/e. Published by Allyn & Bacon, Boston, MA. Copyright © 2002 by Pearson Education. Adapted by permission of the publisher.

24. _____ impression	24. _____ im	24. _____ sion
25. _____ independence	25. _____ in	25. _____ ence
26. _____ international	26. _____ inter	26. _____ al
27. _____ invasion	27. _____ in	27. _____ sion
28. _____ irresponsible	28. _____ ir	28. _____ ible
29. _____ midnight	29. _____ mid	
30. _____ misunderstand	30. _____ mis	
31. _____ musician		31. _____ ian
32. _____ nonliving	32. _____ non	32. _____ ing (drop e)
33. _____ overpower	33. _____ over	
34. _____ performance	34. _____ per	34. _____ ance
35. _____ prehistoric	35. _____ pre	35. _____ ic
36. _____ prettier		36. _____ er (y - i)
37. _____ rearrange	37. _____ re	
38. _____ replacement	38. _____ re	38. _____ ment
39. _____ richest		39. _____ est
40. _____ semifinal	40. _____ semi	
41. _____ signature		41. _____ ture
42. _____ submarine	42. _____ sub	
43. _____ supermarkets	43. _____ super	43. _____ s
44. _____ swimming		44. _____ ing (double m)
45. _____ transportation	45. _____ trans	45. _____ tion
46. _____ underweight	46. _____ under	
47. _____ unfinished	47. _____ un	47. _____ ed
48. _____ unfriendly	48. _____ un	48. _____ ly
49. _____ unpleasant	49. _____ un	49. _____ ant (drop e)
50. _____ valuable		50. _____ able (drop e)

Personal Report of Communication Fear (PRCF)

McCroskey & Richmond, 1991, pp. 41–43.

Directions: The following 14 statements concern feelings about communicating with other people. Please indicate the degree to which each statement applies to you by circling your response. Mark "YES" if you strongly agree, "yes" if you agree, "?" if you are unsure, "no" if you disagree, or "NO" if you strongly disagree. There are no right or wrong answers. Answer quickly; record your first impression.

1. Talking with someone new scares me.

   YES   yes   ?   no   NO

2. I look forward to talking in class.

   YES   yes   ?   no   NO

3. I like standing up and talking to a group of people.

   YES   yes   ?   no   NO

4. I like to talk when the whole class listens.

   YES   yes   ?   no   NO

5. Standing up to talk in front of other people scares me.

   YES   yes   ?   no   NO

6. I like talking to teachers.

   YES   yes   ?   no   NO

7. I am scared to talk to people.

   YES   yes   ?   no   NO

8. I like it when it is my turn to talk in class.

   YES   yes   ?   no   NO

9. I like to talk to new people.

   YES   yes   ?   no   NO

10. When someone asks me a question, it scares me.

    YES   yes   ?   no   NO

11. There are a lot of people I am scared to talk to.

    YES   yes   ?   no   NO

12. I like to talk to people I haven't met before.

    YES   yes   ?   no   NO

13. I like it when I don't have to talk.

    YES   yes   ?   no   NO

14. Talking to teachers scares me.

    YES   yes   ?   no   NO

Scoring: YES = 1, yes = 2, ? = 3, no = 4, NO = 5.

To obtain the score for the PRCF, complete the following steps:

   Step 1. Add the scores for the following items: 2, 3, 4, 6, 8, 9, and 12.

   Step 2. Add the scores for the following items: 1, 5, 7, 10, 11, 13, and 14.

   Step 3. Compute the following: 42 (plus) total of Step 1 (minus) total of Step 2.

   Your score should be between 14 and 70.

The normal range of scores on the PRCF is between 28 and 47. Students who score above 47 are most likely communication-apprehensive. These are the children who need very careful, special attention. Those who score below 28, on the other hand, are very low in communication apprehension. These children are likely to be highly verbal, and they often will be the students who are most disruptive in the classroom. They are also those who most likely will do well in a traditional instructional system. In addition, they are frequently well liked by other students and, unless they are particularly disruptive, well liked by their teachers.

Scoring Rubric for Oral Expression

CRITERIA	NEEDS WORK (1)	MAKING PROGRESS (2)	DOING GREAT (3)	ABOVE AND BEYOND (4)	SCORE
Speaking	Monotone; speaker seemed uninterested in material.	Little eye contact; fast speaking rate, little expression, mumbling.	Clear articulation of ideas, but apparently lacks confidence with material.	Exceptional confidence with material displayed through poise, clear articulation, eye contact, and enthusiasm.	1 2 3 4
Creativity	Delivery is repetitive with little or no variety in presentation techniques; lacks visuals.	Material presented with little interpretation or originality; visual aid fails to grab attention and/or fails to communicate information.	Some apparent originality displayed through use of original interpretation of presented materials visually and/or orally.	Exceptional originality of presented material and interpretation both visually and orally.	1 2 3 4
Content	Results are unclear and information appears randomly chosen.	Results are clear, but supporting information is not available.	Results are very clear; many relevant points, but they are unaddressed.	Exceptional use of material that clearly relates to a focused thesis; abundance of varied supportive materials.	1 2 3 4
Clarity	No apparent logical order of presentation; unclear focus.	Content is loosely connected; transitions lack clarity.	Sequence of information is well organized for the most part, but more clarity with transitions is needed.	Development of thesis is clear through use of specific and appropriate examples; transitions are clear and create a succinct and even flow.	1 2 3 4
Presentation Length	Greatly exceeding or falling short of allotted time.	Exceeding or falling short of allotted time.	Remained close to the allotted time.	Presented within the allotted time.	1 2 3 4

Am I a Good Listener?

Circle Y for "Yes" and N for "No" after each question about your listening habits and attitudes.

1. I like to listen to others.   Y   N

2. I listen even if I do not like the person talking.   Y   N

3. I listen even if I do not like the topic.   Y   N

4. I treat all people the same when I listen to them—
   whether or not they are friends, family, adults,
   children, male, female, or from a different country.   Y   N

5. I stop what I am doing so that I can give the speaker
   my full attention.   Y   N

6. I look at the speaker.   Y   N

7. I let the speaker finish what she/he is saying before   Y   N
   I begin talking.

8. I sometimes repeat back to the speaker what she/he   Y   N
   said to see if I got it right.

9. I ask questions if I don't understand an idea.   Y   N

10. I try to improve my listening.   Y   N

Source: Cooper, P. & Morreale, S. (Eds.) (2002). *Creating Competent Communicators,* p. 95. Scottsdale, AZ: Holcomb Hathaway.

Student Self-Assessment Checklist for Effective Writing

Name: _____ Title(s) of Work Assessed: _____

Did I . . . ?

○ have a plan before I started writing?

○ write complete sentences that are not run-on sentences?

○ write some compound sentences that are connected with and, or, but?

○ write a good topic sentence for each paragraph?

○ write supporting sentences that help support the topic sentence in each paragraph?

○ write accurate nonfiction that is also interesting?

○ provide good transitions between paragraphs?

○ write a story that has a beginning, a middle, and an end?

○ write a story with a problem and a solution?

○ describe the main character well?

○ include dialogue in my story?

○ use correct punctuation in any dialogue?

○ use interesting and vivid words?

○ confer with others to revise?

○ edit my drafts?

Scoring Rubric for Expository Essay

CRITERIA	NEEDS WORK (1)	MAKING PROGRESS (2)	DOING GREAT (3)	ABOVE AND BEYOND (4)	SCORE
Understanding of Material	Apparent misunderstanding of material.	Limited understanding of material displayed by vague, unclear language.	Developing understanding of material.	Clear understanding of material displayed by clear, concrete language and complex ideas.	1 2 3 4
Structural Organization	Essay lacks logical progression of ideas.	Essay includes brief skeleton (introduction, body, conclusion) but lacks transitions.	Essay includes logical progression of ideas aided by clear transitions.	Essay is powerfully organized and fully developed.	1 2 3 4
Sentence Fluency (Flow)	Repetitive sentence patterns. There are no connecting words between sentences. Many sentences run into each other.	Sentence patterns are generally repetitive, with occasional variance. There are usually connecting words between sentences, where appropriate. Some sentences should be merged; others should be made into two or more sentences.	Sentence patterns are generally varied, but sometimes variations seem forced and inappropriate. There are connecting words between sentences, where appropriate. Each sentence contains a complete thought; there are no run-on sentences.	Varied and interesting sentence patterns. There are connecting words between sentences, where appropriate. Sentences are complete thoughts, with no run-ons.	1 2 3 4
Support	Few to no solid supporting ideas or evidence for the essay content.	Some supporting ideas and/or evidence for the essay content.	Support lacks specificity and is loosely developed.	Specific, developed details and superior support and evidence in the essay content.	1 2 3 4
Mechanics	Frequent errors in spelling, grammar, and punctuation.	Errors in grammar and punctuation, but spelling has been proofread.	Occasional grammatical errors. Spelling has been proofread.	Nearly error free. Reflects thorough proofreading for grammar and spelling.	1 2 3 4

Checklist for Observations of Progress Toward Standards[*]

NAME: _____   GRADE: _____

STANDARDS	CONTEXT	DATE OBSERVED	CONTEXT	DATE OBSERVED	CONTEXT	DATE OBSERVED
1. Reads a wide range of print and nonprint texts						
2. Reads a wide range of literature (many time periods, many genres)						
3. Applies a wide range of strategies to comprehend, interpret, evaluate, and appreciate texts						
4. Adjusts use of spoken, written, and visual language to communicate effectively						
5. Employs a wide range of strategies for writing and different writing process elements to communicate effectively						
6. Applies knowledge of language structure, conventions, media techniques, figurative language, and genre to create, critique, and discuss print/nonprint texts						
7. Conducts research by generating ideas and questions, and by posing problems						

STANDARDS	CONTEXT	DATE OBSERVED	CONTEXT	DATE OBSERVED	CONTEXT	DATE OBSERVED
8. Uses a variety of technological and informational resources to gather/synthesize information and create/communicate knowledge						
9. Understands and respects diversity in language use, dialects, cultures						
10. If SLL, makes use of native language to develop English competency						
11. Participates in a variety of literacy communities						
12. Uses spoken, written, and visual language to accomplish own purposes						

*The standards used in this checklist are the NCTE/IRA Standards for the English Language Arts. Any state standards could be used and the checklist can be made grade-level specific as well.

Intermediate-Grade Literacy Observation Checklist

NAME: _____ GRADE LEVEL: _____ TEACHER: _____

CONTENT STANDARDS	DATE						COMMENTS
Reads narrative text with fluency							
Reads expository text with fluency							
Identifies main events of the plot							
Makes inferences using text							
Makes inferences using illustrations							
Identifies structural patterns in expository text:							
—compare and contrast							
—cause and effect							
—order (enumeration or sequential)							
Asks questions							
Makes predictions							
Monitors own understanding							
Applies appropriate fix-up strategies							
Creates mental images while reading							
Retells to include salient points							
Makes text-to-self connections							
Uses clues to determine word meanings:							
—word clues							
—sentence or paragraph clues							
—background knowledge							

A Self-Evaluation for Literacy Instruction

Name _____   Date _____

	Yes	Somewhat	No
1. I can recognize and describe the characteristics of emergent literacy.	○	○	○
2. I can list whole-group, small-group, and individual activities for the development of reading.	○	○	○
3. I can make a basic developmental reading lesson plan.	○	○	○
4. I know the components deemed necessary for a comprehensive, balanced reading program.	○	○	○
5. I can correctly write objectives (with three parts) for lessons.	○	○	○
6. I can describe and list at least 20 techniques for motivating children to read.	○	○	○
7. I can describe a variety of top-down and bottom-up approaches to teaching reading and the strengths and weaknesses of each.	○	○	○
8. I can explain how listening, speaking, reading, writing, viewing, and visually representing are related.	○	○	○
9. I understand the usage of authentic reading materials and how literature-based reading supports this.	○	○	○
10. I can develop and employ tools for diagnosing reading ability, including portfolios.	○	○	○
11. I am familiar with the basal readers adopted by the State of _____ for use in elementary classrooms.	○	○	○
12. I know the terminology used by reading teachers (e.g., guided rdg., shared rdg.) including abbreviations (IRI, DRTA, IRA)	○	○	○
13. I can develop and analyze types of questions to get at various levels of comprehension and analyze students' answers.	○	○	○
14. I can identify and demonstrate techniques for teaching word analysis skills.	○	○	○
15. I can identify and demonstrate techniques for developing students' vocabulary.	○	○	○

	Yes	Somewhat	No
16. I can list and develop techniques for teaching the various comprehension skills.	○	○	○
17. I can plan and describe activities to aid special need students (e.g., gifted, physical handicap, special ed.)	○	○	○
18. I can plan and describe activities to aid students with language differences.	○	○	○
19. I can identify sources (places, journals, magazines) for instructional materials and teaching strategies.	○	○	○
20. I understand the components of cooperative learning (and how it differs from group learning) and can incorporate it into my reading lessons.	○	○	○
21. I can list activities for *meaningful* seatwork or learning centers to supplement the basic reading program.	○	○	○
22. I can define basic linguistic terminology and describe the contribution of phonics to reading acquisition.	○	○	○
23. I can use diagnostic techniques to identify the strengths and weaknesses in reading of the students in a class and devise a plan of remediation for identified areas of need.	○	○	○
24. I can plan reading lessons that are interdisciplinary.	○	○	○
25. I know the professional organizations and journals that have reading as their focus.	○	○	○
26. I am familiar with the purpose of the state framework, district benchmarks, and social improvement plan.	○	○	○
27. I know various methods of presenting a children's book to students whether one copy or multiple copies are available.	○	○	○
28. I enjoy reading and can be a good role model for children.	○	○	○
29. I know the components of writer's workshop and could incorporate it in my classroom.	○	○	○
30. I can design a literature-based three-day reading unit plan that includes reinforcement and enrichment tasks.	○	○	○

APPENDIX E

Fry Readability Graph

Randomly select three average passages of exactly 100 words each. For each passage, count the number of sentences in the 100 words, estimating the length of the fraction of the last sentence to the nearest one-tenth. Count the number of syllables in each passage. If no hand counter is available, put a mark over every syllable *over* one for each word (e.g., a two-syllable word gets one mark); then when you get to the end of the passage, count the number of marks and add 100.

After you have completed these steps for all three passages, plot the *average* sentence length and *average* number of syllables on the graph. Where the two lines intersect, draw a dot. This point indicates the approximate grade level. See the next page for an example.

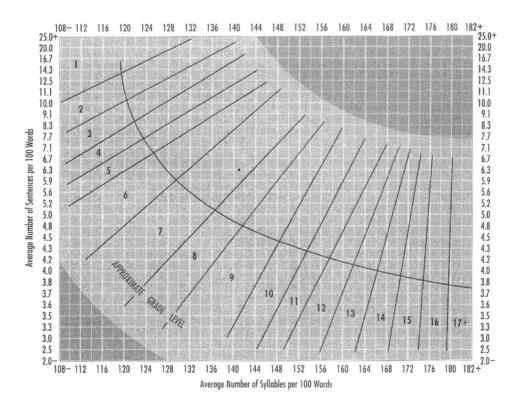

Choose additional passages if great variability is observed among the three original passages, recognizing that the book may have uneven readability.

Example:	Syllables	Sentences
1st Hundred Words	124	6.6
2nd Hundred Words	141	5.5
3rd Hundred Words	158	6.8
Average	141	6.3

Readability 7th Grade (see dot plotted on graph)

Source: Fry Readability Graph by Edward Fry. Reproduction permitted.

GLOSSARY

Glossary

acceleration Progress through the curriculum at a faster rate.

accuracy The ability to recognize words correctly.

achievement test A formalized test that measures the extent to which a person has assimilated a body of information or possesses a certain skill after instruction has taken place.

affixes Bound morphemes that change the meaning or function of a root or stem to which they are attached, as the prefix ad- and the suffix -ing in adjoining.

alliteration A pattern in which all words begin with the same sound.

alphabetic principle The principle that there is a one-to-one correspondence between phonemes (or sounds) and graphemes (or letters); letters represent sounds.

analog A strategy of comparing patterns in words to ones already known.

anecdotal notes Written observations taken by the teacher—usually on a clipboard—of literacy-related behaviors in an authentic literacy context.

anticipation guides A prereading tool used to activate schema and engage readers.

antonyms A pair of words that have opposite meanings.

Asperger's syndrome A mild form of autism.

assessment The process of gathering information about students' abilities using a variety of means and tools, both formal and informal.

assistive technology Any technology designed or modified specifically for use by individuals with disabilities.

augmentative communication systems Any system or device designed to enhance the communication abilities of individuals who are nonverbal or have speech too difficult to understand.

authentic assessment Assessment representing literacy behavior in the community and in the workplace.

autism A disability characterized by extreme withdrawal and underdeveloped communication or language skills.

automaticity Fluent performance without the conscious deployment of attention.

basal reader series A coordinated, graded set of textbooks, teacher's guides, and supplementary materials from which to teach reading.

basic words Commonplace words that are the building blocks of everyday language.

behavioral disorder A disability in which students are characterized by inappropriate school behavior.

big books An enlarged version of a book used by the teacher for mediated reading instruction so that students can track the print and attention can be focused on particular phonemic elements.

blend A consonant sequence before or after a vowel within a syllable, such as cl, st, or br; the written language equivalent of a consonant cluster.

book clubs Another term for (see) Literature Circles.

book contract An individual contract of literacy activities based upon a self-selected book.

book talk Brief teasers that teachers present to interest students in particular books.

camouflage A vocabulary-enriching activity in which learners must try to disguise a chosen word by creating an oral story using several words above their normal speaking vocabulary. The other students must try to guess the hidden word.

clarifying table A graphic organizer used to help children understand the meaning of complex terms.

closed sorts Word sorts that classify words into predetermined categories.

cloze test An assessment device in which certain words are deleted from a passage by the teacher, with blanks left in their places for students to fill in by using the context of the sentence or paragraph.

code switching The use of English for known words and the home language for words not yet acquired in English.

compound words A two-syllable word composed of two separate words that have meaning on their own, such as baseball and lipstick.

comprehension The interpretation of print on a page into a meaningful message that is dependent on the reader's decoding abilities, prior knowledge, cultural and social background, and monitoring strategies—the "essence of reading."

concept-oriented reading instruction (CORI) An integrated curriculum approach.

concepts about print Concepts about the way print works, including directionality, spacing, identification of words and letters, connection between written and spoken language, and understanding the function of punctuation.

construct validity When test items assess the skills, knowledge, and understandings that most experts agree comprise the area being tested.

constructivist model of learning A learning theory suggesting that students are active learners who organize and relate new information to their prior knowledge.

content area literacy Reading, writing, speaking, listening, viewing, and visually representing with a focus on the bodies of knowledge in the academic curriculum; e.g., English, science, social studies, mathematics.

content standards Stated expectations of what students should know and be able to do in particular subjects and grade levels.

content validity When test items assess the ability needed to perform the behaviors expected in the course or curriculum.

context clues The syntactic and semantic information in the surrounding words, phrases, sentences, and paragraphs in a text.

context–relationship procedure A strategy utilized to help students integrate new words into their meaning vocabularies.

contract spelling Children have a written agreement with the teacher each week to learn specific words.

controlled vocabulary A system of introducing only a certain number of grade-level appropriate words before the reading of each basal story, with periodic review.

conventional spelling stage The final stage of spelling development, in which the child has mastered the basic principles of English orthography and most words are spelled correctly.

conversation clubs Small, student-led groups established to enhance oral language in an informal, enjoyable setting.

cooperative learning An instructional model in which students work together as a team to complete activities or assignments.

correct spelling stage See conventional spelling stage.

criterion-referenced assessment An assessment designed to reveal what a student knows, understands, or can do in relation to specific objectives or standards.

criterion-referenced test A test for which scores are interpreted by comparing the test taker's score to a specified performance level rather than to the scores of other students.

critical reading Reading to evaluate the material being read.

cubing A writing scaffold used for students to model how to organize a six-paragraph essay.

cuing systems The four language systems that readers rely upon for cues as they seek meaning from text: graphophonic (based on letter–sound relationships), syntactic (based on grammar or structure), semantic (based on meaning), and pragmatic (based on social and cultural norms).

curriculum-based assessment The process of matching the curriculum to the content standards assessed in a testing program to ensure that teachers will cover the material assessed.

data chart A table or grid for recording answers to specific research questions (columns) gathered from a variety of sources (rows).

decodable text Beginner-oriented books that contain the same letters or word patterns currently being studied, or those previously taught.

decoding The translation of written words into verbal speech for oral reading or mental speech for silent reading.

deduction The process of helping students to construct meaning by going from the general to the particular, through explanation.

derivational relations stage A spelling stage characterized by the ability to recognize and spell bases and roots correctly. Correlates to an advanced stage of reading and writing.

developmental spelling stages Stage-like progressions that children advance through when learning to spell, characterized by increasingly complex understandings about the organizational patterns of words, including precommunicative, prephonetic, phonetic, transitional, and conventional spelling stages.

diagnosis The act, process, or result of identifying the nature of a disorder or disability through observation and examination, often including the planning of instruction and the assessment of the strengths and needs of the student.

diagnostic tests Age-related, norm-referenced assessment of specific skills and behaviors children have acquired compared with other children of the same chronological age.

dialogue journals Journals that provide a means of two-way written communication between learners and their teachers, in which learners share their thoughts with teachers, including personal comments and descriptions of life experiences, and the teachers, in turn, write reactions to the learners' messages.

differentiated instruction Instruction designed to meet the needs of all students by adjusting content, process, or product.

direct instruction Teacher control of the learning environment through structured, systematic lessons; goal setting; choice of activities; and feedback.

directed reading thinking activity (DRTA) A time-honored format for guiding students as they read selections, usually from basal reading programs.

directionality of print The concept that, in English, writing goes from left to right and from top to bottom. Directionality of print varies among languages.

discussion Oral communication in an informal setting, involving an exploration of an issue or topic; problem solving by cooperative thinking.

dramatic play Simulating real experiences with no set plot or goal.

dyad reading A paired reading activity in which students alternately read aloud or listen and summarize what their partner has read.

dyslexia A developmental reading disability, presumably congenital and often hereditary, that may vary in degree from mild to severe.

echo reading A strategy where a lead reader reads aloud a section of text and others follow immediately after it, or echo the leader's reading.

editing The process of reviewing text in draft form to check for correctness of the mechanics and conventions in writing.

ELL (English language learner) A person who is in the process of acquiring English as a second language.

emergent literacy A developing awareness of the interrelatedness of oral and written language that occurs from birth to beginning reading.

encoding Transferring oral language into written language.

engagement A process involving a complex set of ongoing activities and activities that occur in the classroom.

enrichment Strategies designed to deepen appreciation for reading selections.

environmental print Print that is encountered outside of books and that is a pervasive part of everyday living.

ESL (English as a second language) A program for teaching English language skills to those whose native language is not English.

etymology The study of the history of words.

evaluation Making a judgment about assessment data or assigning a score or grade to assessment data.

experience–text relationship A lesson format for narrative text that helps students to develop prior knowledge and relate it to what they read.

experiential background The fund of total experiences that aid a reader in finding meaning in printed symbols.

experimental spellings Unconventional spellings, or approximations, resulting from an emergent writer's initial attempts to associate sounds with letters.

expository frame A basic structure for expository text designed to help students organize their thoughts for writing or responding to text.

expository structures Content organized around a main idea and supporting details.

expository text A text written in a precise, factual writing style.

expressive writing Personal writing that expresses emotion such as diaries or letters.

FLIP strategy A strategy readers use to examine a text for reader-friendliness, language, interest, and degree of prior knowledge needed to understand the text.

fluency Achieving speed and accuracy in recognizing words and comprehending text, and coordinating the two.

fluent reader A reader whose reading accuracy and rate meet or exceed normal expectations with respect to age, ability, and grade level; an independent reader.

formal assessment Commercially designed and produced tests given on single occasions.

formal (standardized) test A testing instrument for which readability and validity can be verified; the results of these tests are based on right or wrong answers, and individual scores are interpreted against national norms.

frustration level A level of reading difficulty at which a reader is unable to cope; when reading is on the frustration level, the reader recognizes approximately 90 percent or fewer of the words encountered and comprehends 50 percent or fewer.

general-utility words More complex words that are used often by proficient readers and speakers but that do not tend to be specific to any particular subject.

GIST (generating interactions between schemata and text) A strategy used by readers to summarize text.

Goldilocks strategy Students examine a book to determine if it is "too easy," "too hard," or "just right" for them to read.

grade-level equivalency score A conversion of a score on a test into one that tells how a child compares with others in the same grade; e.g., a grade equivalent score of 4.5 on a reading test would suggest that the child is reading as well as children in the normative sample who are in the fifth month of fourth grade.

graded word list A list of words at successive reading levels.

grand conversation A response to text strategy whereby students share personal connections to the text, make predictions, ask questions, and show individual appreciation.

grapheme A written symbol that represents a phoneme.

graphic organizer A visual representation of facts and concepts from a text and their relationships within an organized frame.

graphophonic cues Cues based on sound or visual similarities.

group profile A listing of scores on a specific reading or writing skill that allows the teacher to view the strengths and weaknesses of the whole class for purposes of reteaching and reporting to parents and others.

guided reading A teacher-mediated instructional method designed to help readers improve skills, comprehension, recall, and appreciation of text.

herringbone strategy A graphic organizer used with expository text to show who, what, when, where, why, and the main idea for a passage.

heterogeneous literature groups Literature circles based not upon reading ability level, but self-selection of a particular book.

high-frequency words Words common in reading material that are often difficult to learn because they cannot be easily decoded.

high-stakes assessments Assessment tools mandated by the state or district in which the teachers work that are often used to determine how well children are doing compared to other children in the area, state, or nation and whether certain programs will be funded.

holistic approach A whole-to-parts approach in which meaning is considered to be more critical than the underlying skills of reading.

holographic stage The earliest language acquisition stage, in which one word is used to represent a concept or idea.

impromptu speech A short speech given on a topic with little or no preparation.

independent level A level of reading difficulty low enough that the reader can progress without noticeable obstructions; the reader can recognize approximately 98 percent of the words and comprehend at least 90 percent of what is read.

individual dictation A strategy in which the student dictates a message while the teacher writes it down, sounding out the words in front of the child.

individualized education program (IEP) A written educational plan specifying a special student's annual goals, current levels of educational achievement, and short-term instructional objectives; prepared by a team that includes the student's parents, teachers, and often the student.

induction The process of helping students to construct meaning by going from the particular to the general, with the help of examples.

informal assessment A nonstandardized measurement in which a teacher seeks to learn about what a student is able to do in a certain area of literacy, interprets the results, and uses those results to plan instruction.

informal reading inventory An informal assessment instrument designed to help the teacher determine a student's independent, instructional, frustration, and reading capacity levels.

informal speaking Oral language of a nonacademic, conversational nature.

information literate Knowing how to locate, acquire, and use information.

informational books Nonfiction books that provide factual information about a topic; expository text.

instructional level A level of difficulty low enough that the reader can be instructed by the teacher during the process; in order for the material to be at this level, the reader should be able to read approximately 95 percent of the words in a passage and comprehend at least 75 percent.

interactive electronic books Computerized programs that allow learners to read books on a computer while responding to questions about the text, exploring various aspects or sidelines of the text, and often even adapting the text.

interactive (story) writing A mediated writing experience used to assist emergent readers in learning to read and write. With help from the teacher, students dictate sentences and the teacher verbally stretches each word so they can distinguish sounds and letters. Students use

chart paper to write the letter while repeating the sound.

interest and attitude inventory An informal assessment device that allows teachers to discover how their students feel about reading and about themselves as readers.

interest groups Students are organized according to a common interest in a topic or book selection.

interest inventory A list of questions used to assess a student's preferences in a particular area.

intervention The corrective instructional program the teacher devises as a result of assessment.

interview An oral language activity consisting of asking another person a specific set of questions.

jigsaw grouping A collaborative learning technique in which individuals become "experts" on one portion of text and share their expertise with a small group, called their home group. Each member of the home group becomes an "expert" on a different part of the text and shares his or her new knowledge with the group so that each group member will get a sense of the whole text.

journals Journals are kept by students in the same way artists keep sketch books. Students write in them regularly to record life events of their choosing or, for very beginning writers, to complete sentence stems offered by the teacher. At the beginning reader stage, journals are often accompanied by illustrations and are rarely corrected.

K-W-L Plus strategy A process intended to help students organize learned information into a coherent paragraph or research report; typically involves a chart with column headings such as "What We Know," "What We Want to Know," and "What We Learned." The "Plus" refers to using additional categories of information, perhaps to write summaries or reports.

language arts The global term for reading, writing, listening, and speaking.

language disorders Communication disorders that involve poor speech or language performance due to various factors, including voice quality, speech fluency, and sound production.

language experience approach (LEA) An approach in which reading and the other language arts are interrelated and the experiences of students are used as the basis for the material that is written and then used for reading.

learning center A location within the classroom in which students are presented with instructional materials, specific directions, clearly defined objectives, and/or provisions for self-evaluation.

learning disability A disabling condition in which a person with average intelligence is substantially delayed in academic achievement because of a processing disorder, not because of an environmental, an economic, or a cultural disadvantage.

learning logs Journals students use to summarize a day's lesson and to react to what they have learned.

letter name/alphabetic stage Spelling characterized by literally matching letters to sounds in a linear sound-by-sound fashion.

letter name stage See phonetic stage.

listening vocabulary The words a person is able to understand aurally; also known as receptive vocabulary.

literacy The competence to carry out the complex reading and writing tasks in a functionally useful way necessary to the world of work and life outside the school.

literacy scaffold A temporary writing structure.

literal comprehension Understanding those ideas that are directly stated.

literary sociogram A diagram used to help students understand the complexity of the relationships among characters in a story or chapter.

literature circles Small, student-led book discussion groups that meet regularly in the classroom to read and discuss self-selected books.

literature double response journal A special type of reading log with quotes from a story or informational book in the left column and a personal reflection on the quote in the right column.

literature response groups Same as literature circles and analogous to writing response groups; in literature response groups students discuss the work of published authors and in writing response groups they discuss the work of their peers.

long vowels Vowels that represent the sounds in words that are heard in letter names, such as the /a/ in ape, /e/ in feet, /i/ in ice, /o/ in road, and /u/ in mule.

look-say method An early meaning-based method of reading instruction requiring children to use the context alone to figure out words they did not know.

low-utility words Less frequently encountered words that are usually found in particular content areas.

masking Using a sliding frame or other device to help children focus on a particular word or part of a word.

Matthew effect The phenomenon that suggests that skilled decoders get better at reading while poor decoders tend to fall further behind.

meaning vocabulary That body of words whose meanings one understands and can use.

mediated reading Large or small group instruction in which the teacher guides the children in selected reading skills.

metacognition A person's awareness of his or her own thinking and the conscious efforts to monitor this awareness.

metacognitive strategies Techniques for monitoring one's own thinking.

metacomprehension Understanding what you know about how you comprehend; self-knowledge about your own comprehension processes.

metalinguistic ability The conscious awareness of sound, meaning, and the practical nuances of language.

minilesson A short lesson on reading procedures, concepts, strategies, or skills taught based on teacher observation of the need for it.

miscue An unexpected reading response (deviation from text).

miscue analysis A procedure that lets the teacher gather important instructional information by providing a framework for observing students' oral reading and their ability to construct meaning.

mock interviews Pretend discussions with deceased or fictional figures.

modeling Showing an instructional strategy through teacher demonstration.

morning message Children observe as the teacher writes a meaningful morning message addressed to all the children on the board about a specific event that is planned for the day, or an interesting question. It is used as an instructional tool for discussing skills children are learning, such as conventions of writing or phonic elements.

morpheme The smallest meaning-bearing linguistic unit in a language.

morphology The aspects of language structure related to the ways words are formed from prefixes, roots, and suffixes (e.g., "re-heat-ing") and are related to each other.

motivation The incentive to do something; a stimulus to act.

multicultural Classrooms are multicultural settings when students from a variety of cultures learn together daily, making it necessary to know how students' perceptions, knowledge, and demeanor are shaped by their experiences at home and in their own community.

narrative text Text that contains the structural features of a story.

nonstage theory A theory that suggests that unskilled and skilled readers use the same strategies to figure out unknown words.

norm-referenced test A test designed to yield results interpretable in terms of the average results of a sample population.

norm (normative) group A large number of students chosen to represent the kinds of students for whom an assessment device is designed.

norms Statistics or data that summarize the test performance of specified groups, such as test takers of various ages or grades.

one-to-one correspondence An awareness that letters or combinations of letters correspond directly with certain sounds in the English language.

ongoing assessment Assessment that occurs within daily lessons and over time, usually through observation and anecdotal notes.

onset All the sounds of a word that come before the first vowel.

open sort A type of picture or word sort in which the categories for sorting are left up to the student.

oral recitation lessons (ORL) Three-part lessons designed to increase oral reading fluency.

oral report A presentation of information for an audience of classmates often using multimedia.

oral synthesis Hearing sounds in sequence and blending them together to make a word; sounding out.

orthographic knowledge Understanding of the writing system of a language, specifically the correct sequence of letters, characters, or symbols.

parent packets Folders containing early reading and writing reinforcement activities that can be completed at home with a child's parents or caretakers.

paragraph frames A scaffold for helping students write paragraphs; transition words are provided and students fill in the substantive content words.

partner reading Also known as Buddy Reading. Oral reading with another student.

peer editor A student assigned to help a classmate evaluate a piece of writing and provide helpful questions and suggestions.

percentile scores Raw scores that are converted to percentiles so that comparisons can be made. Percentiles range from 1 to 99, with 1 being the lowest and 99 being the highest.

performance descriptors The criteria that help communicate to teachers and students the standards that will be used to evaluate students' work.

phoneme The smallest unit of sound in a language.

phoneme blending Blending individual sounds to form a word.

phoneme counting Counting the number of sounds in a word.

phoneme deletion Omitting the beginning, middle, or ending sounds of a word.

phoneme isolation Identifying the beginning, middle, and/or ending sounds in a word.

phoneme substitution Substituting beginning, middle, or ending sounds of a word.

phonemic awareness The ability to hear, identify, and manipulate individual sounds in spoken words.

phonemic segmentation The process of separating sounds within a word.

phonetic stage The third stage of spelling development, in which consonants and vowels are used for each spoken syllable.

phonics Instruction in the association of speech sounds with printed symbols.

phonics generalizations Rules that help to clarify English spelling patterns.

phonology The study of the sound system of language.

picture sort A precursor to the word sort activity in which children categorize pictures according to their common sounds.

picture walk An instructional strategy in which the teacher guides students through the text by looking at and discussing the pictures before reading the story.

play centers Areas of the classroom containing inviting props and set aside for spontaneous dramatic play.

polysemantic words Words that can have different meanings depending on the context in which they are used.

portfolio Place to collect evidence of a student's literacy development. It may include artifacts collected by the student, the teacher, or both.

portmanteau words Words created from a combination of two existing words (e.g., motel = motor + hotel).

precommunicative stage The initial stage of spelling development, in which the child scribbles random letters with little concept of which letter makes which sound.

predictable texts Books that use repetition, rhythmic language patterns, and familiar patterns; sometimes called pattern books.

predictive questions Questions designed to activate students' prior knowledge before they read in order to focus their attention on key ideas as they read.

prefixes Meaningful chunks attached to the beginnings of words, such as re + play = replay.

preliterate stage See prephonetic stage.

prephonetic stage The second stage of spelling development, in which the child becomes aware of the alphabetic principle.

prewriting The initial creative and planning stage of writing, prior to drafting, in which the writer formulates ideas, gathers information, and considers ways in which to organize a piece of writing.

primary language The first language a child learns to speak, or the child's home language.

process-oriented assessment A teacher's direct observations of students' reading and writing abilities for the purpose of noting which specific behaviors or strategies students use.

professional teaching standards Standards related to how well the teacher performs.

QARs (question–answer relationships) A strategy in which students become aware of their own comprehension processes, particularly the importance of the knowledge they bring to text and their role as active seekers rather than passive receivers of information through reading.

r-controlled vowels Vowels that occur in a syllable preceding an *r* and the vowel sound is modified, such as the /r/ in car.

readability An objective measure of the difficulty of written material.

readers theatre A form of drama in which participants read aloud from scripts adapted from stories and convey ideas and emotions through vocal expression. This oral interpretation strategy helps students to see that reading is an active process of constructing meaning. Unlike a play, there is no costuming, movement, stage sets, or memorizing of lines.

reading The construction of meaning from coded messages through symbol decoding, vocabulary awareness, comprehension, and reflection.

reading buddies A social reading activity in which students read and reread books with a partner who may help them with unfamiliar words and encourage them to continue reading.

reading capacity level The highest level of material children understand when the passage is read to them.

reading interest inventory An informal assessment device used to determine a child's interests so that the teacher can match appropriate reading material to them.

reading process The steps a reader goes through to construct meaning from what the author has written.

reading product Some form of communication that results from the reading process.

reading rate Speed of reading, often reported in words per minute.

reading readiness The level of preparedness for formal reading instruction.

reading response journal A journal in which readers record their first reactions to something they have read.

reading vocabulary The words a person is able to understand in written form; also part of receptive vocabulary.

realia Concrete pictures and other items used to show the meaning of words and concepts.

reciprocal teaching A technique to develop comprehension and metacognition in which the teacher and students take turns predicting, generating questions, summarizing, and clarifying ideas in a passage.

recreational reading An independent reading activity for motivating voluntary reading interest and appreciation rather than instruction.

reliability When a test consistently measures the same behavior with each administration of the test.

repeated readings The process of students rereading a selection for a different purpose and thinking again about what they have read. Rereading helps improve a young reader's speed, accuracy, expression, comprehension, and linguistic growth.

response guide A set of suggestions designed to help peer editors provide helpful feedback to other student writers.

retelling The process of teachers analyzing students' retellings of text to gauge their level of comprehension and use of language. In examining the retellings, teachers look for the number of events recalled, how students interpret the message, and how students use details or make inferences to substantiate ideas.

revising The process of changing a piece of writing to improve clarity for its intended audience and make certain that it accomplishes its stated purpose.

rime The first vowel in a word and all the sounds that follow.

role playing A form of dramatic play that involves having children act the part of another child or a fictional character.

root word A word to which prefixes and/or suffixes are added to create new, but related, words.

roots Base words.

ROW Read, organize, write: a strategy used to help students write summaries.

rubber-banding The process in which the teacher stretches out all the sounds in a word so learners can pay attention to each phoneme or sound.

running records A procedure for analyzing students' oral reading and noting their strengths and weaknesses when using various reading strategies.

scaffolding A support mechanism by which students are able to accomplish more difficult tasks than they could without assistance.

schema A preexisting knowledge structure developed about a thing, a place, or an idea; a framework of expectations based on previous knowledge.

scoring rubric A tool describing the levels of performance a student must demonstrate relat-

ed to a particular achievement goal, whether it is written or oral.

self-monitoring The mental act of knowing when one does and does not understand what one is reading.

semantic cues Meaning clues.

semantic feature analysis An instructional activity in which students select a group of related words and then create a chart to classify them according to distinguishing characteristics.

semantic field A range of similarity among words.

semantic gradient A vocabulary-enriching activity that allows children to discuss the many shades of meaning of words, beginning with a word and ending with its opposite.

semantic map A graphic representation of the relationship among words and phrases in written material.

sentence fluency The careful crafting of sentences so that paragraphs flow smoothly and effortlessly.

sentence stems The first two or three words of a sentence followed by blank spaces offered to students to support initial attempts at writing.

sentence strips Rectangular pieces of tag board or construction paper upon which are written individual sentences from a story students have read.

service learning Curriculum projects that involve and enhance the surrounding community.

shared reading A mediated technique whereby the teacher reads aloud while students follow along using individual copies of the book, a class chart, or a big book.

sheltered English Lessons taught in a multisensory, multi-intelligence way to ensure understanding by English language learners.

short vowels Vowels that represent the sound of /a/ in apple, /e/ in end, /i/ in igloo, /o/ in octopus, and /u/ in bus.

showcase portfolio A collection of artifacts taken from the working portfolio that demonstrates excellence in achievement.

sight vocabulary Words that are recognized by the reader immediately, without having to resort to decoding.

sight word A word that is immediately recognized as a whole and does not require word analysis for identification.

Six Traits approach The important aspects of writing including ideas, organization, voice, word choice, sentence fluency, and conventions.

speech disorders Disabilities characterized by deficits in speech, receptive language, and/or expressive language.

SQ3R (Survey, Question, Read, Recite, Review) A study strategy that asks readers to first survey the material, form questions based on that survey, then read, restate in their own words, and review or rehearse what was read to help their comprehension and memory of the material.

Squire's model The notion that reading and writing are related because they place similar demands on one's thinking.

stage theory A theory that suggests that children go through three stages in acquiring literacy: the "selective cue stage," the "spelling-sound stage," and the "automatic stage."

standard deviation The number (usually (1, 2, or 3) used to refer to the variability in the scores as indicated by their distance from the mean, or average.

standard error of measurement The number representing the error associated with a test.

standardized reading tests Achievement tests that are published, norm-referenced, group-administered, survey tests of reading ability.

standardized testing The use of norm-referenced tests to measure reading and writing skills as well as their subskills.

standards Broad curricular goals containing specific grade-level targets or benchmarks. They represent systematic ways for educators to ask themselves, What is it that we want our students to be able to know? and What do we want them to be able to do?

standards-based performance assessment Assessment tasks designed to show what has been learned as it relates to a particular content standard.

stanine scores Scores that have been converted into nine equally spaced groups, with 1 being the lowest and 9 the highest.

story frame A basic outline for a story designed to help students organize their ideas about what they have read.

story grammar A set of rules that defines story structures.

strategic reader model A view of reading instruction that focuses on teaching readers a wide variety of strategies to use before, during, and after reading.

structural analysis Examination of words for meaningful parts (affixes, contractions, endings, compound words).

structured listening activity An activity in which students listen to a story accompanied by visuals that support the action in the story, and then retell the story with the help of the visuals.

suffix A meaningful chunk attached to the end of words, such as play + ing = playing.

summative assessment A compilation of summary data provided at program endings, units of study, or other intervals to report progress.

sustained silent reading (SSR) A program for setting aside a certain period of time daily for self-selected, silent reading. During SSR time, each student chooses material to read for a designated period of time, typically 10–15 minutes for beginning readers. Everyone, including the teacher, reads without interruption.

syllabication Breaking words into syllables; "chunking."

syllable juncture stage *See* Syllables and affixes stage.

syllables The units of pronunciation that include a vowel sound.

syllables and affixes stage Spelling stage characterized by considering the conventions of preserving pattern-to-sound relationships at the place where syllables meet.

synonyms Groups of words that have the same, or very similar, meanings.

syntactic cues Clues derived from the word order, or grammar, of the sentence.

T-chart A two-column list used to compare the information in the column heads.

talk-to-yourself chart A chart to help children self-assess their ability to read and spell new words.

teachable moments The spontaneous, indirect teaching that occurs when teachers respond to students' questions or when students otherwise demonstrate the need to know something.

teacher observational portfolio A progress file containing observations and informal assessments of children's reading and writing behaviors and accomplishments.

telegraphic stage The language acquisition stage in which an idea or concept is represented by two words.

think aloud A strategy in which the teacher models aloud for students the thinking processes used when reading or writing.

think, pair, and share A cooperative learning strategy in which children listen to a question, think of a response, pair to discuss with a partner, and then share their collaboration with the whole class.

think sheet A written format used to help students with behavioral disorders devise better choices for ways to behave.

tiered activities Activities that are modified to meet the differentiated needs of learners.

time/order chart Sequencing to show chronological order.

time-out Removing a student acting disruptively from the immediate vicinity of instruction for a specified period of time, or until he or she can return and behave appropriately.

topic and details maps Charts showing relationships of details to main topic.

tracking Indicating understanding of the one-to-one correspondence of spoken and written words by finger-pointing.

trade book Any book that can be purchased by the general public in bookstores, through mail-order houses, or at book fairs.

transactional model A perspective of early reading instruction from cognitive psychology and psycholinguistic learning that views children as bringing a rich prior knowledge background to literacy learning.

transfer words Words containing elements that are also found in many other words.

transitional reader A reader aware of letter pattern units, or word families, and frequently occurring rimes.

transitional stage The fourth stage of spelling development, in which the child is able to approximate the spelling of various English words.

transmission model A perspective of early reading instruction from behavioral psychology that views children as empty vessels into which knowledge is poured.

validity The degree to which a test measures what it purports to measure.

Venn diagram A set of overlapping circles used to graphically illustrate the similarities and differences of two concepts, ideas, stories, or other items.

vicarious experiences Indirect experiences, not involving the senses.

vocabulary The knowledge and use of words.

voice The writer's personality emerging through words.

web A graphic organizer used to involve students in thinking about and planning what they will study, learn, read about, or write about within a larger topic.

within word stage See transitional stage.

word attack An aspect of reading instruction that includes intentional strategies for learning to decode, sight read, and recognize written words.

word bank A collection of sight words that has been mastered, usually recorded on index cards.

word building An activity in which students arrange letter cards to spell words, practicing phonics and spelling concepts.

word choice The element of writing that involves using fresh and colorful language to make certain passages memorable and worthy of reading aloud.

word families Common rimes useful for creating many words by onset substitution.

word hunt An activity in which children search for words that correspond to a certain pattern that has been identified by them or by the teacher.

word map A visual illustration of a word showing its meaning by offering examples, explaining what it is, and what it is not.

word play A child's manipulation of sounds and words for purposes of language exploration, practice, and pleasure.

word sort An activity in which students sort a collection of words into two or more categories.

word study Analyzing words to discover the regularities, patterns, and rules of English orthography needed to read and spell.

word wall A chart or bulletin board on which are placed, alphabetically, important vocabulary to be referred to during word study activities.

wordless books Picture story books without words.

working portfolio A collection of completed work samples or works in progress that may be chosen for placement in a showcase portfolio.

writer's workshop A writing program that implements the writing process by having students write on topics that they choose themselves, assuming ownership of their writing and learning.

writing folder A folder where students keep rough drafts in various stages of the writing process and other daily compositions or reports, topics for future writing, and notes from minilessons.

writing process The process by which a piece of writing is completed for publication, involving prewriting, drafting, revising, editing, and publishing.

writing prompts Motivational ideas or structures that are offered by the teacher to inspire students to write.

INDEX
Author Index

INDEX
Subject Index